FILM FESTIVAL YEARBOOK 4:

Film Festivals and Activism

Edited by

Dina Iordanova

and Leshu Torchin

St Andrews Film Studies
St Andrews
2012

First published in Great Britain in 2012 by
St Andrews Film Studies
99 North Street, St Andrews, KY16 9AD
Scotland, United Kingdom
Publisher: Dina Iordanova

Secure on-line ordering:
www.stafs.org

British Library Cataloguing-in-Publication Data
A catalogue record for this book is available from the British Library.

ISBN 978-0-9563730-5-2 (paperback)

The book is published with the assistance of the Centre for Film
Studies at the University of St Andrews, the Leverhulme Trust,
the Carnegie Trust for the Universities of Scotland and The Royal
Society of Edinburgh.

St Andrews Film Studies promotes greater understanding of, and
access to, international cinema and film culture worldwide.

University of
St Andrews

The University of St Andrews is a charity registered in Scotland,
No. SC013532

Cover design: Duncan Stewart.
Cover and pre-press: University of St Andrews Print & Design.

Front cover illustration: Festival Internacional de Cine del Sahara; photo by
Andy Isaacson (www.andyisaacson.net).
Part 1: The Human Rights Watch Film Festival; photo by Leshu Torchin.
Part 2: Nick Higgins (director), Javier Ruiz Perez (Acteal representative),
José Alfredo (Acteal representative) and Pablo Romo (human rights negotiator)
at the Morelia International Film Festival, 2007; photographer unknown.
Part 3: Screening of *Budrus* in the Occupied Palestinian Territories; photo by
Ronit Avni.

Printed in Great Britain by Lightning Source.

Contents

Part 3: Resources

Acknowledgements

Looking at issues beyond national borders is a key feature of our approach in the *Film Festival Yearbook* series. For this volume, we have once again brought together the academic study of film festivals with the day-to-day work of international festival practitioners.

We would like to thank all the contributors and interviewees who have made this volume what it is. As with previous volumes, this one brings together people from various corners of the world – Europe (the Czech Republic, Germany, Italy, the Netherlands, Serbia and the UK), North America (Canada and the U.S.) and elsewhere (Australia, India and Israel). Indirectly, contributors referred to experiences linked to even more countries, including Bosnia-Herzegovina, Bulgaria, Chile, Mexico, Morocco, the Occupied Palestinian Territories, Romania, Spain, Uruguay and West Sahara.

We would also like to thank Alex Marlow-Mann, for handling production and for editorial assistance, Steve Blackey, for copy-editing and proof-reading, Duncan Stewart, for his design work, Margaret Smith for typesetting, Andy Isaacson for granting us the right to use the photograph on the cover, as well as the book's anonymous peer-reviewers.

The Leverhulme Trust provided funding which made the Film Festival Yearbook series possible. A research grant from The Carnegie Trust for the Universities of Scotland enabled interviews and site studies, which greatly enhanced our work. The Royal Society of Edinburgh funded further work on the topic of film festivals and activism and supported the publication of this volume. We are grateful to them all.

Leshu Torchin would also like to acknowledge the contributions of Faye Ginsburg (New York University), Christine Squires (Human Rights Watch), Andrea Holley (Human Rights Watch International Film Festival) and Sky Sitney (AFI-Discovery Channel Silverdocs).

Dina Iordanova would also like to thank her friends at the film festival in Douarnenez, who first revealed to her what a great activist film festival can achieve, Benoit Ginisty of FIAPF in Paris, Alberto Elena and the members of the Southern Platform of Film Festivals and the Cines del Sur festival in Granada, Spain, as well as the Busan Cinema Forum in South Korea.

A Note on Referencing and Interviews

Film Titles

All films are referenced in the following fashion: Original title (English language title [where applicable], Director, Country of Origin, Date). The only exception is the case of industrial videos or items produced by non-governmental (NGO) and supra-national organisations. The director's name has not been included in the case of industrial videos, whose organisational provenance is more important. The UN-produced videos could be said to have the provenance of all the member states (or none of them as its own entity), and NGO-produced videos offer challenges for their independence from government affiliations. In the case of the NGOs we have opted to provide the names of the nation(s) housing the organisations, although this admittedly omits issues of funding from global donors and sponsors and risks marrying the independent bodies with the states named.

Referencing of Other Volumes

Many of the essays in this volume reference texts published in the earlier volumes of the *Film Festival Yearbook* series. In the interest of brevity and to avoid pointless repetition of publication details, these have simply been referenced throughout as *FFY1: The Festival Circuit*, *FFY2: Film Festivals and Imagined Communities* and *FFY3: Film Festivals and East Asia*. For example: Iordanova, Dina (2009) 'The Film Festival Circuit', in *FFY1: The Festival Circuit*, 23-39. We have also abbreviated the references to the manual published by People in Need, as it is equally frequently referenced. For example: in Tereza Porybná (ed.) *Setting Up a Human Rights Film Festival*. Prague: People in Need, 14-25.

Websites

The URLs for film festival websites are cited in parentheses the first time the festival is mentioned in a chapter. In the case of interviews these are presented in square brackets, since they constitute editorial interventions and do not form part of the interview itself.

Interviews

The opinions expressed in interviews reflect the views of the interviewees and do not necessarily correspond to those of the editors or of St Andrews Film Studies.

Contributors

Ronit Avni is an award-winning filmmaker and human rights advocate. She is the founder and Executive Director of Just Vision, an organisation dedicated to increasing media coverage and support for Palestinian and Israeli efforts to end the occupation and the conflict without arms. Her work has been featured in nearly every major international news outlet. Ronit produced the 2009 film *Budrus*, which was hailed in The New York Times as 'this year's must-see documentary'. She also directed and produced the critically acclaimed film *Encounter Point*. Previously, she trained human rights defenders to incorporate film into their advocacy efforts while working at Peter Gabriel's human rights organisation, WITNESS. She now sits on the WITNESS board. Ronit is a Young Global Leader through the World Economic Forum and a Term Member of the Council on Foreign Relations.

Igor Blažević was born in Bosnia and Herzegovina and graduated from the Faculty of Philosophy in Zagreb, Croatia. Since 1992, he has been involved with People in Need (PIN), a Prague-based non-profit organisation whose mission is 'to inspire a largeness of spirit in Czech society by helping others in need, and to promote democratic freedoms for all'. PIN complements and supports its relief work with a vigorous advocacy for human rights and democratic freedoms, and is one of the largest organisations of its kind in post-communist Europe, having administered projects in more than 40 countries over the past 17 years. Igor Blažević is also founder and, for 11 years, was Director of One World, the biggest European human rights film festival, which attracts audiences of over 100,000. He is currently working on educational and training programmes for Burma activists.

Jasmina Bojic has taught at Stanford University for the last 17 years. She has been working as a journalist more than 25 years, covering many political and cultural events, including the Academy Awards® and numerous international film festivals, as well as interviewing noted politicians, scientists, directors, producers and actors. Ms Bojic has served on juries at many international film festivals and has extensive connections with filmmakers and within the film industry worldwide. She has worked as a producer/director on several documentaries and TV programmes dealing with human rights issues. Fourteen years ago she conceived and organised what has become one of the oldest international documentary film festivals in the U.S. – UNAFF (United Nations Association Film Festival) at Stanford University, which became the Traveling Film Festival in 2000.

Bruni Burres is a New York-based film producer whose work focuses primarily on film and arts initiatives exploring contemporary human rights themes. She is a consultant with the Sundance Institute's Documentary Program and the Open Society Foundation's (OSF) U.S. National Security and Human Rights Campaign. Recently, she authored a report for the OSF's Central Asia Program on the plausibility of a year-round, long-term film centre in Tajikistan. In 2011, in collaboration with the International Center for Transitional Justice (www.ictj.org), Bruni produced the feature length documentary *La Toma* (*The Siege*), which explores the lasting cultural and political impact of the 1985 siege of the Palace of Justice in Colombia (www.latoma.info). She was also co-founder and director of the Human Rights Watch International Film Festival (www.hrw.org/iff) from 1991-2008.

Amalia Córdova is the Latin American programme manager at the Film and Video Center of the Smithsonian National Museum of the American Indian (NMAI) in New York City where she has organised Latin American indigenous screenings, video tours, the Native American Film + Video Festival and the showcase First Nations/First Features, as well as presenting with the Museum of Modern Art and New York University in 2005. She is an international correspondent of the Latin American Indigenous Peoples' Film and Video Coordinator (CLACPI) and has published articles, curated screenings and juried at numerous film festivals, including the International Indigenous Peoples' Film and Video Festivals in Santiago, Chile (2004) and Quito, Ecuador (2010). She is a former trustee of the Flaherty Film Seminar. She holds an MA in Performance Studies and is a PhD candidate in Cinema Studies at New York University. She is from Santiago, Chile.

Greg DeCuir, Jr. is a doctoral candidate at the Faculty of Dramatic Arts in Belgrade, Serbia. His writing has appeared in *Cineaste, Jump Cut, Studies in Eastern European Cinema* and *KinoKultura*; his book *Yugoslav Black Wave: Polemical Cinema from 1963-72 in the Socialist Federal Republic of Yugoslavia* was published by Film Center Serbia in 2011. He has served as a jury member for Balkanima – the European

Animated Film Festival (Belgrade) – and for Film Front – the Festival of Small and Independent Film Production (Novi Sad); he is a programmer for the festival ±40 Years: 1968-2008 (Belgrade), and is the selector/ programmer for the Alternative Film/Video Festival in Belgrade.

Marijke de Valck is Assistant Professor in the Department of Media Studies at the University of Amsterdam, the Netherlands. She is a well-known specialist on film festivals whose work includes the monograph *Film Festivals: From European Geopolitics to Global Cinephilia* (2007), as well as articles in *Cinema Journal*, the *International Journal of Cultural Studies* and the *Film Festival Yearbook* series. Together with Skadi Loist she founded the Film Festival Research Network (FFRN).

Sean Farnel is currently an unrestricted free agent, having departed his post as Director of Programming at Hot Docs (Toronto, Canada), North America's largest documentary festival, market and conference, in 2011. Sean was recruited to this newly-created position in November 2005, following six years as a staff programmer for the Toronto International Film Festival. At Hot Docs, Sean was responsible for managing all festival programming, including film curation and the industry conference. He also created the popular Doc Soup screening series, as well as the Doc Mogul Award, and managed the Shaw Hot Docs Fund. Sean is a graduate of Cinema Studies from one of Canada's most respected film schools, Concordia University. Upon graduation he received the Motion Picture Foundation of Canada Award for Most Outstanding Achievement. His occasional blog is RippingReality.com.

Alex Fischer is The Leverhulme Trust Research Associate at the Centre for Film Studies of the University of St Andrews where he works as part of the Dynamics of World Cinema team. He has extensive international experience as a filmmaker and film festival manager. Alex has given talks in the context of international film festivals in Australia, Russia, the U.S. and elsewhere, and has published work in *Film Festivals and East Asia* (2011) and *Digital Disruption: Cinema Moves On-line* (2012). He is working on a monograph, which examines film festival operation through an open system paradigm.

Georgekutty A. L. is the founder and editor of *Deep Focus Film Quarterly* and the Secretary of the Bangalore Film Society, India. He holds diplomas in film studies from the National Film Archive of India, the Film and Television Institute of India, Pune, and in Human Rights from the Institute of Social Sciences, The Hague. He was a jury member of the Environmental Film Festival, Freiburg, Germany, 2004 and is also the founding Director of Voices from the Waters' International Travelling Film Festival. He organises film festivals and conferences on contemporary social issues for institutions and the public with a view to exploring their cultural politics and how they effect and shape modern cultural practices, politics, aesthetic sensibilities and social behaviour. He is also one of the founder members of Open Cinema, an international consortium of environmental and social film festivals.

Mariagiulia Grassilli is Artistic Director of Human Rights Nights (an annual festival on human rights in Bologna, Italy), Chair of Human Rights Film Network and Officina Cinema South-East. Since 2000, she has been a consultant involved with organising communication campaigns on migration, human rights and development for film institutions (Cineteca di Bologna), festivals (Venice Film Festival, Africa at the Pictures UK), film production companies (Channel 4 BRITDOC Foundation), public institutions and NGOs (Bologna Municipality, Oxfam, AfricanBamba, Senegal). She holds an MA in International Relations and Development Studies (University of East Anglia) and a PhD in Migration Studies (Sussex University). Currently she is Research Associate at the School of Oriental and African Studies, University of London, in the Department of Anthropology and Sociology.

Judith Helfand is a filmmaker, activist and educator known for her ability to make resonant and entertaining films from stories of chemical exposure and environmental injustice. Receiving Emmy nominations and Sundance and Peabody awards, her films include *The Uprising of '34* (1995, with George Stoney), the 'toxic comedy' *Blue Vinyl* (2002, with Daniel B. Gold), its prequel, *A Healthy Baby Girl* (1997, a video-diary about her experience with DES-related cancer) and *Everything's Cool* (2007, with Gold). Co-founder of Working Films, which links non-fiction filmmaking to activism, and of Chicken & Egg Pictures, which provides grants and mentorship to women filmmakers, Helfand strives to balance her commitment to the field with her own filmmaking and community engagement. In 2007, she was awarded a United States Artist Fellowship, one of 50 awarded to 'America's finest living artists'. She is presently working on *Cooked*, a story about heat, poverty and the politics of disaster.

Nick Higgins is an award-winning documentary filmmaker and senior lecturer at the University of Edinburgh, Scotland. His first films, *Hidden Gifts* (2004) and *Women in Black* (2004), have been broadcast on several European television channels and have picked up awards and nominations at many international festivals. His 2006 documentary short, Mentiras, screened at over 20 festivals worldwide, including touring 16 cities in Mexico. In 2007, Nick completed his first feature documentary, *A Massacre Foretold*, which subsequently won the WACC/SIGNIS award for best human rights documentary. In 2008, Nick originated and co-produced the multi-directorial feature documentary, *The New Ten Commandments*, which premièred at the 2008 Edinburgh International Film Festival and continues to screen at film festivals internationally. He currently runs the PhD course in Transdisciplinary Documentary Film at the University of Edinburgh.

Raluca Iacob is a doctoral candidate in the Department of Film Studies at the University of St Andrews. Her research focuses on understanding the reception mechanisms of recent Romanian art cinema and the formation of an audience. This includes a study of the Transylvania International Film Festival, as a mediator between films and filmmakers and between local communities and audiences.

Dina Iordanova is Professor of Film Studies and Provost of St Leonard's College at the University of St Andrews in Scotland. She is the conceptual leader of the *Film Festival Yearbook* series and the Principal Investigator on The Leverhulme Trust-sponsored project, Dynamics of World Cinema. Engaged with initiatives in the areas of publishing, festivals and global creative industries, she has organised a variety of events related to the study of film festivals, has attracted substantial funding and has attended some of the world's most interesting festivals. Dina has published ten books dedicated to matters of international cinema and her work has been translated into over 20 languages. She is a Fellow of the Royal Society of the Arts and a member of the Institute of Directors. She also serves as a Trustee of the Board of the Edinburgh International Film Festival.

Skadi Loist is Junior Researcher at the Institute for Media and Communications at the University of Hamburg. She sits on the board of the Hamburg International Queer Film Festival and is editor of the festival's anniversary anthology *Bildschön: 20 Jahre Lesbisch Schwule*

Filmtage Hamburg (2009). Her PhD project analyses queer film festivals in the U.S. and Germany/Austria. In collaboration with Marijke de Valck she co-founded the Film Festival Research Network, www. filmfestivalresearch.org. Her work has been published in German and English in edited volumes, in journals such as *Screen* and in the *Film Festival Yearbook* series.

David Mitchell and **Sharon Snyder** edit the Corporealities: Discourses of Disability book series for the University of Michigan Press. They are the authors of two books – *Narrative Prosthesis: Disability and the Dependencies of Discourse* (University of Michigan Press, 2001) and *Cultural Locations of Disability* (University of Chicago Press, 2006) – an edited collection of essays on disability history and representation – *The Body and Physical Difference: Discourses of Disability* (University of Michigan Press, 1997) – and nearly 30 refereed journal essays on various aspects of disability culture, art and history. They founded the independent production company Brace Yourselves Productions and are the creators of four award-winning documentary films: *Vital Signs: Crip Culture Talks Back* (1996), *A World Without Bodies* (2002), *Self Preservation: The Art of Riva Lehrer* (2004) and *Disability Takes on the Arts* (2005). Their most recent work centres on disability education, independent disability films and neo-liberal medical networks.

Clare Muller worked with the Australian Human Rights Arts and Film Festival (HRAFF) as Production Manager during 2009 and 2010. Over this time, Clare was involved in all facets of festival planning, coordination and management, both in Melbourne and interstate. This work formed part of a professional internship component to her final year studies in the BA (International Studies) program at RMIT University. Clare became particularly interested in the unique position that HRAFF holds within Melbourne's strong film festival culture.

Robert A. Rosenstone, Professor of History at the California Institute of Technology, is a leading scholar in the field of film and history. He has written two books – *Visions of the Past: the Challenge of Film to Our Idea of History* (1995) and *History on Film/Film on History* (2006) – and has edited a collection of essays on the topic. Rosenstone acted as historical consultant for several films, including the Academy Award®-winning *Reds* (1981), founded the journal *Rethinking History* as well as the film section for *American Historical Review*. Other books on history include *Crusade of the Left: The Lincoln Battalion in the Spanish Civil War, Romantic Revolutionary: A Biography of John Reed and Mirror in the Shrine: American Encounters with Meiji Japan.* He has also published works of fiction, has lectured on six continents and has been a visiting professor at universities in the UK, Spain, Italy, Japan and Columbia.

Isabel Santaolalla is Professor of Spanish and Film Studies at Roehampton University, London. She has published on postcolonial literature, cultural studies and film, with special emphasis on the representation of ethnicity and gender in the cinema. She is the editor of *'New' Exoticisms. Changing Patterns in the Construction of Otherness* (2000) and is the co-editor of *The Transnational in Iberian and Latin American Cinemas* (2007). She is also the author of *Los 'otros': Etnicidad y 'raza' en el cine español contemporáneo* (2005). In company with a team of EU-funded interns, she delivered an audiovisual workshop in the Saharawi refugee camps in May 2009 as part of the 6th Edition of Festival Internacional de Cine del Sahara (FISahara). She is currently a Trustee of Sandblast, a London-based arts and human rights charity working to empower the Saharawis to promote their culture and earn a living through the arts.

Kathleen Scott is a PhD candidate in Film Studies at the University of St Andrews. Her thesis explores the intersections between haptic film theory, feminist politics and spectatorship ethics in the context of viewing explicitly violent imagery. Her research interests include phenomenology, horror films and the philosophy of Gilles Deleuze.

Stefan Simanowitz is a writer, journalist, broadcaster and human rights campaigner who writes regularly for publications, including, *The Independent*, *The Guardian*, *The Financial Times*, *The Washington Times*, *Huffington Post*, *Salon.com*, *Mail & Guardian*, *Contemporary Review*, *The New Statesman*, *The Tribune*, *Christian Science Monitor*, *Prospect*, *In These Times* and *New Internationalist*. He broadcasts regularly on channels including Al Jazeera English. Simanowitz worked for the ANC during South Africa's first democratic election campaign and has filed reports from mass graves in Somaliland and Indonesia, from prisons in Cameroon and South Africa, and from the deserts of Mali. In 2009, he covered the Festival Internacional de Cine del Sahara (FISahara) for *The Independent* and returned in 2010 and 2011 to be involved in the international organisation for the festival. He also chairs the global campaigning initiative, the Free Western Sahara Network, www.freesahara.ning.com.

Beatriz Tadeo Fuica is a PhD candidate working on an interdisciplinary project involving the Departments of Spanish and of Film Studies at the University of St Andrews. Her thesis examines the emergence of Uruguayan cinema between 1960 and 2010, exploring its relationship with Third Cinema and New Latin American Cinema, and also cinema under dictatorship and cinema after the re-establishment of democracy. Her research interests include Latin American Cinema, cultural identities and memory studies.

Leshu Torchin is a Lecturer in Film Studies at the University of St Andrews, where she works on the subject of film, genocide and human rights advocacy. Co-author of *Moving People, Moving Images: Cinema and Trafficking in the New Europe* (St Andrews Film Studies, 2010), her work has appeared in *Third Text*, *Film & History*, *American Anthropologist* and *Cineaste*. Her book, *Creating the Witness: Documenting Genocide in Film, Video and the Internet*, is due out from University of Minnesota Press in 2012.

Ger Zielinski is Assistant Professor of Media in the Department of Cultural Studies at Trent University, Canada. He completed his doctoral dissertation on the cultural politics of LGBT film festivals in the Department of Art History and Communication Studies at McGill University and a two-year postdoctoral research fellowship in the Tisch School of the Arts at New York University (2008-10). He has also served as a member of the board of directors of the Images Festival of Independent Film and Video, as programmer for the nomadic experimental film and video art exhibition group Pleasure Dome (Toronto) and as awards juror for the Inside Out Toronto LGBT Film and Video Festival. He has been a member of the editorial team for *Alphabet City: Culture, Politics, Art* (MIT Press) for many years.

Želimir Žilnik was born in 1942 and is currently based in Novi Sad, Serbia. From the late 1960s, his socially engaged films and documentaries in former Yugoslavia earned him critical accolades (*The Unemployed* – Best Documentary at the Oberhausen festival, 1968; *Early Works* – Best Film at Berlin Film Festival, 1969), but also, in the 1970s, censorship for his unflinching criticism of the government apparatus. Low budget filmmaking and challenging political themes mark Žilnik's prolific career, which includes over 50 feature and documentary films and shorts. More recently, his focus has shifted beyond the divided Balkans to question that area's relationship with the tightening controls of European borders, delving into the heart of issues of refugees and migrants. For more information, visit: www.zilnikzelimir.net

Patricia R. Zimmermann is Professor in the Department of Cinema, Photography and Media Arts at Ithaca College, Ithaca, New York. She is also co-director, with Tom Shevory, of the Finger Lakes Environmental Film Festival. She is the author of *Reel Families: A Social History of Amateur Film* (1995) and *States of Emergency: Documentaries, Wars, Democracies* (2000), and is co-editor of *Mining the Home Movie: Excavations in Histories and Memories* (2007) and *The Flaherty: Four Decades in the Cause of Independent Cinema* (1995). She previously taught at the University of Iowa, U.S. and at the Nanyang Technological University, Singapore. She is currently collaborating with Scott MacDonald on a book analysing the 50-year history, activism and impact of the Robert Flaherty Film Seminars. Her blog, Open Spaces (www.ithaca.edu/fleff10/blogs/open_spaces/), explores international public media.

PART 1

CONTEXTS

Networked for Advocacy:
Film Festivals and Activism[1]

Leshu Torchin

This book explores the relationship between activism and film festivals through a range of perspectives from filmmakers, activists, programmers and academics. The array of participants helps to tease out the variety of investments and practices that make film festivals a site for social advocacy, in addition to their role in commercial agendas of distribution, exhibition and acquisition. Bringing these perspectives together helps to identify and define the concept of 'activist' as applied to films or film festivals, whilst intervening into the (still persistent) formulation that suggests immediate audience transformation upon viewing, or that exposure inevitably leads to action (Cohen 1996; Keenan 2004).

When Igor Blažević, the founder of the One World festival in Prague (www.oneworld.cz), defines the human rights film as 'information and testimony rather than art and entertainment' (2009: 15), he indicates, whether intentionally or not, the transformative expectations embedded in such films and their screenings. Despite its seeming self-evidence and absence of jargon, 'testimony' is a loaded term. Historically understood as the truthful first-person narration of suffering to transform the world, the word testimony resonates with juridical and Christian arenas, whether it be from a person sworn in as witness to testify to an event in order to bring about justice, or from the Christian martyr (Ancient Greek for 'witness') who testifies to Christ in order to hasten the Second Coming. Shoshana Felman and Dori Laub address these features in their performative and therapeutic models of testimony, where testimony becomes a transformative 'speech act' that occasions beneficial change; in this case, psychological recovery and the formation of a community conducive to listening and responding (Felman and Laub 1992). Meanwhile, the Latin American genre of *testimonio* makes its political potential manifest within its definition: truthful speech deployed 'in the cause of denouncing a present situation of exploitation and oppression or in exorcising and setting aright official history' (Yudice 1996: 44). In this regard, the human rights film, or more broadly speaking, the activist film, functions as a truthful narration of a situation, presented with the intention of bringing about beneficial change. Meanwhile, the emphasis on 'truth' indicates the prominence of documentary film in this field; as Sean Farnel notes in his interview, the overlap does not suggest that activist films and documentary films are necessarily the same thing but, rather, express a mutual interest in the state of the real world, as well as an interest in change persist. The number of documentary filmmakers appearing in this volume suggests as much; Želimir Žilnik, interviewed for this volume, enters into this realm with his semi-fictional narratives and non-professional participants that transform his work into 'urgent street-level communiqués on current problems' (DeCuir, in this volume).

Nevertheless, the processes of this transformation are hardly straightforward, even as the expectations linger. Digging below the surface is in order. For instance, in April 2011, acquaintances of mine attended the Uist Eco Film Festival (uistfilm.org), an environmentally themed three-day film festival in Scotland's Outer Hebrides. When they reported back, they expressed an appreciation of the project, but wondered as to its activist potential, stating that the films were not cinematic ('infomercial' was the word they used to describe certain films), and that the festival seemed to do little more than 'preach to the converted'. Another attendee privy to this exchange reacted with surprise at their commentary. The evening events she had attended had hosted speakers offering a range of important perspectives, she thought. More than that, she wondered if perhaps the festival was not so much intended for outsiders seeking a cinema event, but rather for the local community who had suffered personal losses due to their land falling into the sea through soil erosion and major weather events. These local tragedies had made both the screenings and the evening discussions resonate within this small, tightly knit community. That some of these discussions were held in Gaelic amplified the local nature of this event, indicating that it may have functioned more to bring a community together, and to explore avenues of conservation and sustainability, than to change hearts and minds.[2]

This example suggests that the transformative and activist functions of the film festival are best explored through an examination of the testimonial encounter: the interface between the testimony or programmed films and the audiences hailed as witnessing publics, viewers who take responsibility for what they have seen and become ready to respond (McLagan 2003; Torchin 2006). Such an exploration requires one to engage with what Sam Gregory has described as the question of the human rights practitioner, '*what* is distributed, and *how* it is distributed' (Gregory 2008: 198), and, in the case of film festivals we need to consider *how* it is *exhibited*.

To better understand these processes, I propose thinking of the film festival as a field of witnessing, a concept that yokes Craig Calhoun's territorial metaphor of the public sphere as 'involving a field of discursive connections' with clusters 'organised around issues, categories, persons, or basic dynamics of a larger society' (Calhoun 1992: 37), to Pierre Bourdieu's field of cultural production (Bourdieu 1977). This framework broadens our understanding of the testimonial encounter as taking place within a range of practices, interests and stakes, and involving an array of players. The transformative power of testimony is not something eternal and enduring, but is enabled through situated activities, many of which are discussed and illustrated by this volume's contributors, who are, yes, programmers, filmmakers and activists, but who are also scholars.

The Film Festival Programme: The Films

The question of programming is always an important one for film festivals and it takes on particular dimensions when one considers their activist potential. Although for some it might seem that 'activist' becomes interchangeable with 'human rights' or 'humanitarian', the issues are much broader, as politics and industry also come into play when investigating the nature of activism. Representing marginalised communities, calling attention to political issues and ushering in underappreciated works and methods, are a few of the ways that a film's content and a film festival come together in activist aims.

These representational interventions may challenge the expected aesthetics. Many film festival programmers, including Bruni Burres in this volume, name cinematic quality as important a criterion as factual accuracy or truthfulness. Yet what exactly constitutes 'cinematic' quality? Although some film festivals with advocacy goals do offer gala events and encounters with celebrity, as indicated in the contributions by Mariagiulia Grassilli, Robert Rosenstone and by Stefan Simanowitz and Isabel Santaolalla, associated costs can be prohibitive and better spent on programme production, panel discussions and community outreach.

In the case of itinerant festivals, such as the Festival Internacional de Cine del Sahara (www.festivalsahara.com), lorries and trucks are more likely to provide the screens than a physical cinema.

The question of quality comes under scrutiny when one considers the 'cultural activism' that Amalia Córdova, a coordinator at the Museum of the Native American Indian Film and Video Center, sees as a function of indigenous film festivals. In these cases, films are the result of 'collective self-productions... [used] to mediate historical and social ruptures' (Ginsburg 1991:120). These collective self-productions need not necessarily adhere to mainstream criteria of quality, as they deploy hybrid aesthetics which communicate the many and varied voices of films produced through 'community consultation and traditions of reciprocity' (Córdova, in this volume). Similarly, one can see challenges to the mainstream made in the Flaherty Seminars discussed by Patricia R. Zimmermann, which advance non-commercial and independently made artisanal films. Such venues function like the earlier European film festivals: as sites for celebrating alternatives to Hollywood, its industry and its aesthetics.

What constitutes this alternative or alterity (cultural otherness) in aesthetics, industry or society is mutable, as evidenced in the contributions from Skadi Loist and Ger Zielinski, and from David Mitchell and Sharon Snyder. In the case of Lesbian, Gay, Transgender, Bisexual (LGTB) or Queer film festivals, the otherness which once demanded tolerance has crept into the mainstream – even if peripherally. LGTB festivals have become more established points in the marketplace, although the introduction of additional letters or the use of the word 'queer' suggests its on-going function of introducing additional communities and concerns to the mainstream. Meanwhile, Mitchell and Snyder trouble the idea of communities as unified, since disabilities are not a monolithic experience nor even necessarily shared within families. Disrupting even kinship formations, the films and the festivals become celebrations of radical alterities and the impossibility of categorisation, thereby charting new ways for all humans to think of themselves. The fact that the films run all lengths, and often in video, suggests further otherness from what typically receives mainstream distribution; the films thus challenge the categories and criteria that produce understanding of the cinematic as much as they challenge categories of normal and atypical bodies.

The word 'infomercial' may resonate with Blažević's description of the human rights film as being more concerned with information than entertainment. However, the term, which refers to long-format television advertisement, may likely be closer to the 'activist' film he describes in his contribution to this volume. Blažević prefers not to programme such films because of their overt didacticism and directed advocacy for a single solution. The likeness to the infomercial in this case ought not immediately be taken as disparagement. After all, commercials could be considered an extreme form of the documentary, marshalling truth-telling devices to convince the viewer of an action to take. In this case, I wonder if such descriptions could also be linked to campaign films, which are short videos produced in the service of particular human rights campaigns, and are typically screened for concerned communities or directly to decision-makers. These films are often peripheral, particularly within larger festival programmes, since their video-production and the overt instruction suggest works best suited for specialised use. However, their life in the festival world is hardly forbidden.

Voices from the Waters (www.voicesfromthewaters.com) programmer, Georgekutty A. L., praises *Cutting Off a Lifeline* (Saraswati Kavula, India, 2007), a film about the livelihoods dependent on the river Musi. This documentary was commissioned by the Nexus Institute (www.nexus-berlin.com) for 'Communication and Cooperation for the Sustainable Development of Megacity Hyderabad/India', a project funded by the Federal Ministry of Education and Research, Germany. Meanwhile, as I note in my chapter, 'Traffic Jam Revisited', the Na-Wa festival, Nigeria (en.adesuwa.org/nawa-festival.html) programmed a UN-produced instructional video. And, by way of another example, the campaign film *Equal Access: Integrated Education for Romani Children* (2006), a co-production between WITNESS and Organisation Drom, found its way into a variety of venues. Released in November 2006, this 14-minute documentary was developed to promote educational desegregation in Vidin, Bulgaria and beyond, through local screenings for parents (Romani and non-Romani) and direct-to-decision-maker screenings for local, national and educational authorities. Screenings were extended to the film festival world where *Equal Access* won the Award for Roma Decade Film at the 5th Annual Golden Wheel Roma Film Festival in Skopje, Macedonia (no website) and was programmed at the 3rd annual New Zealand Human Rights Film Festival (www.humanrightsfilmfest.net.nz) in 2007 (Torchin 2008: 391-2); although perhaps not typical, campaign films nonetheless appear in many activist festival programmes.

Festivals as Fields of Witnessing:
How the Films are Exhibited

The pathways of these films, their audiences and their screening circumstances, all contribute to the field of witnessing that enables, or factors into, the transformative capacity of the testimony on display. By fleshing out the contexts, adding details, depth and practices to screenings, the contributions to this volume further aid in determining the activist potential of the film festival, regardless of an individual film's own identity as 'activist'.

I return again to my acquaintances' (informal) comments on the Uist festival, and particularly to the phrase 'preaching to the converted'. This phrase is something of a sensitive issue, often being used by the news media to question the activist potential of a festival or a documentary. Such a claim underscores the expectation of transformation, as well as the demand for outreach, on a massive scale. That is certainly a goal to some extent, but it possibly misses the other activist values and works of the film festival. Singer-activist Harry Belafonte responded to this oft used dismissal when he was special guest star of the 2011 Human Rights International Film Festival (HRWFF; www.hrw.org/en/iff) New York Festival Centrepiece, *Sing Your Song* (Susanne Rostock, U.S., 2011). Following the screening of this biographical documentary, Belafonte reminded the audience of the importance of such gatherings: if one stops preaching to the choir, they may stop singing. In this phrase, he echoes the characterisation of festivals as 'tonic' advanced by Blažević in his chapter. These are places for renewal of commitment, where one sheds the yoke of cynicism by watching empowering stories and mingling with equally committed people.

It is tempting, in fact, to take the house of worship analogy further – and not simply because religious institutions have historically hosted live testimonies and film screenings as components of human rights and humanitarian campaigns (Torchin 2006). The sermon does not necessarily aim to convert its audience so much as to provide information and guidance – theological, philosophical and practical. In fact, the sermon – be it given in a church, mosque, shul or any gathering house – is only one component in a larger community-based organisation that seeks to provide material and spiritual assistance to its congregation and beyond. So, too, as we see in many of the contributions to this volume, festival screenings are only one component of the festival practices that contribute to its definition as activist, as advocating for social justice and change, and seeking to engage a community.

Providing a Pulpit

One overarching value of film festivals is their ability to garner media interest. This can be useful in generating buzz around a film or filmmaker, or in directing attention to an issue or cause. Filmmaker Nick Higgins notes how the inauguration of the 2007 Morelia International Film Festival (www.moreliafilmfest.com) by the President of Mexico, Felipe Calderón, yielded multiple newspaper stories on the topic of the festival's identity and its role in addressing the recent history of Mexico. In her interview, filmmaker Judith Helfand specifically offers advice on the creation of a media story as something that increases both the likelihood of a film's acceptance at a festival and the possibility for community engagement. Frequently, it would appear that the emergence of some festivals coincides with governmental initiatives. As Burres notes, the HRWFF was launched as part of the Fortieth Anniversary of the UDHR (Universal Declaration of Human Rights) and Voices from the Waters launched in 2005, thereby coinciding with the start of the UN International Decade for Action 'Water for Life' (2005-2015) (www.un.org/waterforlifedecade). Although Georgekutty A. L. does not expand on sources of funding, the potential for investing partners to benefit from a demonstration of participation seems likely. The idea that the film festival functions as a performative platform – demonstrating participation in governmental and nongovernmental expectations – underlies Rosenstone's account of Rencontres méditerranéennes cinéma et droits de l'homme (Mediterranean Encounters: Cinema and the Rights of Man, www. rmcdh.ma). Here, one wonders if the heightened involvement of His Majesty, King Mohammed VI, and the uncharacteristic gala events at this human rights film festival, serve to present the nation as a good human rights citizen to a global audience. Could this be one of the risks of governmental use of a film festival, as Grassilli warns?

Building Context

Context emerges as an essential factor in all the contributions. Many chapters in this volume discuss the use of panel discussions and question and answer sessions, and consider them key to providing additional information and connecting the audience with activist programmes; festivals become sites of capacity-building harnessed by the filmmaker/activists and facilitated by the festival programmers. The stars of the documentary films, the sufferers of injustice turned community activists and the filmmakers themselves, can provide crucial backstories, extending the emotional engagement into the off-screen space. Meanwhile, speakers, such as community organisers and experts can provide basic information as well as social, historical, political and practical information for taking action.

Audiences, too, play a crucial role in this formation of context, particularly in cases where direct-to-decision-maker screenings are provided. Grassilli discusses this practice in the case of Festival International du Film et Forum sur les Droits Humains (Geneva) (www. fifdh.ch) and other festivals also facilitate such screenings. For example, AFI-Discovery Channel Silverdocs Festival (silverdocs.com), located in a suburb of Washington, DC, makes use of its location by helping filmmakers to set up specialised screenings at the Capitol Hill Visitor's Center. Although these screenings are seen as independent of the festival, the organisers have connections at the Center and are active in the promotion of the screenings.

The materiality of the encounter contributes to the formation of illuminating and engaging contexts. The screening of *A Massacre Foretold* (Nick Higgins, UK, 2007) at Morelia included a question and answer session with community-members from Acteal, who received a rare moment of full attention from a largely non-indigenous audience. Higgins' observation of this detail reminds us how film festivals can function as spaces that redesign alignments and power structures, even if only temporarily. Meanwhile, Žilnik's staged happenings further point out the occasion that festivals of all kinds offer for destabilising expectations and assumption. Disabilities film festivals, in particular, indicate how the physical construction of film festival venues becomes an expression of community demands and requirements. Describing her participation in the development of ReelAbilities: NY Disabilities Film Festival (www.reelabilities.org), Faye Ginsburg has referred to the challenges of organising screenings in spaces that required wheelchair accessibility and films that provided both subtitling or sign language translation along with audio-description.[3] Even time was reconfigured as screenings had to allow for the inevitable challenges of access to the site, an issue that emerges in Mitchell and Snyder's contribution to this volume. Preparation for the film festival itself contributes to a developing awareness and redesign of sites, creating a transformative platform in advance of the screening. Not only do host cities and institutions shift their perspectives, but visitors can also see the possibilities of inclusive spaces.

Outreach, Circuits, Networks

These festival contexts, in their many permutations, serve to engage communities through affective pleas and practical instruction. In her case study of the Human Rights Arts and Film Festival in Australia (hraff.org.au), Clare Muller suggests that the festival takes on a Human Rights Education model advanced in the UN Decade for Human Rights Education (1995-2005). And as Grassilli points out, there are cases of the development of a general human rights culture in a host city. At the same time, a filmmaker can leverage a film festival, inviting niche audiences to a screening for purposes of capacity building, as Ronit Avni describes in her interview. However, many of the festivals described in this volume 'push out' – reaching beyond the physical space and set dates of the event – into cities, villages and classrooms. Educational institutions play significant roles in these festivals, often as the site of origin, as in the case of UNAFF (United Nations Association Film Festival), started by Jasmina Bojic at Stanford University (www.unaff.org). Meanwhile, Blažević discusses the outreach into the schools and the partnerships developed therein, with teachers becoming volunteers and students developing film clubs to continue festival screenings. For Georgekutty A.L., the travelling of the Voices from the Waters Film Festival to various villages, schools and universities throughout the region, transforms the festival from simply an event into a movement.

Although 'festival circuit' is an oft-used term – and one actively interrogated within the *Film Festival Yearbook* series – 'network' may be the better term in the case of film festivals with an activist function. The value of networking that takes place at, and behind the scenes of, film festivals cannot be underestimated. It appears in varying forms: the casual alliances built among audience members according to shared taste and interests, the card swapping of professionals in the lobby, the pick-me-up of communing with the similarly socially engaged. There are the more formal organisations of the One World Network and Human Rights Film Network, which pool information resources to explore how best to promote human rights values through film culture. And there are informal arrangements arising from collegial relationships.

AFI-Discovery Channel Silverdocs and the New York HRWFF will occasionally share the cost of travel for some international guests who are attending both festivals, which overlap in dates and take place in relative proximity of one another. This sharing of resources is particularly valuable for the documentary-activist filmmaker, who can see these festivals as part of the desirable circuit that includes not only prominent sites such as the Sundance Film Festival (www.sundance.org/festival) and Berlin International Film Festival (www.berlinale.de), but also the documentary festivals such as IDFA – International Documentary Film Festival Amsterdam (www.idfa.nl), Yamagata International Documentary Film Festival (www.yidff.jp), Hot Docs – the Canadian International Documentary Festival (www.hotdocs.ca) in Toronto, Full Frame Documentary Film Festival in Durham, North Carolina (www. fullframefest.org), Sheffield Doc/Fest (sheffdocfest.com), Human Rights Watch International Film Festivals in London and New York (hrwff.org) and AFI-Discovery Channel Silverdocs in Silver Spring, MD. Affiliations and connections further heighten the value of these festivals: HRWFF for its association with Human Rights Watch and AFI-Discovery Channel Silverdocs for its proximity to Washington, DC, which, as discussed above, the festival programmers help the filmmakers to leverage.

At the same time, the circuit for the activist filmmaker is hardly limited to the niche or specialist festival; the capacity for activism and community engagement can take place at any festival. According to Avni, Tribeca Film Festival (www.tribecafilm.com/festival) provided a supportive platform for outreach and publicity whilst, for Žilnik, Berlin offered a site for student protests and radical articulations. Helfand, meanwhile, offers instruction on how a filmmaker can transform any film festival into a platform for engagement. The festivals become sites for all manner of alliance building that aids those looking to mobilise their films in the pursuit of justice and community action. Festivals are places for cultivating alliances and for mounting campaigns that can enhance a film's impact.

Conclusion

In a discussion about documentary and urban activism, social justice filmmaker George Stoney said, 'I'm not happy until my media lead to face to face interaction'. It is precisely this sort of engagement that film festivals offer, so making them a place where activism can take place. One could find a component of activism in many festivals, and not simply those explicitly identified as activist, as these are spaces that enhance the testimonial encounter between viewer and screen witness through discussions, activities and links to action. This volume encourages another, if still virtual, interaction, by uniting a range of perspectives in order to sketch out the numerous and varied relationships between programmers, filmmakers, press, audiences, invited guests and local communities. In doing so, we aim to provide resources for methodological considerations – both for activists and filmmakers wishing to explore the potential of screen media and festivals as sites for community engagement and for the scholar seeking resources and methods to better understand the phenomena of festivals and activism.

Works Cited

Blažević, Igor (2009) 'How to Start', in Tereza Porybná (ed.) *Setting Up a Human Rights Film Festival*. Prague: People in Need, 14-25.

Bourdieu, Pierre (1977) *Outline of a Theory of Practice*. Cambridge: Cambridge University Press.

Calhoun, Craig (1992) 'Introduction: Habermas and the Public Sphere', in Craig Calhoun (ed.) *Habermas and the Public Sphere*. Cambridge, MA and London: The MIT Press, 1-50.

Cohen, Stanley (1996) 'Government Responses to Human Rights Reports: Claims, Denials, and Counterclaims', *Human Rights Quarterly*, 18, 517-43.

Felman, Shoshana and Dori Laub (1992) *Testimony: Crises of Witnessing in Literature, Psychoanalysis and History*. New York and London: Routledge.

Ginsburg, Faye (1991) 'Indigenous Media: Faustian Contract or Global Village?', *Cultural Anthropology*, 6, 1, 92-112.

Gregory, Sam (2006) 'Transnational Storytelling: Human Rights, WITNESS, and Video Advocacy', *American Anthropologist*, 108, 1, 195-204.

Keenan, Thomas (2004), 'Mobilizing Shame', *The South Atlantic Quarterly*, 103, 435-49.

McLagan, Meg (2003) 'Principles, Publicity, and Politics: Notes on Human Rights Media', *American Anthropologist*, 105, 1, 605-12.

Torchin, Leshu (2006) '*Ravished Armenia:* Visual Media, Humanitarian Advocacy, and the Formation of Witnessing Publics', *American Anthropologist*, 108, 1, 214-20.

_____ (2008) 'Influencing Representation: *Equal Access* and Roma Social Inclusion', *Third Text*, 22, 3, 387-96.

Yúdice, George (1996), 'Testimonio and Postmodernism', in Georg M. Gugelberger (ed.) *The Real Thing: Testimonial Discourse and Latin America*. Durham and London: Duke University Press, 42-57.

Notes

[1]   In addition to all of the contributors and to the casual conversations with programmers, activists and filmmakers, I am particularly grateful to Sky Sitney (AFI-Discovery Channel Silverdocs Festival), Andrea Holley (Human Rights Watch International Film Festival) and Christine Squires (Human Rights Watch), who gave generously of their time to provide insights that have informed my own contributions to this volume.

[2]   Thanks to Professor Jan Bebbington, the Director of St Andrews Sustainability Institute, for her account of the festival which provided details regarding the community-centred nature of the event.

[3]   From the session 'The Future of Documentary Studies', *Visible Evidence XVIII*, New York (12 August 2011).

[4]   From the session 'Race, Class, and Community: American Non-fiction Media and Urban Activism', *Visible Evidence XVIII*, New York (13 August 2011).

Film Festivals and Dissent:
Can Film Change the World?

Dina Iordanova

> Hundreds of film and video makers around the world believe that their work can make a difference. Not all of these films or videos initiate concrete help immediately [...] As with human rights work these films expose and publicize human rights abuses occurring throughout the world, using a medium perhaps more powerful than the written word.
>
> Bruni Burres and Heather Harding 1997: 333.

Activist filmmaking and activist film festivals have at least two things in common. Firstly, they are engaged in an effort to correct the record on a certain issue by highlighting lesser known aspects for the benefit of improved public understanding. They are driven by intentionality, be it to increase awareness, to expose, to warn, to prevent and sometimes change the course of events. Secondly, they embody the belief that film is powerful enough to have an impact.

Like other mainstream or genre festivals, activist events also create a temporary venue for the showcasing of new films. The driving force here, however, is a certain cause that has found sufficient expression in cinematic works, which, if showcased, could assist in winning over further supporters for the cause.

In addition, activist festivals have a specific set of stakeholders. Unlike other film festivals, where regional/local authorities or film industry interests have immediate concerns, activist film festivals do not usually see much direct interference from the government or the film industry; equally, they cannot expect much support from them. More often than not activist film festivals have some form of affiliation with existing organisations, usually bodies that qualify as non-government organisations (NGOs) and function in relation to a variety of civil society groups and causes.[1]

Amnesty International, Human Rights Watch and People in Need, are just a few of the parent organisations referenced in the context of this volume.[2] Some of the sponsoring bodies are locally or regionally focused (e.g. CLACPI, discussed here by Córdova), whereas others function globally (United Nations, Greenpeace). Thus, most activist film festivals rely on the continuous financial support and guidance of a parent organisation and often seek further funding from various charitable trusts.[3]

In turn, the parent organisations and groups have a vested interest in using film events because, as Bruni Burres puts it in her interview for this volume, film supplies the human face and the story and provides the much-needed narrative background for activist work. Burrres notes that using film and post-screening debates to communicate contemporary human issues is likely to reach 'a broader and more diverse audience than a 200-page report or the legal briefing on these same issues [...] a great film can emotionally move and affect an individual in a way that no legal report can'. Throughout this book, authors repeatedly stress the importance of accessibility: films make the highly abstract categories of human rights discourses easier to grasp and understand.

The goals of activist film festivals – to correct the record, to enlighten, to mobilise – also set them apart from other film festivals. A special feature of activist festivals is their frequent involvement with educational institutions, which also function as implied stakeholders in the project to mobilise public opinion and nurture committed cultural citizens. The targets are high schools, universities and a variety of other educational bodies.[4] In such a context, the Flaherty Seminar should indeed be considered as an early example of an 'activist educational organisation', as Patricia R. Zimmermann describes it in her essay in this volume, since it is involved with the study of film, not as entertainment, but as a serious means of communicating information and shaping perceptions about the world; and this constitutes a *sui generis* activism. Indeed, pedagogy and activism are so closely correlated that many contributors to this volume (Muller, Blažević, Bojic, Farnel, Helfand and Burres) discuss educational linkages explicitly as an integral part of their film festival project.[5]

Public intellectuals are often involved with activist film festivals and represent a special group of stakeholders in such events: their 'stake' is of a moral rather than material nature. Many activist festivals, for example, feature concurrent debates, discussion forums and conferences, which provide a tribunal beyond the traditional confines of academic institutions. Such is the case, for example, with the Subversive Film Festival in Zagreb, Croatia (www.subversivefilmfestival.com), where high profile commentator Slavoj Žižek brings like-minded intellectuals and academics together for political debates on matters such as '68, the legacy of Maoism and so on. Another example of such public involvement is the festival started by dissident documentarian Michael Moore in Traverse City, Michigan (www.traversecityfilmfest.org).

It is along similar lines of public visibility that activist film festivals often pursue the involvement of celebrities. The approach is similar to the longstanding practice of UN agencies and other large NGOs enlisting ambassadorial assistance. While mainstream events rely on quasi-professional activist personages such as Bianca Jagger, Bono or Bob Geldoff, some activist causes receive prominence due to the involvement of celebrities who become personally engaged: such as trafficking and sex slavery (Demi Moore, Ashton Kutcher and Mira Sorvino), indigenous concerns in Ecuador linked to Joe Berlinger's anti-Chevron environmental documentary *Crude* (U.S., 2009) (Darryl Hannah), or the proposed Tobin tax on banks in the aftermath of the 2008 financial crisis (Bill Nighy).

As Nick Higgins points out in this volume, rather than relying solely on celebrities, human rights film festivals also make an effort to get the subjects of the films to attend screenings. In this way ordinary heroes are recognised and celebrated in a highly personalised way that 'helps to amplify the story', as Farnel remarks in his interview here. They are the true celebrities of the activist festival circuit.

Alongside educational links, outreach and community building are equally important for the activist film festival; they allow it to build awareness and trust, as well as to enlist support and mobilise for the specific cause that the festival and the respective backing organisation(s) stand for. These are achieved by a combination of extras that enhance the screening of films, such as discussions and Q&A sessions, but also by the production of supporting information and website campaigns. Another important specific feature is the travelling festival: taking a selection of films that played at the festival proper for outreach screenings in remote communities, is as typical for the New York HRWIFF (www.hrw.org/en/iff) as it is for Voices from the Waters in Kerala, India (www.voicesfromthewaters.com). Such outreach activities help in developing new audiences, building and strengthening local communities and capitalising on the network potential of the festival by expanding it far beyond its main location. In some instances specific to activist festivals – like the Festival Internacional de Cine del Sahara (www.festivalsahara.com) featured in this volume or the festival in Douarnenez, Brittany (www.festival-douarnenez.com), which focuses on ethnic minorities, guests stay in the homes of local people, thus becoming involved and getting to share and learn more about their lives. The topical debates are probably the single most important feature that makes a festival activist: it is in the context of these discussions that a more complete understanding of a film can crystallise and a call to action can take place. In fact, as becomes clear from the case studies and interviews included in this volume, the discussion is as important as the film screening and undoubtedly constitutes an inherent part of the festival structure. In this respect, discussions at activist film festivals differ from the Q&A sessions at mainstream festivals: the goal is not to receive insight and information about the film's making and message, but to go beyond the film and address the issues that the film is concerned with, as well as to influence the thinking of the audience. Thus, audience engagement is of prime importance. As Sean Farnel puts it in his interview, 'the whole point of having this type of film festival is the transfer that takes place from the screen to the audience'.

Circuit and Networks

Is there a circuit for activist film festivals? Do they form clear networks? Do films travel on from festival to festival in a coordinated manner?

A few years back I put forward the view that festival networks function as relatively independent parallel circuits (Iordanova 2009). Leshu Torchin also asserts this standpoint, remarking in her introduction that, in the case of film festivals with an activist function, it may be more appropriate to talk of a 'network' than of a 'circuit'. Indeed, the evidence is that many of the specialist festivals do not interact much with their mainstream counterparts, but rather enter into specific consortia and coalitions with one another. One example is described in Mariagiulia Grassilli's essay, which talks of the Human Rights Festivals Network and its respective charter. Another is the One World Network, whose members also produced the practical guidebook that is reviewed here. Yet another example relates to specialised GLBT/Queer film festivals, which 'have built their own circuits and are part of niche industries' (Loist 2011: 281).

The evidence that emerges from the case studies and interviews suggests that, when a film focusing on an activist cause is involved, there is something akin to a two-tier festival system at play. First, there is the top tier of desirable mainstream festivals that would supposedly give excellent exposure to issue-based films. These are usually identified as Cannes (www.festival-cannes.fr), Berlin (www.berlinale.de) and Sundance (www.sundance.org/festival), but also Toronto (tiff.net), Hong Kong (www.hkiff.org.hk) or Abu Dhabi (www.abudhabifilmfestival.ae). These are followed by a second tier of niche, but inclusive, documentary and human rights festivals; most often the festivals listed in this category include the IDFA – International Documentary Film Festival Amsterdam (www.idfa.nl), Hot Docs in Toronto (www.hotdocs.ca), AFI-Discovery Channel Silverdocs in Maryland (silverdocs.com), Sheffield Doc/ Fest (sheffdocfest.com), Cinéma du réel in Paris (www.cinemadureel. org), Visions du réel in Nyon, Switzerland (www.visionsdureel.ch), the Yamagata Documentary International Festival (www.yidff.jp) in Yamagata, Japan, the Al Jazeera Documentary Festival in Doha, Qatar (festival.aljazeera.net), Movies That Matter in The Hague, Netherlands (www.moviesthatmatterfestival.nl) and so on.[6] This is further enhanced by rounds of dedicated screenings, television broadcasts, DVD and on-line distribution and, occasionally, a wider theatrical run, which usually comes at the very end of the cycle.

In deciding on tailor-made festival trajectories for a specific film, filmmakers would choose, depending on the entry point in the annual calendar and on the geography of the issues at stake, from a combination of large established festivals (especially if they want to target the Establishment)[7] and a line-up of niche (documentary, issue-based) festivals; thus the film would travel through a two- (or more) tiered system.

As the case study of *A Massacre Foretold* (Nick Higgins, UK, 2007) demonstrates, in such a system of circulation for activist film, singular festivals constitute the nodes in the network, whereas established documentary festivals, such as those in Amsterdam, Sheffield or Yamagata, assume the role of hubs from which material is redistributed.

The sustainability of these events often depends on the sheer number of films that are made in a given area of concern: one needs to have sufficient material, a critical mass of films produced during the year on a certain topic, to secure a full festival programme.[8] This is why, perhaps, general documentary and human rights festivals have the highest visibility and impact in correcting the public record. Due to their all-inclusive stance, such festivals receive more submissions than they could possibly screen and can therefore afford to be selective.

The topics covered by such festivals invariably shift over time, in keeping with the changing nature of the human rights agenda and on-going political concerns. Part of this correcting of the record involves highlighting instances of control, and a number of mainstream and specialist festivals commit to renouncing censorship, as this issue not only cuts across the human rights agenda, but also undermines artistic creativity. Such instances include recent festival campaigns in support of censored Iranian filmmaker Jafar Panahi and Chinese installation artist Ai Weiwei. The origins of Arsenals (arsenals.lv), a film festival based in Riga, Latvia, can be traced to 1986 and the end of the Soviet *perestroika* era, when it took systematic, activist steps to combat censorship and assert the principles of *glasnost* in society.[9]

On checking the trajectory through the circuit of two prominent independent documentaries – *Petition* (Zhao Liang, China/Switzerland/ UK/France/Belgium/Finland, 2009) and *Burma VJ: Reporter i et lukket land* (*Burma VJ: Reports from a Closed Country*, Anders Østergaard, Denmark/Sweden/Norway/UK/U.S./Germany/Netherlands/Israel/Spain/ Belgium/Canada, 2008) – the two-tier mixture of niche/specialist and mainstream festivals is confirmed; in each case it is enhanced by a limited distribution deal once the festival circuit has been exhausted.

Petition, which chronicles the desperate and ultimately hopeless plight of ordinary Chinese who are determined to seek justice and take their complaints to the central government, opened with showings at a combination of major and secondary mainstream festivals, such as Cannes (22 May 2009), Locarno (www.pardo.ch) (7 August 2009), Bangkok (www.bangkokfilm.org) (28 September 2009), Vancouver (www.viff.org) (2 October 2009), Gent (www.filmfestival.be) (5 November 2009), Amiens (www.filmfestamiens.org) (17 November 2009), Hong Kong (2 April 2010) and Melbourne (miff.com.au) (25 July 2010), but it also ran through a dedicated circuit of documentary festivals, which included specialist forums like the AFI Fest (www.afi.com/afifest), AFI-Discovery Channel Silverdocs (for which it was selected by programmers in November), the IDFA (November), Watch Docs (www. watchdocs.pl) in Poland (December), the Thessaloniki Documentary Festival (tdf.filmfestival.gr) in Greece (March 2010) and the Buenos Aires International Festival of Independent Cinema (www.bafici.gov.er) (April 2010). It gained awards both at mainstream events such as the Bratislava (www.iffbratislava.sk), Hawaii (www.hiff.org), Hong Kong and Tiburon (www.tiburonfilmfestival.com) International Film Festivals and at specialist events in Buenos Aires and Thessaloniki. In January 2011, about 18 months after its festival première, *Petition* received a theatrical release in the United States.

Burma VJ, an international co-production featuring rare footage of the democracy demonstrations in this closely-guarded country, showed at dedicated documentary festivals – IDFA in Amsterdam, CPH-DOX (www.cphdox.dk) in Denmark and the Thessaloniki Documentary Festival – at mainstream indie festivals (Sundance) and at dedicated human rights film festivals such as the One World Film Festival (www.oneworld.cz) in Prague; but it was also shown at mainstream generalist international festivals that screen controversial documentaries, such as Vancouver and Seattle (www.siff.net), Vienna (www.viennale.at), San Francisco (www.sffs.org), Jakarta (www.jiffest.org) and Bangkok. After screening at the UNHCR's-sponsored Refugee Film Festival in Japan (unhcr.refugeefilm.org), *Burma VJ* received theatrical distribution in Denmark and played on television in the co-producing countries. Eventually it was released on DVD in the UK and is now available for purchase on the Internet.

Internet-enabled Developments: Space of Flows

> The world of cinema is changing in every way, and that extends to the new world of film festivals.
> Geoffrey Gilmore, Chief Creative Officer, Tribeca Enterprises, 2011.

The dramatic disruptions in the cycle of filmmaking, distribution and reception enabled by technological changes, are being rapidly embraced by activists at the same time as new, previously unavailable opportunities for increased exposure become available (Dargis 2010). Crowdfunding for independent low-budget features and documentaries seems to have become the feature of the day, with filmmakers not only raising production funds through a variety of sources, but also selling their films directly from websites or making them available for streaming through dedicated outlets.[10] The implications for activists of new technologies in production, distribution and exhibition are felt most productively in areas where the democratic and ethical dimensions of the activist forum pair up with full-scale digital disruption (see Iordanova and Cunningham 2012).

The new dissemination model for activist films relies on a combination of festival screenings (by using Withoutabox for submission;

see Fischer 2011), specially organised showings to communities, a website DVD release (often with differential pricing) and on-line streaming that enables the filmmaker to reach out much more efficiently than before. What would previously be described as 'guerrilla' marketing nowadays becomes a viable model that allows activist films (and their causes) to travel much farther and gain global exposure. For example, Robert Greenwald's documentary, *Iraq for Sale* (U.S., 2006), which uncovers war profiteers, is available for viewing on-line. Norwegian activist documentarian Line Halvorsen distributed her films *USA vs. Al-Arian* (Norway, 2007) and the anti-capitalist *Living without Money* (Norway/Italy, 2011), through a combination of festival and special screenings, a crowdsourcing campaign that funded a DVD release and Web-based streaming via Snag Films (Halvorsen 2011). The same pattern is followed by Swedish documentarian Terje Carlsson, whose *Israel. vs. Israel* (Sweden/Israel/Occupied Palestinian Territory, 2010) received numerous awards at the festival circuit in 2011 (http://www.israelvsisrael.com/). Sites such as Vodo (vodo.net) or Spanner Films (www.spannerfilms.net) are among those pioneering this new model of distribution. The main preoccupation of Snag Films (www.snagfilms.com) is to showcase films that would not otherwise reach an audience. Other video streaming sites, such as Hulu (www.hulu.com) or Vimeo (vimeo.com), carry diverse material of this type as well. For example, *Gaza-strophe* (Samir Abdallah and Khéridine Mabrouk, Palestine/France, 2010), a film that has been in theatrical distribution only in France, can be seen in full on the Vimeo site. A distinct hub for activist causes is the Web-based activist forum Explore (www.explore.org), which features a range of specially commissioned videos on different concerns.[11]

YouTube, in existence since late 2005 and nowadays the third most popular website in the world, can be best described with Manuel Castells' concept of 'space of flows', one that implies 'the material arrangements that allow for simultaneity of social practices without territorial contiguity' (2005 [2001]: 628). Having rapidly become a key hub for an alternative public sphere that fosters new attainments in participatory communication (Burgess and Green 2009), YouTube transforms the whole game of cinematic circulation by making content available outside territorial and temporal limitations and by providing a forum for global discussion. It gives permanent access to many films that could previously only be seen in the context of activist film festivals: from Bill Nighy and Richard Curtis's short video backing the Robin Hood tax on banks (*The Banker*, 2009) and a range of anti-trafficking messages fronted by celebrities, through *Good Kurds, Bad Kurds: No Friends But the Mountains* (Kevin McKiernan, U.S., 2000), targeting the double standards of Western coverage of independence movements in the Middle East, to *Hacking Democracy* (Simon Ardizzone and Russell Michaels, U.S., 2006), exposing serious shortcomings within the U.S. electoral system.

The radical digital disruption adds a new dimension to burgeoning developments with regard to the showcasing of films for activist causes. A realm that until recently was preserved for festivals is now being taken over by new models of combined circulation. In this changed context, the film festival will remain a key component of the activist dissemination strategy only for as long as festival showings are found to be a good way to reach out to audiences.

For the time being, festivals still play an important role in this cycle of DIY filmmaking and distribution. Circulation via the activist festival circuit generates sufficient word-of-mouth to establish filmmakers' reputations and enable them to sell DVD copies directly out of websites, as well as to successfully crowdfund further projects. The decreasing costs related to submitting, transporting and screening films, make it increasingly easy to mount new festivals. It would be logical to expect further proliferation in the number of activist-led festivals. There is also likely to be a proliferation in one-off events, as it is no longer necessary to stage festival gatherings on a regular basis.

Indeed, new digital dimensions diminish the importance of physical presence. Thus, festivals that opt to turn into 'space of flows' and stream part of the festival content on-line for the benefit of viewers that could not be physically present are a prime example of early adoption of new possibilities. Both the wealthy Tribeca Film Festival (www.tribecafilm.com/festival) and the Festival Internacional de Cine del Sahara tried outreach on-line streaming in 2011 for the benefit of audiences who could not attend live screenings. Some festivals arrange for close tie-ups with television, where material shown at the festivals is also featured on niche, yet global, digital TV channels (e.g. the Sundance Channel in the U.S., but also Al Jazeera or Russia Today) and simultaneously streamed through websites; a suitable example is the practice of the Amnesty International-sponsored Movies That Matter in The Hague, Netherlands. Yet other festivals moved entirely on-line as they assessed that a global audience of like-minded spectators was more important to them than limited local exposure. The best-known example, perhaps, is the on-line festival Media That Matters (www.mediathatmattersfest.

org), which is dedicated to showcasing 'short films that inspire action'. Even this on-going festival, however, is known to stage its premières and various other events in the real world, usually in New York City, the festival's headquarters (de Valck 2012).

In this new set-up, an interesting combination emerges between the activist film festival and its on-line dissemination, where filmmakers create a method of distribution that combines a variety of channels to secure maximum exposure for their message. Festivals and YouTube are often seen to coordinate efforts for such dissemination, often resulting in a hybrid model whereby films are shown at a festival, but then also make their way to the Web, where they can be seen by those who reach them through word-of-mouth, to ensure the widest possible dissemination.

The unprecedented level of exposure that new technologies enable inaugurates a new era for activism: film festivals are enhanced by the additional dimension of on-line streaming and can therefore reach out far beyond the post-screening discussion. It is possible to see a film at a festival and then e-mail or tweet your friends to encourage them to view it over the Internet. In this new dissemination model, a variety of activist projects that link contributors and individuals from around the world becomes possible: Pangea Day (10 May 2008), which links filmmaking efforts from Cairo, Kigali, London, Los Angeles, Mumbai and Rio de Janeiro,[12] or Kevin McDonald's globally crowdsourced project Life in a Day (U.S./UK, 2011).

It is particularly important for activist filmmakers that their films are easily accessible across the globe and can be disseminated further in an uninhibited manner. Sharing and further disseminating the film is explicitly encouraged and seen as acting 'for the planet'. One of the best examples of such wide, free circulation concerns the carbon-offset themed Home (Yann Arthus-Bertrand, France, 2009), a mobilising environmentalist film which was in mainstream distribution, but also played at festivals while simultaneously being made available for viewing in at least three locations on the Web. As a result, Home has been acknowledged as having had a significant influence on public opinion.[13]

The innovative dissemination approaches enabled by new technologies are likely to intensify even further in a context in which activism, particularly in cyberspace, is changing outcomes and influencing new developments. The 'hacker' attitude has now entered the mainstream and one can only expect further developments; new social movements have been facilitated by the growth in social media, which activists have embraced and put to new uses. Enabled by technology, for the first time in history millions of people can tell their stories in film and see them disseminated to global audiences. This is a unique opportunity to radically undermine double standards in reporting and hypocrisy in rhetoric. Festival-goers themselves can now be involved more directly, both in the making and dissemination of films, as well as via commentary and recommendations.

In this new configuration of activist film dissemination, the film festival plays an important community-building role, in supplying legitimacy to what could otherwise still be seen as a marginalised cyberspace project. Previously a hub of alternative activity, the festival gradually becomes a node in a system of complex approaches to dissemination.

It so happens that this book on film festivals and activism is being produced during a particularly intense period. The festivals that form the focus of our attention take place alongside a wide range of street protests and grassroots political activities – from 'Los Indignados' in Madrid and the rampant crowds of Cairo, Manama and Sana'a, to the 'Occupy Wall Street' protesters in New York City and far beyond. The growth in general dissent and disillusionment over political hypocrisy and corruption is palpable and the impact of political mobilisation and civil disobedience is being felt throughout the world, from the Arab Spring to the Seattle protests and on the streets of Western capitals (Athens, Paris, London).

Today, activism takes many shapes and forms: from celebrity chef Jamie Oliver's televised school dinners 'revolution' in the UK, to Banksy's 'art terrorism' as seen in *Exit Through the Gift Shop* (Banksy, U.S./UK, 2010); from Julian Assange's publicity-seeking WikiLeaks provocation, to the unobtrusive but influential arrival of non-Western alternative economic thinkers, such as Bangladesh's Mohamad Yunus or Peru's Hernando de Soto. Some of the most visible dissident media personalities who are fighting the double standards in international politics, each from their own corner (José Bové, Noam Chomsky, Adam Curtis, Robert Fisk, Al Gore, Naomi Klein, Lawrence Lessig, the Yes Men) are directly or indirectly involved with film and film festivals. [14]

Yet isn't it also true that each and every festival is an act of activism in its own way? The range of causes and agendas that film festivals serve is truly diverse: combatting poverty, fighting slavery and false imprisonment, exposing and condemning discrimination on the basis of race and sexual orientation, securing the future of the planet against excessive and destructive industrial growth, and much more. A much wider variety of film festivals than we have space to discuss in this book would qualify as activist, and they perpetuate a variety of agendas – from Cines del Sur in Granada, Spain (www.cinesdelsur.com), which seeks to consolidate the global South (see Iordanova 2010), to Emir Kusturica's maverick Küstendorf Film and Music Festival (www. kustendorf-filmandmusicfestival.org), which reflects a singular and idiosyncratic, yet profoundly anti-establishment politics. These events all reflect the 'rise of the rest' and a growing diversity of environmental, political and financial agendas which are no longer underpinned by the West's geopolitical interests, but are instead proliferated in the context of diverse economies and cultures as part of what Fareed Zakharia has dubbed the 'Post-American world' (2008).

Works Cited

Broderick, Peter (2009) 'Crowd-funding,' *The Distribution Bulletin*, 9, 10 March. On-line. Available HTTP: http://www.peterbroderick.com/distributionbulletins/distributionbulletins.html (20 June 2011).

_____ (2011) 'Crowd-funding Takes Off,' *The Distribution Bulletin*, 15, 24 February. On-line. Available HTTP: http://www.peterbroderick.com/distributionbulletins/distributionbulletins.html (20 June 2011).

Burgess, Jean and Joshua Green (2009) *YouTube: Online Video and Participatory Culture*. London: Polity Press.

Burres, Bruni and Heather Harding (1997) 'Human Rights Filmmaking Today,' *Visual Anthropology*, 9, 329-33.

Castells, Manuel (2005 [2001]) 'Grassrouting the Space of Flows,' in Ackbar Abbas and John Nguyen Erni (eds) *Internationalizing Cultural Studies: An Anthology*. Oxford: Blackwells, 627-36.

Coss, Simon (2009) 'Movies Can't Change the World, Say Israeli, Palestinian Filmmakers,' *The Daily News Egypt*, 17 February. On-line. Available HTTP: http://www.thedailynewsegypt.com/archive/movies-cant-change-the-world-say-israeli-palestinian-filmmakers.html (11 July 2011).

Dargis, Manohla (2010) 'Declaration of Indies: Just Sell It Yourself!' *New York Times*, January 14. On-line. Available HTTP: http://www.nytimes.com/2010/01/17/movies/17dargis.html?scp=1&sq=declaration%20of%20indies&st=cse (20 June 2011).

de Valck, Marijke (2012) 'Screening the Future of Film Festivals? A Long Tale of Convergence and Digitisation in the Age of YouTube,' in Dina Iordanova and Stuart Cunningham (eds) *Digital Disruption: Cinema Moves On-line*, St Andrews: St Andrews Film Studies.

Fischer, Alex (2011) 'Film Festival Submission: Case Study,' *Dynamics of World Cinema*. On-line. Available HTTP: http://www.st-andrews.ac.uk/worldcinema/index.php/resources/research/82-submission (18 October 2011).

Gilmore, Geoffrey (2011) 'How the Internet is Changing the Film Festival Experience,' *Tribeca Blog*. On-line. Available HTTP: http://www.tribecafilm.com/tribecaonline/future-of-film/How-the-Internet-is-Changing-the-Film-Festival-Experience.html (20 June 2011).

Gündoğdu, Mustafa (2010) 'Film Festivals in the Diaspora: Impetus to the Development of Kurdish Cinema?' in Dina Iordanova with Ruby Cheung (eds) *FFY2: Film Festivals and Imagined Communities*, St Andrews: St Andrews Film Studies, 188-98.

Halvorsen, Line (2011) Unpublished interview with the author, August.

Hessel, Stéphane (2011) *Time for Outrage: Indignez-vous!* New York: Twelve.

Iordanova, Dina (2009) 'The Festival Circuit,' in Dina Iordanova with Ragan Rhyne (eds) *FFY1: The Festival Circuit*, St Andrews: St Andrews Film Studies and College Gate Press, 23-40.

_____ (2010) 'From the Source: Cinemas of the South,' *Film International*, 8, 5, November, 95-9.

Iordanova, Dina and Stuart Cunningham (eds) (2012) *Digital Disruption: Cinema Moves On-line*, St Andrews: St Andrews Film Studies.

Klinger, Gabe (2011) 'The Old Soldier,' *Sight and Sound*, August, 52-5.

Loist, Skadi (2011) 'On the Relationship between Film Festivals and Industry,' *Busan Cinema Forum: Seeking the Path of Asian Cinema*. Busan: BIFF, 280-90.

Rangan, Pooja (2010) 'Some Annotations on the Film Festival as an Emerging Medium in India,' *South Asian Popular Culture*, 8, 2, July, 123-41.

Ross, Miriam (2011) 'The Film Festival as Producer: Latin American Films and Rotterdam's Hubert Bals Fund,' *Screen*, 52, 2, Summer, 261-8;

Zakharia, Fareed (2008) *The Post-American World*, New York: W.W.Norton & Co.

On-line Availability of Films Referenced:

The Banker (Richard Curtis, UK, 2009). On-line. Available HTTP: http://www.
youtube.com/watch?v=qYtNwmXKIvM&feature=related (20 July 2011).

Gaza-strophe: The Day After (Samir Abdallah and Khéridine Mabrouk, Occupied
Palestinian Territories/France, 2010). On-line. Available HTTP: http://
vimeo.com/9882505 (15 August 2011).

Good Kurds, Bad Kurds: No Friends but the Mountains (Kevin McKiernan, U.S.,
2000). On-line. Available HTTP: www.youtube.com/watch?v=x33grBe_
wjQ (31 October 2011).

Hacking Democracy (Simon Ardizone and Russell Michaels, UK, 2006). On-line.
Available HTTP: http://www.youtube.com/watch?v=-hNxBa6KENE (22
August 2011).

Home (Yann Arthus-Bertrand, France, 2009). On-line. Available HTTP: http://
www.homethemovie.org; www.home-2009.com; http://www.youtube.com/
watch?v=jqxENMKaeCU (21 August 2011).

Iraq for Sale: The War Profiteers (Robert Greenwald, U.S., 2006). On-line.
Available HTTP: http://iraqforsale.org (22 August 2011).

Israel.vs. Israel (Terje Carlsson, Sweden/Israel/Occupied Palestinian Territory,
2010). On-line. Available HTTP: http://www.israelvsisrael.com;
http://www.youtube.com/watch?v=Btr1IQ-7xmA (8 December 2011).

Living without Money (Line Halvorsen, Norway/Italy, 2011). On-line. Available
HTTP: http://livingwithoutmoney.org/ (20 August 2011).

No Child Is Born a Terrorist (Douglas Thompson, U.S., 2010). On-line.
Available HTTP: http://www.explore.org/videos/player/me-no-child-is-
born-a-terrorist (15 August 2011).

USA vs. Al-Arian (Line Halvorsen, Norway, 2007). On-line. Available HTTP: http://
www.usavsalarian.com;
http://www.snagfilms.com/films/title/usa_vs_al_arian (25 August 2011).

Notes

[1]   The parent body can also be a media organisation, as it is in the case of
the Al Jazeera Documentary Festival (festival.aljazeera.net). Sometimes, it
is a film body that works across various areas. The London Palestine Film
Festival (www.palestinefilm.org/festivals.asp), for example, is produced by
the Palestinian Film Foundation (www.palestinefilm.org), an organisation
that also engages in other film-related activities and is supported by the
electronic newspaper Electronic Intifada (electronicintifada.net).

2   An example is Breakthrough, an international human rights organisation that uses media, new technologies and popular culture for community mobilising in urban and rural areas in India and the United States, to address gender-based violence, sexual and reproductive health rights, racial justice and migrant rights, and to deal with issues of violence against women, sexuality and HIV/AIDS. One of its initiatives was the Tri Continental Film Festival (www.breakthrough.tv/events/tri-continental-film-festival), which has links to Asia, Africa and Latin America. Further examples include the growing number of environmental festivals sponsored by organisations concerned with climate change, such as the Monsoon Film Festival (active since 2005; website unavailable) and the Vatavaran Environment and Wildlife Film Festival (active since 2006; cmsvatavaran.org), which are discussed in other contexts by Pooja Rangan (2010), or the Uist Eco Film Festival (uistfilm.org), which was launched in 2011 on the remote Scottish island of Benbecula in the Outer Hebrides.

3   The Sigrid Rausing Trust (publisher of *Granta* magazine), for example, supported the Russian LGBT film festival, Bok o Bok/Side by Side (www. bok-o-bok.ru; www.sbsff.com/en), permitting it to stage a Siberian edition.

4   A related example given in Robert Rosenstone's chapter of this book concerns Professor Abdhelhay Mouddon, a politically active academic who has organised debates on matters such as cinema and the university curriculum in the context of the Rencontres méditerranéennes cinéma et droits de l'Homme (www.rmcdh.ma) in Morocco.

5   Some critics – such as Spanish philosopher Joaquin Herrera Flores and Hong Kong lesbian activist Denise Tsang, referenced here in the essays by Grassilli and by Loist and Zielinski – have expressed reservations in regard to the inherently Western-centric scope of cause-based film festivals. A simple observation has it that the West supplies all these festivals and that it essentially controls the access to production and dissemination technology, as well as to equipment and training opportunities. Raising these matters of control is an important consideration in a context in which the West is increasingly exposed and can less and less take the position of impartial moral arbitrator – in particular as it is seen to engage in the dispensation of selective air-bound 'justice' and routine 'blood for oil' practices – all of which triggers scepticism towards both Western-made films and Western-based venues. A group of Latin American filmmakers, for example, recently published a manifesto to object to the trend of 'pornomiseria' (porno-misery), which presupposes that films from these countries are expected to primarily focus on the political situation, poverty

and misfortune, in order to get funding and exposure (Ross 2011: 262). Israeli and Palestinian filmmakers have also expressed disillusionment over the narrow range of themes and approaches that they are expected to cover in the context of their filmmaking in order to make their work fit the demands of the exhibition and festival circuit (Coss 2009). On the other hand, the proliferating number of issue-based festival venues creates a growing opportunity for non-Western filmmakers to have their work seen internationally; not only in the West, but across a number of other countries. One example is the Peruvian documentarian Javier Corcuera whose exploration into the plight of Kurdish exiles, *La Espalda del Mundo* *(The Back of the World*, Spain, 2000), was seen by members of another displaced group, the Saharawi refugees in West Sahara, resulting in the director's commitment to the creation of the uniquely activist Festival Internacional de Cine del Sahara (www.festivalsahara.com).

6   Bruni Burres observes in her interview that mainstream festivals integrated the human rights agenda only after the specialised human rights festivals had successfully developed it.

7   Environmental concern documentaries such as *The 11th Hour* (Leila Conners and Nadia Conners, U.S., 2007) with Leonardo di Caprio, and *An Inconvenient Truth* (David Guggenheim, U.S., 2006) with Al Gore, screened at Cannes in 2007 and 2006 respectively. A veteran of Latin America's Cinema Novo, Fernando Solanas, chose the Berlinale for the première of his documentary *La dignidad de los nadies (The Dignity of the Nobodies*, Argentina/Brazil/Switzerland, 2005), which focuses on poverty in Argentina. *Promises* (Carlos Bolado, B.Z. Goldberg and Justine Shapiro, U.S., 2001), a moving account of the filmmakers' attempts to bring together Palestinian and Israeli children, played at three mainstream festivals in the northern summer of 2001: Karlovy Vary (www.kviff.com), Locarno and Toronto.

8   As the interview with Bruni Burres reveals, Human Rights Watch did not decide on a festival format immediately; they just knew of films that needed showing. The realisation that the festival format is the most suitable one for showcasing them only came later. It is the availability of a critical mass of material that often proves most important. Thus Jewish, GLBT festivals are viable as recurring events, while others are more suited for one-off events.

9   Festivals engaged with fighting around a sovereignty cause occupy a special position in the activist taxonomy. Usually clustered in larger cities, such festivals attract an array of activists to propagate their specific cause. London, for example, is home of a Palestine Film Festival (staged by the Palestinian Film Foundation, www.palestinefilm.org), a Kurdish Film

Festival (www.lkff.co.uk), a Tibetan Film Festival (www.day-for-night.org/ tibetfilmfestival), as well as many more cause-specific events. These festivals not only screen cause-focused films made by international filmmakers but also showcase the output of filmmakers from the respective group who work in complex conditions of marginality (Gündo du 2010).

10   Peter Broderick, one of the leading propagators of these new distribution models, quotes the example of British filmmaker Franny Armstrong, who used crowdfunding to raise over £590,000 for the production and distribution of her docufiction climate change hybrid, *The Age of Stupid* (UK, 2009), and £164,321 for the accompanying social action campaign called 'Not Stupid' (Broderick 2009). He claims that crowdfunding has now become a key element of indie film financing, with the most successful film projects now raising hundreds of thousands of dollars as opposed to the tens of thousands just a few years ago (Broderick 2011).

11   A useful structural division applied by Explore can be adopted in a possible taxonomy for the activist film festival. It evolves around two major categories, which, while overlapping, provide a good navigation tool: Places and Causes. On the one hand, under Places, one can find films related to concerns and issues specific to a given country or region. On the other hand, the Causes section features material that treats anxieties and ills that spread out and affect humankind supranationally, such as slavery and trafficking, climate change or homosexual rights. Explore, for example, features the short *No Child Is Born a Terrorist* (Douglas Thompson, U.S., 2010).

12   A crowdsourced filmmaking project, *Can Your Film Change the World?* (www.youtube.com/watch?v=Pl3xHIsvF9o) is linked to the idea of Pangea Day, 10 May 2008. It invited individuals from around the world to make a film that expressed their concern and then upload it in order to reach out to others; 'Pangea Day plans to use the power of film to bring the world a little closer together. We're divided by borders, race, religion, conflict [...] but most of all by misunderstanding and mistrust. Pangea Day seeks to overcome that – to help people see themselves in others – through the power of film. [...] sites in Cairo, Kigali, London, Los Angeles, Mumbai and Rio de Janeiro will be linked to produce a 4-hour programme of powerful films, visionary speakers and uplifting music. The programme will be broadcast live to the world through the Internet, television, digital cinemas and mobile phones. Your film could be part of it. The online video revolution has helped spawn a new generation of grass-roots film-makers worldwide [...] Movies can't change the world. But the people who watch them can'.

13   The commentaries from the YouTube Home site show that viewers react to the film as an inspirational and life-changing spiritual experience. One of the commentators insists that 'Everyone on this planet should have seen this!' Another describes *Home* as 'possibly one of the most eye opening, educational, and critical 90 minutes any Human Being can invest of their time'. Another user admits she was so moved that she cried while watching the film.

14   In France, activism seems to be subsumed under the category of 'indignation', a category introduced by the nonagenarian Stéphane Hessel, who, in an influential pamphlet entitled Time for Outrage (Indignez-vous!), spoke of a permanent stance of anger towards the corruption prevalent in politics. 'The motif of resistance, this is indignation' (2011: 11), he wrote, linking indignation to the war-time virtues of the Resistance, identifying a range of causes that trigger indignation at the present time and talking extensively of 'disobedience'. Jean-Luc Godard's recent *Film Socialisme* (Switzerland/France, 2010) references a similar range of influences (Klinger 2011). While such intellectuals are often regarded as 'armchair radicals', younger French activists often follow their lead; for example, the Cinémaligre Film Festival (www.cl-aligre.org) in one of the central Parisian neighborhoods, the 'free communie of Aligre', coincided with mass protests during 2010 and evolved around the theme of 'disobedience'.

Human Rights Film Festivals:
Global/Local Networks for Advocacy[1]

Mariagiulia Grassilli

Human rights film festivals recognise films as powerful tools for advocacy. Through a combination of film screenings, arts and music exhibitions and debates and discussions with filmmakers and activists, festivals create a space for the investigation of human rights issues that encourages networking on all levels. One can see this from the very beginnings of human rights film festivals. Billed as 'the world's oldest environmental and human rights film festival', the Vermont International Film Festival (VTIFF) (www.vtiff.org) was developed with the aim of promoting the ideals of peace, human rights and environmental conservation, among others.[2] First held in 1985 at Marlboro College, VTIFF sprang from the local anti-nuclear movement and the original programmers were inspired by the success of their film *From Washington to Moscow* (George and Sonia Cullinen, U.S., 1981). As recipients of the UNESCO prize at the 1983 Hiroshima International Film Festival in Japan (website unavailable), they were excited by the possibilities of using film in social justice movements. Twenty-six years later, VTIFF is still running strong and revisiting its community mission, exploring collaborations to enhance the availability of films for the region and 'build relationships with community members'.

Human rights film festivals have proliferated in the decades since VTIFF appeared. Only three years later, in honour of the Fortieth Anniversary of the 1948 Universal Declaration of Human Rights (UDHR) and its own Tenth Anniversary, Human Rights Watch held its first festival in New York. By 1994 it was the Human Rights Watch International Film Festival (www.hrw.org/iff), co-presented with the Lincoln Film Center, and in 1996 a second flagship was launched in London. In the 1990s, the world saw the appearance of the Amnesty International Film Festival (now Movies that Matter; www.moviesthatmatterfestival.nl) in The Hague (1995), DerHumALC (www.derhumalc.org.ar) in Buenos Aires, Argentina (1997) and the One World Festival (www.oneworld.cz)

in Prague (1998). Such festivals continue to appear around the world and for a range of reasons, including: Festival Internacional de Cine de los Derechos Humanos (www.festivalcinebolivia.org; also known as Septimo Ojo es Tuyo) in Sucre, Bolivia, the Addis Ababa Film Festival (www.addisfilmfestival.org) in Ethiopia, the Refugee Film Festival (www.refugeefilm.org) in Tokyo, the Nationality: Human, Travelling Film Festival (www.yachelovek.caucasus.net) in the Caucasus and the Bahrain Human Rights Film Festival (www.bhriff.com), the first of its kind in the Middle East.

This list only scratches the surface. Today human rights film festivals are being staged in all parts of the world, throughout the year – from Seoul to Amsterdam, from Johannesburg to Bologna, from Los Angeles to British Colombia, from Buenos Aires to Warsaw. The growth has been such that, in 2003, festival directors and advisers from the Amnesty International Film Festival (The Hague),[3] Human Rights Nights (Bologna) (www.humanrightsnights.org) and Festival du Film et Forum International sur les Droits Humains (Geneva) (www.fifdh.ch), convened in Locarno and conceived the Human Rights Film Network (HRFN) (www.humanrightsfilmnetwork.org) – an international network of major film festivals dedicated to human rights. The network was launched in 2004 at the One World Festival with 14 founding festival members present. By 2011, the Human Rights Film Network counted 32 members and is typically expanding by two or three more festivals each year.

What Are Human Rights? A Question for Festivals

Criteria for belonging to the Human Rights Festivals Network begin with understanding the concept of human rights. Despite being seemingly self-evident (all humans have basic rights conferred by their very existence as human beings), the notion of human rights is actually the product of many societies, political systems, religious beliefs and philosophical debates, and film festivals take part in this process. The Human Rights Festivals Network uses the definition advanced by the Universal Declaration of Human Rights, the Charter of which states:

> The Network strives to promote a broad concept of human rights, on the basis of international standards as embedded in the Universal Declaration of Human Rights and other international law. These rights include:

- Integrity rights, such as the right to be protected from torture, killing and arbitrary detention, and the right to be free from discrimination and repression based on nationality, ethnic origin, gender and other personal characteristics.
- Political and civil rights, such as the right to freedom of expression and the right to participate in public life, in government and in private organizations.
- Social, economic and cultural rights, including the rights to basic needs such as food, water, work, housing, health, a clean environment, as well as participation in cultural and scientific life and copyright protection.

We recognise these human rights as universal. Human rights cannot be annulled or diminished on the basis of 'tradition', 'culture' or any other excuse. As stated in the Universal Declaration of Human Rights, 'every individual and every organ of society [...] shall strive by teaching and education to promote respect for these rights and freedoms...' Governments, or others who are in actual control of an area, are primarily responsible for the protection of such rights. Governments also have an obligation to take measures to prevent and redress violence and injustice among private persons, such as violence targeted at women, children and minorities. (Human Rights Film Network, 2004)

Most festivals recognise and abide by this definition of human rights, which includes the protection of human dignity and the opportunity for all to live safely and well. As Mona Rai from the Document Festival in Glasgow (www.documentfilmfestival.org) says,

Human rights are to have food on the table, to sleep peacefully without fear, to have equal rights and be respected in the workplace, to have access to good education for yourself and your children, to be respected for your cultural/sexual/ethical beliefs, no matter where you find yourself on the planet. (Rai 2011)

Even with this Charter in place, however, human rights are not a fixed and defined concept, but are constantly being negotiated at local, regional and global levels. Historical and geographical specificities shape the various interpretations and understandings of human rights and these aspects inform the visions of a festival. In the last 60 years, the Universal Declaration of Human Rights has been contested by those claiming its 'universal' principles to be Western in origin and potentially imperialist in intent. The late Spanish human rights philosopher Joaquin Herrera Flores, for example, is known for his denouncement of human rights as a cultural product of the West where concepts of living a life with dignity are nevertheless tied to a social context based on capital (Herrera Flores 2005).[4] The ideas and debates around universalism and cultural relativism dominate the discussion of human rights internationally. For example, when asked, 'What are human rights for you?', Bolivian festival director Humberto Mancilla of the Bolivian Festival Internacional de Cine de los Derechos Humanos, answers that the general conceptual framework of human rights treats Western concepts as universal while disregarding culturally-specific beliefs. Mancilla continues, however, with an appreciation of what human rights means, noting a way through this rift:

> 60 years after the Universal Declaration of Human Rights, this same vision has renewed, the people of our culture now embrace this philosophy to advance and meet justice [...] Human Rights trace a path towards real horizons: a new transformative vision in defence of the environment has emerged out of the encounter with indigenous people. The individual focus has left ways for a more collectively oriented community vision, as the final destiny is for all to be responsible, isolating and punishing those that instead create damage to our common house. (Mancilla 2011)

From this point of view, human rights become a site for debate and exploration, where one weighs individual rights against those of the collective. And to extend from that, one can see the malleability of the notion, when those advocating for women's rights, children's rights and gay rights, draw on the notion of human rights, and thus press against and expand its borders.

Human rights film festivals provide a place in which these debates, discussions and definitions can be clarified and where cultural specificity develops and builds on notions of human rights. Festivals that grow from a political legacy of genocide and torture, such as the DerHumALC in Buenos Aires, might emphasise the cause of such inhumanity and advocate for a life free from violence. At the same time, some festivals may move away from such topics. The Rwanda Film Festival (www.hillywood. com) was founded in 2004 by genocide survivor and film producer Eric Kabera as an initiative of the Rwandan Cinema Centre. The festival features Rwandan stories told by Rwandan filmmakers, a mission that combines concerns of representation with the development of a local film industry. Although it started mainly by showing films on genocide, the festival has gradually shifted its programme away from that topic, in part to advance a new Rwandan identity, to include romantic comedies, and is now not solely defined by its tragic past. Could this move away from a focus on an 'Africa in crisis' to a more diverse programme be part of a much needed move to restore dignity, and thus itself constitute a human rights impulse, even if the festival had never explicitly articulated such intentions? Free Zone in Belgrade (www.freezonebelgrade.org) is one of many such festivals which embrace a human rights vision, but others, in order to avoid alienating their potential audiences, steer away from using the widespread human rights terminology which has become associated with adverse experiences related to the region's tragic past (see Popovic 2009).

In other cases, certain not yet universally recognised 'human rights' are being debated in the context of mainstream film festivals. For instance, at the Venice Film Festival (www.labiennale.org/en/cinema) in 2005, the jury members of the Human Rights Film Network awards discussed whether to treat Alejandro Amenábar's acclaimed film *Mar Adentro (The Sea Inside*, Spain/France/Italy, 2004) as a human rights film.[5] The film explores euthanasia and the individual's right to die, issues not covered by the Charter. In the end, the jury held to the Charter definition and decided that the film did not qualify under its remit. Meanwhile, Human Rights Nights (www.humanrightsnights.org) in Bologna has adopted a broader understanding and is exploring the possible inclusion of a 'right to happiness' and 'human development' (as measured in terms of 'gross national happiness' as opposed to purely economic indicators). It has also accepted that issues related to climate change and the environment belong in the festival programme as well.

Human rights are a dynamic concept, whose meaning is shaped by a range of forces: historical experience, industrial concerns and political, social, religious and legal discourses. Film festivals are a part of this terrain, which contributes to debates around programming and the bestowing of awards.

What Is a Human Rights Film?

The definition of a human rights film may be as broad and potentially malleable as the film festival's notion of human rights. 'Human rights films', according to the Human Rights Film Network Charter,

> are films that reflect, inform on and provide understanding of the actual state of past and present human rights violations, or the visions and aspirations concerning ways to redress those violations. Human rights films can be documentary, fiction, experimental or animation. They can be short, medium or feature length; have a 35mm, 16mm, video or other format; can be experimental through the use of 'new media' or any other artistic and technological visual means.
>
> Human rights films may be harshly realistic, or highly utopian. They may offer gruesome pictures, or show the bliss of peaceful life. They may report, denounce or convey an emotional message. They may forcefully present the views of one group or individual only, or try to convey the opinions of as many of those involved as possible. They may be a highly accurate report of facts, or offer surreal provocation.
>
> We strive to promote films that have good cinematographic quality in photography, narrative, rhythm, audio and other technical characteristics – films that are 'engaging' in the sense that they keep the attention of a large audience. However, due to the difficult circumstances in which many human rights films are made, we recognize that also films that do not come up to standards of optimal cinematic quality can be forceful and convincing testimonies of human rights violations and ideals. The Network promotes films that allow silenced and marginalized voices to be heard, as a contribution to their empowerment. (Human Rights Film Network, 2004)

The human rights film can belong to any genre, but it exists primarily to inform and inspire. For Maurizio Del Bufalo of Cinema e Diritti, Naples (www.cinemaediritti.org), it is 'a story that leaves a deep impression on those who sees it [...] a discovery, an invitation to reflection' (Del Bufalo 2011). For Mona Rai (Document Film Festival, Glasgow, www.docfilmfest.org), it is a 'film with a strong clear narrative which forces the viewer to look, think, engage and perhaps act long after the film is over' (Rai 2011). Writing in this volume, Igor Blažević (One World, Prague) shares that sentiment, but with a proviso: the human rights film motivates people to take action, particularly when combined with a good campaign strategy.

Human rights films should educate and excite. They should fight hatred and discrimination against groups or individuals. They need to avoid propaganda and assure authenticity of information. The films should inform, but not intentionally misrepresent the facts or the views and words of those portrayed. To this end, the Human Rights Festivals Network emphasises the need for truthfulness and impartiality in human rights films, as well as independence from purely political or commercial interests. As will be discussed below, this need for independence extends to festivals as well.

What Is a Human Rights Film Festival?

The Human Rights Film Network sets forth some basic requirements that need to be satisfied before a festival may join its ranks: The festival must mainly programme films dedicated to the analysis and exploration of human rights issues. It has to be a regular event (annual or bi-annual) and must have completed at least two editions before entry into the network. One-off events cannot be members of the network.

A human rights film festival, however, is defined not only by its thematic programming, but also by its mission. It is born out of a desire to communicate and inspire justice, and this passion for justice informs the festival and its managing organisation. Unlike other festivals, the films are not simply a main feature of the programme; they are tools for a higher objective: raising awareness. While artistic quality is a much-needed component of a film, the human rights content is absolutely and unquestionably essential here. A human rights film festival may bring in celebrities to shine a spotlight on issues, but its real stars are the peaceful warriors of the films, the people who struggle everyday for basic human rights.

Human rights festivals are started by a variety of organisations, such as universities, cultural foundations and governmental and inter-governmental institutions. They can also be launched by, and have close links with, non-governmental human rights organisations. Movies that Matter developed from the Amnesty International Film Festival and enjoys a close partnership with the organisation. The Human Rights Watch International Film Festivals form a division of the organisation of the same name, while the Helsinki Foundation for Human Rights in Poland helped to launch Watch Docs (www.watchdocs.pl), and One World came from People in Need, a Czech relief organisation that provides development assistance. Universities and cinema-based institutions also come to the cause, as with the case of the Cineteca di Bologna (Bologna Film Archive), which produced Human Rights Nights, or of the joint programme between the University of Sarajevo and the University of Bologna that launched the Sarajevo-based Pravo Ljudski (www.pravoljudski.org).

Other festivals are initiated by the need of the festival director or founder to communicate and reach out on human rights issues because they are themselves activists, refugees, artists and intellectual warriors for human rights. For instance, Julio Santucho started DerHumALC upon his return to Argentina after he had escaped the brutality of the dictatorial regime responsible for thousands of Desaparecidos. Despite the differences in their foundational support, human rights film festivals do share a particular form of support: they are backed and run by a passionate team of film and human rights professionals and sustained by donors, volunteers and partners, all of whom value the ability of film to engage and mobilise an audience.

Although each festival has its own unique story, many have been forged in the pursuit of a specific cause. The first festival in Vermont was born out of the anti-nuclear movement of the 1980s; Amnesty International Film Festival started in 1995 within the framework of the Women's Conference in Beijing, China; Festival Internacional de Cine de los Derechos Humanos started in 2005 during the massive demonstrations against the privatisation of the Bolivian gas industry that came to be known as the hydrocarbon protest, and which resulted in radical political shifts; Document Film Festival in Glasgow was founded in 2003 in response to negative media reporting on asylum seekers and refugee issues. Cinema e Diritti (Naples) began as a community response to the shameful waste crisis in the city, where rubbish was left uncollected in the streets. The AfricanBamba Human Rights Arts and Film Festival (www.africanbamba.webs.com) started within the framework of Human Rights Nights (Bologna) as a music programme with locally-based African and Asian artists and musicians. It has now moved to Senegal (Camp Thiaroye, Dakar) and changed its focus to migration and the environment in order to help build local communities and prevent further devastating losses of that country's population to emigration. Post-war reconstruction and conflict resolution have provided fertile occasions as well. Pravo Ljudski in Sarajevo and Free Zone in Belgrade (www.freezonebelgrade.org) were both started in the mid-2000s by a young generation of activists and filmmakers striving to move beyond the legacy of the Balkan wars and usher in a movement of social concern and human rights. The Autumn Human Rights Film Festival in Kabul, Afghanistan (www.facebook.com/pages/Autumn-Human-Rights-Film-Festival), set to launch in October 2011, was founded following new calls for democracy and aims to showcase the works of those who have been marginalised by oppressive authoritarian regimes.

The Festival as Forum

A human rights film festival is more than its film programme and exceeds the duration of the festival event, whether that be one or 10 days. Festivals organise additional events around the films on show. Making use of its cultural capital as the home of human rights, Geneva's Festival et Forum des Droits de l'Homme (Geneva FIFDH) organises film screenings alongside debates with the aim of producing a forum for discussion and exploration. Human Rights Nights selects three subjects of focus each year (in 2011 these were climate change and the environment, food justice and the Arab Spring digital social revolutions), and produces a selected programme of arts and music to accompany the core cinema screenings. This multi-media programme aims to lighten the festival experience, creating a sharing, collaborative and participatory community space in the festival hub.

Additional art programmes and discussions help to create a community space, as does the extension of a festival's activities beyond the location of the main event. The event itself is typically one of many other events scheduled by partner organisations, a component in their campaigns as well as a network hub for activists, filmmakers and NGOs. Meanwhile, the festival may extend its programmes across the year and beyond its central location, with monthly film screenings, education seminars, travelling film festivals, projections in schools and other non-theatrical screenings. For instance, after the main festival in Sucre has concluded, Festival Internacional de Cine de los Derechos

Humanos tours the Bolivian countryside. The festival's director explains the rationale: 'The festival reinforces the community and the community embraces the festival [...] culture is a two ways experience. In Bolivia we say, "you need to give in order to receive"' (Mancilla 2011). To this end, the festival holds free screenings, not only in cinemas, but also in psychiatric hospitals, detention centres, universities and parks. The goal is to integrate the festival with the community and to foster an interest in human rights throughout the region.

Maurizio Del Bufalo (Cinema e Diritti) views the festival as a 'network with long legs that reaches remote neighbours, villages and urban suburbs' (Del Bufalo 2011) in order to give access to images and information to those who do not have the opportunity to attend the festival proper or establish information networks on their own. According to Del Bufalo, the events provide more than just data, as the films help communities to find voices of their own. When festivals do not travel, they bring people in to further strengthen network associations:

> We promote international cooperation between social actors from territories that we put in connection through the festival. For example, in Naples we invite people from the Balkans; we then try to establish partnership relations between universities, filmmakers and associations of the two sides, and so on [...] this dramatically empowers our efforts to give roots to our festival [...] we are more like a popular movement than a traditional film festival. (Del Bufalo 2011)

Similarly, from my own perspective as its director, Human Rights Nights (Bologna) is no longer just a festival, but rather the centre of a network of local-global relations focused on human rights. It offers a neutral site for encounters and dialogue among activists, filmmakers and the community, and, in so doing, fosters a 'transversal socialisation', a reference to the way this formation cuts across borders of discipline, nation, community and difference. The festival moment is only the visible celebratory event within the city, but the potential of Human Rights Nights to instigate change is actually expressed through the invisible and constantly growing interactions and synergies between all actors and agencies who work together throughout the year. The festival and its interactive website offer two nodes within an on-going exchange; all influence radiates from there. Since Human Rights Nights has come into existence, Bologna has redefined itself as a city of human rights, initially drawing on its record as the first city, in 1256, to abolish slavery and later on by remaining active in the present by participating in global networks involved in human rights, the fight against racism and xenophobia, and by supporting environmental issues such as green energy. The festival supports this identity-building process, promoting a diverse and plural Bologna by offering awards to migrant filmmakers and by involving the many diverse communities that are part of the city's cultural life. There is a synergy between the festival and the city, which has developed into a human rights community.

A festival connects people and can provide a way to re-connect with one's own community and initiate a dialogue over issues when there is a dissonance of perspectives. Hence the aim of Laye Gaye from AfricanBamba, to use that festival format to reach back to the community in Senegal, to relay a direct and real vision of the experience of migration and to dispel the myth that surrounds the dream of Europe (Gaye 2011).

Some festivals make political advocacy and lobbying a specific focus of their work. Geneva FIDFH, for example, strategically times its festival to run in parallel with UN meetings; the forums produced through the combination of screenings and debates become occasions to advance claims and incite the invited officials to participate.[6] Jeffrey Hodgson of Geneva FIFDH sees this work as developing 'with civil society and [serving] as a relay for human right defenders' (Hodgson 2011). Movies that Matter, which is based in the Hague, home to the International Criminal Courts, invites politicians, policy-makers, ambassadors, journalists and other influential people, to screenings directly related to their work and interests. The festival organises private screenings in the workplace in order to directly engage decision-makers, be they advisers and policy officers of the Human Rights Department at the Ministry of Foreign Affairs or employees of companies that do business in China (De Jong 2011).

This kind of political engagement can make the human rights film festival a target for those with agendas of their own. Governmental hostility can make it difficult to screen films by closing access to venues, as happened to the Seoul Human Rights Film Festival (www.sarangbang. or.kr), which was prevented from holding outdoor screenings. Opposition can also foster a harsh climate for fundraising, as in Addis Ababa, where limits to foreign aid for human rights organisations and festivals were introduced. Sometimes the situation is untenable and the festival has no option but to close down, as occurred in Cameroon, where the Yaoundé Human Rights Film Festival (website unavailable) was cancelled after its first edition.[7]

At the same time, a festival can provide an appealing opportunity for image laundering and propaganda. Both the public and private sectors can benefit by becoming investing partners and associating their brands with a high-level ethically and socially responsible public event. They can in turn, however, use their funding to pressure or influence the programme according to their own needs and wishes. A festival director must therefore always be on the alert to safeguard the festival's integrity and ensure the safety of its team, partners and guests. Thus, generally speaking, partnerships and sponsors are selected with great care. Festival programmers accept funding from ethical sources only and tend to avoid support from major corporations, unless the company has been fully vetted. Public funding will only be accepted on a 'no strings attached' basis.

The power of a festival and its role within the community make integrity of paramount importance. This concern extends not only to the festival backers, but also to the celebrities associated with the festival. At Human Rights Nights, we value celebrities because they attract the attention of the popular press and increase the chance that the festival and its issues will receive coverage. Celebrities and high profile events become platforms for expression in their own right. Since 2005, the Human Rights Film Network has bestowed the International Human Rights Film Award at the Cinema for Peace Gala, a celebrity-supported charity gala held during the Berlin International Film Festival (www. berlinale.de).[8] Here, members of the film community, humanitarian and human rights activists and other international public figures, come together to honour a selection of cinematic works that raise awareness of important humanitarian and environmental issues. Still, as is the case with sponsors, care must be taken to preserve the integrity of the festival. Celebrities are often drawn to charity and activism merely as a means to rehabilitate a flagging public image and are sometimes focused only on self-promotion; this kind of work can be seen as a 'sexy' way to be branded as socially committed. Such interest means that film festivals must monitor these developments, ensuring that original objectives are not lost and that the film festival remains true to its mission: to investigate and explore human rights issues through human rights films.

This concern is shared by the Human Rights Festivals Network, which recognises the need for its members' independence from influence and undue pressure, whether that be from individuals or organisations (governmental and non-governmental) at all levels – local, regional, national and international. Festivals must be free to select and present the films of their choosing, to extend invitation to the film professionals and activists of their choosing and to raise and disburse funds as they see fit. The Network upholds the principle of freedom of expression and information, whatever may be the members' affiliations and sources of funding and assistance.

Definitions and Beyond

The human rights film festival serves as an inspiration for active participation in advocacy and social justice. It is a place where campaigns can be launched and nurtured. The films inform audiences of human rights abuses locally and globally. The festivals lobby for justice and capture the attention of the news media, which then disseminate information about the issues and campaigns. The existence of the festival itself can foster the growth of a human rights culture beyond in its primary location, fostering and reinforcing a network for action.

Prior to the 1990s, human rights film festivals were few and far between, but today such festivals proliferate, inspired by one another and interlinked in a network of commitment. New digital technologies have assisted further developments and increased access to new mechanisms for exhibition and distribution. Today, a festival can be launched with just a projector and a community, or as an on-line globally networked event, with its capacities for local and global promotion of campaigns exponentially enhanced. Thanks to podcasts and debates and films streamed on-line, people can participate in festivals from a distance and over time. All of these opportunities amplify the potential of a human rights festival as a space for raising awareness on human rights, community building and advocacy. The festival community is not bound to the transient occurrence of the actual festival, but can now be permanently connected through social networks, regardless of time and space.

Works Cited

Afronline (2011) 'Cameroon: Government Suspended Human Rights Film Festival', *Afronline*, 15 April. On-line. Available HTTP: http://www.afronline. org/?p=14787 (10 October 2011).

Blažević, Igor (2009) 'Raising Funds to Support a Human Rights Film Festival', in Tereza Porybná (ed.) *Setting Up a Human Rights Film Festival*. Prague: People in Need, 42-68. On-line. Available HTTP: http://www.oneworld. cz/2011/userfiles/file/OW-cookbook_web.pdf (11 October 2011).

De Jong, Matthea (2011), Unpublished interview with the author, June.

Del Bufalo, Maurizio (2011) Unpublished interview with the author, June.

Dembour, Marie-Bénédicte (2001) 'Following the Movement of a Pendulum: Between Universalism and Relativism', in Jane K. Cowan and Marie-Bénédicte Dembour (eds) *Culture and Rights: Anthropological Perspectives*. Cambridge: Cambridge University Press, 56-79.

Gaye, Laye (2011) Unpublished interview with the author, June.

Herrera Flores, Joaquin (2005) *Los derechos humanos como productos culturales. Crítica del humanismo abstracto*. Catarata: Madrid.

Hodgson, Jeffrey (2011) Unpublished interview with the author, June.

Human Rights Film Network (2004), 'Charter: Statement of Principles and Practices'. On-line. Available HTTP: http://www.humanrightsfilmnetwork. org/content/charter (11 October 2011).

Ignatieff, Michael (2001) *Human Rights as Politics and Idolatry*. Princeton: Princeton University Press.

Mancilla, Humberto (2011) Unpublished interview with the author, June.

Popovic, Marko (2009) 'Building Up Human Rights Awareness in Post-War Serbia – Free Zone', in Tereza Porybná (ed.) *Setting Up a Human Rights Film Festival*. Prague: People in Need, 182-94. On-line. Available HTTP: http://www.oneworld.cz/2011/userfiles/file/OW-cookbook_web.pdf (29 July 2011).

Porybná, Tereza (ed.) (2009) *Setting Up a Human Rights Film Festival*. Prague: People in Need. On-line. Available HTTP: http://www.oneworld.cz/2011/ userfiles/file/OW-cookbook_web.pdf (11 October 2011).

'Presentation. Human Rights Opinion Column' (2011). On-line. Available HTTP: http://www.fifdh.org/2011/index.php?lan=en&rubID=9 (10 October 2011).

Rai, Mona (2011) Unpublished interview with the author, June.

Notes

1   This paper is the result of direct input from numerous festivals and networks: the Human Rights Film Network; Movies That Matter; Festival Internacional de Cine de los Derechos Humanos (a.k.a. El Septimo ojo es tuyo, Bolivia); the Festival International des Droits de l'Homme, Switzerland; Document Human Rights Film Festival, Glasgow, Scotland; DerHumALC, Argentina; One World Film Festival, Prague, Czech Republic; Human Rights Nights Film Festival, Bologna, Italy; AfricanBamba Human Rights Films and Arts Festival, Thiaroye, Senegal; and Cinema e Diritti, Naples, Italy.

    It also draws from a number of case studies published in Porybná (2009): Perspektive, Nuremberg, Germany; Cine Droit Libre, Ouagadougou, Burkina Faso; Free Zone Belgrade Film Festival, Serbia. Finally, it draws, too, on the author's first-hand knowledge as a partner of, or audience member at, the following festivals: Latin American Network of Social Cinema and Human Rights Festivals; Addis Ababa International Film Festival, Ethiopia; Rwanda Film Festival/Hillywood, Rwanda; Pravo Ljudski, Sarajevo, Bosnia Herzegovina; Human Rights Watch, London and New York.

    I would like to thank especially Daan Bronkhorst (Amnesty International) with whom we co-drafted the Human Rights Film Network Charter, festival directors Humberto Mancilla (Festival Internacional de Cine de los Derechos Humanos, Bolivia), Jeffrey Hodgons (Geneva FIFDH), Mona Rai (Document Glasgow), Julio Santucho (DerHumALC, Buenos Aires), Maurizio Del Bufalo (Cinema e Diritti, Naples), Laye Gaye (AfricanBamba, Senegal), Igor Blažević (One World, Prague) and international programme coordinator Matthea De Jong (Movies that Matter, Amsterdam), who were very kind in responding to my interview requests and providing precious data for this paper.

2   For more information see the website of the festival at www.vtiff.org/about (accessed 11 October 2011).

3   The Movies That Matter Film Festival is the successor to the Amnesty International Film Festival; after 10 editions in Amsterdam, in 2009 the festival moved to The Hague, city of peace and justice.

4   On the universalism versus cultural relativism debate on human rights, see also Dembour, 2001 and Ignatieff, 2001.

5   The Human Rights Film Network Award was established in 2004 at the Venice Film Festival, in recognition of the important role played by filmmakers and the cinema in denouncing human rights abuses and

providing a deeper understanding of contemporary world issues. Until 2008, a jury composed of Human Rights Film Network festival directors and renowned film critics conferred awards at the Venice Film Festival. Winning films over the years were: *Melancholian 3 huonetta (Three Rooms of Melancholia*, Piro Honkasalo, Finland/Denmark/Germany/Sweden, 2004) and *Yizo Yizo* (Angus Gibson, Teboho Malhatsi, Andrew Dosunmu and Barry Berk, South Africa, 2004), *La dignidad de los nadies (The Dignity of the Nobodies*, Fernando E. Solanas, Argentina/Brazil/Switzerland, 2005), *When The Levees Broke: A Requiem In Four Parts* (Spike Lee, U.S., 2006), *Jimmy Carter Man from Plains* (Jonathan Demme, U.S., 2007) and *The Hurt Locker* (Kathryn Bigelow, U.S., 2008). The award was also presented at the Cape Town World Cinema Film Festival/Sithengi Film and TV Market (www.sithengi.co.za) and at Mar del Plata (www.mardelplatafilmfest.com) and is currently conferred at the Dubai International Film Festival (www. dubaifilmfest.com). Since 2006, the Human Rights Film Network also confers a prize at the annual Cinema for Peace Gala at the Berlin Film Festival, to honour activists featured in human rights films.

6   On its website, the Festival International et Forum des Droits de l'Homme describes itself thus: 'An annual event in Geneva, international capital of human rights, its aim – in relation to the UN Human Rights Council – is to serve as an "opinion column" or space where ideas are freely expressed and shared. A platform for dialogue between human rights activists, film-makers and members of civil society, the FIFDH fearlessly denounces attacks on human dignity' (Presentation. Human Rights Opinion Column, undated). The festival invites officials from international institutions (including the UN and the EU), journalists, activists, intellectuals and filmmakers to discuss specific issues in forums organised alongside film screenings. For details of previous contributors, see: www.fifdh.org/2011/index.php?rubID=94&lan=fr (accessed 11 October 2011).

7   'The first edition of the Yaoundé International Human Rights Film Festival has been suspended by the Cameroonian authorities. This comes just after a week when government banned mobile twitter in an attempt to stop future unrest in the country so that the West African state does not face the Middle Eastern clashes. On the 12th April, the Yaoundé prefecture issued a suspension of a public event authorisation, thereby calling off this first edition of the International Human Rights Film Festival in Yaoundé. [...] This suspension occurs in such an international political context as to explain somewhat the nervousness around discussing certain human rights issues

in Cameroon. "Given the reasons specified by the authorities, we think that this is a politically-motivated refusal to discuss problems relating to human rights in Cameroon. We deplore this situation and regret that dialogue around human rights can not be held dispassionately in Cameroon," said festival director Vincent Mercier' (Afronline 2011).

[8] The annual Cinema for Peace Awards (www.cinemaforpeace.com) seek to promote valuable films and attract worldwide attention to important social issues covered in films. The Cinema for Peace Gala is a charity event and a platform for discussing issues of global peace and tolerance. Since 2002, the Cinema for Peace initiative has invited members of the film community, humanitarian and human rights activists and international public figures, to its annual Gala in Berlin to honour a selection of cinematic works that raise awareness of important humanitarian and environmental issues. In addition to bestowing awards, the Cinema for Peace Gala aims to illustrate the influence of films on the perception and resolution of important global issues, while also raising funds for the Cinema for Peace Foundation and other charities. The Awards include: Most Valuable Film of the Year, Most Valuable Documentary of the Year, the International Green Film Award, the Award for Justice, the International Human Rights Film Award (in cooperation with Amnesty International and the Human Rights Film Network) as well as various Honorary Awards.

On the Development of Queer Film Festivals and Their Media Activism

Skadi Loist and Ger Zielinski

In 1977 the very first edition of what today is known as the Frameline Festival (www.frameline.org) took place in San Francisco under the name of the Gay Film Festival of Super-8 Films. As co-founder Marc Huestis has recounted in interviews (e.g. Wiegand 2003), the event was held in a community centre with projection onto white bed sheets. A motley group of young filmmakers who regularly convened at Harvey Milk's Castro Camera shop to develop their films, decided to stage a festival of screenings in order to see each other's work, but they were also keen to open it up to an unknown but imagined public. They had no idea whether anyone would actually attend. As the story goes, the planned screenings sold out, both seats and standing room. More screenings were added. The festival instantly found a public and continues to be popular to this day. Gay and lesbian film festivals have been proliferating unevenly around the world since that time.[1] In this essay we will attempt a critical survey of the activist politics of these festivals from the 1970s on.

Ever since their festive, humble beginnings, lesbian and gay film festivals have been deeply implicated in various waves of activist causes; they have adapted and continue to adapt to the changing concerns of specific communities of members with diverse intersectional affiliations. To be sure, the queer film festivals of today owe much to earlier developments and experiments. Historically, several types of identity-based film festivals, which share a corrective and self-affirming ethos, stem from the social movements centring on identities and representational politics of the 1970s. Second-wave feminism enabled women's and feminist film festivals across North America and Europe, particularly the Ann Arbor Women's Film Festival (1970-4), while the civil rights movement produced African American film festivals, with the Newark Black Film Festival (from 1974; www.newarkmuseum.org/NBFF.html) being the longest running. The Native Rights movement produced the American Indian Film Festival (from 1975; www.aifisf.com), based in San Francisco. Also important to the development of gay and lesbian film festivals was the sexual revolution following the 'Summer of Love' in 1967, the invention and ready availability of contraceptives and, crucially, the relaxation of anti-pornography laws in the U.S. under Nixon, which spawned a sudden but brief wave of feature-length pornographic films and erotic film festivals in San Francisco, New York and Amsterdam (Zielinski 2008; Gorfinkel 2006).

These social movements and their respective festivals, along with other activist and exhibition practices, such as clip-show lectures and screenings at community centres, public libraries, bars and cinemas (Zielinski 2008), served as the basis for gay and lesbian film festivals. Gay and lesbian film festivals were started by filmmakers or activists who wanted to show (realistic, positive) representations of queers that would not otherwise find a public screen. The Hollywood production code, which had explicitly banned representations of 'sexual deviance' such as homosexuality, had gone out of practice by the late-1960s. Nevertheless, films with gay characters were still scarce in the mainstream media. Thus, gay film festivals were established as much to re-present gays to an interested audience as to provide a showcase for gay filmmakers who had few, or no, other opportunities to screen their work publicly. These festivals were a space where a group of individuals could meet and create a community. As such they were counter-public spheres, where the films were as important as the staging of the event. Thus, the functions of queer film festivals were, and still are, to represent the community cogently in its diversity – in terms of sexuality and gender as much as race, ethnicity, dis/ability and age – and to constitute their respective counter-publics. As part of political movements, these volunteer-run festivals were themselves politically positioned and offered interventions into hegemonic representational regimes. As such, they constitute an activist act through their interventionist counter-publics (Ommert and Loist 2008: 126; Rastegar 2009; Kim 2007).

The history of queer film festivals is quite distinct from the so-called International Film Festivals (IFFs). While queer film festivals were founded by activists as grassroots and identity-oriented events, IFFs were established from the top down; originally initiated by national governments, up until the early 1970s they were treated as a mode of international diplomacy under the control of ministries of foreign affairs, either nationalist or following Cold War political divisions. Since the 1970s, they have retained more regional political affiliations, with relative programming autonomy, but emphasis continues to be placed on promoting a city's image, a national or regional identity and the local film industry (Zielinski 2008; Strandgaard Pedersen and Mazza 2011). As a result of this background, the community-oriented, identity-based film festivals differ in their organisational structures and funding patterns (Loist 2011). This is clearly visible in smaller organisations with very few or no paid staff positions, as this usually has an impact on the tasks and functions a film festival can fulfil.

The constant changes in the naming of these festivals indicate real changes in the politics of the respective festivals from 1977 on, alongside changes in the movement (Gay; Lesbian; Gay-Lesbian; Lesbian-Gay; Lesbian-Gay-Bisexual; Lesbian-Gay-Bisexual-Transgender; Queer). The act of naming any organisation requires great care and the consideration of many possible nuances and associations. As a matter of shorthand we have been calling these festivals 'queer film festivals' and elsewhere 'lesbian and gay' or 'LGBT', but this is strictly for convenience rather than historical accuracy. The cumbersome nature of the long descriptive names is no secret and presents practical difficulties when discussing the festivals. To be sure, these festivals have gone through a number of important name changes over the years that reflect, to varying degrees, changes in their structure and policies regarding content, effectively revealing their self-understanding and how they want to be understood, which includes, moreover, the sort of counter-publics they want to attract. This continuing process of naming and renaming is part of what Martha Gever suggests as that special reciprocal (creative) dynamic between festival and audience, namely that such a counter-public sphere could serve as 'a collective experience and a literal site of critical reception' (Gever 1990: 74). There have been several distinct phases in the historical development of the festivals, which require some attention and hint at the specific cultural politics of their times.

Not only have their names changed, but so also has the meaning of the words comprising them. In the 1970s they began as gay film festivals, organised and run mainly by gay white men – independent filmmakers and film buffs alike – primarily for one another and with very little lesbian content.[2] As women became more present and vocal, both within the organisation and as members of the festival audience, demands for greater lesbian representation increased. Consequently, the San Francisco festival shifted its name to 'gay and lesbian film festival' to become more inclusive in 1982. Furthermore, to forefront lesbian visibility and the need for more work by and concerning women, many other festivals made the semiotic shift to 'lesbian and gay film festival'. Frustration with the imbalance in programming resulted in the so-called Lesbian Riot at the 1986 Frameline Festival, which compelled programmers to seek out and uncover work by lesbians to screen (Siegel 1997). More recently, similar controversies arose in 2007 over Catherine Crouch's short video *Gendercator* (U.S., 2007). After vocal criticism of the film by transgender activists, Frameline pulled the film from the line-up over fears that it might insult members of the transgender community. This fuelled discussions between conflicting transgender and lesbian viewpoints and members of the latter group counter-charged that it was an act of censorship (Bajko 2007). Many festivals have not yet adequately addressed their position on transgender issues; it is likely that further controversies and discussions will compel them to reconsider their policies and attitudes.[3]

When looking at the established first wave of gay and lesbian film festivals in North America and Western Europe, one can see that the kind of activism they once practiced has since changed. While their initial aim was to advocate by way of showing films and the bringing together of a community, later festivals have become part of a film industry or ecosystem specialising in LGBT film. The basic reasons or foundation for the expansion and growth of such festivals – and also their difference from the newer festivals elsewhere – can be found in the social and media context in which these festivals operate:

- Since the basic activism of the 1970s, gay rights have been secured through the struggles of the gay liberation movement.

- The success of New Queer Cinema in the 1990s made films with a political and aesthetic edge visible and marketable. These films became part of a developing cross-over art house market and helped pave the way for a growing niche market for gay film.

- Mainstream visibility grew: gays and lesbians are now frequently seen in ads, on network television and in mainstream film.

- A 'queer ecosystem' – a term coined by queer film historian Jenni Olson (2002) – of independent film has developed. The indie boom, and increasingly affordable video technology, enabled the production of more independent queer film. At the same time distribution companies were founded that dealt solely with, or specialised in, LGBT film.[4]

• Funding strategies have been developed for larger queer film festivals that enable the organisation to function year-round and at least partially compensate the festival workers. These factors are the basic context in which queer film festivals could grow and develop their agenda further.

With the expansion of the LGBT festivals came a shift in their functions and their relation to the (independent queer) film industry. With the niche marketing of New Queer Cinema and the growth of an ecosystem, the festivals – like other LGBT organisations (Stone 2010) – became more professionalised and focused on industry tasks and diversity management (due to funding politics) rather than on dissent and on being actively involved in activist radicalism. On a positive note, these festivals are in a better position to help queer filmmakers and their work by becoming 'business festivals' (Peranson 2008) within the queer film festival circuit.

The ways in which film festivals are connected by the flow of films and people between festivals has been described as the film festival circuit. Dina Iordanova has pointed out that there is not one film festival circuit, but rather several parallel circuits (2009: 31-2). The queer film festival circuit is connected to the larger film festival circuit, but it also forms a separate parallel entity. This network can be further differentiated into several levels. Going top-down one can differentiate between the queer-friendly 'A-list' festivals and markets, 'wholesale' (Bachmann 2000) or 'business' queer film festivals and a large number of smaller 'retailer' festivals.[5] The Berlin International Film Festival (www.berlinale. de) is the only 'A-list' festival with a long-running tradition of programming queer film and awards the Teddy (since 1987); the Venice Film Festival (www.labiennale.org/en/cinema) has had a Queer Lion since 2007 (www.cinemarte.it) and the Cannes Film Festival (www.festival-cannes. com) has conferred the Queer Palm (www.queerpalm.fr) since 2009 (Loist 2010). Because of this focus, international queer film festival programmers come to Berlin to scout and network. Thus, the Teddy can be seen as operating within the network like a wholesale-queer film festival, even though (or because) it is not a distinct queer film festival.

Next, there are long-running, established queer film festivals, such as Frameline, Outfest (www.outfest.org), Torino GLBT Film Festival (www. tglff.com) and the London Lesbian and Gay Film Festival (www.bfi.org. uk/llgff), which exert regional impact on programming within the queer circuit. Then there are a number of established medium-sized queer film festivals with impact on a national scale, which are followed by smaller locally-oriented queer film festivals showcasing recent queer film that might not show otherwise in that region.

The service of the festivals within the queer circuit began with the practical goal of enabling not only the exhibition of relevant films but also of nurturing talent from within its associated community and this has extended into establishing networks of distribution and production. The tasks themselves comprise the following set of screening-related functions:

- To showcase, promote and launch a film with the aim of generating interest for later theatrical exhibition or direct DVD sales.

- To offer a platform for films to find a (regional) distributor.

- To offer an opportunity for buyers or cinema programmers to view films with an audience.

- To host industry meetings and establish networking opportunities for the development of future projects.

These functions might be facilitated professionally and emphasised in the form of a film market attached to a film festival.[6] Festivals are no longer just facilitators; rather, they have become part of the industry itself by making advances into classic industry tasks. Like festivals on the international film festival circuit, queer festivals have shifted their position and expanded and now also function as producers and distributors. Minority festivals started to provide those functions as a necessity early on to help circulate, or even create, representations that were not available otherwise. International film festivals seem to have taken on this role only later as a result of the shifts in independent film distribution and the exhibition market.

- Frameline started its Completion Fund as early as 1990, in an attempt to help complete films by under-resourced parts of the LGBT community (for instance, women and queers of colour); the Los Angeles-based Outfest offers a Scriptwriting Lab; and on a smaller scale, the Tel Aviv International LGBT Film Festival (www.tlvfest.com), MIX NYC (www.mixnyc.org) and the Hamburg International Queer Film Festival (www.lsf-hamburg.de), have offered smaller film workshops, enabling participants to make films in a one-week hands-on workshop.

- Frameline also started a distribution arm, which at first operated for the festival circuit and later also branched out into the American educational DVD sector and home video.

The majority of LGBT/queer film festivals beyond North America and Western Europe have developed since the 1990s. When looking at these festivals it is necessary to pay attention to the complex developments of global LGBT activism, with its geo-temporal disjunctions, seriality, coincidence and stories of progress (Mizielińska and Kulpa 2011). Events like queer film festivals betray the local inflection of global queer politics and culture, as well as a connection to Western queer politics and organising, which potentially reveal problematic neoliberal and neo-colonial tendencies when models like 'queer diaspora' and global liberal cosmopolitanism are mobilised (Rhyne 2011). For instance, Denise Tse Shang Tang, director of the Hong Kong Lesbian and Gay Film Festival (www.hklgff.hk) in 2004-5, has reflected on the problematic post-colonial dynamics when European-owned film distributor Fortissimo Films became a main sponsor of the Hong Kong festival after 2000. She points out that while the affiliation with Fortissimo 'allowed the festival to obtain internationally renowned films, it further constructs the identity of the festival as a foreign import, an expatriate hobby and a middle-class gay male event'. She cautions that an internationally-focused selection of films, mostly in English without Chinese subtitles, and the close alignment 'with the film industry can also take a festival and its meaning easily away from what is happening on a community level' (Tang 2009: 176).

The disintegration of the Soviet Union in 1991, and the consequent reorientation of its former satellite countries towards the West, brought with it sexuality and gender rights movements, typically sponsored by various international agencies. With the prospect of joining the European Union (EU), the governments of the interested countries had to demonstrate their commitment to human rights as detailed by the EU. As queer film festivals cautiously sprang up, international experts lent their advice and experience to the new organisations. Initially, each of the festivals experienced local resistance – and sometimes violence – but often overcame the problems by adapting and learning tactics for survival, such as invoking police protection and the use of foreign cultural agencies and venues.

The violent closing of the 2008 Queer Sarajevo Festival (www.queer.ba), the first such festival in Bosnia-Herzegovina, came as quite a shock to those who had not been following the events. The festival had been organised by an LGBTIQ activist group named Organisation Q to commemorate its sixth year of existence. The organisers had prepared well and established relations with highly-experienced festival directors and programmers in Western Europe and North America. Every element seemed highly-professional and comparable to any similar festival in the rest of Europe or North America. The local press vilified the organisation and the festival for its frank and positive representation of homosexuality in a part of the world where it is typically and paradoxically considered both immoral and a medical pathology. The festival was profoundly unlucky in its choice of dates: election campaigns were being held and politicians were making opportunistic use of the controversy; Ramadan was also underway, a coincidence which offended a fundamentalist Imam and his followers. Sanja Kajinic's recent analysis of the events brings out the liberal news media's framing of the debates in terms of cosmopolitanism versus parochialism unique in the history of the multi-ethnic, multi-denominational (Muslim, Roman Catholic and Eastern Orthodox) city of Sarajevo (Kajinic 2010).

Later the same year, Saint Petersburg's Bok o Bok (Side by Side) LGBT Film Festival (www.bok-o-bok.ru) struggled to put on its screenings when, at the last minute, the authorities cancelled their venues one by one, citing building code infractions and fire or tax issues. There was no violence, simply obstructionism after weeks of public vilification in the media. According to the organisers, Manny de Guerre and Ksenia Zemskaya, the local politicians felt pressure to prevent the festival as it prepared to launch (de Guerre 2011). The surprise cancellation of the venues prompted an improvised samizdat network by cell phone which gave safe directions to contacts who wanted to attend the festival (samizdat being the term for the illegal underground, clandestine social networks established during the period of the Soviet Union). In 2008, the actions of the festival were clearly not illegal, while those of the anonymous municipal authorities were, on the other hand, in all likelihood, not legal in their deliberate, fabricated obstructionism. Since then, the festival has learned to deal with similar political problems in other provincial cities through which it tours, namely Novosibirsk, Arkhangelsk, Kemerovo and, most recently, Tomsk. The situation in Saint Petersburg has improved, too, since the festival started making use of local foreign cultural venues, such as the Goethe Institute, the British Council and Dutch, Swedish and Norwegian agencies.

Queer film festivals have prospered in Asia, with major annual events taking place in Hong Kong, Japan, South Korea, Taiwan and Indonesia, to name a few. Important underground (officially not public) festivals are also being organised in Mainland China. Each has its own history of adaptation.

In 2002, a group of journalists, advertising agents and cultural bodies, organised the Q! Festival (www.q-munity.org) in Jakarta, Indonesia, the first ever LGBT film festival in any Muslim-majority country – a fact which is proudly declared in English on the festival website. Now it is the largest festival in the country and has touring programmes to several other cities throughout Indonesia. While the organisers occasionally receive death threats from conservative Islamist groups, no violence has transpired and no edition has ever been wholly cancelled (Badalu 2011). The festival receives no government support, and very little from corporations as they fear that their brand might be damaged; instead it relies on individual donations to Q-Munity and the use of venues offered free-of-charge by foreign cultural agencies. It has established strong ties with the Berlin International Film Festival and the Hamburg International Queer Film Festival, and has organised programme exchanges with festivals in India and elsewhere in Asia. The festival has found its way and is remarkably successful at sustaining itself as a vibrant cultural hub, both nationally and internationally.

China is a fascinating case, as the country continues to liberalise and become more open to the world. Its highly centralised bureaucracy requires approval from government officials for any cultural events, and the state is suspicious of homosexuality as a foreign issue. As 'LGBT' or 'queer' finds its way onto the promotional material for the festivals, it is often left in English to serve as a shibboleth. A cogent example of this can be found in recent work on how Chinese is adapting the word 'queer' as 'ku er' and placing it alongside the older term 'tongzhi' which means 'homosexual', but by way of an appropriation of 'comrade' from the communist nomenclature (Yang 2010; Bao 2010; Rhyne 2011). However, once officials are able to notice and decode the neologism or polysemic terms, they will likely take action, as they did in the northern summer of 2011 at the Beijing Queer Film Festival (whose website is tellingly unavailable).

In a quite different socialist country – Cuba – the first ever gay cinema week (website unavailable) began in Havana in 2005. This case is interesting for the way it frames the festival in terms of health, hygiene and cinéphilia. As co-organiser Raul Regueiro writes, echoing queer film festivals elsewhere but without the emphasis on rights:

> The ultimate goal is to broaden the scope of the initiatives undertaken since the year 2000 to diminish the vulnerability of the gay, lesbian, bisexual and transsexual (GLBT) community and to promote greater social acceptance of sexual diversity. The gay cinema week follows in the footsteps of the video screening and discussion sessions held twice monthly for the past five years and other similar activities organised in different provinces throughout the country. The HSH project is part of a national AIDS education and prevention programme undertaken by the Cuban Ministry of Public Health, with the help of financing from the Global Fund to Fight AIDS, Tuberculosis and Malaria. (Regueiro in Acosta 2005)

Although same-sex relations have been legal in Cuba since 1979, there is still no freedom to associate or meet as a group. Even street life is met with harassment by local police. From the late 1990s, and since the fall of the Soviet Union and the beginnings of economic liberalisation, new social problems have arisen, primarily due to increased sexual tourism. In contrast with the Chinese approach, this festival is supported from the top-down by the Cuban Government.

As we argue above, the formation of the queer film festivals owes much to the activist media practices and theories of (positive) representation of earlier social movements, particularly women's and gay liberation and civil rights movements. Historically, they presuppose a liberal rights discourse and seek recognition, equal rights and representation, increased production of film, by and for the members of the LGBT community, as well as the strengthening of skills and development of audiences. This early period changed with the celebrated cross-over films of the early 1990s (the New Queer Cinema) and the additional emphasis on distribution and production grants. To be sure, the original idea of putting up a bed sheet to share films with fellow filmmakers and a potentially interested audience has been radically developed into a sophisticated global network of queer film festivals – however unevenly distributed – with many shared aims that are often dependent on their respective contexts. While many queer film festivals in the West may have reached maximal audience size, there is no indication that the appearance of new festivals elsewhere is slowing down.

Note: *I wish to thank Professor Kay Armatage who generously arranged for my research stay at the Cinema Studies Institute at the University of Toronto during the northern spring and summer of 2011, during which I wrote most of my contribution to this article. (Ger Zielinski)*

Works Cited

Acosta, Dalia (2005) 'Out of the Closet, onto the Big Screen', *Inter Press Service (IPS)*, 16 September. On-line. Available HTTP: http://eforums.healthdev.org/read/messages?id=7897 (7 July 2011).

Bachmann, Gideon (2000) 'Insight into the Growing Festival Influence: Fest Vet Discusses "Wholesale" and "Retail" Events', *Variety*, 28 August. On-line. Available HTTP: http://www.variety.com/article/VR1117785609.html (26 July 2011).

Badalu, John (2011) Unpublished email interview with Ger Zielinski, 7 June.

Bajko, Matthew S. (2007) 'Frameline Yanks Film', *Bay Area Reporter*, 24 May. On-line. Available HTTP: http://www.ebar.com/news/article.php?sec=news&article=1840 (7 July 2011).

Bao, Hongwei (2010) 'Enlightenment Space, Affective Space: Travelling Queer Film Festivals in China', in Mikako Iwatake (ed.) *Gender, Mobility and Citizenship in Asia*. Helsinki: Department of World Cultures, University of Helsinki, 174-205.

De Guerre, Manny (2011) Unpublished email interview with Ger Zielinski, 10 June.

Gever, Martha (1990) 'The Names We Give Ourselves', in Russell Ferguson, Martha Gever, Trinh T. Minh-ha and Cornel West (eds) *Out There: Maginalization and Contemporary Culture.* Cambridge, MA: MIT Press, 191-202.

Gorfinkel, Elena (2006) 'Wet Dreams: Erotic Film Festivals of the Early 1970s and the Utopian Sexual Public Sphere', *Framework*, 47, 2, 59-86.

Iordanova, Dina (2009) 'The Film Festival Circuit', in Dina Iordanova with Ragan Rhyne (eds) *FFY1: The Festival Circuit.* St Andrews: St Andrews Film Studies, 23-39.

Kajinic, Sanja (2010) '"Battle for Sarajevo" as "Metropolis": Closure of the First Queer Sarajevo Festival According to Liberal Press', *Anthropology of East Europe Review*, 28, 1, 62-82.

Kim, Jeongmin (2007) 'Queer Cultural Movements and Local Counterpublics of Sexuality: A Case of Seoul Queer Films and Videos Festival', trans. Sunghee Hong, *Inter-Asia Cultural Studies*, 8, 4, 617-33.

Loist, Skadi (2010) 'Queer Film and the Film Festival Circuit', curator's note, *In Media Res*, 14 September. On-line. Available HTTP: http://mediacommons. futureofthebook.org/imr/2010/09/14/queer-film-and-film-festival-circuit (26 July 2011).

_____ (2011) 'Precarious Cultural Work: About the Organization of (Queer) Film Festivals', *Screen,* 52, 2, 268-73.

Mizielińska, Joanna and Robert Kulpa (2011) '"Contemporary Peripheries": Queer Studies, Circulation of Knowledge and East/West Divide', in Robert Kulpa and Joanna Mizielińska (eds) *De-Centring Western Sexualities: Central and Eastern European Perspectives.* Farnham: Ashgate, 11-26.

Olson, Jenni (2002) 'Film Festivals', *glbtq: An Encyclopedia of Gay, Lesbian, Bisexual, Transgender, and Queer Culture.* On-line. Available HTTP: http://www.glbtq.com/arts/film_festivals.html (7 July 2011).

Ommert, Alek and Skadi Loist (2008) 'Featuring Interventions: Zu queer-feministischen Repräsentationspraxen und Öffentlichkeiten', in Celine Camus, Annabelle Hornung, Fabienne Imlinger, Milena Noll, Isabelle Stauffer and Angela Kolbe (eds) *Im Zeichen des Geschlechts: Repräsentationen – Konstruktionen – Interventionen.* Königstein/Taunus: Ulrike Helmer, 124-40.

Peranson, Mark (2008) 'First You Get the Power, Then You Get the Money: Two Models of Film Festivals', *Cineaste*, 33, 3, 37-43.

Rastegar, Roya (2009) 'The De-fusion of Good Intentions: Outfest's Fusion Film Festival', *GLQ: A Journal of Lesbian and Gay Studies*, 15, 3, 481-97.

Rhyne, Ragan (2011) 'Comrades and Citizens: Gay and Lesbian Film Festivals in China', in Dina Iordanova and Ruby Cheung (eds) *FFY3: Film Festivals and East Asia*. St Andrews: St Andrews Film Studies, 110-24.

Siegel, Marc (1997) 'Spilling Out onto Castro Street', *Jump Cut*, 41, 131-6.

Stone, Amy L. (2010) 'Diversity, Dissent, and Decision Making: The Challenge to LGBT Politics', *GLQ: A Journal of Lesbian and Gay Studies*, 16, 3, 465-72.

Strandgaard Pedersen, Jesper and Carmelo Mazza (2011) 'International Film Festivals: For the Benefit of Whom?', *Culture Unbound: Journal of Current Cultural Research*, 3, 139-65. On-line. Available HTTP: http://www.cultureunbound.ep.liu.se/v3/a12 (16 June 2011).

Tang, Denise Tse Shang (2009) 'Demand for Cultural Representation: Emerging Independent Film and Video on Lesbian Desires', in Olivia Khoo and Sean Metzger (eds) *Futures of Chinese Cinema: Technologies and Temporalities in Chinese Screen Cultures*. Bristol/Chicago: Intellect, 169-90.

Wiegand, David (2003) 'Marc Huestis Grew Up Wanting to Be Either an Actor or President. Now the Filmmaker and Camp Impresario is Using His Showmanship to Promote Peace', *The San Francisco Chronicle*, 16 July, Section D1.

Yang, Yang (2010) 'De "Queer" à "Tongzhi": Etude comparative transnationale des festivals de films thématiques ayant trait aux questions de la sexualité et du genre en Belgique et dans les trois Chines', unpublished Master's thesis, Université libre de Bruxelles.

Zielinski, Ger (2008) 'Furtive, Steady Glances: On the Emergence and Cultural Politics of Lesbian & Gay Film Festivals', unpublished PhD thesis, McGill University, Montreal, Canada. On-line. Available HTTP: http://digitool.library. mcgill.ca/webclient/StreamGate?folder_id=0&dvs=1321962526615~555 (10 November 2011).

Notes

[1] New York (1979-87; from 1989); Chicago (from 1981); Los Angeles and Pittsburgh (from 1982); Ljubljana, former Yugoslavia, now Slovenia (from 1984); from 1986 on in Copenhagen, Brussels, Turin and Milan; 1988 in Montreal; 1989 in Paris; 1990 in Hamburg; 1991 in Toronto; and many others thereafter. An extensive database currently lists more than 180 queer film festivals worldwide (see www.queerfilmfestivals.org).

[2] One notable exception is the 1977 San Francisco Gay Video Festival, organised by N. A. (Nikos) Diaman, which had a remarkably equitable representation of various groups.

3   Even more recently, there were lively discussions regarding the scarcity and perceived misplacement of queer and intersex films in a programme labeled 'transgender' at the 2010 Hamburg Queer Film Festival, which resulted in the renaming of the programme to 'Gender Bender'.

4   In Germany, the most prominent are Edition Salzgeber (founded 1984), ProFun (1993) and GMFilms (1995); in the U.S., they are Wolfe Video (founded 1985), Strand Releasing (1989) and TLA Releasing (2001); and in the UK, Tartan Films (1982-2008) and Peccadillo Pictures (2000).

5   Gideon Bachmann (2000) differentiates between 'wholesale' and 'retail' festivals, while Mark Peranson (2008) talks about festivals based around business models versus those based around audience models.

6   After a failed plan by Frameline in 1995, in 2009 LesGaiCineMad – Madrid International LGTB Film Festival (www.lesgaicinemad.com) launched the Spanish Film Market, which promotes Spanish-language LGBT film through the Iberoamerican LGBT Film Network, CineLGBT (www.cinelgbt. com).

Towards an Indigenous
Film Festival Circuit

Amalia Córdova

Since the 1980s, indigenous communities in the Americas have been producing audiovisual media and organising news collectives, websites, community radio and photography and film and video workshops, forming a field that has come to be known as indigenous media. The results of an array of organisational processes, these films and videos encompass the full generic range, including fiction, animation, music videos, video-letters and various forms of documentary. Although much has been written on the appropriation of new technologies, little of these media are broadcast, and specialised criticism may be even rarer. Yet, despite these challenges, as well as the lack of funding and distribution, indigenous filmmaking is flourishing on a global scale, in part due to the growing number of film festivals that now screen this work. As it makes its way out to larger audiences, however, this unwieldy corpus – one often rooted in local indigenous community life – becomes entangled with the funding and exhibition circuits of Europe and North America.

The struggle for representation, political and otherwise, gained force in the four decades following the 1960s. In the 1980s, local and regional indigenous political organisations formed an international, pan-indigenous movement. This eventually led to the drafting and adoption of the United Nations Declaration on the Rights of Indigenous Peoples in 2007, which formalised indigenous peoples' demands for political inclusion on a global scale. This declaration recognised the existence of indigenous peoples globally and granted them a common framework for situation assessment and mobilisation. Before then, in the 1970s, indigenous filmmakers and film festivals had already begun to appear in North America. Video, in particular, was adopted as the preferred tool for expanding awareness of indigenous issues and continuing the struggle for recognition on local and global scales. Portable and cost-effective, video also offered an accessible means for teaching filmmaking. Meanwhile, film festivals provided an outlet for the circulation and exhibition of these proliferating works – from grassroots screenings to international film festivals.

The sites of these festivals are essential for considering the indigenous struggle for representation. The transmission of these works takes place locally through grassroots screenings, before making the leap to global markets by screening at international indigenous film festivals, often bypassing the national film arena. In addition to offering venues for the celebration of artistic and cultural achievements, indigenous film festivals become meeting grounds for the community of filmmakers themselves. They offer a locus for the recognition of indigenous groups and individual directors, for garnering production funds and for strengthening awareness on pressing social and political concerns faced by communities. This chapter provides an overview of how such film festivals perform key roles in the production and circulation cycle of indigenous film, and in conveying a sense of solidarity with indigenous struggles.

Indigenous Media: A Challenging Category

What constitutes indigenous media is a question as often debated as definitions of 'indigenous' or 'indigeneity'. In each case, discussions revolve around the expectations these terms generate and the communities they benefit. The growth of indigenous film festivals worldwide has both amplified these concerns and provided an occasion for their continued definition, as programmers and juries assess works for inclusion and reward. Moreover, film festivals have developed specifically to show and discuss this work, from academic conferences to native-run film festivals, creating a host of indigenous film festivals worldwide. As more indigenous film festivals appear, their organisers are faced with defining their scope within today's mediascape. Programmers and juries must discern which works best represent the current spectrum of indigenous work. It is a process that is prone to reawakening such debates each time a new group of jurors or curators convenes. Who or what makes a film indigenous?

Faye Ginsburg, who has written extensively on aboriginal and First Nations and on indigenous media, uses the term 'cultural activism', as a feature of indigenous media, which she suggests is

significant not simply as a transformation of Western technologies, but also as a new form of collective self-production that is being used self-consciously by indigenous producers to mediate historical and social ruptures within their own cultures and to assert the presence and concerns of First Nations peoples in the broader societies that encompass them. (Ginsburg 1997: 120)

Regardless of their differences, what these works do share is a concern over representation, allowing traditionally silenced people to respond to 'the structures of power that have erased or distorted their interests and realities' (Ginsburg et al. 2002: 7).

Nevertheless, many indigenous film practitioners are uncomfortable with such an overarching qualifier for their work. Although aware of its political value, they worry that the ethnic label keeps the discourse at the periphery, or implies a lesser quality, thus potentially undoing the media's potential for professional validation or social transformation. Others embrace the idea of indigenous video, film or media, as a cohesive descriptor with gravitational and performative functions. These situations strengthen networks of solidarity with the struggles of indigenous peoples, and have 'reconnected Aboriginal and Native Americans in new ways [...] bringing us into contact with other indigenous peoples' (Singer 2001: 58).

Re-inscribing and curating indigenous films from within the perspective of national cinemas, from which they are strikingly absent, is complicated by the fact that the historically and colonially-determined borders of today's republics often violate and divide the geography of traditional indigenous territories. Indigenous nations claiming sovereignty stand in direct confrontation with the nation-state occupying their land and seeking cohesion through imposed policy, language, calendars and, of course, national media. Further complications in territorialisation and identity emerge as indigenous nations are displaced or migrate. In the Americas, large indigenous populations are moving to the global North, where they may not readily identify with, or find recognition as, Native American, American Indian or 'Latino'. In the U.S., indigeneity is formally determined by federally recognised tribal enrolment, where affiliation criteria vary from state to state. This official system excludes many 'undocumented' Native and indigenous peoples, particularly from regions where indigeneity is unfavourably associated with class background, or is naturalised (implicit) due to regional origin or language proficiency, as is the case in many regions in Latin America. Definitional categorisations are further complicated in light of *mestizaje*, or 'mixed' identities. Potentials for exclusions abound in the top-down quests for specificity.

Such social exclusions, as well as both historical and on-going violence, drive the goals of indigenous media, namely to highlight the struggles of native peoples. The works – fictional and documentary – counter official stories of the national media, providing community perspectives on matters of human rights abuses and violations of indigenous territories. Through each of their works, indigenous filmmakers are exploring how film can serve as a tool for advocacy, to document alternative histories and project their concerns and visions towards future generations, to strengthen contemporary community identity, traditions and language and to help dispel the pervasive myths of the 'noble savage' and 'disappearing native'.

Festivals have also developed their own criteria for what counts as an indigenous work. The network of indigenous video producers affiliated with the Latin American Coordinator of Indigenous People's Film and Communication (Coordinadora Latinoamericana de Cine y Comunicación de los Pueblos Indígenas-CLACPI), published its own definition of 'indigenous video':

> For organisations and individuals who make up CLACPI, indigenous film and/or video includes works, and their directors and filmmakers, that apply *a firm commitment to give voice and vision worthy of the knowledge, culture, projects, claims, achievements and struggles of indigenous peoples.* Implicit in this definition is the notion that this work requires a high degree of *sensitivity and the active participation* of those who appear on-screen. Put another way, indigenous film and video offers a tool to foster self-expression and strengthen the real development of indigenous peoples. (CLAPCI 2009; author's translation, emphasis added)[1]

This definition appears to clarify to the outside world what CLACPI considers to be indigenous film and video: a status earned by practices such as respectful consultation and representation of communities, and by stressing the agency and voice of indigenous peoples in the productions while downplaying technical specifications, locations or roles, in specific productions. The CLACPI position is radically different from that of other festivals, such as Toronto's ImagiNATIVE Film and Media Arts Festival (www.imaginenative.org), which was founded in

2001 and only accepts works directed, written or produced by tribally affiliated indigenous peoples, regardless of subject matter. For CLACPI festival selectors, comprised of indigenous and non-indigenous jurors alike, the dignified treatment of indigenous themes may outweigh indigenous authorship.

Definitions aside, the films themselves provide points of challenge for many film festivals, be they peripheral, mainstream or otherwise. The look of the film can be distinctive, as indigenous festivals often screen works developed in training workshops where the appearance has the rough feel of an exercise, as opposed to a more 'polished' aesthetic. The inclusion of the workshopped film reveals a democratising drive in programming, fused to the commitment of the indigenous training process, all of which appear on screen in what Juan Salazar has called a 'poetics of imperfect media' (Salazar 2004: 7), following Julio García Espinosa's notion of an 'imperfect cinema' (García Espinosa 1979: 24). Funding, too, influences this look. Indigenous media-makers almost everywhere face extremely limited funding and distribution, either relying on grants from advocacy organisations or state bodies, or opting for self-funding. The reliance on others, and the commitment to sustainable filmmaking, leads to projects grounded in community accountability and infused with a community's pressures and interests. These works, which can use unconventional film styles, such as static shots of lengthy speeches in an indigenous language, become more geared towards the local audience rather than towards an audience trained in mainstream cinema. Meanwhile, the hybrid, heteroglossic nature of films produced through workshops, community consultation and traditions of reciprocity, further challenges mainstream aesthetics.

These practices of collective production affect more than aesthetics, as production schedules and running times vary widely. In turn, these processes affect availability, programming, planning for premières and other logistical aspects. In addition, works may exist in different versions for screening to internal and external audiences and are rarely 'packaged' with trailers, websites, promotional materials or print-quality stills. In fact, some works have been taken out of circulation entirely at the filmmaker's request.[2]

Fictional works are often based on traditional stories, involving collective memory and consultation with elders to verify the accuracy of the working version of the tale. Many indigenous directors aspire to recreate important historical events that have been erased or misrepresented by the official (national) history in a contrapuntal approach that asserts the contemporary reality of indigenous communities in the wake of forced assimilation and pressures towards globalisation.

The voice(s) of these films are often dialogical, multivocal and polyphonous and favour collective views and authorship. For example, Latin American works are usually produced in indigenous languages, with a community audience in mind and then subtitled into Spanish or Portuguese for a wider audience. These efforts, however, and those to translate and subtitle works from indigenous languages into French, English or Spanish to secure further distribution, involve costs prohibitive to the independent filmmaker. Such practical and aesthetic issues factor into the distribution of these indigenous works; opportunities for distribution and broadcasting are still limited.[3] These issues also factor into festival programming, whilst simultaneously engaging questions of the film's voice, function and audience: Who is telling the story? Who is the intended audience? What are the goals to be accomplished? Film festivals specialising in this work must be flexible and conversant with these issues in order to successfully engage with the producers of indigenous media. Hence the need for culturally sensitive, transnational and interdisciplinary approaches, if one is to participate in and study the circulation of indigenous media.

First Gatherings and Festivals

Several organisations and individuals intervene and collaborate at different levels around indigenous film and video, to stimulate the training of indigenous peoples and support the circulation of their work, gathering at international meetings, conferences and festivals. The main space for articulation and growth of this particular transnational community is the indigenous film festival, where indigenous media reaches urban, regional and international audiences and filmmakers interact and discuss pressing issues with their peers and collaborators. These are emblematic events that make visible a global indigenous film community, bringing together widely-dispersed works and often disenfranchised producers, opening up generative spaces for debate around rights and representation, creating links of support and exchange and facilitating circulation to indigenous communities and beyond.

Alliances of local, national and global nature are often created at such festivals, such as the Aboriginal Film and Video Arts Alliance in Canada (now the Aboriginal Arts Program at The Banff Centre, www. banffcentre.ca/aboriginal_arts), first proposed at the 1991 International

Indigenous Film Festival in Japan (website unavailable) and the Native American Producers Alliance, organised at the 1993 Two Rivers Native American Film and Video Festival (www.walkerart.org) in Minneapolis, Minnesota (Singer, 2001: 96-7). Along with the Native American Public Broadcasting Consortium (NAPBC) in the U.S., these organisations create circulation and support networks for and of indigenous filmmakers, even if the film festivals whence they emerged do not continue.

As with other ethnic, identity-based or special interest festivals (de Valck 2009: 182), networks form around 'specific agendas that focus on fostering and showcasing (and not distributing) a certain type of cinematic product' (Iordanova 2009: 32). The stakeholders include: scholars and film programmers, independent producers; regional, national and state film agencies; international non-governmental organisations and private foundations; indigenous training centres and regional organisations, archives and festivals; and indigenous television broadcasters. By working with indigenous communities and their media, participants of this wider circle become involved with indigenous issues. Indigenous film festival programmers must be active curators and take a self-reflexive approach to engage with and secure these works (Ross 2010: 171).

What follows next may be best described as a set of mini-case studies representative of the specific respective subheading. Each section addresses the work and specific effort of these festivals.

American Indian Film Festival

The American Indian Film Festival (www.aifisf.com) is the oldest indigenous film festival in existence. It was founded in 1975 in Seattle by Lakota (Sioux) activist Michael Smith, as part of the surge in Native American political and cultural affirmation, which characterised that decade (American Indian Film Institute 2011). Since 1977 the annual festival has taken place in San Francisco, screening works by or about indigenous peoples of Canada and the U.S. selected by Smith and a group of local Native American collaborators. The non-profit organisation behind the festival, the American Indian Film Institute (AIFI), runs a youth filmmaking initiative, the Tribal Touring Program that tours a selection of works in reservations and features a week-long digital video workshop for youth led by Native American directors. The AIFI maintains a website and publishes ICED (Indian Cinema Entertainment Destination) and Indian Cinema Entertainment (1993-2000).

Native American Film and Video Festival (Smithsonian)

What is now known as the Smithsonian Institution's Native American Film and Video Festival (nativenetworks.si.edu/nafvf/index.aspx) broadened its scope beyond North America to include all the Americas. The programme built on work begun by the original Museum of the American Indian (MAI), founded in 1916 by the collector of Native American Art George Gustav Heye as a site for exhibiting his considerable collection. In 1979, a decade before its incorporation into the Smithsonian Institution, the MAI produced its first festival as part of a weeklong celebration of Native American arts called The Ancestors. Due to the limited number of works actually made by indigenous directors at the time, the organisers Elizabeth Weatherford and Emilia Seubert decided to screen ethnographic films and other works about indigenous communities directed by non-natives. The museum's collection and exhibitions were from North, Central and South America, so works by or about indigenous peoples from all these areas were also considered. The Ancestors film programme grew into a singular showcase, outgrowing its initial scope and leading to the founding of the museum's Film and Video Center (FVC) and its on-going Native American Film and Video Festival (launched in 1982). The National Museum of the American Indian (NMAI) generates and maintains an extensive study collection of festival works at its Film and Video Center in New York City and at the museum's Cultural Resource Center in Suitland, Maryland.

Native American, First Nations and Latin American indigenous media makers, cultural activists and staff, comprise the Smithsonian's biannual Native American Film and Video Festival selection committee. Presented in New York City at the George Gustav Heye Center, the festival partners with other host organisations, including the American Indian Community House, the American Museum of Natural History, New York University and consular cultural offices. Structurally, the NAFVF facilitates the production of the festival as a gathering space for indigenous communities, filmmakers, film trainers, funders and advocates. The Festival is free for audience and filmmakers (it has no admission or submission charges), is non-competitive (it does not grant awards) and provides services for its invited participants, including travel, lodging and interpretation.[5] The NAFVF is one of the few indigenous festivals to publish a multilingual Call for Entries (in English, Spanish and occasionally Portuguese). The FVC also produces an important resource on indigenous filmmaking, Native Networks, a bilingual website devoted to Native media (in English at www.nativenetworks.si.edu and in Spanish at www.redesindigenas.si.edu).

Festival Internacional de Cine y Vídeo de los Pueblos Indígenas and The Latin American Coordinator of Indigenous Peoples' Film and Communication/Coordinadora Latinoamericana de Cine y Comunicación de los Pueblos Indígenas

The Latin American Coordinator of Indigenous Peoples' Film and Communication/Coordinadora Latinoamericana de Cine y Comunicación de los Pueblos Indígenas (CLACPI, www.clacpi.org) was founded in 1985 by a group of ethnographic filmmakers and 'indigenist' activists in Mexico City, at the first Latin American Indigenous People's Film Festival. Called Festival Latinoamericano de Cine de los Pueblos Indígenas at this first edition, the festival has grown and has changed its name a few times. In 1992, it changed to Festival Americano de Cine y Vídeo de los Pueblos Indígenas to include North and Central America, and in 2004, it became Festival Internacional de Cine y Vídeo de los Pueblos Indígenas (www.clacpi.org).

Since its inception, CLACPI has organised festivals, training workshops and seminars devoted to strengthening the development of indigenous media in Latin America. While not founded by indigenous peoples, CLACPI aspires to be a platform for indigenous filmmaking and is gradually being appropriated by indigenous filmmakers working with committed non-indigenous collaborators. Its festival is itinerant and roughly biennial, having staged events in Mexico (1985 and 2006), Brazil (1987), Venezuela (1990), Peru (1992), Bolivia (1996 and 2008), Guatemala (1999) and Chile (2004). Over the years, the festival has grown interested in films coming from outside Latin America, increasingly showing works made by or about indigenous peoples worldwide. This organisation presents the most visible discourse on indigenous video in Latin America, yet faces particular challenges due to its ambitious scope and rotational structure.

Unlike mainstream European and industry festivals, CLACPI festivals are de-territorialised, moving every two or three years to a different location in order to support emerging local processes. While the festival is recreated in a new location each time, its overall structure tends to stay the same: training workshops and community screenings usually precede a main event in an urban centre with an opening night event and a closing awards ceremony. The festival accepts submissions of work in diverse languages, negotiating translation and subtitling for accepted works, then circulating curated programmes after each festival. Participants are selected to present screenings, moderate roundtable discussion, translate and to write commentary. In exchange, they are given travel, food and lodging.

Following indigenous organisational practices, CLACPI conducts an Assembly after each festival, thus determining (by vote) the next festival location and drafting pronouncements and declarations. These declarations often address pressing social concerns, such as the plight of indigenous peoples in particularly conflicted areas, or reiterate the need for self-representation (see the Indigenous Agreement on Audiovisual Production [1992] in Harvey 1993: 176; and the Continental Network of Indigenous Communicators' 1996 Cochabamba Declaration, in Kalafatic 2002). Like the Havana International Film Festival (www.habanafilmfestival.com), CLACPI festival award categories reflect social commitment and are determined by a mixed indigenous and non-indigenous jury. Most of the time, the award is a gift of locally-produced artwork; however, on occasion a partner organisation will provide a prize of film production grants, equipment or scholarships.

CLACPI's contributions go beyond its own festivals. Although not a formalised distribution network, the organisation has collected a vast video archive of submitted works in La Paz, Bolivia. It participates in other festivals, playing a leading role in the itinerant Anaconda Awards (www.fundapraia.org),[6] a competitive biennial film festival focused on the Amazon and tropical rainforests of Latin America, and presenting works from its own festivals at European and Latin American showcases.[7] CLACPI also advises on indigenous training plans and film festivals throughout Latin America.

The methodologies instituted by CLACPI are the result of over two decades of experience in taking the festival to different locations and working with a growing network of indigenous and non-indigenous filmmakers, advocates, funders and scholars. Many, but not all, Latin American indigenous media projects form part of CLACPI. Each festival it organises has its own local character, achievements and challenges, but an influx of more steady support has enabled CLACPI to stabilise itself as an organisation, drawing up a Code of Ethics (2006), maintaining a Spanish-language website and holding more regular meetings throughout the year.

Programming in CLACPI festivals (and NAFVF) aims to provide a wide range of works, rather than the 'best' or most representative works of any region, nation or genre. Because so many of the works focus on matters of human and territorial rights, either denouncing violations or examining strategies of traditional justice and conflict resolution, programmes tend to be thematic, rather than regional.

Since 2006, CLACPI festivals have continued to broaden, moving beyond the hemispheric to the international. In 2006, CLACPI included work from Africa and the afro-mestizo communities of the Americas, bringing Senegalese director Mansour Sora Wade to present his films at the eighth CLACPI festival in Oaxaca, Mexico. Chadian director Mahamet Saleh Haroun's feature *Daratt* (*The Dry Season*, Chad/France/Belgium/Austria, 2006) screened at the ninth festival in La Paz, Bolivia in 2008 and afro-Colombian cultural activist Gustavo Balanta juried the tenth festival in Quito, Ecuador in 2010. That year the festival's jury awarded a prize to the documentary *Demam: Indigenous Peoples and Climate Change* (released as *Fever – a Video Guide on Climate Change for Indigenous Peoples*, Serge Marti and Gemma Sethsmith, Indonesia/UK, 2010), the second South Asian-based work to win an award at CLACPI. Although CLACPI began as a Latin American, 'Americanist' or continental project, it has since become global, stimulating intercultural and pan-indigenous exchanges.

Towards an Indigenous Festival Circuit

There are over 65 film festivals worldwide that specialise in, or show work exclusively related to, indigenous peoples, of which approximately half are held in the U.S. and six in Canada. Fifteen film festivals are held regularly in Latin America, in addition to one-time sidebars and regular showcases presented in Australia, Europe (France, Germany, the Netherlands, Norway and particularly Spain), India (iffi.gov.in) and Indonesia (www.indonesia.embassy.gov.au). Indigenous film festivals are also running in Australia, the Czech Republic, Finland, Germany, Nepal, New Zealand, Norway, Spain, Taiwan and the UK, with most having emerged after 2000.[8]

A few non-indigenous-themed international festivals have created permanent sections that focus on indigenous works, such as the Sundance Institute Native Forum (www.sundance.org/festival/film-events/native-forum) and the Morelia International Film Festival's Indigenous Peoples Forum (www.moreliafilmfest.com). Indigenous works are also screened by a host of special interest festivals (African diaspora, animation, documentary, environmental, ethnographic, experimental, human rights, Latin American, Latino, women's and youth film festivals) or showcased regularly at smaller festivals whose local or regional constituency is indigenous.

Several European film festivals have recognised key indigenous-produced films, such as the Amiens International Film Festival (www. filmfestamiens.org), which has presented thematic showcases on Native peoples of the Americas since 1995, and the Festival de Cinéma de Douarnenez (www.festival-douarnenez.com) which has presented regional indigenous showcases. The Berlin International Film Festival (www.berlinale.de) distinguished Inupiaq director Andrew Okpeaha MacLean's feature *On the Ice* (U.S., 2011) with the Crystal Bear award for best debut film. The first indigenous-directed feature film, *Atanarjuat* (Zacharias Kunuk and Norm Cohn, Canada, 2001), produced by the Igloolik Isuma collective, won the Camera d'Or at Cannes for Best First Feature Film. The film, made in the Inuktitut language, played extensively on the mainstream festival circuit, including the festivals in Toronto, Rotterdam, Mar del Plata and Tokyo, among others.

In primarily Anglophone regions, including Australia, New Zealand, North America (Canada, Hawaii and the U.S.), the Pacific and Northern Europe, filmmakers, funders and festivals, are developing a circuit of what we could call an international indigenous cinema, but there has been little participation by indigenous communities in the global South.[9] While indigenous producers working in Latin America undoubtedly face similar colonial conditions as their aboriginal/Native American/First Nations counterparts and are interested in their visual and political work, occasions for exchange and reciprocity have been rare, perhaps due to lack of access to each other's work as well as multiple language barriers.[10] Few indigenous works from the global North are ever subtitled into languages other than English and French, or submitted to Latin American indigenous film festivals.

By contrast, many Latin American indigenous film festivals regularly programme diasporic and indigenous cinema from the global North (as well as from Africa and Asia), both as models for alternative cinematic practices and as works that resonate thematically with indigenous audiences. This rather unacknowledged North-South divide within indigenous cinema can be seen in the nature of the works themselves, in their modes of production and, most evidently, in their uneven access to global circulation.

Conclusion

There is no consensus as to what constitutes an indigenous film. The notion is largely held together by approaches to making audiovisual work from indigenous perspectives and is supported by a vast, transnational network of activists, filmmakers, journalists, scholars, funders and programmers, that (in one way or another) connects a dispersed community of indigenous video producers and helps circulate their work. Indigenous film is positioning itself as a distinct field of cultural production – a signifying practice, distinct from national cinemas, popular and community video and tactical media practices. While it has created its own representational space, with parallel circuits of production and circulation through festivals, increasingly the works are flowing into broader circuits, as audiences gain interest in hearing indigenous perspectives on environmental and indigenous rights issues.

Although indigenous media has gained visibility both politically and academically, effective collaboration with indigenous producers remains problematic for most academic institutions, distributors, curators, museums, broadcast channels and state and non-governmental institutions. This is partly due to the demands of navigating the diverse cultural protocols, restrictions and potential implications that come with collectively-produced, socially-embedded indigenous narratives. It also implies working in several languages and allowing for slippage in translation. The traditional circulation spaces of national, regional ('Latin American') and 'world' cinema are culturally unprepared to negotiate with the community-based practices prevalent in indigenous film and video, which carry distinct social concerns and commitments. In fact, mainstream film festivals and distributors can occasionally become new 'contact zones', where marginalisation is re-inscribed or tokenism takes the place of thoughtful engagement.

Circulating indigenous media calls for the decolonisation of media practice and scholarship, moving from the dominant industry's film and nation-making conventions to the involvement of non-indigenous producers, funding agencies and non-governmental organisations in its production and circulation. There is an urgent need to relay the messages contained in this media, but to do so effectively, agreements must be reached with the producing communities on respectful, reciprocal terms. This inevitably involves unthinking Eurocentric notions implicit in most cultural and creative agencies and seeking out the indigenous thinking around media.

Works Cited

Academia de Lenguas Mayas de Guatemala 'Bienvenidos' (2011) On-line. Available HTTP: http://www.almg.org.gt (1 July 2011).

American Indian Film Institute (2011) 'History', *American Indian Film Institute*. On-line. Available HTTP: http://www.aifisf.com/history.php (1 July 2011).

CLAPCI (2009) Blog posting, *CLAPCI* Website, 29 June. On-line. Available HTTP: http://www.clacpi.org/index.php?/quienes-somos/clacpi.html (10 December 2011).

Continental Network of Indigenous Communicators (1996) 'Declaración de Cochabamba'. *V Indigenous Peoples Film and Video Festival.* Cochabamba: CLACPI.

Córdova, Amalia and Gabriela Zamorano (2004) 'Mapping Mexican Media: Indigenous and Community Video and Radio', *Native Networks*. On-line. Available HTTP: http://www.nativenetworks.si.edu/eng/rose/mexico.htm (14 August 2011).

de Valck, Marijke and Skadi Loist (2009) 'Film Festival Studies: An Overview of a Burgeoning Field', in Dina Iordanova and Ragan Rhyne (eds) *FFY1: The Festival Circuit,* St Andrews: St Andrews Film Studies, 179-215.

García Espinosa, Julio (1979 [1969]) 'For an Imperfect Cinema', trans. Julianne Burton, *Jump Cut: A Review of Contemporary Media*, 20, 24-6.

Ginsburg, Faye (1997) '"From Little Things Big Things Grow" Indigenous Media and Cultural Activism', in Richard G. Fox and Orin Starn (eds) *Between Resistance and Revolution, Cultural Politics and Social Protest.* New Brunswick: Rutgers University Press, 118-44.

Ginsburg, Faye, Lila Abu-Lughod and Brian Larkin (2002) 'Introduction', in Faye Ginsburg, Lila Abu-Lughod and Brian Larkin (eds) *Media Worlds: Anthropology on New Terrain.* Berkeley: University of California Press, 1-36.

Guitérrez, Franklin (2008) *El Camino de Nuestra Imagen: Un proceso de comunicación Indígena.* Pueblos Indígenas y Comunicación, 1, La Paz: Plan Nacional Indígena Originario de Comunicación, 214-6.

Harvey, Penny (1993) 'Ethnographic Film and the Politics of Difference: A Review of Film Festivals', *Visual Anthropology Review*, 1, 9 March, 164–176.

Iordanova, Dina (2009) 'The Film Festival Circuit', in Dina Iordanova and Ragan Rhyne (eds) *FFY1: The Festival Circuit,* St Andrews: St Andrews Film Studies, 23-39.

IsumaTV (2011) *Isuma TV* Website. On-line. Available HTTP: http://www.isuma.tv (30 June 2011).

Kalafatic, Carol (2002) 'CEFREC: Media in Bolivia', *Native Networks*. On-line. Available HTTP: http://www.nativenetworks.si.edu/eng/rose/cefrec. htm#open (14 August 2011).

Molina Ramírez, Tania (2009) 'En *de Raíz Luna* buscamos la parte de identidad que se queda entre pueblo y ciudad: Carballo', *Periódico La Jornada*. On-line. Available HTTP: http://www.jornada.unam.mx/2009/06/12/index.php? section=espectaculos&article=a10n1esp (12 June 2011).

Programa Universitario México Nación Multicultural, *Proyecto México Multicultural*, Universidad Nacional Autónoma de México. On-line. Available HTTP: http://www.nacionmulticultural.unam.mx/Portal/Derecho/ MULTIMEDIA/ppm.html (16 December 2010).

Ross, Miriam (2010) 'Film Festivals and the Ibero-American Sphere', in Dina Iordanova and Ragan Rhyne (eds) *FFY1: Film Festivals and Imagined Communities*, 171-83.

Salazar, Juan Francisco (2004) *Imperfect Media: The Poetics of Indigenous Media in Chile*. Unpublished thesis submitted to the University of Western Sydney in partial fulfilment of the requirements for the Degree of Doctor of Philosophy, 82-92.

Singer, Beverly (2001) *Wiping the War Paint Off the Lens: Native American Film and Video*. Minneapolis: University of Minnesota Press.

United Nations Permanent Forum on Indigenous Issues (2007) 'United Nations Declaration on the Rights of Indigenous Peoples Adopted by the General Assembly 13 September 2007'. Geneva: United Nations. On-line. Available HTTP: http://www.un.org/esa/socdev/unpfii/en/declaration.html (7 July 2011).

Notes

[1]   The Coordinadora Latinoamericana de Cine y Comunicación de los Pueblos Indígenas, CLACPI, was formerly known as the Latin American Council of Indigenous People's Film and Video (Consejo Latinoamericano de Cine y Comunicación de los Pueblos Indígenas).

[2]   *Ritual Clowns* (Victor Masayesva Jr., U.S., 1988) drew some controversy, leading the filmmaker to withdraw it from circulation because it showed culturally sensitive aspects of Hopi tradition.

[3]   In the U.S. and Canada there are few distributors specialising in this kind of media or carrying a line of indigenous work; those that do include Documentary Educational Resources, First Nations Films, the National Film Board of Canada, Third World Newsreel, Video Databank, Visionmaker

Video (run by Native American Public Telecommunications) and V-Tape, among others. International distribution networks for indigenous film outside North America are almost non-existent, with the exceptions of Video Nas Aldeias of Brazil and Promedios/Chiapas Media Project of Mexico, both of which have U.S.-based international distribution and are run by non-indigenous, English-proficient directors.

Broadcast spaces for this work are also extremely limited, with the exception of Canada's Aboriginal Peoples Television Network (APTN), a national channel devoted exclusively to indigenous production, and IsumaTV (www.isuma.tv), an Inuit web portal that enables producers to start their channels and upload their content directly for streaming or download. In Latin America, Mexican public television regularly broadcasts indigenous-produced documentaries through a series called *Pueblos de México*, and a programme called *De Raiz Luna* focuses exclusively on Mexican indigenous cultural expressions. In 2009, Guatemala's Ministry of Education and Sports and the Academia de Lenguas Maya de Guatemala (ALMG) launched TVMaya, a dedicated aboriginal television channel. Since 2004, Bolivia's aboriginal producers affiliated by CAIB (Coordinadora Audiovisual Indígena Originaria de Bolivia) have produced community television in the lowland region of Beni as well as a weekly indigenous program, *EntreCulturas*, which airs on national television (Gutiérrez 2008: 214).

4   In 1989, the collection was incorporated into the Smithsonian Institution and its exhibition venue and administrative staff moved to the former U.S. Customs House, now the George Gustav Heye Center, home to the New York branch of the Smithsonian National Museum of the American Indian and of other federal agencies.

5   Along with the Latin American Indigenous People's Film Festival (Festival Latinoamericano de Cine de los Pueblos Indígenas) founded in 1985 in Mexico City, the Smithsonian's festival provides a unique gathering place for an otherwise dispersed community of indigenous film trainers, producers, funders and advocates who rarely have the means to gather.

6   The full name of the festival in Spanish is Premio Anaconda al Vídeo Indígena Amazónico del Chaco y los Bosques Tropicales de América Latina y el Caribe. It has been co-produced since 2000 by the Fundación PRAIA and CLACPI. It has no website of its own but periodically launches its call for entries from its partners' sites: www.fundapraia.org and www.clacpi.org.

7   These showcases are all called El Universo Audiovisual de los Pueblos Indígenas (The Audiovisual Universe of Indigenous Peoples) and versions

have occurred sporadically in Peru (Lima, 2007, and Ayacucho 2010, www. chirapaq.org.pe), Santiago de Chile (since 2007, cineindigena.blogspot. com/), at diverse cities of the Basque Country in Spain since 2002, with the support of the non-profit organisation Mugarik Gabe, (www.mugarikgabe. org), and more regularly as itinerant showcases supported by the Spanish international Cooperation Agency (www.aecid.es) in Barcelona, Córdoba, Madrid, Sevilla and Valencia.

[8] In addition to the aforementioned festivals, there are several significant, international festivals worth noting. They include: in the U.S., the All Roads Film Festival (www.nationalgeographic.com/allroads), the Festival of Native Film & Culture (www.accmuseum.org), First Americans in the Arts Film/TV/Theatrical Awards (www.firstamericans.org/call4entries. htm), Indigenous Film & Arts Festival (www.iiirm.org), Indigenous World Film Festival (www.alaskanative.net) and the International Cherokee Film Festival (www.internationalcherokeefilmfestival.com); in Canada, Dreamspeakers Film Festival (www.dreamspeakers.org), First Peoples' Festival Film & Video Showcase/Présence authoctone (www.nativelynx. qc.ca), Weeneebeg Aboriginal Film and Video Festival (www.weeneebeg. ca), Winnipeg Aboriginal Film and Video Festival (www.aboriginalfilmfest. org); in Latin America, Argentina's Festival de Cine de los Pueblos Indígenas of Chaco (www.deceachaco.blogspot.com); in Colombia, Daupará-Muestra de Cine y Video Indígena (www.daupara.org) and the Festival de Cine y Video Rodolfo Maya (festivalrodolfomaya.blogspot. com); in Mexico, Puebla's Festival de Cine y Video Indígena (www.wix. com/ficvi2011/cinearte), Morelia's Festival de Video Indígena (www.cdi. gob.mx) and Geografías Suaves (yoochel.org) in the Yucatan; and the Muestra de Cine Indígena of Venezuela (www.fundacenafv.gob.ve). In Australia there is, The Dreaming-Australia's International Indigenous Festival (www.thedreamingfestival.com) and Message Sticks Indigenous Film Festival (www.sydneyoperahouse.com); in New Zealand, the Wairoa Maori Film Festival (www.manawairoa.com). In Europe, Indianer Inuit: North American Native Film Festival (www.nordamerika-filmfestival. com) in Germany; the Native & Indigenous Film Festival in the Czech Republic (www.naiff.eu); Native Spirit, which takes place in the UK and Spain (www.nativespiritfoundation.org); there are also two Sámi film festivals – the Sámi Film Festival in Norway (www.samifilmfestival.no) and Skábmagovat Film Festival (www.skabmagovat.fi) in Finland. Finally, of note is the Nepal International Indigenous Film Festival (ifanepal.org. np), established in 2006 in Kathmandu; the World Indigenous Television Conference (www.witbc2010.org) which took place in New Zealand (2008)

and Taiwan (2010); and the Festival of Indigenous African Language Films (fiafng.com), undoubtedly fuelled by Nigeria's prolific film industry and independent of an indigenous festival circuit.

[9] In 2005, the Museum of Modern Art, New York University and the Smithsonian National Museum of the American Indian produced First Nations/First Features (www.moma.org/visit/calendar/films/724), a unique, one-time retrospective of world indigenous cinema in New York City, featuring 26 groundbreaking indigenous films and directors from the Americas, Europe and the Pacific.

[10] International video tours have facilitated exchange between indigenous filmmakers and audiences in different countries. In 1998, the tour Video América Indígena/Video Native America was organised by the Film and Video Center of NMAI in collaboration with indigenous media organisations in Mexico to have Native American directors present their work in indigenous villages in the states of Oaxaca, Morelos and Michoacán. In 2003 NMAI partnered with Ojo de Agua Comunicación to present Video México Indígena/Video Native Mexico, travelling Mexican indigenous filmmakers to screen at diverse community venues in four U.S. states. In 2004, the Chiapas Media Project toured works of indigenous videomakers from Chiapas and Guerrero across Australia, in collaboration with aboriginal media associations (Córdova and Zamorano, 2004).

Permutations of the Species: Independent Disability Cinema and the Critique of National Normativity

David Mitchell and Sharon Snyder

Contemporary Disability Films and Film Festivals

Seeds of this analysis first took hold during a screening of the short film, *I'm in away from Here* (Catriona MacInnes, U.K., 2007), at The Way We Live International Short Film Festival in Munich (www.abm-medien. de) in November 2009. The film begins with a man masturbating on a public beach. He is interrupted as an older woman calls his name. As the film progresses, more information arrives: the man, Archie, is identified as neuro-atypical and on the autistic spectrum and the woman turns out to be his mother, but at the start, we don't know exactly how to place Archie in a cultural or geographical sense. We do not know why he sleeps by the side of a bank, or why the woman is trying to gain his attention. The audience awakens with Archie, suddenly and without warning. Signalled by audio and video distortions, the world crashes in upon us, as well as upon the protagonist; we cannot interpret the story amidst these sensorial intrusions coming from every direction. The film ultimately leaves Archie and the audience immersed in an experience that belongs to neither; an enigmatic story marked by little more than a shared inability to keep the interruptions at bay.

To begin *in media res* is nothing new. Both popular and avant-garde film movements have provided abrupt entry into film's narrative spaces for decades. Here, though, it takes on additional significance as part of the upending of all comfortable coordinates that comes not only with contemporary independent disability films, but also with their places of exhibition: the independent disability film festival circuit. Both the films and the festivals challenge expectations and understandings of normative narratives, spaces and people, allowing for the raising of issues related to the place of disabled people in the world and the readjusting of perspectives on the subjects and on the systems that assign these definitions and categories.

When we speak of independent disability films, we refer to predominantly video-based works created on low budget (less than U.S.$100,000 but in many cases below U.S.$10,000) and without the backing of a multi-national, corporate, commercial, mainstream U.S. film industry. Independent videos derive from local community contexts but speak globally to people with disabilities living around the world. The intersections of local and global usher in the first complexities around definitions and categorisations: typically funded by arts-based governmental organisations supporting the promotion of national identity abroad, these films represent those typically omitted from the national narrative.

This peripherality extends to the aesthetic realm, as many independent disability films are non-narrative, eschewing conventions of exposition, conflict and denouement. The style is more akin to a 'slice of life' – a brief examination as different variants of embodied life come into contact with social barriers. This tendency toward a refusal of narrative arc might be understood as the film equivalent of what queer theorist Lee Edelman (2004) calls 'no future'. Like 'non-reproductive' queer and trans-gendered bodies, people with disabilities find themselves denied ways to narrate viable futures for themselves, and thus they explore alternative modes of transmission and expression. Because traditional story mediums such as film have proven largely disinterested in imagining productive life stories for disabled people where the target group is projected into successful futures, independent disability film responds by narrating the results of truncated storylines and lives within the strict confines of a truncated form: the film short.[1] In a great number of independent disability films, social roles are reversed and disabled people perform acts of counter-cultural resistance commonly denied them by hetero-normative circuits of desire.[2] Perhaps, ironically, these counter-cultural acts of resistance often entail pursuing normative practices denied to those in non-normative bodies.

These films tend not to receive local theatrical release, but instead share a distribution network of independent disability film festivals held in major metropolitan centres such as London (London Disability Arts Festival: www.disabilityartsonline.org.uk/ldaf-film-festival), Melbourne (The Other Film Festival: www.otherfilmfestival.com), Moscow (Breaking Down Barriers Film Festival: festival-eng.perspektiva-inva.ru), Munich (The Way We Live International Short Film Festival: www.abm-medien.

de), Berkeley (SUPERFEST International Disability Film Festival: www.culturedisabilitytalent.org/index.html), Athens (Emotion Pictures: www.ameamedia.gr), Calgary (Picture This: www.ptff.org/ptff_main/2011-festival.html) and Helsinki (KynnysKINO Disability Film Festival: www.kynnys.info.) among others. The festival venues operate as cosmopolitan gathering points for showcasing independent works about the struggles, triumphs, exclusions, successes and everyday living experiences of disabled people. The films offer aesthetic interventions, challenging narrative standards and continuity editing, while de-privileging normative body movements and appearance through the casting of disabled people in the roles of characters with disabilities. Key filmmaking norms are sent into hiding and, in doing so, are exposed as the conventions of a normative visual media artifice. The events and characters now appearing on screens at disability film festivals chart reactions to the historical 're-entry' of disabled people into normative social orders that are specific to their respective nations, in the wake of histories of formalised exclusion from the most rudimentary aspects of human community. These films (and festivals) begin to defy entrenched attitudes toward people with disabilities as non- (productive) citizens and to challenge host governments to create more flexible policies and access to infrastructure for all. The festival screenings themselves may provide such impetus not only on, but also off-screen, as venues must be made physically accessible to all attendees. Even the timing of events is relevant, as programmers account for the numerous difficulties faced by people with disabilities in everyday travel.

In effect, the main function of independent disability cinema, a term that embraces both the films and the conditions of viewing, lies in critiquing the exclusionary social orders that we call 'national normativities'. National normativities work to police the local boundaries of physical, cognitive, sensory and aesthetic foundations of embodiment. Normative values grounded in a narrow concept of bodily acceptability produce disabled bodies as exceptionally deviant. By default, the various national concepts of body norms are often complicit with 'ableist' sensibilities that cherish the 'abled' body as normal and advance this norm as a pre-condition for social inclusion and acceptable citizenship. Disability film festivals counter this foundational exclusion at the heart of national formulas of belonging; they engage alternative ways of 'being disabled' as an antidote to histories of social rejection by inflexible and unaccommodating norms. This is achieved by showcasing independent films and promoting stories that feature different kinds of bodies, capacities, sensory experiences and subjectivities. The experience of independent disability film is one of immersion and exposure to atypical lives.

Multiple Subjectivities on Screen: *Jak to jest byc moja matka* (*What It Is Like To Be My Mother*, Norah McGettigan, Poland, 2007)

As an example of the immersion and exposure to atypical lives that independent disability films offer, the short film *What It Is Like To Be My Mother* evolves around the encounter of a non-disabled daughter with her mother, who has recently undergone a double amputation. When shown in the context of a disability film festival, it offers an opportunity for reflexive exploration of multiple and conflicting expectations and identities.[3] The film uses a family drama to stage a now common political conflict about the necessity of policing the borders of disability representation between disabled people and non-disabled image-makers. At the same time, it raises questions about the nature of disabled community, where kinship and commonality are often fraught, given the competing demands of access and limited resources.

In the opening scene we learn that the daughter has made a film about her mother's struggle to 'regain independence', and the video has been selected for screening at a disability arts and film festival. The mother, who is introduced lying on her back working with weights on a padded therapy table, expresses disapproval of her daughter's desire to show the film at the festival because the would-be filmmaker 'doesn't have a disability' and therefore cannot represent her effectively. What can display accomplish?

Once the daughter convinces her mother that the film festival screening could be a positive move toward a future career, the mother agrees to attend and even to make an appearance on stage prior to the screening. After being introduced by the festival host, the mother moves to centre stage and insists on making a dangerous transition from her wheelchair to a precarious standing position on crutches hovering above the audience. The festival participants clap following the mother's banal, yet successful effort to stand on prosthetic legs. Holding their attention, she tells them to give her daughter a hand now, in case they end up not liking the movie. The event turns into a humiliating experience for the daughter.

During the screening the mother grows increasingly upset and rolls out of the theatre before the film concludes. In the following scene, she wheels herself stubbornly in the rain while the cab follows behind. Later, mother and daughter are reunited in the cab; the mother grudgingly admits that the daughter has made a 'good film', while the daughter grumpily refuses to return the mother's hug. Ultimately, the daughter demonstrates indifference to the mother's sense of violation by resting on the laurels of film festival acclaim and replacing one kind of recognition (parental) with another (artistic). This scene depicts more than the micro-politics of a family: it calls forth the larger political context of disability cinema with the potential for social rejection experienced by both subjects and filmmakers.

Initially, the daughter's intention to have the film shown at the festival appears potentially exploitative. Later on, however, when they get to the festival, the mother engages in attention-seeking behaviour, undermining her daughter's aspirations to be taken seriously as a filmmaker. While, from the outset, the mother suspects her image may be exploited, toward the end of the film the daughter is put off by her mother's attention-grabbing behaviour at the festival. The two individual stories that evolve here – of the mother and of the daughter – reflect the various agendas, benefits and downfalls of film and festival display.

Likewise, the audience's allegiances shift from one character to the other as the film asks the viewers to contemplate whether direct identification is a pre-condition to the creation of a successful portrayal of disability. It also asks an even more difficult question: Whether an artistically worthy film should be shown without the consent of the disabled subject being filmed.

To highlight this point, the film stages an interview sequence showing the filmmaker/daughter awkwardly asking the subject/mother: 'Did your disability impact on your life?' Besides taking an amateur interlocutor's approach at asking impossibly open-ended questions, the daughter's query is laden with assumptions about asexuality, unemployability, incapacity to parent and failure to maintain the interests of a lover. The below-the-knee double amputee mother pauses before answering with a cool retort: 'I used to buy shoes – now I buy gloves'.

What It Is Like To Be My Mother examines critical questions about film images of disabled bodies and narrative recreations of lives lived with disability as re-told by filmmakers. Questions of objectification proliferate as able-bodied image-makers and disabled individuals are on display for the festival audience, receiving accolades, awards and moments of glory, but much of it feels as if it is at the expense of a further degree of public objectification. At the same time, *What It Is Like To Be My Mother* purposefully avoids delivering an answer to its titular thesis. A more accurate title might be 'What is it like to be the daughter of a disabled mother?' or, better yet, 'How my mom's disability looks from the perspective of an able-bodied daughter seeking to adjust to her alternative embodiment?'.[4] The innovation of the film is in its argument that there is no such thing as authentic subjectivity of disability. The daughter imposes her version of what it is like to be a disabled mother, while the mother's participation in the filmmaking process proves fully performative in its own right. Ultimately, *What It Is Like To Be My Mother* contemplates how film belies the illusion of direct access to disability experience, and depends on bodily spectacle as well as an attendant level of personal violation for its power.

Challenging Definitions

The oscillation between exploitation and objectification, and between acceptance and rejection, illustrates many of the tensions around identity production in disability film festivals. As discussed above, the films are often produced in a national context but aimed at transnational audiences. Yet each stop offers a moment to intervene into the local discourse that establishes these exclusionary power relations (which manifest themselves in other discourses, whether legal, political or cultural). Perhaps most notable, though, is the way that disability challenges identity-based projects, calling attention to the permeability and mutability of identity.

The alternative universes showcased at disability film festivals strain the boundaries of national norms. Independent disability film festivals upset the sanctity of the able body; they parade a pastiche of oddities as foundational to the social and material dynamics of disabled bodies in tension with social norms. Disability itself provides challenges to identity production since it implies a medical condition, confers a legal status and describes a state of being. The festivals accept – and even promote – this complexity, which challenges the political efforts to forward a less challenging social message about experiences of disability, such as, that disabled people are just like everyone else. Rather, disability film festivals share a social model of disability that is an identity of difference based on shared experiences of exclusion.

Yet, while exclusionary experiences of stigma-based rejection are common, disability film festivals show disability as a strategy of referencing identity in the absence of a coherent and universally shared experience of embodiment. This strategy questions containment of any sort, fighting against the forms of identity-building that contribute to exploitation and exclusion. They are not to be counted among the various social missions of fixing and stasis 'wishing to contain the messiness of identity within formulaic grids' such as diagnosis, special education, rehabilitation and prosthetic supplementation (Puar 2007: 212). The curated programmes offer a tactical deployment of body chaos and demand critical engagement from a range of audiences, including policy-makers, employers, government officials, teachers, parents, therapists, medical personnel and commercial business operators. The films require the accommodation of the arrival of new generations of politicised disabled people in public and private spaces.

Disability film festival programming embraces a collective identity of distinct experiences. The festivals gather together a variety of human differences and place them on display in non-sequential and/ or non-thematic relation to each other. The screenings tend to avoid grouping films according to conditions, parallel kinds of discrimination, or other organising principles, since the act of categorising disabilities represents a form of oppression in and of itself. Without this conscious orchestration of films into normative narrative groupings of disability as deviance festival audiences become connoisseurs of human variation and aficionados of diverse bodies. They dabble in the persistent nuances of biological differences, social constructions and mutating screen presences. They are not meant to become therapeutic or diagnostic experts, cultivating skills to manage these unruly bodies.

The festival circuit offers a tactical vantage point that is not easily duplicated in other contexts, particularly insofar as the venues sweep up a wide net of new video productions from around the globe and stage them for simultaneous consumption over a condensed period of several days. The cumulative programming effect results in an opportunity for audiences to assess the range of experiences across the world, and pick out possible trends. With its orchestrated influx of international filmmakers, actors, experts, producers and activists, the disability film festival gives voice to otherwise estranged artistic and documentary points of view and highlights the situation of an alienated people navigating disabilities in a variety of barrier-ridden social milieus. As such, disability film festivals provide us with a useful barometer for understanding the degree to which disability rights, identity and representational strategies are transforming (or not) our understanding of people with disabilities.

The festival circuit – by definition – recognises disability as a contextual phenomenon of ever-mutating proportions. Disability film festivals are consciously created contexts that bring together surveys of disability that are carried out in various contexts; without this contextual analysis, close readings of individual films have relatively little to tell us about the nature, reception and impetus for the creation of alternative cinema. The multiplicity of screening venues at the festivals enables an important context for the understanding of disabled concerns 'at large'.

The films themselves become essential agents in this definitional process, not only as sites for determining trends and issues, but as a key way in which disabled people might be able to communicate through the physical barriers of mass transit inaccessibility, intensive immigration restrictions and poverty. Disability films transcend barriers toward acquiring the degree of extra-national mobility that is often denied people with disabilities; and to achieving improvements in access. Consequently, the array of offerings at independent disability film festivals provides an overview of the global 'health' of disabled populations as they navigate increasingly diffuse, and largely inhospitable, social networks.

Moreover, these challenges to the system, these bodies on the periphery, may offer something else: a chance to reconsider all forms of social identity, and not merely the formations on the fringe. Disabled people represent boundary creatures at a contemporary historical juncture, akin to the sea serpents, the dragons and the 'deformed' native beings seen at the edges of world maps in the context of early colonial cartographies. Whereas these extra-human figures previously marked unexplored geographies of the primitive, disability film festivals recognise the margins of the species as the locations of what discredited evolutionary biologist Richard Goldschmidt once referred to as 'hopeful monsters' (Goldschmidt 1982: 205-6), a case of rapid evolutionary change in individual organisms that holds promise for the longevity of the species as a whole.

We approach disability film festivals as sites for change on a massive geological scale. The festivals offer meeting places that reveal national constructions of disability and call attention to the dynamic cultural contexts that shape the concepts of disability as difference. No longer inevitable and enduring, these formations are inherently mutable and contingent. The festival puts social norms under scrutiny because the diversity of disability on view here exhausts any pretension to an overarching human 'commonality'. The disability film festival does not advocate clichés such as 'We are all alike' or 'Disabled people are just like everyone else', although a few frequenters of these festivals are still prone to making such naturalising claims. Rather, it expands our knowledge of human difference in seeking to document exhaustively experiences of embodiment that, by definition, cannot be exhausted.[5]

Not only are individual disability predicaments not well understood (you've seen one disability, you've seen *one* disability), but disability filmmakers venture out into the peripheries of peripheral locations for their subject. Within such an effort to gather up those on the margins of the margins, cultural norms become recognised for what they really are: inelastic standards of homogeneity incapable of accommodating a wide array of human diversity.

Disability film festivals, as gatherings that function both onscreen and off, allow for radical self-reflection. The collection of films revels in displays of difference to the point that identity-making practices are what come under scrutiny. We are not claiming that film festivals produce the change to which their individually showcased products aspire, but as programmes and meeting places, they draw up the permutations of a species (i.e. people with disabilities) into one net and lay them out for reflection on the nature of the year's 'catch'. How plentiful is the species? How successful the survival campaign? How great or insubstantial the migration? In what environments does co-habitation prove most viable? How much innovation can be detected? What corners of the species are most endangered? From where do the greatest threats derive? What is the firmest evidence for adaptation? Film festival audiences serve as amateur investigators of the exclusions that persist across cultural contexts, even as film offers the inclusive medium capable of representing unfamiliar bodies, attending festivals inaccessible to certain disabled persons and communicating across cultures.

Conclusion: Cinematic Interdependencies

Actual attendance at these film festivals is rarely the point (although they all undertake Herculean marketing struggles to get their local clientele to participate). Filmmakers, producers, actors and invested individuals populate the majority of the festival's audience and seek each others' assistance in deepening their own art, as well as in securing the birth of a next generation of disability filmmakers, commentators and participants. With this relatively specialised audience in tow, film festival conveners actively orchestrate a choir of voices regarding disability and, in doing so, expose relatively non-disseminated work projects to a wider, international, film art audience. Participants bargain and trade film works with the intentions of bringing the products of others' video labour back to their home countries for future screenings and further conversations. Disability is conceived largely as an opportunity to stage otherwise muted cultural conversations about the value of greater intimacy with human diversity.

Improvement of conditions for people with disabilities in the host country of the festival is more rare than real. In some rare cases, however, film festivals succeed in bringing about real change. Such was the case with the 2007 'Emotion Pictures!' film festival held in Athens, Greece (www.ameamedia.gr), where, following a series of protests, the local disabled student organisation, received assurances from the Minister of Cultural Affairs that a dedicated disability programming channel would be made available nation-wide. In most places annual events fizzle from lack of funding and/or political infighting before such measurable and tangible social effects can be realised.

Yet, in many ways, the results of political praxis remain beside the point. Independent disability film festivals stage their projects as a necessary coping device of subcultural resistance to national normativity. Disability film products are not David versus Goliath, but are rather more akin to David in a wrestling match to the death bereft of even a slingshot. The more modest goal of the disability film festival is to generate a discourse on film about the meaning of disability as if it were 'up for grabs'. Disability film festivals enable a critical space that opens up disability to the true multiplicity of its expression across the species. Rather than being treated as exemplifying unviable lives, disability at the disability film festival records the messy networks of human materiality as they interact with technological spaces such as human-made environments, prosthetics, media-made contexts and nature.[6] The point of gathering together so many diverse examples of human differences is the creation of a catalogue of multiplicities that threaten to fray the already decaying fabric of narrow human norms bequeathed by history.

Disability film festivals document individual space lived expansively within the limited national spaces of social mobility; disability studies scholar Celeste Langan (2001) calls the phenomenon 'mobility disability'. For instance, in the award-winning film *Body and Soul: Diane and Kathy* (Alice Elliot, U.S., 2007), one of the disabled protagonists is seriously wounded by an inattentive train conductor who drives her wheelchair into a wall while attempting to board. Ironically, the two disabled women of the film's title are on their way to protest the incarceration of fellow disabled citizens in state-funded institutions. As a result of the injury suffered, the two women find themselves spending the rest of the film immobilised within their own house and responding to the medical mismanagement of the victim's broken hip. Throughout independent disability films we witness the efforts of loose confederations of 'families' (biological or chosen) akin to the conscious interdependency of Diane and Kathy. Similarly independent disability films document the choices of disabled individuals and their advocates as they elect to untether themselves from complex medical equipment requiring their permanent isolation in hospitals and clinics, and where trained professionals suited to operate such apparatus have inflexibly congregated.

Documenting such health-based decision-making allows audiences to imagine disability unleashed from isolated corners of existence and brings about relief. Such films follow the precarious entry of people with disabilities and their advocates into the dangers of a life lived by those who insist upon an active relationship to other others; an elected habitation of those who exemplify the permutations of the species that will not be shuttered up in a laboratory akin to the specimen jars in a previous century's curiosity closet.

Works Cited

Charlton, James (2009) 'Peripheral Everywhere', unpublished paper presented at Temple University, Philadelphia, U.S., in the Geo-Politics of Disability Lecture Series, February 2009.

Edelman, Lee (2004) No Future: Queer Theory and the Death Drive. Durham: Duke University Press.

Goldschmidt, Richard (1982) The Material Basis for Evolution. New Haven: Yale University Press.

Langan, Celeste (2001) 'Mobility Disability', Public Culture, 13, 3, Fall, 459-84.

Lee, Spike and Lisa Jones (1989) Do the Right Thing. New York: Fireside.

Powers, Richard (1992) Three Farmers on Their Way to a Dance. New York: Harper Perennial.

Puar, Jasbir (2007) Terrorist Assemblages: Homonationalism in Queer Times. Durham: Duke University Press.

Singer, Peter (2007 [1974]) 'All Animals are Equal', in Hugh LaFollette (ed.) Ethics in Practice: Third Edition. Malden, MA: Blackwell, 171-80.

Notes

1   For instance, in the short *Yolk* (Stephan Lance, Australia, 2008), an adolescent girl with Down's Syndrome is forced to return a copy of *The Joy of Sex* that she has stolen from the local bookmobile after her mother discovers it hidden between her mattresses. The imperative of a 'non-reproductive' life for disabled women is crystallised in the scene of returning the forbidden knowledge to the bookmobile. Yet the daughter belies her obedience to the mother's dictates by hiding the book beneath her farmer's bib. The bell to her experience as a sexual being cannot be unrung, however, and the film leads us on to witness the overhead shot of an intellectually disabled girl's *jouissance* in the fantasy sequence that follows.

2   One further instance occurs in the short *Outcasts* (Ian Clark, UK, 2008), wherein a disabled woman joins forces with three other disabled characters to kidnap a charity-minded able-bodied entertainer, a hyper-sexualised Mick Jagger-like rock singer, dressed in a cheap sequined shirt, touring patient rooms at a hospital. Instead of acquiescing to the untenable results of consignment to an asexual future, two members of a disabled foursome abduct the singer, stow him in the trunk of their car and meet the other members of their group at a pre-arranged liminal space on the edge of some untended corn fields near a nuclear power plant. The kidnapped figure represents the equivalent of a captive audience – a debased sexualised attraction admired within the narrow aesthetic interests of a homogenising middle class pop culture. The rock singer's captive presence makes him available for active ideological and aesthetic re-programming regarding demeaning views on disability. In staging this absurd situation, the film asks audiences to contemplate a coercive seduction fantasy, briefly played out on film, wherein disabled people insist on their attractiveness and successfully argue on behalf of their own worthiness for love. The film turns the tables on the rejected body's exclusion from romantic entanglement by challenging a representative of the normative sexual culture. The dark humour of forcibly absconding with a figure of debased mainstream sexual desire provides the disabled cast with a momentary outlet for expressing their own sexual frustrations and progressivist social fantasies. In the process, their surreal scheme insists on the legitimacy of its result, if only able-bodied culture would give it a go.

3   The films discussed here were screened at Munich's The Way We Live International Short Film Festival, www.abm-medien.de.

4 The film works to foreground the fact that disability film is filtered through the point of view of able-bodied narrators; of protagonists equivalent to those whom the African-American filmmaker Spike Lee (1989) calls 'gatekeepers' in reference to white characters who draw predominantly white audiences into racial community experiences.

5 Such a project is akin to the efforts of photographer Auguste Sanders, as portrayed in Richard Powers' novel *Three Farmers on Their Way to a Dance* (1992), in his failed fin-de-siècle project to collect all physiognomic facial types of the American people.

6 Philosopher Peter Singer (2007 [1974]) insists that it is possible to make a hierarchical list of organisms that would place some animal species as more 'valuable' than some classes of people with disabilities.

Traffic Jam Revisited: Film Festivals, Activism and Human Trafficking[1]

Leshu Torchin

Since 2005, mainstream film festivals have gained momentum as sites for advancing political agendas and promoting anti-human trafficking initiatives. In 2007, for example, the Jackson Hole Film Festival (www. jacksonhole.bside.com) hosted a forum sponsored by the Humpty Dumpty Institute[2] and the United Nations Office on Drugs and Crime (UNODC) on the subject of the global crime and the role of film and media in raising awareness. The event included a screening of *Human Trafficking* (Christian Duguay, Canada/U.S., 2005) and a panel featuring representatives of the UNODC, UN Goodwill Ambassador and actress Julia Ormond, activist and former victim of trafficking Shakira Parveen, and the film's producers.

Meanwhile, specialised human rights film festivals, such as the One World Festival (Prague) (www.oneworld.cz) and the Human Rights Watch International Film Festival (HRWFF)[3] (New York and London) (www.hrw.org/iff), regularly programme films on the subject of trafficking. For the HRWFF, the goals are threefold: to provide stories that animate the testimony and evidence collected by Human Rights Watch (HRW); to build awareness of human rights as a legal and political concept and of the violations worldwide; and to promote action. To this end, they choose films that adhere to the high standards of credibility and accuracy that Human Rights Watch is known to use internally and externally, and screen them within a context that allows for emotional and intellectual responses, as well as continued engagement.

A more recent phenomenon involves dedicated anti-trafficking film festivals that highlight the issue of modern slavery whilst engaging in fundraising and community building. Often these are one-off projects sponsored by non-government organisations (NGOs), which have adopted film and celebrity to attract audiences. Frequently, they are developed though organisational partnerships and rely on shared political affinity to foster communities of concern and to develop activist publics. Whether as a single screening, a one-time event, or as an on-going festival, these programmes add value to the anti-trafficking campaign, not simply for highlighting issues of human trafficking through film, but for producing an occasion in the process.

The term 'occasion' is fruitful for its multiple evocations of ceremony, favourable opportunity and cause for action; moreover the combination of these three definitions aid in thinking about the use of film or video in an activist campaign. As mentioned in my introduction to this volume, all too often an Enlightenment-style confidence in visuality persists, encouraging belief that exposure leads to justice, or that if people know they will act accordingly (Cohen 1996; Keenan 2004). Examining the way in which a film is used in a campaign helps fill in the gaps in this seemingly seamless transition from seeing to doing, from being a member of an audience to becoming part of a witnessing public, recipients of testimony who take responsibility for what they have seen and become poised to act (McLagan 2003). In this regard, it is useful to explore the uses of film, video (and Internet) in activist campaigns by addressing the strategies of representation (such as questions of format, genre and voice), the modes of production, distribution and exhibition, and the interaction of the two aspects (texts and contexts) (e.g. Gregory 2006; Torchin 2006; Torchin 2008). Such an approach can find theoretical scaffolding in Michael Warner's view of publics as being hailed into existence by speech (2005) and Craig Calhoun's formulation of publics as contingent, fluid and clustered around issues (1992). On the one hand, there is the text that excites audiences and potentially unites them; this demands studying for the tactics it employs to achieve this response and for the way it frames and represents an issue. On the other, there is the context, which fosters this creation of a public, providing both points around which publics are clustered and the means for them to take action. The platforms and mechanisms for encouraging action can be as diverse as the types of texts deployed to hail the audience, and frequently questions of representational strategy dovetail with considerations of the selected context. However, in this chapter's brief overview of anti-trafficking campaigns in relation to the occasions for promotion and mobilisation offered by a film festival, it is the context that receives the bulk of attention.

Screen Media and the Anti-Trafficking Campaign

Films and other screen media are widely used by governmental and non-governmental organisations to promote awareness of human trafficking, as well as to publicise and implement a range of initiatives. These uses are far ranging. Public Service Announcements (PSAs) have been used as a deterrent, as in the case of the short spot *Witness* (Germany, 2006) produced by Terre des Hommes Germany (www.tdh. de), which was screened as in-flight viewing on planes en route to sex tourism destinations. The documentary B*ought & Sold* (Gillian Caldwell, U.S., 1999), produced by U.S.-based organisations WITNESS and Global Survival Network, was not only featured on many national news broadcasts, including BBC, CNN and ABC, but was also distributed, with an accompanying manual, to over 2,000 organisations, and is used as a training tool by the U.S. Department of State, Department of Justice and American Embassy and Consular officials worldwide. MiraMed, an anti-trafficking coalition based in Russia, has been showing the film to multiple audiences, including young women at risk to trafficking, NGOs, educators and parents.

The use of the feature film *Holly* (Guy Moshe, U.S./France/Israel/ Cambodia, 2006) is representative of the strategic benefits of media in an anti-trafficking campaign. Produced by Guy Jacobson, founder of the Redlight Children Campaign (RCC) (redlightchildren.org) which seeks to rescue children from exploitation and lessen occurrences of underage prostitution, the film was a centrepiece in a wider media campaign.[4] With an internationally recognised cast that included Udo Kier, Virginie Ledoyen and Ron Livingston, *Holly* was more readily distributed and publicised than the documentaries that RCC had produced. Although *Holly's* commercial release was relatively limited, the film enjoyed substantial media attention, with interviews and short pieces running on radio and television in the U.S. (CNN and ABC-TV news) and in print (Glamour, The New York Times and the LA Times). Such coverage served to promote not only the film, but also the campaign's cause and additional programmes, building the outreach potential in advance of screenings. Meanwhile, partnerships with NGOs and corporations further enhanced capacity building. Joint programmes yielded film screenings accompanied by talks and panels with experts on trafficking, filmmakers, government officials and activists. The public debates offered opportunities to promote the organisations and engage the audiences in specific action plans. The RCC website helps in direction. In the section marked 'Take Action', a visitor can sign up for more information and volunteer opportunities, submit a donation, contact a state representative, or even learn how to organise a public screening (the RCC supplies a complete guide from procuring the DVD to leading an effective discussion and hosting a reception for guests). The RCC is clear on the value of a *screening* (not just a film) as 'a platform for publicity and media for your organisation and as an opportunity to bring in new members or keep in touch with existing ones'.[5]

HRWFF and *The Price of Sex*
(hrw.org/en/iff and thepriceofsex.org)

The film festival can provide an equally productive platform for promotion, outreach and support of a campaign. In 2011, the New York City edition of HRWFF screened *The Price of Sex* (Mimi Chakarova, U.S./United Arab Emirates/Bulgaria/Moldova/Greece/Turkey, 2011), a beautifully shot feature-length documentary that investigates the world of sex-trafficking from Eastern Europe to the Middle East and Western Europe through in-depth interviews with survivors and hidden camera footage, a testament to the unprecedented level of access Chakarova was able to attain. The filmmaker received the Nestor Almendros Award for courage in filmmaking, which confers prestige and a prize of U.S.$5,000 – valuable support for any documentary filmmaker.

While the film left the audience deeply moved, the Q&As that followed each screening helped spectators intellectualise their emotions and contributed to the formation of an improvised, temporary public sphere. Chakarova told stories of the participants and the process. Expert panellists, such as Human Rights Watch representative and Senior Legal Advisor Aisling Reidy and local activist Danielle Malangone of the Midtown Community Court New York, provided greater insight into the phenomenon. These presentations alerted the audience to root causes (such as the dire poverty that inspires migration and the impediments to justice, such as state corruption and the criminalisation of the victims) and to the action people were taking. Discussions enhanced the process. After one screening, a man inquired into the possibility of boycott, a question that led to an exchange regarding the global nature of human trafficking and sex slavery. But why not begin here and now? Another audience member asked, in the same vein, how he might recognise trafficking locally and what could he do if he stumbled across a situation of forced victimisation.

Opportunities for engagement extended beyond the walls of the auditorium. A reception enabled continued discussion among participants and audience members, and for the activists in the crowd, cards were exchanged and contacts forged. Tables staffed by volunteers offered more ways to be in contact with HRW or partner organisations. Press in attendance, lured by the presence of the filmmaker, prepared items for publication. Even further, the film's website offered (as it still does) the opportunity for extended storytelling, with a multi-media series and additional interviews, as well as resources for taking action. According to director Chakarova, in one case viewers of the film were so upset by the story of a woman disabled in her attempt to escape her captors that they collected money to help her pay for surgery – and they used the website as point of contact.

In this regard, the activism of a festival is not located in its ability to immediately bring an end to trafficking through the screenings, but to produce sites for discussion, exchange, networking, name capture and promotion of the work being done.

The rest of this essay offers brief glimpses of anti-trafficking film festivals around the world, addressing their contributions to the cause.

Unchosen: Bristol Film Festival against Human Trafficking (UK)
(unchosen.org.uk)

Unchosen is a Bristol-based UK festival launched in 2008 with the aim of raising awareness and funds. The festival took place over the course of a week, with screenings accompanied by speakers, performances and the distribution of literature. Each night featured a single film and guest. The line-up included features, such as *Ghosts* (Nick Broomfield, UK, 2006), *Sex Traffic* (David Yates, UK/Canada, 2004), *It's a Free World...* (Ken Loach, UK/Italy/Germany/Spain/Poland, 2007), *Amazing Grace* (Michael Apted, UK/U.S., 2006), a recounting of the eighteenth century campaign against the slave trade, and the aforementioned *Holly*. There were also documentaries, such as *Our Big Fair Trade Adventure* (Richard Pollack, UK, 2008), which follows three British school children to India as they visit garment factories and cotton fields in search of an ethically-produced school-uniform. Covering a diversity of subjects related to trafficking – from the historical slave trade to sexual slavery to the place of trafficked people in the economy – the programme lends itself to educational purposes. While *Ghosts* and *It's a Free World* illustrate the shady benefits of exploitation, *Our Big Fair Trade Adventure* reveals the abuses implicit in free trade policy. Thanks to the sponsors (which included Pathé International, Christian Aid, Century Films, Lafayette Films, Priority Films, Momentum Pictures, Hot:Haus, Hope and Bible Society), the entire proceeds from ticket sales could go directly to nominated charities, such as Daughters Day Centre (Phnom Penh, Cambodia), Morecambe Bay Victims Fund (UK) and Stop the Traffik, a global coalition of anti-trafficking organisations (www.stopthetraffik.org).

In subsequent years, the festival developed more sidebars, as well as specialised screenings in schools with Q&A sessions aimed at 9 to 13-year-olds and topical awareness evenings. During the 2009 edition, partner organisations, supported by 100 volunteers, organised topical exhibitions. In 2010, Unchosen developed a 'How to Respond Pack', a toolkit for activists that assembled information from multiple sources with the intent of assisting new campaigners. The programme contained information about the films and a checklist to identify signs of trafficking.

Anti-Human Trafficking Film Festival (Taiwan)
(No official website)

Organised by the Garden of Hope Foundation (www.goh.org.tw) and receiving sponsorship from MTV-EXIT, this film festival ran for two years (2007 and 2008) with the goal of raising 'social awareness of the worsening problem of human trafficking'.[6] Support also came from the American Institute in Taiwan, the Taiwan Foundation for Democracy and the Human Rights Research Centre at the College of Law, National Taiwan University. The screenings were free and frequently accompanied by 'expert discussions' where audiences could learn more about the problem and about the action others are taking. In 2007, the line-up included five films made by both professionals and amateurs and that focused on women and children and the ways in which developments in global transportation aided the practices of trafficking. The following year, the agenda was broadened to include films featuring the abuse of undocumented migrants in labour sectors spanning beyond sex work.

Of Inhuman Bondage (Kolkata/Calcutta, India)
(No official website) [7]

Taking place in 2009 at the Indian Council of Cultural Relations, Of Inhuman Bondage was a two-day film festival organised around Women's Day through a partnership between NGOs Apne Aap Women Worldwide and the American Center. The event was part of a larger general education programme of workshops, films and discussion panels held by the consulate in Calcutta and throughout the northeast regions. Celebrities such as dancer Gita Chandran and actor Jaya Seal Ghosh were in attendance. The programme line-up boasted a series of films focused on prostitution and trafficking, such as *Kaal* by Bengal director Bappaditya Banerjee (India, 2007), which looks at women tempted by the money and allure of working abroad and *Mondo Meyer Upakhan* (*A Tale of a Naughty Girl*, Buddhadev Dasgupta, India, 2002), which contrasts the story of a Lati girl whose mother is a prostitute in rural India with the stories of three prostitutes in Calcutta. The festival also featured *Chameli* (Sudhir Mishra, India, 2003), a Bollywood production about a chance encounter between a widowed banker and a prostitute named Chameli in Bombay's red light district. Alongside the programme of educational events and screenings, the festival aimed to trigger action by collecting signatures under petitions asking for trafficking legislation.

Na Wa Film Festival (Nigeria)
(www.nawafestival.org)

The Na Wa Film Festival took place over 10 days in June 2011 as a multi-sited event organised by EXIT, a Vienna-based NGO founded by Nigerian author and activist Joana Adesuwa Reiterer. The festival was supported by the United Nations Office on Drugs and Crime (UNODC) and the International Organization for Migration (IOM) in the framework of the United Nations Global Initiative to Fight Human Trafficking (UN. GIFT). Travelling through three Nigerian states – Abuja (13-14 June), Edo (15-17 June) and Lagos (18-21 June) – the festival aimed to build awareness of human trafficking among at-risk communities. In particular, EXIT sought to use Na Wa as a platform to facilitate discussion and inform audiences about the threats of trafficking in the channels of irregular migration. The press release invited an audience to the screenings, 'so that you can help yourself to never be a victim or help somebody else by telling them the truth about the criminals who so frequently deceive them'. The majority of the programmed films were documentary shorts that communicated this truth through the testimony of former victims, including *Better Life* (Joana Adesuwa Reiterer, Austria, 2011) and *Sisters of No Mercy* (Lukas Roegler, Germany/Nigeria, 2007); other films, such as *Is Europe an Option?* (Johanna Tschatscher, Austria, 2009), featured stories of young men exploited while attempting to migrate to Europe. An entry notable for its clearly different intended audience is *Affected for Life* (UNODC, 2009), described in the programme as a training film 'designed to assist prosecutors, judges, law enforcement officers and other specialized anti-trafficking officials working to prevent and combat human trafficking'.

Although the institutional support of the festival suggests strong involvement of activists from outside the global South (and may even be seen as a covert effort in European border maintenance against Nigerian immigrants), the support was also found at the ground level in the Nigerian-based National Agency for Prohibition of Traffic in Persons and Other Related Matters (NAPTIP) and Girls Power Initiative Nigeria (GPI), selected because of their expertise in tackling human trafficking in Nigeria. These stakeholders helped to coordinate activities ranging from book readings, panel discussions and strategic receptions with government agencies, NGOs and Nollywood figures, including Uche Jumbo and Segun Arinze (the President of the Actors' Guild of Nigeria).

Human Rights and Sex Trafficking: A Film Forum (U.S.)
(www.bitahrfilmforum.org)

This event took place at the Brattle Theatre in Cambridge, Massachusetts, in December 2010. Organised by Alicia Foley Winn, the Executive Director of The Boston Initiative to Advance Human Rights (BITAHR) (www.bitahr.org), who spoke of film as the driving force behind her decision to pursue human rights-oriented work, and by Kate Nace Day, a law professor at Suffolk University, the event was alternately described as a forum and a festival. It took on a reflexive dimension, combining film screenings and panel discussions in order to 'investigate the power of film in effectuating a movement to combat commercial sexual exploitation and modern-day slavery'. [8] Twelve films were programmed, including *Anonymously Yours* (Gayle Ferraro, U.S., 2002), *Fatal Promises* (Katharina Rohrer, U.S./Austria, 2009), *The Day My God Died* (Andrew Levine, U.S., 2003) and *The Selling of Innocents* (Ruchira Gupta, Canada, 1997). The line-up offered perspectives both from survivors of trafficking and from NGO workers. The animated film *Red Leaves Falling* (Monica D. Ray, Philippines/Denmark 2009), part of a project of animated films directed towards at-risk children, was also screened for the benefit of campaigners.[9]

The invited panellists included people who had grown to prominence in the anti-trafficking movement, whether as survivors, organiser-activists, researchers, filmmakers or journalists. Guy Jacobson of Red Light Children was in attendance, as was Ruchira Gupta, a journalist, filmmaker and former Director of the UNIFEM's (United Nations Development Fund for Women) Media Unit who founded and now directs the aforementioned NGO, Aapne Aap. Others in attendance were Joshua Rubenstein of Amnesty International, survivor and activist Maria Suarez, as well as Audrey Porter of the My Life My Choice Project (www.jri.org/mylife), which is dedicated to mentoring survivors and changing legislation (Yerman 2010). The festival functioned as a consortium, offering up a mixture of information, social networking and inspiration.

Conclusion

This is only a most cursory look at a proliferating field. Campaigns repeatedly rely on film and video to attract attention, as well as to educate and excite publics to action. This is not a matter for easy celebration, as some of my earlier examples may have intimated. If anything, this is an invitation to a more sustained analysis of each case and its many facets. It is important to consider matters of representation and production, while looking into questions related to context and reception, such as:

- **Exhibition and Distribution**: The ways a film can be used are many and varied. There are fundraisers. There are screenings with panel discussions and Q&A sessions. There are in-flight PSAs and even websites that provide short films and spots. Who is using these films? Where and under what circumstances are these films screened? In what ways do the strategies around exhibition make the films effective in the fight against trafficking? Do they attract volunteers and sponsors? Do they serve to warn potential victims? How are these to be crafted according to the parameters of the platform and their intended function?

- **Audiences**: As indicated above, this is a key question. For whom are the films made and directed? Potential victims? Bystanders hailed as activists? Policy makers? Or even perpetrators (warned or shamed)? The answer to these questions determines representational and exhibition strategies. How is the message and desired effect best directed to audiences on the verge of becoming publics?

These constitute only a few of the considerations involved in determining the best use of film in an activist campaign and the function of a film festival therein.

While excellent and important work examines the phenomenon of human trafficking through legal, political and activist lenses (Bales 2004; Kara 2009; Kempadoo et al 2005; Kyle and Koslowski 2001; Lee 2007), there is a dearth of discussion on films and screen media within the context of this analysis, and little or no political reform. The role of film and other screen media in anti-trafficking campaigns has been examined only rarely.[10] The scholarship on trafficking sometimes points to the role of media in promoting awareness, where giving heightened visibility to a hidden crime like trafficking could effectively prevent it, but critical consideration of the media's work needs to go beyond the simplistic formulation that if people see something, they will do something. This is a shortcoming that can be addressed, to some extent, through the study of festivals.

Works Cited

Andrijasevic, Rutvica (2007) 'Beautiful Dead Bodies: Gender, Migration, and Representation in Anti-Trafficking Campaigns', *Feminist Review*, 86, 24-44.

Bales, Kevin (2004) *Disposable People: New Slavery in the Global Economy*. Berkeley: University of California Press.

Brown, William, Dina Iordanova and Leshu Torchin (2010) *Moving People, Moving Images: Cinema and Trafficking in the New Europe*. St Andrews: St Andrews Film Studies.

Calhoun, Craig (1992) 'Introduction', in Craig Calhoun (ed.) *Habermas and the Public Sphere*. Cambridge, MA and London: The MIT Press.

Cohen, Stanley (1996) 'Government Responses to Human Rights Reports: Claims, Denials, and Counterclaims', *Human Rights Quarterly* 18, 517-43.

Gregory, Sam (2006) 'Transnational Storytelling: Human Rights, WITNESS, and Video Advocacy' *American Anthropologist*, 108, March, 195-204.

Kara, Siddharth (2009) *Sex Trafficking: Inside the Business of Modern Slavery*. New York: Columbia University Press.

Keenan, Thomas (2004) 'Mobilizing Shame', *The South Atlantic Quarterly* 103, 435-49.

Kempadoo, Kemala (ed.) (2005) *Sex Trafficking and Prostitution Reconsidered: New Perspectives on Migration, Sex Work, and Human Rights*. London and Boulder: Paradigm Publishers.

Kyle, David and Rey Koslowski (eds) (2001) *Global Human Smuggling: Comparative Perspectives*. Baltimore and London: Johns Hopkins University Press.

Lee, Maggy (ed.) (2007) *Human Trafficking*. Portland: Willan Publishing.

McLagan, Meg (2003) 'Principles, Publicity, and Politics: Notes on Human Rights Media', *American Anthropologist*, 105, 605-12.

'"Na Wa" Festival Coming to Nigeria in a City near You!', Na Wa Festival Press Release (4 June 2011). On-line. Available HTTP: http://en.adesuwa.org/uploads/6/4/1/6/6416995/joint_press_release_na_wa_festival_final.pdf (2 August 2011).

Torchin, Leshu (2006) '*Ravished Armenia:* Visual Media, Humanitarian Advocacy, and the Formation of Witnessing Publics', *American Anthropologist*, 108, March, 214-20.

_____ (2008) 'Influencing Representation: Equal Access and Roma Social Inclusion', *Third Text*, 22, 387-96.

_____ (2010) 'Traffic Jam: Film, Activism and Human Trafficking', in William Brown, Dina Iordanova and Leshu Torchin, *Moving People, Moving Images: Cinema and Trafficking in the New Europe*. St Andrews: St Andrews Film Studies, 218-36.

Warner, Michael (2005) *Publics and Counterpublics*. New York: Zone Books.

Yerman, Marcia G. (2010) 'Human Rights and Sex Trafficking: A Film Forum', *Huffington Post,* 4 December. On-line. Available HTTP: http://www.huffingtonpost.com/marcia-g-yerman/human-rights-and-sex-traf_b_792094.html (11 October 2011).

Notes

[1] This essay is an updated version of the chapter 'Traffic Jam: Film, Activism, and Human Trafficking' that I contributed to *Moving People, Moving Images: Cinema and Trafficking in the New Europe* (2010).

2   According to their mission statement, The Humpty Dumpty Institute (established in 1998) 'forges innovative public partnerships to find creative solutions to difficult humanitarian projects' (www.thehdi.org). One of their present projects is to foster U.S.-UN dialogue.

3   Although HRW describes these film festivals as 'International', the division is referred to as Human Rights Watch Film Festival, hence the acronym HRWFF.

4   The RCC has launched the K-11 project to lead the awareness campaign. In addition to the feature-length narrative *Holly*, the project comprises two documentaries, *The Virgin Harvest* and *The K-11 Journey*.

5   See redlightchildren.org/take-action (accessed 11 October 2011).

6   'Anti-Human Trafficking Film Festival,' Taiwan Culture Portal, culture.tw/index.php?option=com_events&task=view_detail&agid=225&catids=13&Itemid=176 (accessed 11 October 2011).

7   No set website exists for this festival and press releases are no longer available on-line. However, for more information, please see 'Consul General Beth A. Payne's Remarks at ICCR on the Inauguration of a Film Festival, "Of Inhuman Bondage"', kolkata.usconsulate.gov/030509cg. html (5 March, 2009) (accessed 11 Ocotber 2011); 'Kolkata intellectuals pledge to combat sex-trafficking at end of anti-trafficking film festival on International Women's Day organized by Apne Aap' apneaap.org/news/media/pressreleases/oldpressreleases/kolkata-intellectuals-pledge-combat-sex-trafficking-end-an (7 March 2009) (accessed 11 October 2011); Anon, 'Film fest on human trafficking kicks off in city' www.expressindia.com/latest-news/Film-fest-on-human-trafficking-kicks-off-in-city/431592/(6 March 2009) (accessed 11 October 2011).

8   B.I.T.A.H.R., 'First Annual Human Trafficking Film Festival and Academic Conference', www.bitahr.org/programs/film.html (accessed 11 October 2011)

9   For more information about this film, visit www.stairwayfoundation.org/stairway/resources/animation-film-toolkits/red-leaves-falling-a-story-of-child-sex-trafficking# (accessed 11 October 2011).

10   To be fair, some work has taken critical approaches to media campaigns, such as Rutvica Andrijasevic's insightful analysis of anti-trafficking posters and the ways in which these constructed highly gendered notions of European citizenship (Andrijasevic 2007).

PART 2

CASE STUDIES

Film Festivals as a Human Rights Awareness Building Tool: Experiences of the Prague One World Festival

Igor Blažević

The One World Human Rights Film Festival (One World) (www.oneworld. cz) started in Prague in 1999, looking much smaller than it does today. Organised by People in Need, a Czech relief organisation dedicated to human rights advocacy,[1] the festival screened 36 films in three venues over a period of five days. The event was predominantly local, attracting an audience of approximately 3,000 and modest media coverage. Also modest was the condition of its production: the budget was small as was the team. Two full-time employees on a part-time salary prepared the festival in less than six months, aided in the last few weeks by a handful of volunteers. Today, 12 years later, One World is the largest European human rights film festival. It runs over 10 days in May, screens 120 films selected from 1,600 entries, invites 100 guests and attracts an audience of more than 100,000. The festival is widely advertised and receives significant media coverage. The social events are many. Czech policy-makers, academics, journalists and civil society activists participate in more than 160 debates staged after the film screenings. Teachers from a third of Prague's primary and secondary schools come with their pupils and students to attend specially organised morning screenings and debates. And the opening ceremony is gala status, with former Czech President and One World patron Vaclav Havel bestowing the Homo Homini human rights award for extraordinary personal courage in defending freedom, rights and justice.[2]

After the main event in Prague, a selection of One World films tours through 33 cities in the Czech Republic. Touring brings more viewers, nation-wide school participation, coverage in local media, local debates and a significant participation by local organisations and youth groups. One World Prague assisted in launching and developing sister festivals in 10 countries in Central, Southeast and East Europe, and three years ago started staging One World in Brussels, which targets an audience from the European institutions. Like many other festivals today, One World is also actively building its presence on the Internet and social networking sites and now streams some films on-line.

With this growth comes impact. The Czech Republic has a reputation in Europe as a nation active on the international stage in promoting human rights and democracy worldwide. One World's prominence, both as event and as topic for reportage, contributes to the shaping of public opinion within the Czech Republic and to its foreign policy. Meanwhile, the invitation of policy makers allows the festival, through screenings and panel discussions, to play a role in appealing to decision makers and setting agendas for legislative discussion. Moreover, the outreach extends well beyond the parameters of the festival event, with the One World for School programme, a year-round partnership aimed at transforming younger generations into engaged and socially committed citizenry.

I am not naïve. The fact that a group of young and educated people in a relatively affluent and free society sits to watch some films in a comfortable cinema does not make the protection of human rights a reality, nor does attending a screening inevitably lead to legislation. The One World festival, however, functions as a form of annual ritual, a public celebration of certain values that fosters a community of 'believers'. Above all, the festival values basic freedoms and respect for universal human rights, but also believes in the importance of a tolerant, inclusive, liberal society which addresses the dark sides of its past through truth, justice and reconciliation, and encourages active citizenship and solidarity with those in need. The festival also advocates for the Czech state to play an active role, through its foreign policy, on behalf of the protection and promotion of the universal human rights. The event acts as a tonic, renewing social commitment among the previously activist and exciting others into the possibilities of political engagement.

The experience counteracts the political and social cynicism that can set in. It inspires people to want to do something. It encourages people, whether youth, educators, journalists, civil servants or politicians to seek to make change. And active and inspired people can make a difference.

The remainder of this chapter explores what One World does to make this happen.

What Makes One World Festival Different from All the Other (Documentary) Festivals?

What distinguishes One World or other human rights film festivals from the more 'traditional' documentary film festival? Not the film programme. In fact, there is typically a great deal of overlap between the One World programme and that of such documentary festivals as IDFA (www.idfa.nl), CPH-DOX (www.cphdox.dk) or the Leipzig Film Festival (www.dok-leipzig.de). This should not come as a surprise, as engaged social and political filmmaking has been the domain of documentary since the time of Joris Ivens and Luis Buñuel, at least. I do not think that there is some specific category or sub-genre of 'human rights' films which human rights film festivals screen (or screen in greater numbers) and which more classical film festivals do not screen (or screen in fewer numbers). The difference lies not in the films they screen, but rather in how the festivals understand their core mission, the motivation behind their screenings and what they want to achieve.

Broadly speaking (and please forgive this coarse, yet functional overview), some festivals function as a marketplace for distribution, even when that is not their principal or publicly-declared mission. For example, while the IDFA hosts a great variety of celebrations of documentaries and documentarians, it is also host to Docs for Sale, a marketplace for documentaries visited by television exhibitors, festival programmers and distributors. Even when not explicitly commissioning agents, festivals can act as sites for networking, as places for securing financial and professional access. In addition, festivals provide the exhibition platform needed for works originating from within smaller nations, or those made within minority language communities, whose films rarely find theatrical or television release.

The categorisation that follows is deliberately simplified. Things are much more complex, of course, yet this simplification is meant to help explain the fundamental difference between human rights and other film festivals. A number of festivals regard films primarily as goods to be put through the channels of television and cinema distribution. Even where selling films is not their main activity or mission, film distribution and film commissioning remain important pillars in the way these festivals approach things and judge their own successes. Such festivals are extremely important because they help filmmakers and producers become financially self-sustainable and to establish and build professional contacts. Festivals that lack the market and commissioning dimension have no value to filmmakers as they do not help them generate returns and, respectively, do not help them pull off new projects that they may be planning to work on. (You only need to speak occasionally to filmmakers to discover the hardship involved in making documentaries and earning a living from such films, and to gain respect for documentary film festivals that also run successful film markets.)

Then there are festivals that treat films primarily as a form of art and as the artistic, intellectual and spiritual expression of its makers. Such festivals are not less important, because they help foster our common cultural identity. Some other film festivals are primarily for entertainment. There are also a lot of film festivals, particularly in smaller countries (and in small provincial cites) with insignificant market potential; they are meant to service an audience that for the most part does not speak one of the major international languages, or that has no regular access to diverse film programming beyond multiplex offerings. The main purpose of such festivals is to enable local audiences to see films that are not likely to find their way to network TV channels or to the cinemas.

The core mission of One World and other human rights festivals is to raise public awareness and to advocate for change. The main difference here is not the films we screen, but what we 'do' with the films and the interpretive contexts we build for their screenings. Of course, it is too simplistic to expect that a single screening of one film at one cinema or one festival is able to guarantee concrete change. Things do not work that way. And when we (or Amnesty International, or Human Rights Watch) organise a film festival, we do not expect it to bring about immediate change to a particular policy or lead to an instantaneous end of the rights violation in question. Staging a film festival and working with the films is part of the on-going, year-round systematic advocacy work of these organisations. And these organisations, through their work, have positive impact on policy, legislation and on the broader cultural climate of human rights. Films are but one of the advocacy tools we deploy to make our work and aims known to a larger audience and more attractive to the press to cover.

Over the years since I first organised a human rights film festival (in 1999), I have been regularly asked whether I think that films have the power to motivate people to take action outside of the cinema. My experience and response is, yes, I do. Film can be quite an efficient tool in advocating for political or social change and can motivate people to take action, but a handful of screenings in the context of a film festival is simply not enough. One needs a campaign strategy, structural support and a committed group of people who use film, other audio-visual media and social networking, together with more traditional tactics of advocacy. Film is just an element in all this, a functional tool. The campaign strategy relies on defining the issues and identifying an acceptable and feasible solution – what is the problem and what action should be taken? This includes identifying the key decision-makers and then finding pressure points through which to mobilise them. One can then either approach them directly, for example, by screening films to parliamentarians or to people who are influential allies in intergovernmental bodies; or one can try to influence decision makers by drawing the media's attention to the problem, or by showing people how they can exert influence as voters or consumers. Successful campaigns work simultaneously on all these levels, targeting directly policy makers while rallying civic activism and the media.

What Are the Benefits of a Human Rights Film Festival?

Other film festivals are organised by film-lovers and people who are in one way or another connected with the film profession. Human rights film festivals are usually organised by film-lovers as well, but also by those who come from non-governmental organisations, civil society or progressive universities. Film screenings and film festivals have come to be seen as vital to attracting the interest of a wider audience. An increasing number of organisations have begun to integrate film screenings in their outreach and communication strategies. The reasons for the appeal are numerous and growing:

BETTER THAN USUAL COMMUNICATION: Film festivals are better equipped than the usual civil society organisations (whose communication tools include websites, newsletters, leaflets, reports, photo exhibitions, happenings and the like) to go beyond the core group of supporters and engaged, concerned citizens and reach out to 'new', broader audiences. Festivals are particularly good at attracting the attention of young people. The reasons for this are simple: film belongs to popular culture and contains elements of entertainment. Film belongs to the dominant mode of audio-visual communication (a picture is worth a thousand words). Film is an effective tool of communication because it engages the emotions as well as the intellect. Film is persuasive. 'Seeing is believing.'

DE-IDEOLOGISATION OF THE HUMAN RIGHTS DISCOURSE: Films are quite useful and effective in taking human rights topics into concrete human, social and political situations and away from the unfruitful, dogmatic, ideological debate about human rights being an imported concept of the West that is subversively used against the rest. Films add flavour and colour to the rather abstract, dry and somewhat didactic concept of human rights with its fondness of charts, covenants and treaties. Films turn the universal ideas of human rights into concrete experiences. Once faced with the stories of actual individuals or groups suffering from or struggling against repression, tyranny, injustice and exploitation, few can continue to argue that people from different cultures are not the same and that all are not entitled to enjoy basic freedoms and rights.

FILMS GIVE MEANING TO WORDS: Films are very good at assigning meaning to words that might otherwise be quite abstract. They can help, particularly in the case of young people, to relate abstract notions to concrete experiences and concrete human stories. For example, what meanings do 'war crime', 'torture' or 'freedom of assembly and speech' have for someone who has never experienced war or conflict? Or who has grown up in an affluent, free and democratic society? When she or he sees films about the real lives of people who are trapped in poverty or war, or who live under repressive and abusive governments, they learn to understand the meaning of the words they read and hear in media news coverage, or in their history books.

GIVING VOICE TO THE VOICELESS; CHALLENGING PREJUDICES AND STEREOTYPES: Marginalised, suppressed social groups are often dehumanised and made invisible and voiceless through social exclusion, stigma and repression. This renders them even more vulnerable and makes prejudices and stereotypes even more entrenched. Films play a mediating role: it is more likely that majority groups will make a reluctant first step over the bridge of understanding if they see a well-made film about a marginalised group than if they are directly confronted by representatives of that minority. Films and human rights festivals cannot eliminate all prejudices and stereotypes – there are no shortcuts – but they can challenge them, and that is already a good first step.

FILM AS THERAPEUTIC TOOL: Films can be used highly effectively in the closed circle of self-help groups and other forms of group therapy.

For example, *My Left Breast* (Gerry Rogers, Canada, 2002) has been successfully distributed in the Czech Republic among self-help groups of women recovering after breast cancer treatment. According to the feedback, the film helped many women deal with the trauma. In a similar way, One World has helped a number of women's groups in the former Yugoslavia obtain films about victims of rape overcoming their trauma; such films have been used in group therapy in post-war Kosovo. There are so many extraordinary films about overcoming the trauma of torture and war, and about survivors of genocide and war crimes, about former political prisoners, war veterans, or about the relatives of people who have 'disappeared'. And about those searching for truth and justice. Many of these films do not just tell stories of cruelty and suffering. They show people who have gone through such painful experiences and who have managed to turn their pain and trauma into action. These are powerful, inspiring, positive stories of people and can – if used properly – help new victims process their pain and begin to heal.

Being myself a migrant out of Bosnia-Herzegovina, and having observed how things develop in many other places – across post-communist Central and East Europe, in Kosovo, Cambodia, East Timor and a few other places – I have learned that dealing with historic collective and individual trauma is usually politically opposed or supressed, socially and culturally burdened (if not fully taboo), and, individually, psychologically extremely difficult. Films that tell stories from other parts of the world have the advantage of obliquely inciting self-reflection and lead to closures which otherwise might be impossible. Facing the stories and (positive) examples of others can break the 'trauma autism' and help overcome stigma and bring about catharsis.

What We Screen: Selection Criteria

A good chunk of One World's programme relies on what I would call 'hard-core' human rights films, by which I mean films that raise awareness about cases or patterns of human rights violations. These films feature stories of civic activism and of people struggling for their rights and freedoms, for justice and for a life lived with dignity. While the first group typically portrays people as victims of some misdeed or abuse of power, the second recounts inspiring stories about people overcoming obstacles to achieve beneficial change. We aim to reach a balance between the two groups, by trying to include more films from the second category, which is the more inspirational. A programme of unrelenting misery, from harsh testimonies to a portrait of seemingly chronic and unstoppable victimisation, will depress and exhaust rather than motivate and inspire the audience. Such programmes risk revelling in trauma. Meanwhile, films about courageous and committed people, who work to unite communities against injustice, have the effect of exciting and of offering role models along with hope. It is worthwhile, therefore, for the programmer to seek an impact on the audience by matching films that expose abuses with films that show the power of the powerless to achieve victories, no matter how small.

One World, however, regularly programmes beyond this 'hard core' category. We aim to include films that transcend the human rights agenda and address major challenges of our times, such as social and cultural diversity and tolerance, climate change, globalisation, Neoliberalism and resources (such as energy and food). We also aim to highlight the ways in which different societies and cultures deal with the legacy of the past in terms of historical crimes and traumas. This is of particular interest for our local audience given the Czech Republic's own skeletons in the proverbial historical cupboard, whether they be the Holocaust, the expulsion of the German minority from the Sudeten areas of Czechoslovakia after the Second World War, or the crimes of the communist era.

We also feature a good number of programmes focusing on the acceptance of otherness and promoting the values of an inclusive, open and tolerant society. Again, this is important because our own society is, in many different ways, not sufficiently open and tolerant.

The selection criteria include more than subject matter; the artistic value of a film is particularly important. The quality of the film has always been as important a selection criterion as the content. It was often the case that we were unable to cover a topic that we would have liked to because at the time we were unable to find films that met our cinematic standards. In addition to artistry, we seek to programme films from all over the world rather than rely on the output from nations with relatively robust documentary industries, good funding opportunities and elaborate distribution and international promotion support systems, such as the U.S., Canada, France, the UK, Israel and the Nordic countries. We want to include films from countries where filmmakers have far less financial and other opportunities and in which distribution and support mechanisms are virtually non-existent.

Sometimes we include a category of film I call 'activist', but we are quite careful and restrictive about doing so, and whenever we do, I feel slightly uneasy. This refers to a film whose background betrays a certain ideology and certain values and which explicitly promotes and propagates certain solutions and approaches. Such works cloud the plurality of testimonies and advocate a singular interpretation and line of action. Effectively, they are telling the audience what it should think. Sometimes, what makes certain films manipulative is not what the filmmakers have included, but what they have left out. Often we choose not to feature a particular film in the programme, even if it covers a relevant topic, because we think that the film is 'too activist', too intrusive, too didactic, too aggressive and too manipulative in promoting its views.

Film as an Educational Tool

For market-based festivals, distribution in the commercial sector is a typical goal. For years, I have been maintaining that filmmakers and producers are, for a variety of reasons, focused on TV broadcasters, TV commissioners and cinema distribution. More recently the Internet and the possibility of streaming film on-line have gained a lot of attention. And while such distribution is not to be discounted, we are interested in the still relatively untapped opportunities for the exhibition of films in the educational system. To address this, we launched an educational project, which resulted in every second Czech primary and secondary school – more than 2,600 in total – using films from the One World festival in their curricula. Thus, I believe, we have managed to do what we have been preaching all along.

Crucial to the success of this is the systematic, patient, dedicated year-round work, much of it carried out by committed volunteers, including teachers, who put in a great amount of (unpaid) effort to implement new didactic methods into school curricula. Funding comes, as with many other civil society projects, from many different sources and from constant, on-going fundraising. The project has been funded by private foundations, EU grants, various ministries and even by private donations from project supporters.

When it comes to media campaigns and film festivals, sending out a single film on DVD is not enough. Schools usually have too many offers, too little time, an overburdened curriculum and underpaid teachers. The problem goes beyond an overburdened infrastructure;

training and resources are essential. Even the best-intentioned teachers can fail if they do not have proper training on how to moderate a debate after a film screening and how to assist their students' understanding of the political and social topics. For example, in the Czech Republic latent racist attitudes against the Roma minority are still quite widespread. In the early stages of our cooperation with schools we offered them films about the Roma minority, but when teachers screened films in their classrooms, they suddenly discovered young neo-Nazis among their students. These young, right-wing activists were better equipped, because of their involvement in their movement, for the debates following the film than were the teachers. They knew how to use simple arguments that were manipulative but effective. The teachers, on the other hand, did not know how to respond to the challenge and, as a result, more students in the class ended up by thinking that the 'Gypsies' were the problem, rather than racism and social exclusion. We learned that in addition to films, we also needed to provide teachers with pedagogic tools and proper training.

Now, during the festival selection process, we identify appropriate films for the One World in Schools program. Films are chosen according to topic, teachable moments, length, quality and their appeal to young people. Then, during the festival, and riding on the wave of media coverage and an advertising campaign, we attract the interest of schools. Trained volunteers approach individual teachers and school management six weeks before the festival and offer a choice of several films to which they can bring their classes. Similarly, when the festival subsequently tours 33 other cities, local volunteer organisers mobilise schools in their areas. All school screenings have follow-up debates. Because they are usually impressed by the impact the films and discussions have had on their students, teachers are ready to sign up for the One World in School training. In this case, the screening generates not only knowledge about an issue, but also volunteers for the future.

After the festival, we determine which films worked well with the young audiences and clear the screening rights for educational purposes. We then prepare pedagogic materials consisting of a synopsis, photographs, teaching guide and background information on the films in a Q&A format. To help in engaging the students, we also include interactive projects (role-playing games, quizzes) and sample worksheets. Teachers who want to obtain DVDs and toolkits are invited to attend two days of training during which they participate in model screenings and debates with experts, learn about modern interactive methods of teaching and hear colleagues who have already been participating in the programme for several years.

So far, One World has provided schools with films on many basic human rights and current affairs topics such as: xenophobia, racism, tolerance, minority rights, gender equality, refugees and asylum seekers, migration, social and lifestyle minorities, drug abuse, environmental issues, the impact of a globalised economy, dealing with the past and many others. I will give two concrete examples here: the Czech Modern History Project and the Who Else Project.

These programmes do not simply focus on human rights issues elsewhere. By working at secondary schools we have discovered that teenagers know very little about recent Czech history, the Second World War, the Nazi occupation and Holocaust, the Communist era and the events of 1989. Regular history classes, which start with ancient Egypt, Greece and Rome, never reach the post-Second World War period. This is not just the consequence of an overcrowded curriculum and insufficient time schedule. There is a reluctance to speak about the recent past. To mitigate the silence, we have taken action. So now, every year in November, in time for the anniversary of the Velvet Revolution, One World provides schools with Czech documentary films about this recent past. Schools are encouraged to organise screenings followed by panels of witnesses and experts. Each year the programme draws significant media attention and instigates a public debate aiming to show the difficulties Czech society suffers in tackling its own past. Public debate is additionally fuelled by the fact that the project is regularly attacked by the Communist Party, which still sits in the Czech Parliament, and by the reluctance of the Ministry of Education to support it.

If the Czech Modern History Project usually raises a lot of passionate debate, the Who Else? Project has received almost universal praise. Schools are provided with collections of films about socially excluded groups. At first, the students and teachers usually organise screenings and debates with guest speakers. After that, students are invited to search in their neighbourhood for similarly excluded social groups and to develop a small project which brings them in contact with their marginalised and excluded neighbours. Finally, the most active students and classes participate in an essay and exhibition competition. The best essays and exhibitions are awarded prizes at the opening of the One World festival.

In addition to recruiting teachers, One World in Schools also recruits and trains active secondary school students. They are also provided with DVDs as well as with guidance on how to organise student film clubs. Today 52 such One World film clubs exist in Czech secondary schools. In addition to regular screenings with guest speakers and Q&As, students have also organised exhibitions, concerts, performances and sometimes even film festivals for their schools. Both the teachers and the student club leaders are in contact with the One World team through regular electronic newsletters, which keep them involved and up-to-date throughout the year. The festival provides space for togetherness and for inspiring one another.

So if you ask me, 'Do film festivals make a difference?' my answer would have to be a resounding 'Yes!'

Notes

1   People in Need (PIN) is a Czech organisation which provides relief aid and development assistance while also working to defend human rights and democratic freedom. In the Czech Republic and Slovakia it administers social integration programs and provides informative and educational activities. It is one of the largest organisations of its kind in post-communist Europe, and since it was established has administered projects in over 40 countries. PIN, in its current form, began in 1992 when dissidents and leaders of the Czechoslovak Velvet Revolution teamed up with conflict journalists. Since then it has developed many public awareness campaigns aimed at providing independent and unbiased information for journalists, opinion makers and the general public. Through campaigns, information projects and media supplements, PIN believes it is possible to support an informed and empowered civil society both at home and abroad.

2   The Homo Homini award is given to exceptional individuals who have made a significant contribution to the promotion of human rights and democracy worldwide (www.oneworld.cz/2011/homo-homini-award). The 2010 award was bestowed on the imprisoned Kyrgyz activist Azimjan Askarov for his continued work in human rights. In operation since 1994, Homo Homini's previous winners include, among others, Aung San Suu Kyi (2009) and Liu Xiaobo (2008). Homo Homini laureates are invited to both the ceremony and the festival as a whole, and they almost invariably attend, although a number have been unable to do so as they are imprisoned. In these cases members of their family or their close friends attend on their behalf. The award is in the form of a photograph or piece of art. The photographs are from the Czech struggle for freedom but symbolise more universal human aspirations for freedoms and rights. There is no money involved, and PIN remains in contact with laureates after the prize has been awarded.

A Cinematic Refuge in the Desert: Festival Internacional de Cine del Sahara[1]

Stefan Simanowitz and Isabel Santaolalla

During the 1960s, when decolonisation movements were sweeping the world, there was a joke that, after achieving independence, a country had to do three things: design a flag, launch an airline and found a film festival (Rich 1999: 79). Western Sahara has a flag but no airline and, despite a struggle that has lasted over three decades, it has yet to achieve independence. The closest Western Sahara comes to its own film festival is the Festival Internacional de Cine del Sahara (FISahara) (www.festivalsahara.com), a festival like no other, which takes place in a refugee camp in the middle of the desert.

Around 165,000 Saharawi displaced from the Western Sahara live in refugee camps around Tindouf (South Western Algeria), awaiting a solution to a political dispute that has kept them in exile from their native land for over three decades. Western Sahara – effectively Africa's last colony – was divided between Morocco and Mauritania when Spain withdrew in 1976, following Morocco's 'Green March' into the territory that had, until then, been a Spanish 'province'. The Popular Front for the Liberation of Saguia el Hamra and Río de Oro (POLISARIO Front), Western Sahara's independence movement, declared the creation of the Saharawi Arab Democratic Republic (SADR) and a 15-year-long war ensued with the Moroccan occupiers (the Mauritanians having withdrawn in 1979). In 1991, the fighting came to an end and, under the terms of a UN ceasefire agreement, a referendum for self-determination was promised. Despite efforts by the international community, however – including over 100 UN resolutions – the referendum has been continually delayed by Morocco, which has remained in occupation of roughly three-quarters of Western Sahara. Over half the Saharawi population live in exile, inhabiting four large camps in the inhospitable Algerian desert, separated from their homeland by a 2,500 km fortified barrier known as 'the Berm'. The POLISARIO is Western Sahara's government in exile and is responsible for the running of the camps, which are referred to as *wilayas* (provinces) and named after the cities the refugees left behind in their homeland: Aoussert, El Aioun, Smara and Dakhla.

It is against the backdrop of this political crisis and the resulting human suffering that FISahara takes place. Now in its eighth year, the festival was the brainchild of Javier Corcuera, a Peruvian documentary filmmaker resident in Spain, who went to the region in 2002 and was moved to act by what he saw there. Corcuera had been invited to visit the camps by members of the Saharawi independence movement who, having seen his first film, *La espalda del mundo* (*The Back of the World*, Javier Corcuera, Spain, 2000), asked him to make a documentary about the plight of the Saharawi. Corcuera considered that a more effective way to support this forgotten people was to organise a film festival, thus combining a cultural service with international media exposure. He sought financial and logistical aid from a number of public and private organisations, and the festival has now become an annual fixture that usually takes place in the months of April or May. Corcuera himself was the festival's sole director until 2009; nowadays the festival has three directors.

It is this genesis that sets FISahara apart. It did not emerge merely as a political film festival but rather as an on-going piece of activism. Although it is an arts festival with clear artistic purposes and merit, it is also a powerful political and politicising event. These two aspects reinforce one another. The festivals organisers, the refugees and much of the audience are, to a greater or lesser degree, activists.

At the festival in 2009, the guest of honour was not a film star but a 19-year-old refugee, Ibrahim Hussein Leibeit, whose leg had been blown off below the knee by a landmine three weeks previous. Leibeit had been at a protest against the 1,550 mile-long fortified barrier known as 'The Wall', which was built by the Moroccans to stop the Sahrawis from returning to their land. In a symbolic gesture, he had attempted to get close enough to the wall to throw a stone to the other side, when he trod on a mine.

In 2010, two dozen human rights activists from occupied Western Sahara addressed the festival; the guest of honour at the 2011 festival was former United Nations Assistant Secretary-General Francesco Bastagli, who resigned from the UN in 2006 in protest over UN inaction on Western Sahara.

The festival is also an extraordinary example of an 'imagined community' in which hundreds of participants from around the world and thousands of Saharawi refugees live together for a week under the same roofs, eating the same food, watching the same films and participating in workshops and other cultural and educational events, temporarily sharing a land that ultimately belongs to none of them, and to which none of them belongs. The situation created by a film festival, which is organised in a refugee camp by outsiders inevitably raises questions about ownership and dependency. In the case of FISahara, a series of issues need to be considered. To what extent does the festival reflect the sociocultural norms, values and beliefs of the refugees? How do the expectations of audiences differ and how are they met? Where are the areas of synergy and how are potential conflicts over artistic and political differences dealt with? How does the festival resolve interrelated questions of post-colonialism/neo-colonialism and globalisation?

Whilst all festivals are somewhat peripatetic in nature – described by Thomas Elsaesser as 'moveable fests and caravans of film cans' (2005: 103) – this is even more the case for FISahara, which, in its first four editions, moved to a different camp each year. Although this nomadic structure might seem appropriate for the desert for logistical and symbolic reasons, it was decided that Dakhla, the most remote of the camps, situated 175 km away from the nearest city of Tindouf, should become the permanent site for the festival. Whilst transporting equipment so far into the desert is obviously more difficult, having a fixed site provides an organisational continuity that was lacking when the festival moved annually. Very little equipment used in the festival remains in Dakhla. Indeed, even the multiplex-sized screen, which is attached to the side of an articulated lorry situated in a spacious, outdoor area in the centre of the camp, is driven off soon after the festival's closing ceremony.

A desert refugee camp is perhaps the least likely setting for an international film festival and yet, for a week each year, Dakhla is transformed into a gala of screenings, workshops and concerts attended by camp dwellers and visitors, including an array of widely acclaimed actors and filmmakers. The festival's programme has steadily expanded over the years. Fifteen films were screened at the first edition in 2003 and at the latest edition in 2011 there were nearly 30 films, including documentaries and animations. The number of workshops held during the festival has also risen, from five in 2003 to 12 in 2011.

Yet, though the festival has grown in scale and ambition, its aims have remained unchanged. These are not only cultural and educational, but also humanitarian and political. Indeed the ultimate goal of FISahara is to bring about circumstances where the festival itself becomes unnecessary: a solution to the refugee crisis and the creation of an independent Saharawi nation will obviate the need for the festival. In this respect FiSahara is – as repeatedly stated by Javier Corcuera – the only film festival in the world that is actively trying to bring about its own extinction.

Life in the refugee camps has deprived the Saharawi people of cultural as well as other opportunities and, even though the open-air screening projected on the side of an articulated lorry cannot offer the perfect cinematic experience, Corcuera aims to recreate it as closely as possible: 'Everybody should have the right to see cinema in its proper conditions, [and] this involves large screens and films on 35mm,' he argues. Film screenings might be seen as an unusual luxury for refugees who are entirely dependent on external aid for most of their basic needs (including water, food and energy), but Danielle Smith, Director of the London-based cultural charity Sandblast, believes that culture is an important and often overlooked aspect of humanitarian aid: '[W]ithout the spirit which is tied to identity and culture, people have less will to survive' (quoted in Newbery 2008: 14).

FISahara is a non-commercial, non-competitive festival and is organised through close collaboration between external groups in Spain and an internal committee within the refugee camp. The POLISARIO is a key partner in the logistic planning of the festival. Indeed the Ministry of Culture of the SADR and the Saharawi Red Crescent (CRS) work closely with festival organisers in Spain, who themselves work in partnership with the National Federation of Associations of Friends of the Saharawi People (CEAS-Sahara). The festival's budget of €300,000 (U.S.$425,000) is paid for through a mix of private funding and institutional sponsorship, above all from the Spanish Cooperation Agency for International Development (AECID) and the Spanish Ministry of Culture, via the Cinematography and Audiovisuals Arts Institute (ICAA). Despite the institutional financial support, the festival is fiercely independent and its directors and organising committee, as well as most of the collaborators, mainly of Spanish origin, work mostly on a voluntary basis. This was always the case in the earlier editions and only more recently, as the festival has grown in size, has it become necessary to hire some extra help for the three- to six-month period preceding the festival.

The numerous practical and conceptual problems facing a festival of this kind include having to cater for two very distinct target groups:

the displaced refugees and the international participants. While the programming of the screenings and workshops is organised with the Saharawi population in mind, other events are laid on specifically for the incoming visitors. Rather than competing or conflicting, however, the requirements and expectations of these two groups seem complementary, and the festival's aim is to provide a space for intercultural exchange. FISahara offers unique opportunities for interaction between the Saharawi and the incoming visitors. The latter, whose numbers have grown from around 250 in 2003 to nearly 500 in 2009, reside with Saharawi families in their tents or mud houses throughout the duration of the festival. The festival is open to anyone on a first-come-first-served basis and visitors are, typically, fairly politicised Spaniards and a limited number of individuals from other nationalities, most with a keen interest in film and visual arts.

Obviously, the possibility that FISahara may be viewed by some as a means of sampling a safe dose of exoticism cannot be fully dismissed. After all, most international participants come from Western societies where ethnically-marked materials and individuals are systematically being fetishised, labelled as 'authentic' and marketed for public consumption (Santaolalla 2000: 10). FISahara's active promotion of a two-way exchange between locals and outsiders is designed to counter the likelihood of such attitudes, as well as the reasonable misgiving that a festival of this kind could be perpetuating the cultural dependency of the Saharawi on the Western organisers. In fact, despite the undeniable imbalance in the material circumstances of the refugees and their temporary visitors, their relationship during the festival comes close to one of interdependence and exchange. Indeed, the international participants are entirely reliant on the warmth and hospitality of their Saharawi hosts for accommodation, food and transport, as well as for the richness of their cultural and educational experience during their stay in the camps. As part of the festival's programme, a series of visits to hospitals, schools and other official institutions is arranged for the outsiders, offering them the chance to appreciate the ways in which the *wilaya* is structured and run. Further cultural activities and entertainment include a live-music concert in the moonlit dunes, a camel race, an 'international' football match and, above all, multiple opportunities for taking the almost mandatory cup of sweet Saharawi tea, both with the families and in the main festival arena, where a showcase of traditional Saharawi culture is set up during the week-long event. This display – referred to as Le Frig – consists of various *jaimas* (traditional tents), each representing a different *daira* (district) of the *wilaya*, and each concentrating on specific aspects of the culture, such as traditional clothing, food, music, dance and literary and religious lore. Its purpose is to give both the international visitors and, interestingly, also the Saharawi youth, the opportunity of familiarising themselves with progressively disappearing Saharawi traditions.

Still, the festival does not simply aim to have an impact on the Saharawi refugees and the few hundred individuals who travel to the camps. It also actively seeks to reach a wider audience through the involvement of the international media, so that worldwide exposure of the plight of the Saharawi people increases pressure for political change. The support of high-profile figures such as Penélope Cruz and Pedro Almodóvar has given the festival prominence, and each year dozens of – so far predominantly Spanish – actors and filmmakers attend the festival and lend their popularity to the cause. In 2008, Javier Bardem was the most well-known participant, and in 2011 guests included actors Luis Tosar (for *The Limits of Control*, Jim Jarmush, U.S./Japan, 2009) and Nora Navas (for *Pa Negre/Black Bread*, Agustí Villaronga, Spain/France, 2010) and film directors Gerardo Olivares (*Entre lobos/Among Wolves*, Spain/Germany, 2010) and Guillem Morales (*Los ojos de Julia/Julia's Eyes*, Spain, 2010). Each year a well-known band plays a concert in the sand dunes or in a schoolyard in Dakhla; previous performers have included Manu Chao and Macaco.

Every year the festival attracts an ever-wider number of international participants. In 2010, a flight was arranged from London to bring to the festival more than 20 British actors who took part in a workshop and shared advice with potential Saharawi filmmakers on how to work with actors. The 2010 and 2011 festivals were attended by artistic and political delegations from South Africa, comprising ambassadors and members of the South African Department of Arts and Culture. In March 2011, a launch event was held in London which was attended by over 150 members of the British film industry including big name actors, directors and filmmakers. Growing international participation has resulted in increased global media coverage which, in turn, has brought political pressure to bear on governments around the world to find a solution to the on-going dispute that conforms to international law.

The festival's actual choice of screenings and guests deserves consideration. Film selection is an ideologically loaded exercise and the programming of a film festival both reflects and leads to an understanding of the message that it is trying to convey. Cultural analysts such as

Bourdieu (1984) have noted that cinematic taste is rooted in economics, class, geography, education and language, and film programmers therefore need to be sensitive to the varying experiences and cultural competences of their intended public.

According to the FISahara organisers, there are no rigid criteria for the selection of films and the titles chosen vary from pure entertainment to serious subjects. There is, nevertheless, a level of cultural and aesthetic policing or self-policing by the programmers, where films are vetted to ensure that they are culturally appropriate for a Muslim audience of all ages. Films that contain sexually explicit scenes are avoided. However, although certain issues are also viewed as inappropriate, there is some room for manoeuvre, as exemplified by the screening, at the 2007 festival, of *Fresa y chocolate* (*Strawberry and Chocolate*, Tomás Gutiérrez Alea, Cuba/Mexico/Spain/U.S., 1994), a Cuban comedy-drama centring on a homosexual character.

Despite the fact that the FISahara Saharawi audience is arguably more homogeneous than that of most other film festivals, the organisers are aware that their local viewers are stratified across all ages and possess different levels of film understanding, all of which leads to diverse film viewing attitudes. Among other things, familiarity with one or more languages besides the native Hassaniya, and disparate experiences of schooling or work abroad, brings considerable variety to individual cinematic expectations and responses.

Some of the films shown are made by the refugees themselves. In an interview, 22-year-old Najla Mahamed says that Saharawi are naturally good storytellers: 'Living in camps has forced us to develop our imaginations,' she says. 'From your earliest days you are forced to imagine your homeland. As you grow up that imagined place grows up with you' (Simanowitz 2011a).

The FISahara festival organisers do not have to worry too much about attracting spectators. Indeed, the camp residents are almost literally a 'captive audience'. Still, a key question revolves around *what* the Saharawi audience wants: sameness, replication, reflection or difference? There is a tendency among festival programmers to assume that 'identification is the principal or only reason to choose a screening: people are interested only in seeing work about others like themselves' (Fung 1999: 91). The FISahara programmers, however, have a broader approach. Whilst films about the experience of the Saharawis are shown – indeed, some are made by Saharawi refugees themselves – the festival also aims to open a window to the experiences of others beyond the boundaries of the camps and engender a sense of greater internationalism. Showing films about the struggle of other oppressed peoples in the world is intended to give the refugees hope and remind them that they are not alone.

Jermal (Ravi L. Bharwani, Rayya Makarim and Orlow Seunke, Indonesia, 2008), an Indonesian film which was shown at the 2011 festival, follows the life of a 12-year-old boy sent to work on an isolated fishing platform in the Malacca Straits. For the refugees, surrounded as they are by desert, watching a film set in a location entirely surrounded by water was no doubt a strangely familiar and fascinating experience (Simanowitz 2011b).

The FiSahara organisers are also acutely aware of the refugees' wish for entertainment. What is mainstream in other parts of the world is novelty here. For that reason, big-budget, commercial films are as welcome in the camps as the more socially committed films that often form the core of film festivals with agendas similar to FiSahara's, such as those of the Southern Film Festivals Platform, which FiSahara joined in 2009. Yet, even in the choice of commercially or critically successful films there is evidence of an underlying vein that seems to favour stories set against the backdrop of struggle and oppression. Proof of this is the fact that three films by British social realist filmmaker Ken Loach have been screened in recent years and that, in 2008, his film *The Wind that Shakes the Barley* (France/Germany/Ireland/Italy/Spain/UK, 2006) won the festival's first prize.

The predominance of films fully or partly produced in Spain is justified by the fact that the festival is a Spanish initiative and that Spanish is the second language of the camps (Arabic or Spanish subtitles are provided for all films and the intention of the organisers is to provide some English subtitling in the future). The 2011 Best Picture, for example, was picked up by Gerardo Olivares for his 2010 film *Among Wolves*. Actor Luis Tosar was given the Jury Prize for the Spanish movie *También la lluvia* (*Even the Rain,* Icíar Bollaín, Spain/France/Mexico, 2010). Logically, many of the films screened have a Saharawi theme and Cuban or Cuban-themed films feature largely in the programme, which is understandable, given the Saharawi's close connection with Cuba (thousands of refugees have benefited from free university education in Cuba since the 1970s).

There has been no systematic research into audience response to the films screened in FiSahara, but anecdotal evidence seems to suggest that films reflecting the Saharawi experience are particularly popular. In his article on the 2009 edition of FISahara, Isaacson notes that

> [s]creenings of foreign and Saharawi-made short films depicting refugee life evoked scenes from *Cinema Paradiso* [*Nuovo Cinema Paradiso*, Giuseppe Tornatore, France/Italy, 1988] with enraptured audiences clapping to recognisable soundtracks and marvelling at the larger-than-life portrayal of a familiar drama. (Isaacson 2009: AR9)

Similarly, films with storylines that connect with the Saharawi lifestyle also have a big following. In an interview, Beatrice Newbery was told that, 'the Mongolian film was about some nomads, and we all loved it. There was a feeling in the audience of recognition, as we are traditionally a nomadic community. The film reinforced our common humanity.' (2008: 15). If there had been an audience prize in 2011, it would probably have gone to *Al-Yidar (El Muro)* (*The Wall*, Leo Jiménez and Fernando Rivas, Spain, 2010), a documentary about the wall that divides Western Sahara in two. 'I have been to the wall to protest, but landmines stopped me from getting too close,' a refugee said. 'This film made me see the wall in a new way' (Simanowitz: 2011a).

The 2011 festival launched a digital streaming facility that enabled festival organisers to reach out simultaneously to audiences via the Internet. All films shown at the 2011 festival were also available on-line thanks to an agreement with the Association of Management of Audiovisual Producers Rights (EGEDA). From 30 April to 9 May the system, nicknamed VeoFISahara, allowed anyone to register and get a free personal code. They could then log on and watch an unlimited number of films from the FISahara programme for free.

Three decades of living a sedentary life in the camps have disrupted many of the rich traditions of this nomadic people, descended from Bedouin Arabs who arrived in the Western Sahara in the thirteenth century and integrated with the Sanhaja population (Simanowitz 2009a: 299). The Saharawi are conscious of this progressive erosion of their traditional ways of life, as well as of the inexorable penetration of alien practices as a result of exile, emigration and the pressure of thousands of youths returning from periods of study abroad. There is great interest among those living in the refugee camps in using audio-visual equipment to document their changing lives and traditions, as well as to give expression to their political demands.

Giving the Saharawi access to filmmaking equipment and training is integral to the festival's objectives, as this is considered an important means of empowerment. According to Omar Ahmed, a member of the festival's organisation, '[t]he Saharawi need to express their ideas from their point of view, not just from that of the Europeans that come to see us' (quoted in Isaacson 2009: AR9). As if taking cue from Benedict Anderson (1983), the Saharawi seem intent on constructing an imagined space based on a shared vision, memory or myth about their homeland. In tune with the contemporary ethos that 'sees nations as narrated' (Shohat and Stam 2003: 9), they are eager to take the lead in the writing of their nation's evolving narrative. And, although the Saharawi may be disinclined to see their border existence as one of communicative and intellectual empowerment, it is perhaps nevertheless possible to argue, with García Canclini, that their experiences of deterritorialisation and reterritorialisation may grant them a unique and distinctive perspective from which to engage in 'new symbolic productions' (1995: 261 and 239).

The FISahara festival, by now part of what Corcuera and the organisers refer to as their larger 'Cinema for the Saharawi People' project, is actively responding to the Saharawis' desire for increased access to the audio-visual medium and for the development of a film culture of their own that helps them in their nation-building process. From its earliest editions, FISahara has been scheduling a series of workshops run by instructors from international film schools, universities and NGOs, where various audio-visual skills are taught to the Saharawi. Beyond the yearly one-week workshops, however, the festival organisers are now also seeking to create more permanent opportunities for audio-visual training. Each camp is being equipped with DVD libraries, video projectors, sound equipment, screens and DVD recorders. Video technicians have been trained to look after each library and a new Film School opened in a neighbouring camp (the 'February the 27th' camp) during the 2011 FISahara. Each year the School will give up to 20 refugees a chance to learn about all aspects of filmmaking and, at the School's opening ceremony on 8 May 2011, actor Carlos Bardem announced that his brother, Javier, had donated €10,000 to help with running costs.

The Cinema for the Saharawi People' project, in its threefold dimension – annual festival, camp-based film libraries and permanent film school – is still managed by Javier Corcuera and the FISahara organisation; however, the objective, as the festival establishes itself, is for the Saharawi to gain greater control over it. With the development of a new Saharawi film culture emerging from the workshops and Film School, and with a programme increasingly listing more films made by Saharawi filmmakers, the balance of ownership of the festival should shift in the forthcoming years.

Through its strategic choices, FISahara seems to be not only offering entertainment, culture and solidarity to a community of displaced people, but also facilitating the encounter of what Laura Marks calls 'different cultural organisations of knowledge'. In turn, this is, as she argues, 'one of the sources of intercultural cinema's synthesis of new forms of expression and new kinds of knowledge' (2000: 6-7). Through artistic and political camaraderie, FISahara creates a platform for powerful intercultural exchange between the Saharawi and the external participants. It offers the Saharawi refugees some respite from their harsh daily routine and is a beacon of hope for the future, providing them with an imaginative space beyond their bleak desert horizons. The festival also plays an important role in increasing awareness of one of the world's longest-running and most forgotten conflicts. 'We don't want to stage a festival here,' insists Javier Corcuera, Festival Director. 'We'd rather hold it in a free Sahara, beside the ocean. But until that day of freedom arrives, FISahara will continue every year in the refugee camps on the *hammada* plains of the Sahara desert.'

Note: *If you would like to support the Cinema for the Sahara People project, attend FiSahara 2012 or submit a film to the Festival, please visit www.festivalsahara.com. You may also contact stefanowitz2@hotmail.com or i.santaolalla@roehampton.ac.uk.*

Works Cited

Anderson, Benedict (1983) *Imagined Communities: Reflections on the Origin and Spread of Nationalism.* London, New York: Verso.

Bourdieu, Pierre (1984) *Distinction: A Social Critique of the Judgment of Taste,* trans. Richard Nice. Cambridge, Mass.: Harvard University Press.

Elsaesser, Thomas (2005) *European Cinema: Face to Face with Hollywood.* Amsterdam: Amsterdam University Press.

Fung, Richard (1999) 'Programming the Public', Queer Publicity: A Dossier on Lesbian and Gay Film Festivals, *GLQ: A Journal of Lesbian and Gay Studies,* 5, 1, 89-93.

García Canclini, Néstor (1995) *Hybrid Cultures: Strategies for Entering and Leaving Modernity*, trans. Christopher L. Chiappari and Silvia L. López. London and Minneapolis: University of Minnesota Press.

Isaacson, Andy (2009) 'A Desert Film Festival Complete with Camels', *The New York Times*, 2 August, AR9, 151.

Marks, Laura (2000) *The Skin of the Film: Intercultural Cinema, Embodiment, and the Senses*. Durham and London: Duke University Press.

Newbery, Beatrice (2008) 'Captive Images', *Developments Magazine* (UK Government Department for International Development), 39, August, 13-5.

Olivieri, Federico (2009) 'The Representation of Africa within (Contemporary) Spaces for African Cinema's Exhibition: A Case Study of the African Film Festival of Tarifa (Spain – FCAT, *Festival de Cine Africano de Tarifa*)', unpublished Masters dissertation, School of Oriental and African Studies, University of London.

Rich, Ruby (1999) 'Collision, Catastrophe and Celebration: The Relationship between Gay and Lesbian Film Festivals and their Publics', *GLQ: A Journal of Lesbian and Gay Studies*, 5, 4, 79-86.

Santaolalla, Isabel (2000) 'Introduction. What is "New" in "New" Exoticisms?', in Isabel Santaolalla (ed.) *'New' Exoticisms. Changing Patterns in the Construction of Otherness*. Amsterdam and Atlanta: Rodopi, 9-17.

Shohat, Ella and Robert Stam (eds) (2003) *Multiculturalism, Postcoloniality and Transnational Media*. New Brunswick: Rutgers University Press.

Simanowitz, Stefan (2009a) 'Not One Grain of Sand: International Law and the Conflict in Western Sahara', *Contemporary Review*, 291, 1694, 299-305.

____ (2009b) 'Riddle of the Sands', *The Independent*, 15 May, 14.

____ (2011a) 'Storytelling in the Desert', *New Internationalist*, 442, 12 May. On-line. Available HTTP: http://www.newint.org/features/2011/05/12/western-sahara-film-festival (4 August 2011).

____ (2011b) 'Pictures in the Desert', *New Internationalist*, 422, May, 39.

Notes

1   This essay is a revised and updated version of an earlier piece by the same authors, 'A Cinematic Refuge in the Desert: The Sahara International Film Festival', in Dina Iordanova with Ruby Cheung (eds) *FFY2: Film Festivals and Imagined Communities*. St Andrews: St Andrews Film Studies, 2010, 136-50.

'Tell Our Story to the World': The Meaning of Success for *A Massacre Foretold*[1] – A Filmmaker Reflects

Nick Higgins

The first time a film is screened for an audience is a nerve-wracking moment for most filmmakers, and for those with ambitions to bring about social change, it can be especially fraught. Will the film work and what exactly would it mean for a film to be politically successful anyway? Documentary theory would seem to suggest that political success runs the full gamut from the emancipation of the spectator, liberated from passivity to engage critically with representations of the world, to the post screening riots of an audience moved to act through a process of Gainesian mimesis.[2] Perhaps, like most politically concerned filmmakers, my documentaries lay claim to reactions that lie somewhere between these two poles. This article will reflect on a few audience reactions and situate their relationship to the festivals and screenings where they have taken place.

Navigating the Circuit

Documentary films that 'travel' will experience a series of premières: worldwide, continental, national, regional and so forth. If successfully negotiated such premières can have a significant effect on the life of a film. There are, if you like, idealised festival scenarios for the release of a feature documentary. Much as with fiction films, the circuit of top tier festivals, for example Cannes (www.festival-cannes.fr), Sundance (www.sundance.org/festival), Berlin (www.berlinale.de), Toronto (tiff.net) and Edinburgh (www.edfilmfest.org.uk), are still the most desirable. The attraction of this circuit is both in terms of a film's potential longevity and of international media exposure. Longevity, because subsequent programming by smaller festivals is near automatic after an appearance within this premier league of festivals, and this combined with press and media attention increases the possibility of a theatrical release. Although once rare for documentaries to circulate in this network, it is now more common. Nevertheless, for what one might broadly term activist documentaries,[3] this sort of festival life remains unusual.

For the activist documentary, a more likely circuit might include the documentary festivals, with screenings at IDFA (Amsterdam) (www.idfa.nl), Hot Docs (Toronto) (www.hotdocs.ca), AFI-Discovery Channel Silverdocs (Silver Spring, Maryland) (silverdocs.com), Sheffield Doc/Fest (Sheffield, UK) (sheffdocfest.com), Cinéma du réel (Paris) (www.cinemadureel.org) and Visions du réel (Nyon, Switzerland) (www.visionsdureel.ch). Here, too, a longer life may follow as smaller documentary festivals will often programme films that have received the mark of quality that premières within such prestigious festivals confer.

In addition to this, there are the human rights film festivals. Within this circuit the issue of territorial premières is not of primary concern to the programmers and it is arguable whether there is even a ranking division at work within this circuit. Selection criteria often revolve around questions of significance, and possibly political urgency. Although there are high profile human rights festivals such as the Human Rights Watch International Film Festival (London and New York) (www.hrw.org/en/iff), One World (Prague) (www.oneworld.cz) and Festival du Film et Forum International sur les Droits Humains (FIFDH Geneva) (www.fifdh.org), the idealised ranking system identified above does not seem to necessarily effect a film's circulation within this network. Screenings at festivals such as Perspective (Nuremberg, Germany) (www.filmfestival-der-menschenrechte.de), Addis International Film Festival (Addis Ababa, Ethiopia) (www.addisfilmfestival.org), Festival de Cine y Video de los Derechos Humanos (Sucre, Bolivia) (www.festivalcinebolivia.org), Festival de Cine de Bogotá (Columbia) (xxviii.bogocine.com), Human Rights Nights (Bologna, Italy) (www.humanrightsnights.org), Pravo Ljudski (Sarajevo, Bosnia Herzegovina) (www.pravoljudski.org) and Document - International Human Rights Documentary Film Festival (Glasgow, UK) (www.docfilmfest.org.uk), could be seen as equally significant by filmmakers.[4] For a documentary film that makes no claims to being an activist film, festival success may well be judged from an idealised festival run, but for filmmakers with aspirations to create social change, even if they achieve success within these circuits, there is often the lingering question as to what difference the film screenings have really made.

Reaching an Audience...

In 2007, after some six years work, my documentary *A Massacre Foretold* (Nick Higgins, UK, 2007) was complete and ready to be shared with the world. The film tells the story of the Acteal massacre that occurred in Southern Mexico on 22 December 1997. Contradicting the 'official version' of events, the film argues that the creation of clandestine paramilitary groups by the Mexican government and military led directly to the murder of 45 indigenous Mayans in December of 1997. At the time of the massacre I was conducting research for my PhD thesis in the highlands of Chiapas where the massacre took place.[5] Roughly a week after the massacre I interviewed survivors from Acteal. It was both a humbling and deeply uncomfortable experience. Humbling, because I was amazed that the survivors had no desire for revenge against the indigenous paramilitaries who had killed their families, and deeply uncomfortable, because I felt that I had intruded on their private grief without having a clear sense of why I was there. It was as I was leaving the refugee camp where they were then living that one of their group insisted that I help them; when I asked him how, he replied, 'by telling our story to the world'. At that time I had never even picked up a video camera, let alone made a film.

The making of *A Massacre Foretold* was, therefore, in many ways the settling of unfinished business. Once I had completed my PhD, I was left with a deep sense of dissatisfaction. I felt that all the most intense experiences of my fieldwork had been written out of the final manuscript. At that time it seemed to me that academia had no place for the emotions, or the immediacy of what it felt like to be in the highly politicised environment of Chiapas of the late 1990s. So in 2002, I returned to Chiapas with a video camera. I made a short video about the Acteal massacre that was screened only once. The screening was with a politically sympathetic audience who were genuinely interested in events in Chiapas and, as I answered question after question, I realised all the things the video had failed to communicate, and with a cold shudder I recognised how much I had to learn about documentary filmmaking.

In the years that followed, I was fortunate enough to have the opportunity to direct two documentary films working with professional crews: *Women in Black* (UK, 2004)[6] and *Hidden Gifts: The Mystery of Angus MacPhee* (UK, 2004). During that time, I was able to learn more about making documentaries and to witness their potential for social change. *Women in Black* tells the story of the international peace movement of the same name from the perspective of three Scottish women who hold weekly peace vigils on the streets of Edinburgh. It is estimated that weekly vigils are held in over 40 countries worldwide and that the Women in Black network numbers some 10,000. The film was broadcast on Scottish television, reaching an audience of approximately 200,000 viewers. Shortly after, I learned of two new regional Scottish protest groups (Dumfries and Aberdeen) launched in direct response to the screening of the film.[7] This, it seemed to me, was about as close to a mimetic response to a film as a filmmaker could hope for, and all the more surprising as it was achieved through the relatively atomised and solitary medium of the television broadcast. My experience with *Hidden Gifts*, which seeks to challenge the way people view mental illness, further convinced me of the potential of broadcast television. A European-co-production, the film was aired multiple times in Scotland, Germany, Austria, Switzerland, Finland, Sweden and the Netherlands, garnering audiences numbering several million.[8] The film also received several awards, but more importantly, through these avenues, came to the attention of mental health professionals who continue to use it in their work today.[9]

Neither film had what could be considered a significant festival life, partially perhaps as their medium length running time may have rendered them difficult to programme but mainly as I neglected to enter the films into festivals as my main preoccupation at the time was the making of my film about the Acteal massacre.[10]

One of the principal lessons I had learnt from making these two short television documentaries was the fundamental importance of trust. The next time I returned to Mexico with a camera, I filmed less and took more time to get to know the community of Acteal. I recognised how they were protective of those who had survived the massacre, and whilst I had come to learn the importance of first hand testimony for powerful documentaries, I had also come to appreciate that people needed to believe in you as a person before they would trust you with their testimony.[11] In many respects this was a two-way street. I also had to believe in myself as being capable of telling their story in a way that would do justice to their trust, and make it possible for them to bear witness to an audience that they could otherwise never reach.[12]

After several shooting periods, and with the support of the Dutch broadcaster VPRO and several smaller funds including the Scottish Documentary Institute, I managed to complete *A Massacre Foretold* in 2007.

Premier League Mexico

As a Scottish filmmaker, my first festival application was to the Edinburgh International Film Festival (EIFF). To my delight the film was accepted and received its world première in August 2007. There were three packed screenings with good question and answer sessions. It was hugely satisfying to watch audiences engage emotionally with the film and in particular with the testimony of Maria as she related how she first heard the news that nine members of her family had been killed at Acteal. This, I suppose, was the politicised Deleuzian affect in action. The film was nominated for the Sky Movies Documentary Award, and it was also at a screening in Edinburgh that members of the WACC-SIGNIS jury decided to honour the film with the Best Human Rights Documentary Film Award for 2007.[13]

It was also around the time of the Edinburgh première that I discovered that *A Massacre Foretold* had been selected for the Morelia International Film Festival in Mexico (www.moreliafilmfest.com). Within Mexico, Morelia has the reputation for being the most prestigious film festival, and outside of Mexico it has a strong reputation for being serious about cinema. For Morelia to select a documentary about a recent and contentious event in Mexican history, made by a non-Mexican, was a bold move and one that both surprised and excited me. To be able to tell my Mexican friends and contributors that the film would première at the most prestigious festival in their country afforded their trust in me a strong sense of validation.

The 2007 Morelia International Film Festival was opened by the President of Mexico, Felipe Calderon. When I arrived the following day, the President's festival inauguration was on the front pages of the national press. Depending on which paper you read, the story either foregrounded the President's support for national cinema, or concentrated on the demonstrations his presence had provoked. Of greater concern were accusations that the festival organisers had jeopardised their independence and, by permitting the President to open it, had allowed the festival to become politically contaminated. The prominence of these debates not only illustrates the politicised crucible within which Mexican film festivals occasionally find themselves operating, but also acts as a reminder of the publicity and media platform that such a festival can potentially deliver. As one of the main contentions of *A Massacre Foretold* is that the ex-President of Mexico, Ernesto Zedillo, was the individual ultimately and criminally responsible for the massacre at Acteal, arriving in the midst of such a media storm was a warning of how the film might be received.[14]

For the festival première, I hoped to arrange for a legal representative from the human rights team dealing with the case, as well as representatives from the community of Acteal to attend. Chiapas, however, was more than a day's journey away by bus and the costs of attendance were prohibitive for the people of the community. To their credit, the festival organisers provided considerable aid by arranging and financing the attendance of two community representatives. It is a testament to their resources, their commitment and perhaps also their wish to distance themselves from the 'official' label, that they should have given such support to the film.

The night of the Mexican première both Javier and Alfredo from Acteal wore their traditional Mayan clothes and, as we arrived at the cinema, we experienced what can only be described as a paparazzi moment. Around 12 cameramen jostled to take our photographs and as we were escorted by festival staff through the crowded cinema lobby, I realised that the massed public were gathered to see our film. Sure enough the cinema was packed; people were even cramming themselves into the aisles and exits so they could watch. Two television news crews stood at the side waiting to record the post film discussion.

Like many filmmakers I cringed and perspired through my own projection, convinced the film looked terrible and that the audience were distracted, but at a certain point I looked round and realised that many people were crying. When the lights came up and the four of us took to the floor for questions, the atmosphere in the salon was charged with emotion. The intensity was so great that no one left the room and the discussion that followed lasted longer than the screening. Yet what really made the screening special was that the survivors from Acteal could provide their own perspective and response. They could speak to the audience outside the confines of the screen. When asked how they felt about the film Javier replied, 'it both pains me and makes me sad to see this film. It hurts, because they are my people that were killed, but it pains me more, because ten years after the massacre there is still no justice'.

Listening to Javier and observing this rare cultural phenomenon of a non-Indian audience listening so intently to an indigenous man, I thought to myself, this is the difference that films and film festivals can make. For a short time, at least, film festivals can reconfigure power relations and act as counter spaces to often violent political realities.[15]

The next day I awoke to find my photograph on the front cover of the national paper, *La Jornada,* with the headline, 'Los sobrevivientes de Acteal quieren justicia, no venganza' ('The victims of Acteal want justice not revenge'; see Marquez 2007). Footage from our post-film discussion had screened on Channel 11 News and many of the papers had picked up the news of the screening and featured photographs from the event. The buzz surrounding the film had led the festival's guests of honour, Stephen Frears and Bertrand Tavernier, to request a private screening of the film. Other festival directors also approached me about screening the film at their festivals, most notably Sean Farnel of Hot Docs. The next day, I received a request from the Sundance Festival to send them a copy of the film. At that moment, it seemed like the film had 'worked' and, in the festival sense at least, was going to be a success.

Screening in Acteal

Several months later, in December 2007, I returned to Mexico to screen the film in the hamlet of Acteal itself. It was the tenth anniversary of the massacre and after the success of the Morelia screening I had been invited to show the film to the whole community as part of their commemorative rituals.

Whilst my wife and I arrived in Mexico, our bags did not. We nevertheless travelled on to Chiapas as I was due to screen the film in San Cristobal de las Casas before travelling to Acteal. Thinking that the screening would have to be cancelled as all my DVD copies were in the bags, I was initially relieved, then concerned, and then flattered when from within the gathered audience there came four offers to screen from their own copies of the film. This was a testament both to the ubiquity of DVD pirating in Mexico and, I felt, to a genuine interest in the film itself.

By the time we set off for Acteal we had been reunited with our bags. The film was to be projected onto a very large white sheet on a specially constructed auditorium above the collective burial crypt of the 45 martyrs, as they are referred to in Acteal. During the projection the predominantly Tzotzil audience would alternate from complete silence to hushed chatter and eventually, when the film ended, there was a collective prayer with music, food and dance. I can honestly say that in all the years I had been visiting, I've never seen the community of Acteal look happier. It was not, of course, because they loved the film but rather, as they explained, 'because their relatives and loved ones had been with them that night, and when you are with family that you have not seen for a long time you are happy'. It was another humbling reminder of the vitality of indigenous culture and for me personally, it was the most rewarding screening experience I have ever had.

Later that evening, members of the community explained how they use the film as a means to educate younger Tzotzil Indians about their history and the events that have defined them. They too had already made copies and distributed them across 45 rural and often isolated communities. The local human rights organisation, Fray Bartolome de las Casas were later to inform me that instead of giving lectures on the massacre they now send the film instead. They told me it meant the story of the massacre had been able to reach communities that are rarely engaged with, such as prisoners in Mexico City.

Festivals, Audiences and Social Change

Sundance never did select the film. Hot Docs also withdrew their invitation to screen the film, weakly arguing that their collaboration with the Ministry of Foreign Affairs in Mexico to create a sidebar entitled Made in Mexico, precluded my inclusion on the basis of being a non-Mexican. By the time I had this news I had already turned down other screening opportunities in North America in an effort to maintain the all important première status. Even with such minor disappointments, the film was far from the end of its festival life. Indeed, the idealised launch that I had once envisaged now fragmented into a different set of calendar screenings that were in no way correlated with the circuit I had envisaged before. This did not impede distribution, however. In addition to a short theatrical release in Scotland, A Massacre Foretold screened at over 20 international festivals everywhere from Norway to Ethiopia.[16] It was picked up for distribution in Europe by Deckert Distribution and for distribution in North America by Icarus Films. It has been broadcast on European terrestrial and international satellite television and continues to receive screenings that cross circuits and networks – at universities and activist meetings in the U.S. and Europe – that have particular significance for the life of the film.[17]

Such alternative screenings have value for social change. One was the screening at the Latin American Studies Association (LASA) congress in Montreal, which brought the film to the attention of an international group of academics and a representative of the U.S. National Security Archive. As the film sets forward an argument that the Mexican administration of President Ernesto Zedillo had created, trained and financed the paramilitary groups, one of which was responsible for the Acteal massacre, it was gratifying that the viewing of the film in part led this representative to undertake further research and ultimately to publish documents that supported the position of the film (see Doyle 2009).

It was also at LASA that the film was first noticed and invited to screen at Yale University. Although the film had already been screened in campuses throughout the U.S., Yale was distinctive, as former Mexican President Zedillo was employed by the University as a professor of Globalisation Studies. It was thus particularly gratifying that the screening was hosted by both the Yale Law School and the Centre for Latin American and Iberian Studies. This screening became part of a wider campaign to have Ernesto Zedillo removed from his position at Yale.[18]

Whilst the survivors of the Acteal massacre continue to campaign for justice and seek to bring several former high-level officials, including Zedillo, to trial, in 2009 this campaign faced a particularly cynical setback. Twenty-nine indigenous men incarcerated for their part in the massacre, many of whom had admitted their guilt, were freed on a technicality. This seemingly perverse legal decision by the Mexican courts outraged many international activist groups and has led them to renew their campaigning efforts against the Mexican government.[19] One consequence of this is that, with my permission, A Massacre Foretold has become widely used by activist groups across Europe as a means of bringing this injustice to an audience.[20]

It is, as the opening paragraph of this reflection made clear, difficult to assess exactly how activist documentaries bring about change. What is clear, though, is that they must be seen to have any effect at all. The role of film festivals is therefore vital in giving a film the political oxygen it needs; but festivals are not the only platforms and political change, as the political theorists have long taught us, does not occur only at the institutional and cultural level, but also at the personal, subjective and psychological level.

As I have been constantly reminded on my trips to Chiapas, activists must be satisfied with small victories and, as the locals there continue to attest, even to be struggling is a kind of victory in itself. Faced with a mainstream media and culture that encourages us to forget and withdraw from wider societal concerns, documentaries that give meaning to otherwise chaotic events, and festivals that give these films a platform, are now more important than ever.[21]

Works Cited

Aguilar Camín, Héctor (2007) 'Regreso a Acteal. I. La fractura', *Nexos*, 358, October, 56-7.

Chanan, Michael (2008) 'Filming the "Invisible"', in Thomas Austin and Wilma de Jong (eds) *Rethinking Documentary: New Perspectives, New Practices*. New York: McGraw-Hill/Open University Press, 121-32.

Doyle, Kate (2009) *Breaking the Silence: The Mexican Army and the 1997 Acteal Massacre*. National Security Archive Electronic Briefing Book No. 283, 20 August, 2009. On-line. Available HTTP: http://www.gwu.edu/~nsarchiv/NSAEBB/NSAEBB283/index.htm (15 July 2011).

Gaines, Jane (1999) 'Political Mimesis', in Jane Gaines and Michael Renov (eds) *Collecting Visible Evidence*. Minneapolis: University of Minnesota Press, 84-102.

Higgins, Nicholas (2004) *Understanding the Chiapas Rebellion: Modernist Visions and the Invisible Indian*. Austin: University of Texas.

Olesen, Thomas (2004) *International Zapatismo: The Construction of Solidarity in the Age of Globalization*. London: Zed Books.

Rabasa, José (2010) 'On Documentary and Testimony: The Revisionists' History, the Politics of Truth, and the Remembrance of the Massacre at Acteal, Chiapas' in *Without History: Subaltern Studies, The Zapatista Insurgency, and the Spectre of History*. Pittsburgh: University of Pittsburgh Press, 206-30.

Rancière, Jacques (2009) *The Emancipated Spectator*, trans. Gregory Elliott. London: Verso.

Sarkar, Bhaskar and Janet Walker (eds) (2009) *Documentary Testimonies: Global Archives of Suffering*. New York: Routledge.

Shapiro, Michael (2008) *Cinematic Geopolitics*. London: Routledge.

Marquez, Carlos F. (2007) 'Camino a una masacre: denuncia del terror paramilitar entre los indígenas', *La Jornada*, 10 October. On-line. Available HTTP: http://www.lajornadamichoacan.com.mx/2007/10/10/index.php?section=cultura&article=016n1cul (4 August 2011).

Notes

1   *A Massacre Foretold* (Nick Higgins, UK, 2007) was produced by Lansdowne Productions and runs at 58 minutes. To purchase or arrange screenings contact Icarus Films on mail@icarusfilms.com (for the U.S.) or Lansdowne Productions on info@lansdowneproductions.co.uk (for the UK and Europe). For more information on the film see www.massacreforetold.com.

2   See Rancière 2009 and Gaines 1999.

3   Activist documentaries can be defined as films that seek to bring about social change. At the most basic level these can be campaigning films that have a clear objective, such as the release of an innocent man from prison. Within the spectrum of activist films, however, I would wish to include films that, whilst perhaps not offering a clearly instrumental objective, nevertheless can be understood as political in their attempt to change the way we understand the world. Such films may tackle often invisible and structural abuses (see Chanan 2008) and involve a level of political engagement that I would wish to include within the term activist. Such an approach might be placed in contrast to those who merely claim to observe.

4   Most of these festivals are members of the Human Rights Film Network (see www.humanrightsfilmnetwork.org).

5   Since published as Higgins 2004.

6   See www.lansdowneproductions.co.uk.

7   For more information on *Women in Black* and to watch a short cinema version of the film, see http://www.lansdowneproductions.co.uk/women.html.

8   *Hidden Gifts* has been broadcast on Grampian Television (Scotland), Scottish Television, YLE (Finland), ZDF/3sat (Germany, Austria, Switzerland), VPRO (the Netherlands), SVT (Sweden) and Al Jazeera International (International Satellite Channel).

9   *Hidden Gifts* won the Jury Award at the Scottish Mental Health and Arts Film Festival in 2008, the Best Documentary Award at the 2005 Britspotting Festival in Berlin and was nominated for both the Prix Italia (Rome) and the Royal Television Society Broadcast Awards in 2005. The film is regularly screened by health care professionals and to client groups in the UK and, since being made available for distribution in the U.S., has been the subject of several professional reviews, such as the *American Art Therapy Association Journal* and the *Journal of the American Psychoanalytic Association*. More recently, the film has formed part of the permanent

exhibit at the Collection de l'Art Brut in Lausanne, Switzerland. See the catalogue entry on the Icarus Films website: icarusfilms.com/new2008/hidd.html (22 July 2011).

10 At that time both films were distributed by Scottish Screen, an organisation now merged with the Scottish Arts Council and renamed Creative Scotland. Creative Scotland no longer distributes films.

11 In this regard I have learnt not only from my own experience, but also from the generous guidance of Patricio Guzman.

12 The testimony in *A Massacre Foretold* is given careful consideration by José Rabasa (2010). See also Sarkar and Walker 2009.

13 WACC and Interfilm-SIGNIS are Protestant and Catholic Christian organisations that run the Ecumenical prizes at a variety of international festivals including Cannes and Berlin.

14 The reception of the film in Mexico is more complex than can be communicated here. It is worth mentioning, however, that whilst the film received attention and praise from certain quarters of the Mexican media, the media outlets most often recognised as having a bias towards the former ruling party of the PRI were notable by their silence. Rather than criticise the film as I had expected, it is perhaps not co-incidental that in the same month of the 'high profile' Morelia screening a renewed campaign of what is know as the 'official version' of the Acteal massacre began. This campaign was led by the publication in 2007 of an article by Héctor Aguilar Camín in the magazine *Nexos* and culminated in the release of 29 of those accused of the Acteal massacre (who had already admitted their guilt) on technical grounds by the Supreme Court of Mexico in August 2009.

15 For more on this see Shapiro 2008: 2.

16 *A Massacre Foretold* has screened at the following festivals: Edinburgh International Film Festival, Scotland, 2007 (www.edfilmfest.org.uk); El Festival Internacional de Cine de Morelia (FICM), Mexico, 2007 (www.moreliafilmfest.com); ¡Vamos! Festival, Newcastle, UK, 2007 (www.vamosfestival.com); Kosmorama Trondheim International Film Festival, Norway, 2008 (www.kosmorama.no); Festival International du Film des Droits de l'Homme, Paris, France, 2008 (www.alliance-cine.org/paris); Montreal First Peoples' Festival, Canada, 2008 (www.nativelynx.qc.ca); Providence Latin American Film Festival, U.S, 2008 (plaff.org); Document Human Rights Film Festival, Glasgow, Scotland, 2008 (documentfilmfestival.org); Planet in Focus Environmental Film Festival (planetinfocus.org), Ontario, Canada, 2008; Columbian Film Festival, London, 2008 (no website); DocsDF International Film Festival, Mexico, 2008 (www.docsdf.org/en); International Festival of Cinema, Peace and Human Rights,

Valencia, Spain, 2008 (no website); Movies that Matter, The Hague, Netherlands, 2009 (www.moviesthatmatter.nl); Festival de Cine y Derechos Humanos, Barcelona, 2009 (www.festivaldecineyderechoshumanos.com/eng/human_rights_filmfestbarcelona.html); Festival Cine Bolivia, Bolivia, 2009 (www.festivalcinebolivia.org); Addis International Film Festival, Addis Ababa, Ethiopia, 2009 (www.addisfilmfestival.org); Docudays International Human Rights Documentary Film Festival, Ukraine, 2009 (docudays.org.ua/2010/en); Cine en Derechos Humanos, Mexico, 2009 (www.cinepolis.com.mx/cine-derechos-humanos); XXVI Festival de Cine de Bogotá, 2009 (xxviii.bogocine.com); Vancouver Amnesty International Film Festival, 2009 (van.amnestyfilmfest.ca); El Mundo Al Revés, Latin American Film Festival, University of Alberta, Canada, 2010 (www.facebook.com/pages/El-Mundo-al-Rev%C3%A9s-Latin-American-Film-Festival/142658115791644). (This list is not exhaustive; please excuse any inadvertent omissions.)

[17] Whilst the film continues to screen, I would nevertheless estimate that the most intense period of festival life occurred between August 2007 and November 2009, a period of roughly two years.

[18] An official complaint against Zedillo has been lodged by the Chiapas-based Centro de Derechos Humanos Fray Bartolome de las Casas (CDHFBC) to the Inter-American Court on Human Rights (IACHR), in which evidence is presented accusing the former president and several military leaders in his administration of supporting the creation of paramilitary groups to suppress sympathisers of the Zapatista Army of National Liberation, and demanding that he face trial as one of the 'intellectual authors' of the massacre at Acteal.

[19] As a consequence, several Human Rights organisations, including Amnesty International, have renewed their call to the Mexican authorities for a full judicial enquiry, and have called upon the Inter-American Court on Human Rights (IACHR) to take action.

[20] Apart from historical links with Spain, Europe remains an important site of activism on Mexican issues mainly as a result of the political experiment of the Zapatista rebel movement that has, in turn, inspired a broad coalition of European leftist and progressive movements that share a degree of co-ordination in relation to visiting speakers and film screenings. For more on this solidarity, see Olesen 2004.

[21] One example of a positive initiative in this regard is the Ambulante touring documentary festival in Mexico. For more information, see: www.ambulante.com.mx.

Voices from the Waters: International Travelling Film Festival on Water

Georgekutty A.L.

Dedicated to the rivers and streams of the universe.

> Everything on earth bristled, the bramble
> pricked and the green thread
> bit, the petal fell
> until the only flower was the falling.
> Water is different,
> has no direction but beauty,
> runs through all dreams of colour,
> takes bright lessons
> from the rock
> and in those occupations works out
> the unbroken duties of the foam.

Water, Pablo Neruda (1997: 221)

Once upon a time, not so long ago, in the1950s, before Nehru started erecting the 'temples of modern India', the waters of India flowed freely. Streams, brooks and rivers were plentiful. Freshwater fish was a delicacy enjoyed daily by villagers. It was there for the asking. Women washed clothes without much worry about where the water came from, children played around the streams. After washing and bathing they could carry water from the same stream for drinking and cooking at home.

Later years brought about the demise of most of the brooks, streams and rivers. The first thing to go was the freshwater fish from the lunch menu of the villagers as the government issued orders banning fishing in the streams and rivers. Then, slowly, the rich farmlands where the vegetation grew in abundance were submerged under the 'modern temple' dams. The waters of the hills, streams and rivers soon dried up as a result of mindless deforestation. The government took control of the waters that remained, preventing farmers from using it for agriculture, in order to replenish underground reserves and prevent the total exhaustion of these supplies within the next five years. Peasants stopped cultivating crops. Some of those who used to cultivate have committed suicide. As time passed, the Narmada River got snared by the Asuras and the Ganges became a cesspool at her holiest site. Sewage and waste contaminated the rivers and lakes of all the major cities in India. Water became a commodity for sale.

Voices from the Waters are the voices of people who are deeply committed to water issues. We take people to the water: to see and listen to her manifold stories. Water is essential for all living things – a fundamental right for humans and all forms of life. We celebrate the right of water to be free from exploitation and commodification.

Voices from the Waters (www.voicesfromthewaters.com) in Bangalore, is the largest international film festival concerned with water. It explores the many dimensions of the water crisis. Our programming educates on environmental issues such as water scarcity and conservation, floods and droughts, global warming and climate change, deforestation and its effects, water and life, and the holistic revival of bodies of water. The festival aims to motivate people to engage in water conservation and sanitation in order to improve the quality of drinking water and the quality of life.

We also take on the human issues of water – the struggles and conflicts, sanitation and health, dams and the displaced, discrimination and distribution. And we show how all these issues are intertwined; like the waters of the earth, these issues come together. Voices from the Waters reaches out to students, filmmakers, artists, water activists, architects, engineers, educators, policy-makers and to other film festivals. A festival by design, it has become a movement in reality.

Voices from the Waters Film Festival is a voyage through the waters of the universe. The festival is a celebration and an act of worship of water. Water brings us joy when it is abundant, pain and sorrow when it is absent. We pray for her mercy when she is a deluge. She is indeed a goddess, albeit much abused across today's world. We proffer this festival to those who cherish water as life, to light a lamp to celebrate her reincarnation in a form as free as we found her once up on a time. We thank the many film directors who for the past five years have lit up the screen of this altar.

Voices from the Waters does not pontificate, but rather expresses anguish and concern at the state of our waters. There is a thread running throughout the festival: we need to liberate rivers and streams from the present utilitarian approach. Water respects neither geographical boundaries nor corporate priorities. Its nature is to be pure and to flow freely, and thus to nurture life and create cultures, civilisations, dreams and metaphors.

The Water Crisis

South India – in fact the whole of India and the Third World – is a hotbed of water issues. Lakes are being auctioned off in the name of urban redevelopment, rivers are leased out to multinational corporations and privatisation leads to the disenfranchisement of the people.

Once the temples of modern India, the country's water sources have now become mechanisms for massive displacement and migration as a result of the mindless construction of mega dams, of bad river management policies, of scarcity and pollution. The country is constantly reeling either from drought or deluge, livelihoods are being lost, access to clean water for the common man is getting more and more difficult, privatisation of water looms large, inequity in water distribution and management is rife, the ancient rivers and their rich ecosystems are fast disappearing and turning into sewage canals under the brunt of urban sprawl, development and the incessant exploitation of resources. With little access to clean water, health crises loom large, as do problems around the availability of food, shelter and the other necessities for life on the planet and for human dignity. In addition to natural and man-made disasters, there is the sensitive issue of territorial rights over border-defining rivers, which has been the cause of much upheaval in different parts of India. From our perspective, the biggest problem is the lack of public awareness, which allows crimes of exploitation to carry on unchecked. These stories of man-made ecological disasters are rarely reported in the mainstream media, making films that feature them crucial to the education process. It is essential that the public be informed and made aware of the urgency of these issues. Otherwise a bleak future awaits us.

The water crisis is global and the regions worst affected are Asia, Africa and South America. In India, clean drinking water is a luxury, not an ever-present staple of life. Uninterrupted water supply to the citizens is non-existent; even the affluent residential areas receive water only once every two days. Every river in every city in India is turned into sewage. The majority of people in all the major cities and towns live on very little water, which is supplied by private tankers and tube wells. Most of the available water is contaminated due to poor sanitation facilities, leading to serious health problems and restricted agricultural activity. In the villages, too, people walk for miles to procure their drinking water and, because their livelihood is affected by having insufficient water to carry on their agricultural activities, they migrate to the cities and towns where they are forced to live in terrible poverty bordering on destitution.

Newspapers carry articles that highlight the enormity of the issue, such as the report published in *The Hindu* stating that a 'drinking water crisis looms large in over 4000 villages and 38 towns in 12 districts of Karnataka' (Kumar 2011). Most states in India suffer from a shortage of drinking water and we all need to act together to avert the catastrophe of a complete depletion of ground water in India within the next decade. All life here will be affected. There is an imminent crisis and we all need to act together to avert a catastrophe-in-waiting. To mitigate this crisis the Bangalore Development Authority has passed an order making it mandatory for all the big industrial and residential structures to have rainwater conservation facilities.

Water and Cinema

Water courses through films. It always has. Thunderstorms, rivers, crashing waves – these constitute metaphors that accentuate the mood and meaning of a scene. Waterfalls bring enchantment; torrential downpours become an expression of turbulence; a swim in calm waters represents redemption and new beginnings. Water is a part of our arts. It is a part of our mood. It is also a crucial part of our social and political worlds; and films address this, too.

Scores of documentary filmmakers across the globe have explored the theme of water, as have filmmakers across India and South Asia. *Thousand Days and a Dream* (C. Sarathchandran and P. Baburaj, India, 1996) documents the five-year struggle against Coca-Cola in Plachimada, a village in Kerala, where excessive mining of ground water resulted in water scarcity and the degradation of water quality. *Cutting Off a Lifeline* (Saraswati Kavula, India, 2006) takes on the pollution of the river Musi, tainted both by industrial waste and sewage, as it flows into the city of Hyderabad, the capital of Andhra Pradesh. The film chronicles the negligence that has ruined the livelihoods of the villagers downstream, who have only this water for their farms and livestock.

Lost livelihood is not the only danger; displacement is another on-going concern. *Village of Dust and City of Water* (Sanjay Barnela and Vasant Saberwa, India, 2006) shows the diversion of water from the villages to the cities. In the face of the resulting shortage, people walk miles to fetch a pot of water, or migrate in droves to the cities. Meanwhile, *Shadows of Tehri* (Anirban Dutta, India, 2009) shows the desolate ruins of the township of Tehri, which is about to be submerged under water due to dam construction.

Then there is Ganges, the spiritual and ecological core of India, which has been the subject of more than a few documentaries. *Ganges from the Ground Up* (Yves Sadurani and Miriam Ciscar, India/France, 2006) offers a portrait of the river and expresses concern over erosion. The erosion and its impact on villagers is also the topic of *Bhangon* (*Erosion,* Sourav Sarangi, India, 2006). Erosion has continued unabated since the Government of India constructed a barrage at Farraka near the border with Bangladesh. Torrential rain in June-July 2011 has left another 20,000 people completely dispossessed. As one of the victims interviewed in the film *Erosion,* asks:

The government doesn't consider loss of property due to erosion a natural calamity, hence no compensation is paid. Over 30 lakhs people lost their livelihood and live in penury due to river erosion in the districts of Malda and Murshidabad in West Bengal. If it is not a natural calamity, then what is it?

The concern over rivers and waters is not limited to documentary. Fiction feature films *Thanneer, Thaneer* (K. Balachander, India, 1981), *Bara* (Mysore Shrivinas Sathyu, India, 1980) and *Bangarwadi* (Amol Palekar, India, 1995), raise the problem of the worldwide shortage of water and the politics it generates. Satyajit Ray's internationally-acclaimed film *Ganshatru* (*An Enemy of the People*, India, 1990), a loose adaptation of Henrik Ibsen's *An Enemy of the People*, tells the story of a doctor who attempts to alert the public to the source of an epidemic: the contaminated water from the town's temple (and primary tourist attraction). The owner of the temple – a powerful industrialist who also owns the hospital – and other town officials reject these allegations, denying that the holy water is tainted and refusing to shut down the temple for repairs. In the process, it is the doctor who is shunned as 'the enemy of the people'.

These are only a few of the many films that address the vast number of water issues at play in India. Natural phenomena like drought and deluge challenge lives and livelihoods, but environmental issues are just as much man-made.

The Festival: Beginnings

In 2004, with these issues in mind, the Bangalore Film Society, together with a few voluntary organisations in Bangalore, initiated a forum titled *Water Journeys, Forum for the Fundamental Right to Water.* It reached out to the youth with the objective of creating awareness of the increasing scarcity of potable water for the poor and of engaging people in water conservation projects. The response to the event was encouraging. We mobilised college students from Bangalore to demonstrate against the privatisation of water by multinational corporations, in particular Coca-Cola and Pepsi. The Government of India is actively promoting the privatisation of water.[2]

At this juncture, however, we also realised that there were water issues not connected with privatisation. For example, the diversion of water from the villages to the cities and the massive use of fresh water by industry and hybrid agriculture, posed additional problems. The first casualty of minerals mining is underground water. Industrialisation and massive urban development have caused river pollution, the deaths of rivers and lakes, floods, droughts, global warming and climate change. Voices from the Waters International Film Festival came about as an attempt to string together the various ways through which water affects our lives and show how universal these issues are.

Excited by the interest our event had created and wishing to extend the discussion beyond that of privatisation, the following year (2005) we launched the first Voices from the Waters International Film Festival. We wanted to reach out to the uninitiated, the general public, with an emphasis on youth and students. And we wanted to bring together grass-roots level water activists, scientists, policy-makers, filmmakers, lecturers, scholars, artists, architects and working professionals from various fields, to engage in a process of learning and debate on various water issues from around the world in an effort to help resolve the growing potable water crisis. The film festival was developed as a tool to counter ignorance and apathy by exposing audiences to these issues, as well as by creating discussion and debate. To us, such awareness building is the first step towards community involvement.

Because the water conflict affects everyone and everywhere in India, from the dry canals of Rajasthan to the sunken town of Tehri, we decided upon a festival that travels across India throughout the calendar year. Although the principal screenings take place in August in six venues in Bangalore (Alliance Française, Jawhar Bal Bhavan, Badami

House, MES College, Suchitra Film Society and YWCA Bangalore), we also show films in other locations (such as St. Joseph's Arts and Science College, Christ College, Mount Carmel College and many high schools located in Bangalore) and organise screenings at different times throughout the calendar year. Prior to the screenings, college students are encouraged to participate in our 'Walk for Water' (an initiative by Samvada, one of the festival's partners, that works primarily with college students). In addition, we visit colleges with films from previous years in order to motivate interest in the issue and boost the upcoming festival's attendance. After an initial trial-and-error period, experimenting with suitable dates, the festival has now settled on the last week of August in order to enable the participation of maximum number of high school and college students. The festival lasts for three days from 10.30am to 8.30pm, with photographic and art exhibitions at the main venue. So far we have been receiving over 100 entries a year from across the world, from which we select about 35 to 40 films. The selection is overseen by a group of documentary filmmakers, film critics and social activists. The festival showcases shorts, animation, full-length features and, occasionally, fiction films, if they are in keeping with the theme of the festival (as in the case of the aforementioned *Bara*). About 6,000 people watch the films each day across the various locations, making it one of the biggest film festivals in the world.

Throughout the main event, we offer panels and Q&As with filmmakers and activists in order to educate the public about water issues and to facilitate networking among those in attendance. Meanwhile, other arts are also marshalled to give greater expression to the issues. Paintings, photographs and art-installations that highlight water issues, are exhibited at the main festival venue, while the recital of songs in praise of water and street theatre contribute to the feeling of a genuine festival in celebration of water. We also work on the publication and distribution of brochures, posters and banners. The festival concludes with a day-long conference on water issues; in 2010, the subject was 'The Politics of Water'. This year the conference theme is ground water, with a view to making recommendations on the ground water policy currently being formulated by the Government of India.

Beyond Bangalore

Because Voices from the Waters is conceived as a travelling film festival, after their première in Bangalore selected films are screened in a variety of locations, including colleges across Karnataka, non-governmental organisations and in small towns and villages across India. These are followed by directed discussion. We see this as one of the festival's most important facets as it significantly extends the outreach work of the festival, showing films and sharing experience with other cities, schools, colleges, small towns and villages. Here we engage audiences young and old and from all walks of life, teaching them about water issues both near and far. The films we include in the travelling programme are not only films on water issues, but also films that offer inspiring portraits of alternative and sustainable projects. We show people the problems and what can be done – what is being done – to help. This outreach is crucial to our success.

Since we began five years ago, our mission has evolved. Awareness remains key, as we want the public to be aware of the shortage of potable water across the globe, and to understand the causes of this scarcity as well as some of the solutions. Festival programmes of screenings and discussion foster explorations of water availability, use and conservation, while the variety of participants, from activists and policy-makers to young people and students, helps to encourage deeper reflection about development practices and policies that would enhance water conservation. The networking that takes place in the festival, the conference and the additional screenings, help to build links among agencies dedicated to protection and preservation (including Voices from the Waters) and these meetings help us in the greater challenge of developing specific critiques of state and central government water policies. These challenges help us to rethink development and economic growth plans in light of environmental concerns. Our village screenings and educational screenings also have aims beyond raising awareness: recently, we discussed traditional and organic farming with village farmers, a project that also involved the use of seeds that need less water and are more cost effective. And in the schools we used screenings to motivate students to participate in reforestation projects around both wastelands and the catchment areas of rivers and streams.

We call the Voices from the Waters International Film Festival a movement and, as a movement, it has been growing. Groups and institutions are coming on board, expressing interest in using this festival to promote the water cause and to involve local activists. We plan to organise more screenings and festivals throughout India, but we also have help. Karnataka Chalanachitra Academy (KCA) is an academy which organises film festivals and film studies in Bangalore, Karnatka, and it has been responsible for taking this festival to all the major cities and towns of Karnataka, including Mysore, Shimoga and Hassan. Similarly, the Bangalore Film Society has taken the festival to Karim Nagar and Vizakha Pattanam in Andhra Pradesh. The Cochin International Film Festival, Kerala, rural colleges in the area of Manathavady, Kerala, Sacred Heart College in Thirupur, Don Bosco Media Institute and Alliance Française de Chennai in Tamil Nadu, have already organised events related to our festival, with many more being planned.

Over the past five years, we have developed partnerships that have strengthened our work at home and abroad. We benefit from the participation of film academies and film societies such as KCA, Suchitra Film Society and the Federation of Film Societies of India (FFSI), cultural organisations such as Alliance Française de Bangalore and educational institutions including CMR College and Christ University. A great many of our partners are social justice organisations. These include the Charter for Human Responsibilities – Asia Chapter; the Society for Voluntary Action Revitalization and Justice (formerly Oxfam India Society); the Young Women's Christian Association (YWCA) at Bangalore; Samvada, a youth-focused organisation dedicated to personal and social change; and Visthar, a secular non-profit organisation focused on issues of poverty, displacement and marginalised communities.

And then, there are the film festival partners. Finger Lakes Environmental Film Festival in Ithaca, New York (www.ithaca.edu/fleff10) has come on as a partner, whilst others across the world have utilised our collection of films for their festivals. The United Nations University in Tokyo (unu.edu) has contacted us with an interest in organising a strand of our festival in Japan. These responses affirm the international relevance of the film festival, its cause, its archives and its practices. Our festival has become a key node in a global movement.

Works Cited

Kumar, R. Krishna (2011) *The Hindu*, 12 April. On-line. Available HTTP: http://www.hindu.com/2007/06/12/stories/2007061213200300.htm (5 August 2011).

Neruda, Pablo (1997) *Full Woman, Fleshly Apple, Hot Moon: Selected Poems of Pablo Neruda*, trans. Stephen Mitchell. London/New York: Harper Collins.

Notes

1   The 'Temples of Modern India' are Nehru's vision of India's progress and development – mega-dams constructed to tame the rivers and generate electricity and water for the irrigation of arid lands; however, these dams have submerged hundreds of thousands of hectares of fertile agricultural land along the river basin and have displaced hundreds of thousands of people from their natural habitat without either proper relocation or the paying of adequate compensation. The biggest opposition to the mega-dams is organised by Narmada Bachao Andolan and led by Medha Patkar; it is still fighting to adequately relocate the displaced tribes. Such opposition to the construction of mega-dams is relentlessly and ruthlessly suppressed. An additional problem faced by the peasants struggling to retain the arable land, is the creation of special economic zones to promote mining and industrialisation, which also impinge on the water required for agriculture.

2   Water Journeys, Forum for the Fundamental Right to Water and Voices from the Waters International Film Festival, are spontaneous initiatives of institutions and individuals who are deeply concerned about the huge water crisis facing the country. The UN Decade of Water has little to do with local initiatives to restore fresh water reserves. UN funds go to large players in the field that organise government-level consultations and to the government departments managing water. The UN Decade of Water did not really help the Festival obtain funds, though we applied to a few donor agencies offering grants for water issues. In 2007 and 2008 we obtained small grants from Arghyam, a local donor agency working on water issues, and in 2010 a small grant from the Ministry of Information and Broadcasting of the Government of India New Delhi. Most of the support for the festival comes through partnerships and individual donations.

Mediterranean Encounters in Rabat: Rencontres méditerranéennes cinéma et droits de l'Homme

Robert A. Rosenstone

An email inviting me to attend a human rights film festival in Morocco in autumn 2009 came as a complete surprise. For one thing, I was only vaguely aware that such festivals existed. For another, I am a historian with a long list of essays and books stretching over four decades, many of them dealing with radical political and social movements, but not a single work of mine has ever taken up in any direct way issues of human rights. My main connection to the topic, other than signing a few petitions, has largely been financial. Every year I make a contribution to Human Rights Watch, and some years I have attended its annual, very glitzy dinner in Beverly Hills, where you get to rub shoulders with international activists and Hollywood celebrities.

However, the organisers of the festival had not made a mistake. The invitation included a request that I appear on two panels – 'Cinema and University Curricula' and 'Cinema and History' – and asked if I would be willing to deliver a similar seminar to students at Mohammed V University. For me, these were perfect subjects, since my research over the last two decades, and my most recent academic books, have been detailed explorations of the problematics of the relationship between history and film (see Rosenstone 1995 and 2006).

Most interesting was the fact that some of the advance material sent to me about the panels for *Rencontres méditerranéennes cinéma et droits de l'Homme* (Mediterranean Encounters: Cinema and the Rights of Man, www.rmcdh.ma) seemed to suggest that a right to history (and cinema?) should be included among the list of human rights. This is certainly a unique and interesting idea: a right to know the past, free of manipulation and interference by governments, school boards and other pressure groups, would no doubt serve to restructure curricula around the world. For history, as taught in the nation state in the last couple of centuries, has certainly been less concerned with locating the truth(s) of the past than with creating good and patriotic citizens.

That the official invitation, which arrived after my initial acceptance, explained that the event was under the patronage of His Majesty King Mohammed VI, made the issue of a possible right to history even more compelling. The idea for and the organisation of the festival did not, however, come from the Palace, but from the Moroccan Consultative Council on the Rights of Man, 'a national and independent institution', according to its press releases 'for the protection and promotion of Human Rights in Morocco'. Founded in 1990, reorganised in 2001, and initially led by Driss Benzekri, who is considered the Nelson Mandela of Morocco, the Council has been presided over since 2007 by Ahmed Herzenni, a PhD in Anthropology from the University of Kentucky who also spent some years as a political prisoner under a former regime.

The festival took place 12-15 November 2009 in Rabat, a town I had avoided on two previous trips to Morocco because of what you always hear – that it is a drab and boring place filled with government bureaucrats and not worth a visit. Not so, I would say now, after having spent 10 days there. Rabat may not have the claustrophobic exoticism of Fez, the carnival qualities of Marrakesh, the (cinematic?) history of Casablanca, or the desert and palm oases which surround Ouarzazate, but it is a small and charming city, with vast and splendid walls, a bustling and colourful Medina, and an elegant European quarter with cafes and arcades that remind you of the fairer side of a colonial heritage.

The organisation of events in Rabat almost made it seem as if two different festivals were in progress. The one during the daytime was as serious and earnest as I, for one, imagined a Human Rights festival would be. From nine in the morning until late afternoon each day there were panel discussions and screenings of documentaries devoted to the multifarious violations of human rights in the countries bordering the Mediterranean, with excursions into distant lands, such as Cambodia and Peru. Films explored violence against women, honour killing in Kurdistan, the death penalty in Turkey, the 'bloody decade' in Algeria, genocide in Srebenica, family law in Morocco and the problem of state terror in various lands. Panels made up of representatives from a wide variety of countries bordering on the Mediterranean – Lebanon, Turkey, Palestine, Morocco, Algeria, Italy, France, Greece, Bosnia, Spain – and comprising activists, attorneys, social workers, psychologists, journalists, educators, writers and directors explored and analysed topics such as the struggles of women both North and South of the Mediterranean, trafficking throughout the region, and questions of immigration from South to North.

Evenings were a very different story, full of bright lights, glamour, TV cameras, red carpets and *paparazzi*, as we filed into the plush Theatre National Mohamed V for a dramatic feature. When the film was finished, official participants – at least a hundred of us – were taken to a fancy restaurant which featured *maitre d's* in tuxedos and waiters in spiffy uniforms. Here, a large orchestra entertained us with Arabic and European musical numbers as we tried our best to work our way through all the varied savoury dishes placed before us in four- and five-course meals that did not end until well past midnight. At the many tables activists and academics mixed somewhat uneasily with officials from various government agencies (the foreign minister was there one night, the head of the treasury another), representatives of the diplomatic corps, students from local universities and members of the Consultative Council on the Rights of Man. From a couple of the latter I learned that the festival did have its doubters and opponents, those who thought such a spectacle a misuse of funds and an inappropriate vehicle for promoting human rights in Morocco. This was the only negative reaction to the event that I encountered. During my ten days in Rabat, there were no visible public demonstrations or anti-government protests over issues of Human Rights.

If the surroundings and format of the evening screenings smacked of Hollywood, or even Cannes, the four feature films did not. Each dealt directly with questions of human rights, even though one of them, *Al Hadoud* (*Borders*, Syria, 1987) by veteran director Douraid Lahham (billed as the Syrian Woody Allen) was a comedy which tells the story of a traveller (played by the director) who loses his passport somewhere between his unnamed homeland and an unnamed neighbouring country (I could not helping thinking Syria and Lebanon). When officials at both borders block him from entering, he sets up residence in the small No Man's Land between the two, and then manages to open a restaurant which becomes so fashionable that he eventually prospers enough to be allowed back into his homeland. Though other filmmakers and actors were present in Rabat, Lahham was clearly the festival's star and the screening of *Al Hadoud* was followed by a televised ceremony paying homage to his entire body of work (30 feature films and numerous television productions).

There was no humour whatsoever in the opening night feature, *Harragas* (Algeria/France, 2009), the seventeenth film by French-

Algerian beur director Merzak Allouache, in attendance alongside his lead actors. *Harragas* is a word used to describe those refugees from all over the continent who try to cross the sea from the Mahgreb to Europe. The film follows one group of Arabs and Africans from farther south as they gather in the northern Algerian port city of Mostaganem, hire a smuggler with a fragile rowboat and launch into the crossing on what proves to be a harrowing, dangerous and, for some of them, fatal journey. A certain amount of dark humour does touch Elia Suleiman's *Le temps qu'il reste* (*The Time That Remains*, France/Belgium/UK/Italy, 2009), a kind of combined autobiography and history of this Nazareth-born Arab-Israeli director's family, from the creation of Israel to the present day. Distanced and slightly surreal in its aesthetic (as befits the status of Arab-Israelis?), the work is less about the iniquities of the Israeli Government than about the futility and absurdities of the situations in which Suleiman and his family live – Palestinian children at school singing patriotic Israeli songs in Hebrew, or the main character, played by the director himself, moving through events without ever uttering a word; a kind of Arab Buster Keaton with a deadpan expression, even during the most troubling of moments.

The fourth and final of the evening dramas was Peruvian director Claudia Llosa's film, *La teta asustada* (Spain/Peru, 2009) – literally *The Frightened Teat*, but translated for presumably puritanical English-speaking audiences as *The Milk of Sorrow* – which won a Golden Bear Award at the Berlin Film Festival and was nominated for an Academy Award® as Best Foreign Language Feature. As with a couple of the documentaries, this was clearly part of an attempt to broaden the scope of the festival by showing connections with human rights questions in other parts of the globe. Issues of both class and violence against women are highlighted in this tale of a poor girl who has been raped by soldiers during the government's suppression of the Shining Path guerrillas.

Forced to work as a maid, she is exploited both financially and culturally by a wealthy concert pianist who steals the girl's native melodies for her own compositions, then throws her out when the young woman dares to mention this aloud. At the dinner following the film, we sat next to the Peruvian Ambassador who was so embarrassed by the film's graphic vision of the hardships and brutality of life in the stony, bleak favelas outside Lima, that he spent most of the evening trying to convince us (unsuccessfully) that this portrait of the extremes in Peruvian society was highly fictionalised and exaggerated.

At first the split between the deadly serious daytime events and the more glamorous evenings bothered the puritan in me (How can you enjoy a splendid dinner in a world of horrors where people are starving, being raped and dying at the hands of death squads?), but I quickly came to appreciate this divided schedule. A single day of documentaries and discussions made me feel as if I were drowning in unsolvable problems, and led me to wonder if other participants felt the same. No doubt if you are an activist, the synergy from meeting others involved in the movement for human rights is tonic. No doubt seeing and hearing about the problems and struggles of others renews your dedication, makes you feel part of a worldwide force, an army working for the good of humankind. For a historian, though, and for this historian, whose writing about serious social issues is cushioned by a distance of years and thus far less immediate and pressing, exposure to so many contemporary atrocities made me feel the need to flee into a lighter world. Every day my wife and I would sneak off to the jumbled and colourful Medina for a while, to hunt for bargains in jewellery, scarves, antiques and rugs. When we inevitably bumped into other participants from the festival, feelings of guilt meant that we all had trouble meeting each other's eyes and, after too-hearty greetings, we'd soon enough go our own ways.

The panels in which I participated were held on the first two days of the festival. While most daytime events were scheduled in a utilitarian government building, the opening event, held before a single film had been shown, took place in the highly ornamented, traditional Andalucían-style headquarters of the Consultative Council. With some 80 people in the audience, a number of them students who had attended my seminar at the university the preceding day, four local teachers and I informally took on the topic of 'Cinema and the University Curricula'. Our discussion quickly made it apparent that a human rights film festival could have ancillary agendas, in this case one of interest to those members of the Council who were academics (including Abdhelhay Moudden, the political scientist who was responsible for my invitation). Clearly there was stiff resistance in Moroccan academia to using film as part of university studies and, just as clearly, my authority as a historian who has published extensively on film was being used to bolster the position of my fellow panellists, that it was high time for film to become part of the curriculum. One does not mind being used in a good cause and I was happy to back up the arguments of the others with examples of how film is so widely used in American and European universities in a variety of fields – literature, history, anthropology, psychology, political science and international relations. All of us agreed that, as educators, our topic is the entire world, and since film is a contemporary way of showing the world in action, it must become part of what we offer to our students.

For the second panel, 'Cinema as a Witness to History', I was joined by three Moroccan filmmakers, Ali Essafi, Hassan Ben Jalloun and Saâd Chraïbi. While I gave a mini-lecture of a kind I have often delivered before – how historical films arise out of the shortcomings of academic history and how we need to communicate the past to the public in a form it understands and likes – my fellow panellists focused more on the reasons why Morocco needed to produce more historical films, both documentaries and dramatic features. Benjelloun, in particular, strongly advanced the argument that film was a good way of raising controversial historical issues which parents refuse to talk about with their children, and that schools tend to ignore. Calling for films that would bypass the self-censorship of academics and inform the world about the 'black' years in Moroccan history (or the Years of Lead as they are called), he insisted that by raising issues on which there has been silence, film can be a major factor in promoting human rights.

That notion runs parallel to a question that seemed to hang over all the proceedings in Rabat, one voiced a couple of times to me by locals: what exactly does a film festival like this one do for human rights? Does Morocco really have something to gain by sharing films, panels, ideas and contacts with activists from around the Mediterranean? Or should the resources going into all this public hoopla be used on more specific problems at home? I certainly cannot provide definitive answers, for they belong to the participants whose life work is involved with human rights. Yet for me the festival was, overall, a bracing event which has some distant parallels in the annual meetings of various historical associations. To be a historian is to be generally misunderstood and, occasionally, insulted (how often when identified at a party to a new acquaintance, does one hear the phrase 'History was my least favourite subject in school'?). Your narrow concerns as a specialist mean that only a small number of people in the world either care, or are interested, in the particular research topics to which you devote most of your waking hours. Annual meetings are a way of encountering those few who are interested in similar issues and ideas, and they allow you to return to your university buoyed up and full of the notion that what you are doing makes a difference to someone. No doubt a festival such as the one in Rabat does the same for those involved in the struggle for human rights.

It also must do something for the general public. The daytime documentaries and panels may not have drawn huge audiences (75-100 was common), but the Theatre National, which holds at least 1,000 people, was jammed for every evening film. One does not need to be a specialist in reception theory to understand that some, perhaps many, people who don't normally worry over issues of human rights were at least exposed to serious social questions during these days. But how to assess the impact? Even the organisers did not seem certain, though my discussions with President Ahmed Herzenni and others involved in the Council suggested that the festival was a kind of experiment, a tentative step of this young organisation to spread the word in the country and abroad, that the important issues of human rights could now be raised in Morocco, and that indeed questions of such rights were something not unique to this country, but were regional, or even worldwide. The debate over the success and future shape of the festival still goes on.

Epilogue: A second Rencontres méditerranéennes took place on 6-9 April 2011 (www.rmcdh.ma). Sitting in Los Angeles and reading the website let me know that the format of the first festival, mixing serious discussion panels and documentaries during the day and big screen dramas in the evening, had continued. Once again topics like human trafficking, slavery and rural education were featured, with one focus on Democracy in the Arab World clearly meant to embrace the recent political upheavals in North Africa and the Middle East. I was happy to see, as at the first event, a panel devoted to Film and History, and particularly gratified to read in the programme that the new tendency to take films seriously as meaningful explorations of the past was founded by none other than Hayden White and yours truly. Now if only they could raise the money to bring me back for the third festival...

Works Cited

Rosenstone, Robert A. (1995) *Visions of the Past: The Challenge to Our Idea of History*. Cambridge, Mass./London: Harvard University Press.
_____ (2006) *History on Film/Film on History*. Harlow/New York: Longman/Pearson.

Human Rights Film Festivals and Human Rights Education: The Human Rights Arts and Film Festival (HRAFF), Australia

Clare Muller

The last two decades have seen the emergence and proliferation of film festivals dedicated to the promotion and encouragement of a global human rights culture. Appearing throughout Europe, Africa, Latin America and the Asia-Pacific region, such festivals aim to explore the complexities and predicaments of the international system of human rights. Their engagement with film brings the often abstract and remote concepts of human rights down to an accessible level, adding a refreshing dimension to the often beleaguered perception of 'human rights'.

Human rights films have a somewhat 'complicated identity' (Lobato 2009: 133) in pairing human rights content with the film festival institution. One World film festival (www.oneworld.cz) director Igor Blažević provides the most succinct definition of human rights festivals as being 'focused on information and testimony rather than art and entertainment' and aiming for 'awareness building and *education*' (2009: 14, emphasis added). Indeed, the growing practice of human rights film festivals should not be seen in isolation, but rather as part of, and pertaining to, a broader, concerted shift in focus towards education that is currently defining the international movement of human rights. More than ever before, humanitarian nongovernmental organisations (NGOs) are moving further away from their original function as providers, distancing themselves from their role as advocates and embracing their new-found responsibilities as educators.

The United Nations Decade for Human Rights Education (1995-2005) proved instrumental in the push to implement worldwide educational programmes designed to create shared values and beliefs and a global ethical system. International institutions and national governments began adopting the rhetoric of human rights education into policies and practices. With this decade now over, the practice of human rights education continues to remain locked in what human rights theorist John Donnelly (1989) has described as a mixture of strong promotion and weak implementation.

Despite their support for a human rights doctrine, nation states have, for various reasons, been largely noncommittal in systematically introducing human rights education into national education systems. The task of fostering a global culture of human rights lies increasingly with the non-profit sector.

By extension, the human rights film festival network is part of this non-profit sector (see Iordanova 2009); its work has developed organically to either fill a void in any systematic national human rights education implementation or to work in conjunction with existing policy and practice. This network of festivals may not see itself as directly involved in a wider transformation of educational agendas, but its primary motivation of fostering a greater global culture of human rights awareness makes its task intrinsically educational. In the provision of a refreshing, alternative and innovative educational experience for audiences who may be 'much more geared towards consuming moving images than the written word' (Bronkhorst 2009: 126), human rights film festivals secure continuous engagement with the human rights movement.

Film education – or, rather, the use of film for teaching and learning purposes – is becoming an increasingly accepted tool in educational practice, particularly within the realm of human rights and peace education. Cinematic education advocate Kevin Sealey, suggests that, alongside normative educational practice, film is a powerful tool whose entertaining qualities allow increased engagement and learning with subject matter which 'has traditionally been considered too tedious or abstract to be taught through written text or discussion' (2008: 10).

The Australian Human Rights Arts and Film Festival

The Australian Human Rights Arts and Film Festival (HRAFF) (hraff.org. au) is a relatively recent addition to the global network of film festivals aiming to continue public engagement and secure government support for the development of a greater culture of human rights. The HRAFF takes place predominantly in May of each year. Following the main event in Melbourne, a selection of the programmes travels to Australian state capitals and regional centres, which, in 2010, included Sydney, Canberra, Brisbane, Adelaide, Perth, Alice Springs and Byron Bay.

The event was modelled directly on its European counterparts. While studying in Copenhagen, HRAFF founder and first director Evelyn Tadros was surprised to discover that, unlike most European democracies, Australia did not have a cultural event dedicated specifically to the representation, discussion and debate of human rights. On her return, she gathered together an enthusiastic and committed group of young professionals and university students from areas as diverse as law, film, art, development and financial services, and launched the Australian Human Rights Arts and Film Festival (HRAFF) in 2007. The first HRAFF festival was held in Melbourne that year.

Since that time, HRAFF has been presenting an expansive and eclectic selection of local and international human rights films. Both in Melbourne and at interstate festivals, the festival has grown significantly in its vision, programme content and quality, with the 2010 HRAFF film component showcasing 40 films from Australian and international directors. Film programmes at HRAFF aim to balance important and relevant political content with exceptional artistic qualities (as defined by Lobato above). The festival also aims to provide a sound and independent basis for the producers of films who often work (and film) in life-threatening and/or strongly-censored political climates (see Bronkhorst 2004).

The institutional structure of the film festival is equally fundamental to the human rights education practice at HRAFF. Dina Iordanova (2009) has previously defined the film festival as a temporary exhibition space, which links together the festival's various stakeholder groups. In an educational context, this unique communal ground provides the means for otherwise unconnected stakeholder groups to foster discussion, debate and action on human rights issues. HRAFF is not only concerned with film, but employs an array of other interactive initiatives, from forum discussions to panel debates and workshops, which are held alongside film screenings. Prominent speakers from a film or human rights-based background are chosen to lead discussions and provide insights and personal experiences or opinions about the causes and potential solutions of the issues presented. The HRAFF annual event also hosts a number of art exhibitions, a poetry slam and presents a full-day music festival, Rhythm and Rights, which showcases local artists from Australia and from overseas. Throughout the year, HRAFF holds a number of fundraisers and corporate screenings and engages with its Schools Education and Outreach Program, which offers an assortment of resources for schools, community groups, government and corporate bodies. Since 2009, HRAFF holds an annual Gala event in Melbourne with a film screening, silent auction and high profile speakers. Through each of these initiatives, discussion and debate on human rights, which develops through the film festival institution, means that, regardless of the opinions presented, a 'culture' of human rights is thus formed.

Despite all the growth of the Outreach Program, however, current educational practice remains somewhat limited. HRAFF is yet to fully recognise and act upon the educational capacities inherent in its use of both film and the film festival structure. A number of practical issues pertinent to the future success and sustainability of HRAFF need to be addressed.

Human rights educator J. Paul Martin, who works on the early stages of development of human rights education programmes, has been calling for a greater degree of 'evaluation and quality control' in the 'recent rapid expansion and popularisation of human rights education' (1997: 599). Through his work, Martin has developed a framework outlining nine primary evaluation categories with educational and human rights-specific criteria, which he regards as key components in the planning and design of human rights initiatives in education. In Martin's assessment, a legitimate and effective human rights education practice requires the successful identification, assessment and implementation of such elements as overall purpose and design, adaptation to local needs, involvement of responsive target groups, planning for continuing institutional development, proven educational leadership and, last but not least, effective educational methods and evaluation techniques (Martin 1997: 599).

This framework offers highly practical and relevant planning evaluation for organisations like HRAFF which are emerging models of human rights education. Accordingly, the following three areas currently stand out as definitive for the human rights education practice at HRAFF.

A. Public Receptiveness and Attendance. The notion that human rights film festivals have a complicated identity stems largely from dilemmas related to what exactly, and to whom specifically, the task of raising awareness and educating about human rights should be focused. Audience receptiveness, attendance and consequent future 'action', are fundamental to providing legitimate and effective human rights education practice. As with all festivals in this network, HRAFF grapples with two seemingly simple yet fundamental questions: whom exactly is HRAFF trying to educate? Who would benefit most from engaging with human rights education through the film festival structure?

The staff at HRAFF are fully aware of this predicament and the harmful consequences of focusing on one specific cohort of the public over another. Each year, they conduct audience polls into public receptiveness and attendance. Poll data supply a good picture of who is attending (and therefore, who is being potentially 'educated'). Audiences fall into two broad yet distinct groups: those highly engaged with human rights issues and those seeking an alternative cinematic experience. The second group do not necessarily consider themselves active members of the human rights movement, yet usually have had some prior exposure to films on human rights topics. Data from 2008 identified that 38.4 per cent of the audience were engaging with human rights for the first time (HRAFF Marketing Report 2009: 16). HRAFF's newly implemented annual Gala, which was hosted in both 2009 and 2010, attracts a slightly broader demographic than the festival itself. Generally speaking, the Gala appeals to a more mature age (and income) bracket and reaches out to a more glamorous, less politicised and, perhaps, more conservative audience.

In 2009, market research into audience demographics at HRAFF identified three target groups, which included HRAFF's current and desirable audiences: (1) the Young Trendy Alternative cohort; (2) the Secure Professional cohort; and (3) the Socially Aware cohort. These categories were considered the most 'leverageable' members of HRAFF's audience to date (HRAFF Marketing Report 2009).

Based on such research data, HRAFF's priority has been to encourage and motivate those members of the community who already have an active interest in human rights issues, and are thus more likely to act upon about the issues raised, thereby making HRAFF's educational practice both successful and effective. Reaching out to those members of the community who hold a 'rudimentary knowledge' (Martin 1997: 602) of human rights, but suffer from a certain 'compassion fatigue', has proven more problematic. Here, HRAFF's educational practice still remains a work in progress and some believe the festival is mainly preaching to the converted.

B. Institutional Patronage and Actors. Access to a steady source of funding is perhaps the most fundamental factor determining the educational potential of human rights film festivals. In 2011, HRAFF's main source of funding came from an educational institution, RMIT University, alongside a variety of contributions from local, national and international humanitarian NGOs (such as Oxfam Australia, PLAN Australia and Make Poverty History) and from private donations. HRAFF also receives some government funding, contributions from grants from the arts/cultural sector and realises revenues from its own tickets sales during festival time. The annual Gala event is a key funding source. Financial stability based on these sponsors can, however, only go so far. HRAFF's ability to mobilise institutional support beyond those already committed to the human rights movement and secure corporate sponsorship, is by far the most challenging, yet fundamental factor for HRAFF's sustainability in the coming years. As leading festival practitioner Igor Blažević remarks, commercial bodies 'in principle do not like to associate their names with issues that are political or controversial and/or critical' and, while there is the option for HRAFF to align itself with businesses whose corporate goals are in line with supporting social justice, Blažević again reminds us that corporate social responsibility rarely refers to simply supporting the broad notion of 'human rights' itself (2009: 56-57).

C. Organisational Management. The leadership, commitment and work ethic of HRAFF's staff in ensuring the continuation of the festival is extraordinary. Festival practice is overseen, coordinated and run, respectively, by the HRAFF Board and the Festival Director, followed by a small cohort of permanent year-long managers and a large cohort of temporary, seasonal staff, all of whom, bar the current Director Matthew Benetti, are volunteers.

Despite this, organisational management is a pertinent issue threatening the long-term sustainability of the festival; not because it has been ineffective in the past, but because of the uncertainty for the future. The festival's bottom-up development has been secured largely through the natural leadership qualities and abilities of former and current festival directors.

Their commitment to and knowledge of the field, whilst highly commendable, poses problems for future leadership: such savvy leaders will be hard to match or replace. Finding appropriate individuals to continue in such demanding roles will be challenging as the work requires leadership paired with a rich and diverse range of skills and knowledge, all functioning in a precarious context of low-wage capacity and reliance on volunteer labour.

Predictably, HRAFF experiences a high turnover of staff. Each year, knowledge and skills are lost and considerable time and effort is put into recruiting and training new staff members. The type of organisational management problems currently defining HRAFF (as well as other human rights film festivals, more generally) are there to stay until the festival is able is provide robust financial support for its staff members.

The Future: Moving Beyond the Cinema Theatre

One needs to move beyond the idea that the festival educates neutrally. HRAFF is not just an impartial facilitator in the not so impartial task of raising awareness and educating about human rights, fostering a human rights culture and, ultimately, advancing the human rights movement. Four decades ago, radical Latin American educationalist and theorist Paulo Freire made it clear that educational practice is never a neutral concept, but is always a site of cultural politics which, once acquired, is used for politicised action (Freire 1972). Although HRAFF never advocates on behalf on any specific causes and presents itself as a neutral facilitator, the mere fact that the festival aims for stakeholder engagement to move towards greater participation means that its overall approach is motivated by a desire to further the global ideology of human rights.

HRAFF also needs to act to make its educational effort more explicit, by reorientating it in a range of different educational settings. Currently, the human rights education practice at the festival is informal. That is, teaching and learning methods are centred on the traditional film festival structure, which requires active participation from various stakeholders who must turn up at a fixed place and time, year after year. Festival participants are mostly the 'aware', who come with an open-minded, enthusiastic mindset about HRAFF as an alternative educational experience. Whilst keeping this strong foundation, HRAFF could consider branching out into more formal curricular work and into a more diverse community-based educational effort.

A. Formal Education. Building on the existing 'Schools Outreach Program' and integrating HRAFF's work into the Australian formal educational system is significant, not only for festival outreach and sustainability, but also for the current plight of human rights education in Australia. In Australian schools, teaching on matters related to human rights remains sporadic in content and differs dramatically across disciplines and institutions. While researching the state of human rights education in state-run schools in Victoria, human rights lawyer and educator Paula Geber discovered that the few teachers who actively sought to include human rights issues in their pedagogy engaged in such teaching for intensely personal reasons and on an 'ad hoc' basis, usually relying on personal background knowledge or previous experiences, rather than on any systematically designed curriculum (Geber 2008: 32).

The educational capacities of human rights film festivals like HRAFF provide an opportunity for the integration of human rights education into normative schooling. It is relatively easy to set up festival space independently within the school grounds and which different student groups would visit in designated timeslots. The teaching could be facilitated by human rights or film education specialists whose familiarity and knowledge would ensure better consistency and wider coverage.

B. Community-based education. Branching into community-based education allows HRAFF to broaden public engagement to groups that are not part of the festival's current demographic. This requires a reorientation of the festival space whereby, rather than waiting for the audience to come to them, the organisers take the initiative to go and seek the audience out. This approach requires an expansion into the use of different, alternative spaces which have wider public exposure, such as public libraries and community halls. HRAFF's audience outreach is significantly hindered by the use of metropolitan, art house cinema venues. A prime example of possible new areas, then, would be to reach out to rural and regional groups.

Such approaches would take considerable time, effort and funding. To manage this process successfully, HRAFF needs to make it a longterm development goal to avoid stretching staff capacities and diminish the 'burning out' effect.

Human rights film festivals provide an unprecedented opportunity to expand and enhance the notion of effective human rights practice. To ensure that HRAFF's capacity for future growth and sustainability is not limited, the festival's design and implementation need to aim directly into the educational spere, branching out across all areas of non-formal, formal and community-based education.

Works Cited

Blažević, Igor (2009) 'How To Start', in Tereza Porybná (ed.) *Setting Up a Human Rights Film Festival*. Prague: People in Need, 14-23.

Bronkhorst, Dina (2004) *The Human Rights Film: Reflections on its History, Principles and Practices*, Amnesty International Film Festival site, On-line. Available HTTP: http://www.amnesty.nl/filmfestival/essay.doc (11 September 2009).

_____ (2009) 'On Human Rights Film Festivals', in Tereza Porybná (ed.) *Setting Up a Human Rights Film Festival*. Prague: People in Need, 120-6.

Donnelly, Jack (1989) *Universal Human Rights in Theory and Practice*, Ithaca, London: Cornell University Press

Freire, Paulo (1972) *Pedagogy of the Oppressed*. Harmondsworth: Penguin.

Geber, Paula (2008) 'From Convention to Classroom. The Long Road to Human Rights Education', in B. Offord and C. Newell (eds) *Activating Human Rights in Education: Exploring, Innovation and Transformation*. Deakin West, ACT : Australian College of Educators, 29-37.

Human Rights Arts and Film Festival Media Kit (2008) On-line. Available HTTP: http://www.hraff.org.au/media.html (12 April 2009).

HRAFF Marketing Team (2009) *Human Rights Arts and Film Festival Marketing Report August 2009*, Melbourne.

Iordanova, Dina (2009) 'The Film Festival Circuit', in Dina Iordanova with Ragan Rhyne (eds) *FFY1: The Festival Circuit*. St Andrews: St Andrews Film Studies with College Gate Press, 23-40.

Lobato, Heidi (2009) 'Of Course Human Rights Are Not Sexy', in Tereza Porybná (ed.) *Setting Up a Human Rights Film Festival*. Prague: People in Need, pp. 130-8.

Martin, J.Paul (1997) 'The Next Step: Quality Control', in G.J. Andreopoulos and R.P. Claude (eds) *Human Rights Education for the Twenty-First Century*. Philadelphia: University of Pennsylvania Press, 599-622.

Sealey, Kevin Shawn (2008) 'Introduction: Film, Politics and Education: Cinematic Pedagogy Across the Discipline', in Kevin Shawn Sealey (ed.) *Film, Politics and Education: Cinematic Pedagogy Across the Discipline*. New York: Peter Lang, 1-17.

Spring, Joel (2004) *How Educational Ideologies Are Shaping Global Society: Intergovernmental Organisations, NGOs, and the Decline of the Nation State*. Mahwah, New Jersey: Lawerence Erlbaum Asociates, Inc.

Humanist and Poetic Activism:
The Robert Flaherty Film Seminar
in the 1950s

Patricia R. Zimmermann

Operating in the liminal zone between international film festivals, cine clubs, museum screenings, film societies, university film education, sponsored films and artistic retreats, The Robert Flaherty Film Seminar (also known as The Flaherty Seminar) demonstrates the complex, uneven ecologies connecting activism, film festivals and cinema. The Flaherty Seminar problematises the idealisation of activism as the realm of oppositional cinema and radical institutions directly fomenting movements of social change. Instead, an historical analysis of the early formative years of The Flaherty Seminar in the 1950s reveals the deep linkages between film education and activism, where both advocated for a cinema that countered Hollywood mass production, and advanced institutions to develop ideas and foster debates; zones for ideas rather than instruments of craft acquisition. The Flaherty Seminar, then, demonstrates that film education and activism for cinema as an art form were inextricably interwoven in the post-War period. At the seminar, engagement in analysis, discussion and debates about non-commercial cinema, underscored the important collaborations between the informal pedagogy of film societies and the inauguration of formal education in cinema in academia: both constituted proactive ways to restore depth to cinema, to rescue it from commercialism and to reform it through art. And both collaborated with each other to forward these goals.

Frances Flaherty's advocacy for 'The Flaherty Way', a combination of Zen Buddhism, participant observation, deep immersion, poetry, non-preconception and anti-commercialism, underpinned the unique methodology of the seminar's structure and constituted its working activist beliefs. From the beginning, the seminar's programming emanated from these principles, bringing together a mix of various film genres, forms and traditions mapping the emerging independent international cinema sector. Designed as a fully immersive, retreat-like experience, the seminar facilitated non-preconception by promoting heterogeneity both in participants and in programming. The seminar assembled a range of people who worked in various sectors of the non-commercial film world of the 1950s: practitioners, curators, academics, film society programmers, librarians and writers. It also mixed together participants at the early stages of their careers with more seasoned film professionals. The programming also worked to explore non-preconception, expanding beyond documentary to include experimental, narrative, sponsored work and ethnographic films.

The Flaherty Seminar is one of the oldest continuously running gatherings for independent film in the world; it was launched in 1955 by Frances Flaherty, widow of the renowned documentary filmmaker Robert Flaherty (1884-1951). Although Robert Flaherty directed landmark documentary films, it was his wife and collaborator Frances who developed a unique cinematic institution, providing screenings, dialogue, camaraderie and debate, which has endured for over 50 years. The Flaherty Seminar, then, merged the anti-Hollywood, pro-international art cinema thrust of film festivals with advocacy for the burgeoning post-War 16mm non-theatrical distribution and exhibition scene. This blending resulted in The Flaherty Seminar engaging in an activism centred on enhancing both formal and informal film education, in order to deepen cinema as both an art form and intellectual endeavour.

The 'Flaherty Way' was not Robert Flaherty's idea: Frances invented it after her husband's death as a means of advocating a more poetic cinema derived from the 'non-preconception' of materials and people. Frances's 'Flaherty Way' offered a more artisanal, personal way to make films than by the formulaic industrial model based on scripts, planning and marketing. Resolutely anti-Hollywood, the 'Flaherty Way' combined the explorer's journey into the unknown, the ethnographer's cultural observation and the Zen mystic's openness to surroundings. The Flaherty Seminar emerged from Frances's contention that seeing in deeper, more complex ways could be learned through intensive film viewing and vigorous discussion.[1]

The Flaherty Seminar emerged as an activity of the Robert Flaherty Foundation, inaugurated by Frances and by Robert's brother David, after the filmmaker's death in 1951. Initially, the Foundation focused on preserving and circulating Flaherty's films. In her lectures at universities and film societies on behalf of the foundation, Frances advanced a poetic, craft-oriented, independent cinema immunised from the commercial Hollywood system. The seminars occupied a vital interstitial zone between emerging parts of alternative film culture in the 1950s: film societies, 16mm exhibition, educational and industrial films, university film education, film festivals, art theatres and independent cinema outside of the studio system.

The seminar did not operate as a film festival with public screenings of theatrical films. Instead, The Flaherty Seminar functioned as almost the complete opposite: a small gathering on the family farm in Vermont. The seminar promoted conceptual thinking about cinema in the loosely defined non-theatrical sector. This emphasis on critical viewing and lengthy and probing post-screening discussion distinguished it from film festivals. Its expressed purpose was educational – cinema needed to become an intellectual art form. David Flaherty noted in 1960, 'Yes, we think "participants" is a better word to use than "students"'.[2]

The Flaherty Seminar advocated for cinema as an intellectual and almost mystical activity. As Frances contended, 'But, simple as they are, [the films] are little understood, simply because they go against the current – the mighty Niagara – of commercial cinema as projected by Hollywood and projected likewise as "documentary"'.[3]

This particular activism was not, however, focused on radical interventions into Cold War political or social structures. Instead, The Flaherty Seminar promoted a humanist, internationalist and pedagogical purpose. Rather than radical restructurings of society, the first five years of The Flaherty Seminar offered less confrontational politics. It created alliances with various arts, cinema and government institutions related to the burgeoning 16mm non-theatrical film exhibition movement and to the development of international film festivals. The seminar operated in a manner both similar to and different from a film festival: like a film festival, it attracted cinéphiles from programming, curating, museums, production, distribution but, unlike a film festival, it focused upon the idea of 'participants' sharing the same experience in a private, closed setting rather than in an open and public theatrical venue.

During the 1950s, The Robert Flaherty Film Seminar proposed the term 'filmmaker' to suggest a more artisanal, non-commercial mode of production where one person controlled the aesthetic structure, time lines and approach. Frances regularly deployed the term 'filmmaker' in describing Robert Flaherty. The term harboured an activist intention: it suggested an artisanal difference from the division of labour in studio films.

During the 1950s, the festival world was relatively small. The Edinburgh International Film Festival (www.edfilmfest.org.uk) started in 1947 and the Berlin Film Festival (www.berlinale.de) in 1951. Although driven by a parallel motivation to advance non-commercial, independent cinema, the Flaherty's emphasis on a closed, retreat-like setting among a small, intimate group, differed from these emerging festivals. In the U.S., film societies and art cinemas screened international films, classics, documentaries and experimental films. A more intellectual film culture was also in ascendance with the publication of *Quarterly Review of Film, Radio and Television* (Berkeley, California, 1951) and *Film Culture* (New York City, 1955). Very few film schools existed beyond the University of Southern California (USC), the University of California at Los Angeles (UCLA) and New York University (NYU) (Grieveson and Wasson 2008: 408-9). As a result, the goal of the non-theatrical film societies to present cinema as art, the burgeoning interest in a more analytical approach to cinema and the void in film education, all converged in The Flaherty Seminar.

The first five years established the seminar's programming strategies, its dedication to sufficient discussion of ideas, its informal, retreat-like isolation, its pedagogical goals, its advocacy for cinema as an art form. Frances sponsored the seminar to 'further an appreciation of her husband's work and method'.[4] The seminar differed from a film festival because it brought together those involved in the non-theatrical cinema world: filmmakers, museum curators, film society programmers, writers, librarians and students. The operational modes of the seminar emerged from a rather odd mix of Frances' interpretation of Zen Buddhism's non-preconception of experiences and objects, Robert Flaherty's legacy of mentoring younger filmmakers, Vermont-based artistic retreats for renewal and Robert's penchant for conviviality and drinking at the Coffee Club in New York City.

Frances initiated the idea for a seminar within the larger context of the continuing quest of the Robert Flaherty Foundation to secure tax-exempt status from the U.S. Department of Treasury, who considered it a family memorial project. The seminars clarified its educational purpose.[5] In 1955, Frances reasoned that 'this first summer we are trying out an intensive study of the films. There has been considerable dispute as to how much can be studied or imparted'.[6] Frances sought to procure scholarships to pay for students to attend.[7] Patrician, intellectual, monastic in her devotion to cinema and 71 years old, Frances held court at the first seminar, explaining the 'The Flaherty Way'. She mobilised the assets at her disposal to mount the seminar: the Flaherty films, the Flaherty name and the farm.

The seminar positioned the Flaherty films as a platform on which to learn what Frances dubbed 'The Way'. 'The Way' combined Frances's experiences on location with her husband, her extensive readings in philosophy and her experiences in the non-theatrical film culture of the 1950s, into a filmmaking catechism: independence from studio control and timelines, mystical engagement with subjects, non-preconception of material and learning through repeated viewings (Flaherty 1952: 52).

Frances possessed a determination to advance cinema as an art form by bringing together master filmmakers and students for its exploration. For her, the Flaherty films provided a path into cinema as a deep experience. She repositioned the Flaherty films as a touchstone for a poetic, independent cinema. 'His filmmaking will probably be of particular interest to independent filmmakers making their own films in their own way,' she wrote. For her, the Flaherty films offered a rubric for the 'fundamentals of cinema'.[8]

The first Robert Flaherty Film Seminar was held on the Flaherty farm in Dummerston, Vermont, in 1955. Robert Flaherty had been buried on the property. The flyer positioned the seminar as a 'course', an important distinction differentiating it from a film society and other non-theatrical screenings. The seminar ran for ten days. Billed as 'an exploration of the world of Robert Flaherty', students would watch the films and listen to Flaherty collaborators. From the crew of *Louisiana Story* (Robert Flaherty, U.S., 1948), cameraman Richard Leacock, editor Helen Von Dongen and sound recordists Benjamin Doniger and Leonard Stark presented. Virgil Thomson, the film's composer, explained the music. Frances Flaherty, who had collaborated on virtually all of Flaherty's films, and David Flaherty discussed the Flaherty production process.

Attendance required an application and approval. The attendance fee was U.S.$75, including lunch, film screenings and lectures.[9] Special, invited guests explained sound, editing and shooting, underscoring the pedagogical impulse. This early seminar emphasised the master filmmaker's passing down of knowledge to a younger generation. Students at the first seminar spanned the non-theatrical world of the 1950s: Jack Churchill, a science filmmaker; Charles Benton from *Encyclopaedia Britannica*; Edith Hutchinson, from *Reader's Digest*; Lynn

Robinson from the New York State Library; Cecile Starr from *Saturday Review*; Michel Brault from the National Film Board of Canada; and Mary Mainwaring, a graduate student from Indiana University.

The first seminar concentrated on *Louisiana Story, The Land* (Robert Flaherty, U.S., 1942), *Moana* (Robert Flaherty, U.S., 1926) and *Nanook of the North* (Robert Flaherty, U.S., 1922) during the day. A key feature of the seminar, though, revolved around its programming together of features, experimental works and documentaries – usually kept separate in other exhibition contexts – thus, evoking the Flaherty tradition of independence, poetry and artistry. The filmmaker, usually part of the East Coast non-theatrical film world, discussed the film afterwards. The evening screenings featured *All My Babies* (George Stoney, U.S., 1953), a Flaherty Award winner; *Corral* (Colin Low, Canada, 1954); *Seifritz on Protoplasm* (Jack Churchill, U.S., 1953), a scientific film; *Pirogue Maker* (Arnold Eagle, U.S., 1949); and *Toby and the Tall Corn* (Richard Leacock, U.S., 1954) (Barnouw and Zimmermann 1995: 431).

In her first 'Report on the Activities of the Robert Flaherty Foundation' (1956), Frances assessed this inaugural edition of the seminar, asserting its orientation towards young people and an activist, forward-thinking, educational goal. 'It was naturally oriented toward the future,' she noted.[10] Richard Griffith from the Museum of Modern Art (MoMA) had opened the seminar, asserting that this gathering was based on inquiry, discussion and controversy. The seminar's unique contribution to an activist film culture hinged on situating the films within a more intellectual context of intense discussion about ideas and strategies, where group interaction around the work received as much time as the screening itself. A step-by-step analysis of *Louisiana Story* occupied four days. Helen Von Dongen explained the editing process over two days. Richard Leacock elaborated on his cinematography. By the second week, David and Frances Flaherty charted the development of the Flaherty process through a chronological survey of his films.

In this first seminar, Frances worked toward opening up the students and attendees to 'letting go' and 'self-surrender' to the material, major components of her idea of 'non-preconception'.[11] The presenters were called 'faculty' and participants were dubbed 'students'. Spurred on by intense engagements with the films, participants wrote that the seminar taught them about a 'way of life'.[12] During the day, session participants analysed the Flaherty films. At night, the classical pianist Rudolph Serkin, a neighbour, played, and later in the week so did folk musician Richard

Dyer-Bennet. Independent, poetic or ethnographic films exemplifying 'the Flaherty tradition' were also screened. Summarising the inaugural seminar, Frances said, 'They came to feel that we were their family and this place their home'.[13] Cecile Starr observed, 'The informality, the prevailing good-will, and the natural beauty of the location added up to an exhilarating, exhausting, unforgettable event' (Starr 1995: 170).

The Flaherty Seminar did not emerge in isolation, however. The idea of a retreat in a pastoral area to renew, explore and foster creativity without distractions had an antecedent in the Breadloaf Writers Conference in Vermont, initiated in 1926 by Middlebury College. By 1951, Rudolph Serkin, the pianist, had inaugurated the Marlboro School and Music Festival, also in Vermont, dedicated to developing chamber music in an intensive setting. At Marlboro, promising young virtuosos could work with established players in the hopes of launching careers (Serkin 1976; Burgwyn 2001). These gatherings suggest a regional context for the emergence of The Flaherty Seminar, with connections between key personnel at Marlboro and Flaherty, such as Amos Vogel, Dorothy Oshlag and Frances herself.

With the success of the inaugural seminar, Frances was even more determined to advance Robert Flaherty's way of making films as her activist agenda. Frances' activist agenda was actually quite simple: for cinema to reach its potential as an art, its concepts and practices needed to be unpacked, deciphered, dissected, discussed, debated and explained. The Robert Flaherty Foundation offered a special scholarship to members of the American Federation of Film Societies (AFFS). The second seminar announced its programme in the Federation's newsletter: Richard Griffith from MoMA; Fred Zinnemann, feature film director of *From Here to Eternity* (U.S., 1953); Amos Vogel, the founder and programmer of New York's premier avant-garde ciné-club Cinema 16; and *Nanook of the North, Moana, The Land, Louisiana Story* and *Man of Aran* (Robert Flaherty, U.S., 1934) (Special Scholarship 1955: 3). Charles Benton from *Encyclopaedia Britannica* encouraged Frances to involve more university professors.[14] Frances reasoned that 'our seminars, I believe, are the only one[s] where students can get this unadulterated approach to the technique and discipline of film as a new art'.[15]

The second seminar replicated some of the first's content with the five Flaherty films. Again, participants included a mix of writers, filmmakers, distributors, museum curators, librarians and students. Screenings and presentations demonstrated a heterogeneous mix of styles, institutions and approaches to cinema. Albert Wasserman presented his Flaherty Award-winning film on mental health, *Out of Darkness* (U.S., 1956) and Jack Churchill reprised *Seifritz on Protoplasm*. Serkin and Dyer-Bennet performed again. Robert Northshield screened his CBS film *The Way of the Navajo* (U.S., 1955) and Robert Gardner, the director of the film study centre at Harvard, screened *The Hunters* (John Marshall, U.S., 1957), a film about South African bushmen. Amos Vogel programmed experimental films from Cinema 16.[16]

Frances and David ensured that the Flaherty films received top billing. Richard Griffiths lectured on *¡Qué Viva México!* (*Thunder over Mexico*, Sergei Eisenstein, U.S., 1933) (Starr 1995: 170). The seminar's participants represented the Toronto Film Society, the Methodist Film Commission, CBS, the National Film Board of Canada, the Puerto Rico Community Education Film Unit as well as Radford College, New York University, Northwestern University and Harvard University.[17] To assist the programmer, an advisory committee featured prominent figures teaching film at major universities: Erik Barnouw, Columbia University; Jack C. Ellis, Northwestern University; Charles Siepmann, New York University; and George Stoney, City College of New York.[18]

In November 1956, Frances Flaherty, Cecile Star, Fred Zinnemann and Hans Richter determined that the seminars should continue, but with additional assistance and expertise. Andries Deinum, a West Coast film scholar, was selected as the programmer of the 1957 seminar.[19]

In 1957, the third Flaherty Seminar at the Flaherty farm signified a turning point in its activism for developing cinema as an art. The publicity emphasised bringing younger filmmakers together to explore 'the nature of film and take a searching look at its future'. Again, the Flaherty films would be intensely studied, as well as films 'in the spirit of exploration which the Flaherty films represent'. The conceptual background, research, production problems, cinematography, editing, music and structure of the Flaherty films, formed the backbone of the seminar during this early period. Prompted by Al Wasserman, a participant in the 1956 seminar, CBS Public Affairs underwrote a student scholarship.[20] The programme replicated the format of previous years, showcasing the Flaherty films. It also significantly expanded its scope to probe the emerging developments in the independent film world, such as ethnographic film, government-sponsored projects and post-war international film movements beyond U.S. shores. John Marshall's *The Hunters* returned. *Night Mail* (Basil Wright, UK, 1936), *The Plow That Broke the Plains* (Pare Lorentz, U.S., 1936), *New Earth* (Joris Ivens,

Netherlands, 1933) and *Pather Panchali* (Satyajit Ray, India, 1955) also screened.

Almost 40 seminarians attended, an increase from the smaller groups of earlier years, representing the U.S., Canada, Puerto Rico and Japan.[21] The spirit of good will, camaraderie and intimacy devolved into what critic Cecile Starr termed 'politics, opportunism and contention' (Starr 1995: 171). Cliques formed among students and guests. The long-standing animosities between film editor Helen Van Dongen and Frances Flaherty flared up in discussions of *The Land*. Van Dongen, the editor, and Frances, co-producer, muse, wife and writer, had many disagreements about what constituted 'the Flaherty Way' of making documentaries: Van Dongen, who had worked as an editor for Joris Ivens shaped *The Land* and *Louisiana Story* in post-production, while Frances claimed more conceptual input on all the Flaherty films. Further, their politics clashed: Van Dongen had been associated with the European political left and radical documentary, while Frances advocated a more humanistic universalism.

The seminar's fourth edition, in 1958, revised the format yet again. Hugh Gray from the Department of Theater Arts at the University of California would lead the seminar discussions, moving towards an academic model of lectures and guided discussion. The 1957 edition, which attracted a larger group of participants from Northeast film culture, had moved away from a sense of unity around the Flaherty works towards more rancorous debate about the form, function and meaning of non-commercial cinemas. Frances reasoned that, with Gray, 'the atmosphere once more will be relaxed and friendly, in marked contrast to last year, when the only guiding idea, so far as I can see, was to stir up antagonisms and animosities where none existed before'.[22]

Gray would collaborate with an advisory committee of Flaherty stalwarts such as Barnouw, Ellis, Seipmann and Stoney. Richard Griffith, documentary scholar and curator from MoMA, and Hans Richter, an experimental filmmaker, were added.[23] Frances continued to lecture, now donating her speaking fees to the seminar's scholarship fund. Concerned about losing the intimacy of earlier seminars, David Flaherty capped attendance at 40 participants.[24]

The Flaherty films, once again, occupied a central position. *The Hunters* and *All My Babies* returned. The programming expanded into a more international perspective, with screenings of *The River* (Jean Renoir, France/India/U.S., 1951), *Les maîtres fous* (*The Mad Masters*, Jean Rouch, France, 1955) and *Oeuverture* (*Overture*, Gian Luigi

Polidoro, Canada, 1959), which was produced by the United Nations Film Unit.

A filmmaker arrived from India whose presence had a great impact on the seminar's trajectory: Satyajit Ray. The U.S. Information Service provided a special grant to bring Ray to the seminar. The first two films of his festival-award-winning trilogy, *Pather Panchali* and *Aparajito* (India, 1956) were screened prior to their theatrical release in the U.S.

Ray embodied the independent cinema Frances championed. He worked outside commercial Indian cinema, employing a poetic realist narrative style with everyday people as actors.[25] The film and television historian Erik Barnouw, who attended the 1958 seminar, contended that Ray 'epitomised what many in the group were reaching for – work done not in an industry process but rather in an artisan tradition, by artists in control of what they were doing'. Ray was a 'filmmaker', a term the seminar regularly used to imply rebelliousness from the industrial system and independence of the burdens of fundraising and distribution (Barnouw 1995: 173).

With Ray's participation the seminar shifted from its almost exclusive focus on the Flaherty films and U.S. produced films towards an engagement with international cinema advancing similar aims. Referencing the seminar, the *American Federation of Film Societies Newsletter* ran an article honouring Satyajit Ray, noting *Pather Panchali*'s poetic beauty and respect for its subjects. 'De Sica, Flaherty, Pudovkin, Renoir and Ford have all profoundly influenced me,' Ray explained.[26]

By 1959, The Flaherty Seminar had adjusted its familialism into a more professional organisation with explicit links to education: UCLA hosted the fifth seminar, which convened at its Santa Barbara campus. Later on, in 1963, an internal history contended that the seminars had achieved 'a prestige which resulted in several universities and other organisations offering to serve as hosts to subsequent Robert Flaherty Film Seminars'.[27] The choice of seminar staff also underscores the growing university connections: six of the 11 staff members were academics. Experimental filmmaker Shirley Clarke, Jack Churchill and Frances Flaherty were also listed as staff. The seminar now operated at the junction of the newly emerging notion of university film education, the expanding world of non-theatrical distribution, the non-commercial film societies and the development of post-war international art cinema in festivals and arthouses.[28]

That year's brochure amplified the seminar's activist educational goals beyond the Flaherty films, emphasising 'an exploration and study of films made in the Flaherty spirit'. The seminar now identified itself as 'unique in scope and method'. It sought the 'power of the camera to enlarge for man a vision and understanding of his environing world'.[29]

The seminar had solidified its pedagogical method: three major open sessions a day, small discussion meetings on staging versus life caught unawares, non-actors, non-preconception, editing, sound, narrative, music, film sponsorship and economics and educational films. The brochure reiterated the idea of 'study' and the commitment to 'internationalism'. The event would screen selected works from U.S., European and Asian filmmakers, focusing on ethnographic filmmaking. French ethnographic filmmaker Jean Rouch was the featured guest, replicating the model of a master filmmaker like Ray from the year before.[30] Rouch did not attend the seminar, however; his wife presented the films instead.[31]

Frances had continued to lecture on the 'Flaherty Way', but now poured her honoraria into scholarships. The Robert Flaherty Foundation's primary activity was the execution and programming of the annual seminar. The idea that the seminar would always be looking towards the future and the next generation intensified. According to Barnouw, from the very beginning, the seminar was 'meant to spur – empower – young cineastes of independent mind' (Barnouw and Zimmermann 1995: 1).

The connection with the University of California generated anxiety, however. The transition from a family-run operation promoting 'The Flaherty Way', towards an academic institutional collaboration, implied less control, less intimacy and less focus on Robert Flaherty. The first four seminars had taken place at the Flaherty farm; the fifth was marked by the increasing involvement of professional educators, curators and critics. Arnold Eagle, a photographer who had worked on *Louisiana Story* and who, in the 1950s, participated on the team advising Frances about The Flaherty Seminar, argued that the UCLA partnership would benefit the foundation, which fulfilled a need for film education in the United States. He worried, however, about a larger seminar. He argued, 'It is the personal touch that you two [Frances and David] provide that gives it the intimate and warm feeling that one gets when attending the seminar'.[32] In response, David Flaherty cautioned, 'the more of the old guard, the faithful, we can muster out there, the better it will be'.[33]

The films selected to screen in 1959 evidenced the most international scope of any seminar up to that point: Les Fils de l'eau (*The Sons of Water*, Jean Rouch, France, 1958) *Mois un noir* (*I, a Negro*, Jean Rouch, France, 1958), three Ray films, *Pather Panchali,*

Aparajito and *Apur Sansar* (*The World of Apu*, Satyajit Ray, India, 1959), a film from Pakistani filmmaker A. J. Kardar, *Jago Hua Savera* (*The Day Shall Dawn*, Pakistan, 1959). Also featured were the four major Flaherty films – *Nanook of the North*, *Man of Aran*, *Louisiana Story* and *Moana* – by this time a seminar tradition. The seminar rescreened works from previous years, indicating its educational intentions rather than curatorial interventions: John Marshall's *The Hunters*, Churchill's *Seifitz on Protoplasm* and Stoney's *All My Babies*.[34]

By 1960, the Robert Flaherty Foundation had dissolved. A new non-profit educational corporation, International Film Seminars, Inc. (IFS) was created to attract tax-exempt gifts. The Flaherty name was removed. Barnouw invented the new name, inspired by Satyajit Ray's influence on the seminar. Barnouw reasoned that the majority of the Flaherty films were produced outside of the U.S.; Frances also nurtured personal connections to film groups in England, Scotland, France, India, Pakistan, Canada and Puerto Rico. Vermont attorney Paul Olson drew up the incorporation papers and travelled to Washington DC with Frances and Barnouw to offer arguments to the U.S. Department of the Treasury. They succeeded: tax exemption was granted.

IFS operated quite differently from the Robert Flaherty Foundation. It functioned more professionally, with a board; the Flaherty family moved to the side-lines. Columbia University's Center for Mass Communication, administered by Barnouw and Oshlag, provided office space. Barnouw was the first president; his term spanning over eight years. Flaherty stalwarts Clarke and Churchill served as trustees with Frances and David, along with Leo Dratfield from Contemporary Films, the filmmaker Hans Richter and Jack Ellis from Northwestern University.[35]

With the institution of the IFS, The Flaherty Seminar's purpose sharpened and clarified. As an activist educational organisation, it advocated the study of film as an art and brought together people from several countries for meaningful discussion about cinema. As a non-profit organisation, it functioned as a nodal point to connect established and emerging practitioners. As an adjunct to the non-theatrical cinema scene, it convened filmmakers, film society programmers, non-theatrical film distributors, museum curators, intellectuals, academics, musicians and scientific, ethnographic and educational film workers to discuss the future of cinema.[36]

The Robert Flaherty Film Seminars evolved from a small gathering of like-minded, mostly East Coast U.S. film people committed to the activist goals of furthering cinema as an art form, into a significant, non-profit media arts organisation dedicated to international gatherings considering emerging, innovative forms of the moving image. The Flaherty Seminar functions in a dialectical relationship to its formative era. On the one hand, it continues to foster a communal space for exploration of moving image (cinema, video, digital, installation) outside mass-produced, commercial formations, where discussion is as important as screenings and where a heterogeneous mix of people and media forms commingles. On the other hand, its initial activist goals advocating for cinema as an art form and an intellectual endeavour have mutated into providing a forum to engage works and movements often overlooked by festivals, museums or universities. Its continuing activism resides not so much in the politics of the films its various programmers select, but in its continuing insistence on providing an intensive, immersive environment, where what is unresolved in contemporary, international moving image culture – political compilation films of the 1970s, hybrid feminist films of the 1980s, world cinemas of the 1990s – can be discussed, debated and contested in post-screening discussions and impromptu seminar parties. 'The Flaherty Way', then, has been transformed from Frances' mystical theory of cinema into an organisational and programming strategy to connect heterogeneous people, film and ideas in ways not possible without the seminar.

Works Cited

Barnouw, Erik (1995) 'Dummerston Days', in Erik Barnouw and Patricia R. Zimmermann (eds), *The Flaherty: Four Decades in the Cause of Independent Cinema*, special quadruple issue of *Wide Angle*, 17, 1-4, 168-76.

Barnouw, Erik and Patricia R. Zimmermann (1995) 'Prologue', in Erik Barnouw and Patricia R. Zimmermann (eds), *The Flaherty: Four Decades in the Cause of Independent Cinema*, special quadruple issue of *Wide Angle*, 17, 1-4, 1.

____ (1995) 'Works Screened at the Flaherty: 1955-1994', in Erik Barnouw and Patricia R. Zimmermann (eds), *The Flaherty: Four Decades in the Cause of Independent Cinema*, special quadruple issue of *Wide Angle*, 17, 1-4, 428-44.

Burgwyn, Diana (2001) *Marlboro Music: A Fifty Year Portrait, 1951-2000*. Marlboro, VT: Marlboro Music Festival.

Flaherty, Frances (1952), 'The Flaherty Way', *Saturday Review of Literature*, 13, September, 52.

Grieveson, Lee and Haidee Wasson (eds) (2008) *Inventing Film Studies*. Durham: Duke University Press, 408-9.

International Film Seminars Papers, International Film Seminars, Inc. (1955-2011). New York: International Film Seminars.

Morrison, Theodore (1976) *Breadloaf Writers' Conference: The First Thirty Years 1926-1955*. Middlebury, VT: Middlebury College Press.

Robert J. Flaherty Papers (1912-1964), Butler Special Collections, Columbia University

Serkin, Rudolph (1976) *Marlboro Music: The First 25 Years 1951-1975*. Marlboro, VT: Marlboro School and Music Festival.

'Special Scholarship' (1955), *American Federation of Film Societies Newsletter*, Spring, 3.

Starr, Cecile (1995) 'Recollections of Frances Flaherty and the Early Flaherty Seminars', in Erik Barnouw and Patricia R. Zimmermann (eds), *The Flaherty: Four Decades in the Cause of Independent Cinema*, special quadruple issue of *Wide Angle*, 17, 1-4, 168-74.

Notes

[1] George Amberg to the Guggenheim Foundation, 1961, *Robert J. Flaherty Papers*, Butler Special Collections, Columbia University (hereinafter *Flaherty Papers*).

[2] David Flaherty to John Adair, 22 March 1960, *Flaherty Papers*.

[3] Frances Flaherty to Armine Wilson, 9 November 1954, *Flaherty Papers*.

[4] Internal Revenue Service Tax Exemption Petition, 1956, *Flaherty Papers*.

[5] David Flaherty to Floria Lasky of Fitelson and Mayers, New York City, 19 September 1955, *Flaherty Papers*.

[6] Frances Flaherty to Virginia Sears, 26 February 1955; David Flaherty to Jean Epstein, 6 January 1955, *Flaherty Papers*.

[7] Frances Flaherty to Natalie Chapin, 5 February 1955, *Flaherty Papers*.

[8] Frances Flaherty, 'Ideas for Development of Flaherty Seminar', circa 1955, *International Film Seminars Papers, International Film Seminars, Inc., New York* (hereinafter *Seminars Papers*).

[9] Robert Flaherty Foundation flyer inviting an exploration of the world of Robert Flaherty, 1955, *Seminars Papers*.

[10] A Report on the Activities of the Robert Flaherty Foundation, 1 July-31 March 1956, 3. *Seminars Papers*.

[11] A Report on the Activities of the Robert Flaherty Foundation, 1 July- 31 March 1956, 4, *Seminars Papers*.

[12] A Report on the Activities of the Robert Flaherty Foundation, 1-July-31 March 1956, 5, *Seminars Papers*.

13   A Report on the Activities of the Robert Flaherty Foundation, 5 July 1954, *Seminars Papers*.

14   Frances Flaherty and Charles Benton exchanged letters regarding increasing outreach to universities, 1955-6. Frances Flaherty to Francis Butler, 28 March 1958; David Flaherty to Jack Ellis, 11 June 1956, *Flaherty Papers*.

15   Frances Flaherty to Jean Benoit Levy, 16 May 1956, 2, *Flaherty Papers*.

16   Invitation to Robert Flaherty Foundation Events, 1956, *Seminar Papers*.

17   A Partial List of Participants, 1962, 109, *Seminars Papers*.

18   Announcement of the Third Annual Robert Flaherty Film Seminar, 1957, *Seminars Papers*.

19   Cecile Starr, Informal Report on Meetings with Frances Flaherty, November 1956, 10-11, *Flaherty Papers*.

20   Frances Flaherty to Al Wasserman, 5 June 1957, *Flaherty Papers*.

21   David Flaherty to Arnold Eagle, 7 August 1957; David Flaherty to Amos Vogel, 1 October 1957, *Flaherty Papers*.

22   Frances Flaherty to Arnold Eagle, 27 February 1958, *Flaherty Papers*.

23   Announcement for the Fourth Annual Robert Flaherty Seminar August 18-28, 1958, *Seminars Papers*.

24   David Flaherty to Arnold Eagle, 12 June 1958, *Flaherty Papers*.

25   Special Announcement of the Robert Flaherty Foundation, 1958, *Seminars Papers*.

26   'AFFS Honors Satyajit Ray,' American Federation of Film Societies Newsletter, October 1958, *Flaherty Papers*.

27   The Robert Flaherty Film Seminars – Background Information, 1963, *Seminars Papers*.

27   Frances Flaherty to Edna Giesen, 1 May 1959; Amos Vogel to Frances Flaherty, 13 May 1959, *Flaherty Papers*.

29   Announcement for the Fiftth Annual Robert Flaherty Film Seminars, 1959, *Seminars Papers*.

30   Ibid.

31   David Flaherty to Empire Films, 31 July 1959, *Flaherty Papers*.

32   Arnold Eagle to Frances Flaherty and David Flaherty, 11 July, 1959, 2, *Flaherty Papers*.

33   David Flaherty to Arnold Eagle, 3 June 1959, *Flaherty Papers*.

34   Announcement for the Fifth Annual Robert Flaherty Film Seminar, 1959, *Seminars Papers*.

35   David Flaherty to Arnold Eagle, 9 November 1960, *Flaherty Papers*.

36   Proposal to the Louis W. and Maud Hill Foundation, 26 May 1961, *Flaherty Papers*.

PART 3

RESOURCES

The Resources: Groundwork Continued

Leshu Torchin and Dina Iordanova

The Resources, an important part of *Film Festivals and Activism*, continues the essential groundwork that we have been carrying out since the inception of the *Film Festival Yearbook* series (Iordanova 2011). We believe that it is essential to increase the concrete knowledge of the ways film festivals come about, operate and proliferate, and we hope to achieve such increase with the manifold voices that we have brought together here for the creation of the material that was specially commissioned and developed for this section.

Tables of film festivals track developments across time and space, aggregating different types of festivals in order to provide useful overviews and contact data. Interviews with practitioners supply first-hand knowledge, helping scholars to reduce unfounded speculation in their research on film festivals. And the bibliographies help summarise the work done so far, and provide a preliminary map of the field.

As with our previous volume, *Film Festivals and East Asia* (2011), contributions to this section have been subdivided into three parts. First, there are interviews with festival programmers, filmmakers and activists (these categories are not entirely discrete, as the interviews demonstrate). Second, there are five tables providing an overview of film festivals in various areas of the activist spectrum. Third, there is a brief overview of work in the field, with a bibliography on the subject of activism, film and film festivals, an update of the bibliography on film festival research, and a review of the *One World Human Rights Film Festival Yearbook* edited by Tereza Porybná.

And, as with our previous volumes, we hope that the material in this Resource section will be of direct use to scholars and practitioners alike.

Interviews: Bruni Burres, Jasmina Bojic, Sean Farnel, Ronit Avni, Želimir Žilnik and Judith Helfand

To better understand how film festivals may serve an activist function, we turned to those who work on the ground: programmers and activist filmmakers whose discussions place them in dialogue with this volume and with each other. The six interviews illustrate the sometimes differing, but more often intersecting, practices and perspectives of how film festivals contribute to social justice agendas.

Alex Fischer's interview with Bruni Burres, Director of the Human Rights Watch Film Festival from its inception in 1991 to 2008, allows insight into the festival's development from a modest screening series into an international festival with flagship events in London and New York and volunteer-run outposts around the world. The conversation reveals the outreach strategies a festival programmer might use to aid activist agendas. The subtext of this exchange hints at a new, post-1989 landscape where non-government organisations (NGOs) gain prominence as agents on a world stage released from Cold War geopolitics. Human Rights Watch was founded in 1978 as Helsinki Watch, which monitored the Soviet Union and Eastern Europe; other committees developed along the way (Americas Watch, Asia Watch, Africa Watch, Middle East Watch) before all were united, in 1988, under the heading of Human Rights Watch.

While Burres' interview tracks a movement from the local to the global, one could see Raluca Iacob's interview with Jasmina Bojic, Founder and Director of UNAFF (United Nations Association Film Festival) as tracing a movement in the other direction. After all, Bojic mounted the festival at Stanford University with the aim of acquainting Americans – and more specifically, a Palo Alto public – with the goals and processes of the UN, a supranational organisation. The interview links to themes present throughout this volume, both in terms of the educational foundation of the festival and its development as a travelling festival. In the process, it reveals the concerns of a grassroots organisation, which appear to differ from those of established NGOs and film festivals.

The interview with Sean Farnel, former programmer of Hot Docs – Canadian International Documentary Festival in Toronto (2005-2011) (www.hotdocs.ca), allows for continued exploration of institutional politics between festivals and the prominence of the documentary mode in activism. There is a strong legacy of interest in social justice, in documentary filmmaking and in documentary scholarship alike. The discussion with Farnel begins to tease out this special relationship between documentary and activism within the film festival realm.

Farnel's interview concludes with his praise for *Budrus* (Julia Bacha, Israel/Occupied Palestinian Territory/U.S., 2009) and *Encounter Point* (Ronit Avni and Julia Bacha, U.S., 2006). This offers a useful segue into Leshu Torchin's interview with filmmaker Ronit Avni, founder and Executive Director of Just Vision, who discusses in greater depth the appeal and potential of film festivals for capacity building and shifting discourse. Avni's previous experience at WITNESS, where she trained communities in the use of video as a tool for education and grassroots mobilising, granted her insights into how to manage a multi-media campaign around the topic of Israel and Palestine.

Greg DeCuir Jr.'s interview with the veteran Serbian activist filmmaker Želimir Žilnik raises essential questions about the uses of a film festival. A dynamic filmmaker, Žilnik believes that the most important work is done before exhibition through close work with subjects, by contact-building and with the production of an advance dialogue. He is doubtful of a film festival's utility, noting the economy of attention that may limit sustained engagement, and prefers what he calls his 'prior activism'. At the same time, the conversation reveals the ways cine-clubs and film festivals, such as Oberhausen, helped to provide spaces where filmmakers from Socialist states could cultivate solidarity and knowledge beyond the mainstream. He then provides a useful corrective, encouraging us to question assumptions about the activism of film festivals post-1989 and, indeed, ever.

Although it would seem that Žilnik's suspicion of a festival's activist potential places him in opposition to American activist and filmmaker Judith Helfand, interviewed here by Leshu Torchin, there is, in fact, much common ground. Both are committed to the community and debate the existence of an 'activist' festival, as both understand the limitations placed on programmers and the event calendar. Helfand, however, understands festivals as sites for testing strategies that can be developed, re-used and, most importantly, exported to other filmmakers and activists. Žilnik's independent distribution is impressive and admirable, and made possible through his force of will and his status as cineaste. Helfand, meanwhile, investigates sustainability – both for the communities using the films for activism, and for filmmakers seeking to make a living and to find lives for their films; this is evident in Avni's own recollections of the assistance her work received.

Helfand's interview concludes this section not to suggest any narrative of progression, but for her key reminder to all of us: the period during which a filmmaker may make use of film festivals is short-lived; this is only one stop in the longer life of a film and its relevance to activist campaigns. Festivals can provide the entry point into this longer-term mission, which includes the needs, and is dictated by the timetables, of communities. This is not just about activist film festivals, but about the activism facilitated by festivals.

'Activist' Film Festival Tables

Our production of tables listing film festivals under particular categories reflects our belief that festivals operate in relatively defined parallel circuits. Not all festivals mentioned in this volume have been included in the tables, as we believe some cases lend themselves better for analytical discussion in the essays, while others are better presented in a table format. A seemingly straightforward endeavour, the production of the tables, all compiled by Beatriz Tadeo Fuica in consultation with our authors, offered challenges from the start. How do we begin to define an activist film festival? What would be our criteria for inclusion and categorisation?

Although almost any festival could be considered activist, we used two guiding principles: issues and identities. In the first instance, festivals built around issues such as human rights (which include economic rights) and the environment were considered activist for their aims of promoting understanding and action. Thus, the table that lists Human Rights-focused film festivals is the first of six tables we have included in this volume. Other issue-based listings here honed in on film festivals that, in one way or another, deal with various aspects of human migration (Table 4) and with environmental concerns (Table 6).

Tables 2, 3 and 5 focus, respectively, on Indigenous events, on Lesbian, Gay, Bisexual, Transgender and Queer Festivals (LGBTQ) and on Disability film festivals, and present listings of what we regard as identity-based festivals. Further to this, we have included a sub-section for Deaf film festivals (Table 5a) within the Disability listing (Table 5), in order to acknowledge – even if clumsily – how deafness is distinguished as both a disability and as a culture organised around language. Such questions of distinctions within identity can factor into other festivals, as with the LGBTQ festivals noted below. These events are not always divorced from an issue-based festival, as advancing human rights can be a basic component in any festival that celebrates and recognises an identity.

Readers may note the absence of other identity-based film festivals, such as women's film festivals, diasporic film festivals, ethnic and cultural minority festivals and so on. Such festivals bring criteria for inclusion to the fore, whether in terms of our drafting of tables, or more crucially, in terms of historical, political, social and industrial recognition.

These festivals, like so many others that might be considered 'non-activist', enable the representation of those marginalised in the field – both onscreen and off. In this regard one can identify an activist sensibility in film festivals more broadly in that they call attention to films and filmmakers that have been marginalised. In light of this broader cultural activism, though, how then to determine what is an 'activist' film festival?

For example, the festivals based on sexual identity, identifying themselves through a various combinations and permutations of Lesbian/Gay/Bisexual/Transgendered/Queer (LGBTQ), raise a key question regarding transition and position: when is an activist film festival not an activist film festival? The table's organisation allows us to see periods of proliferation and change. With LGBTQ festivals, this may provide additional insights into a phenomenon already suggested in Skadi Loist and Ger Zielinski's contribution to this volume: assimilation into the mainstream. In the case of LGBTQ festivals, some of these issues may be written in the title: do festivals take on additional letters, enhancing the 'Lesbian and Gay' designation that once seemed foreign, but is today increasingly familiar? What is the distinction between LGBT festivals, which may seek to normalise the different, and 'Queer', which proudly champions its difference? How do we understand these shifts in terms of global geography? Categorisation and inclusion become issues even before we move outside a seemingly cohesive group.

Similar questions coalesce around culturally-oriented film festivals, whose aims we might consider to include the bringing to light of the particular political and social issues facing the community, and which work on broadening the cinematic and industrial representation of those communities. The tables that emerged grew unwieldy and demanded further consideration before their inclusion. In addition, many of the identity and issue-based festivals that would be of pertinence here were already included in the second volume of the *Film Festival Yearbook* series, which was dedicated to *Film Festivals and Imagined Communities* (2010). That volume features tables devoted to African Film Festivals outside Africa (Lindiwe Dovey, 2010: 266-7), Jewish Film Festivals (Jerome Segal, 2010: 271-2) and Palestinian Film Festivals (Serazer Pekerman, 2010:273), among others,. We will be looking to compile tables of women's/feminist film festivals in future volumes of the *Film Festival Yearbook*.

So, too, will we look into compiling tables of documentary and independent film festivals, which have been omitted here for reasons similar to those listed above. Although documentary has a long-standing relationship with social justice, and is typically the mode of choice for the activist filmmaker (whether for economic or ideological reasons), the documentary festival is not solely dedicated to activism. The documentary format, however, remains a more peripheral presence in cinemas and thus benefits from the exposure and the combined efforts to ensure audiences, income, awards and other forms of useful industrial capital. Similarly, independent film festivals ostensibly support the films produced outside national or commercial industries. And yet, here is where problems of mainstreaming are thrown into relief: in the context of the U.S., at least, many independent film festivals have functioned primarily to ensure the continued visibility of white men from the Global North, even if they began with the best of intentions. This is the reason for which many of the important festivals mentioned repeatedly in this volume – such as Hot Docs, AFI-Discovery Channel Silverdocs (silverdocs.com) or the International Documentary Film Festival Amsterdam (IDFA) (www.idfa.nl) – do not figure in the tables.

Organisational and conceptual questions aside, practical challenges emerged. Our table compiler Beatriz Tadeo Fuica was often faced with film festivals that were staged only occasionally, with inactive URLs, or with NGOs that overshadowed or obscured the festivals they ran, making the search for information difficult. In many cases, the existence of some festivals is threatened by inconsistent economic or institutional support. Many of them cannot take place every year but instead take place biennially or triennially, and in some cases are sporadic and mobile. Yet festivals continue to proliferate, and many more keep coming to our attention. For instance, while writing this introduction, we received the announcement of the 3rd Black Panther Film Festival taking place at the Maysles Institute in New York (www.mayslesinstitute.org/cinema/bpp.html), which, according to its on-line mission statement, 'exhibits independently curated films to inspire dialogue and action'.

Organised by decade, and with locations noted, the tables allow us to chart developments across time and space and reveal moments when a certain type of festival has proliferated. The website references not only provide contact information, but also some insight into institutional relationships. We know the tables may not be fully complete or comprehensive, but we hope that they provide a starting point for research and will make scholars aware of some hidden or lesser-known festivals.

Writing and Scholarship

The section begins with Alex Fischer's review of the *One World Human Rights Film Festival Yearbook*, which fleshes out a reference found many times within this volume. Fischer's experience in film festival organisation and study makes for a robust investigation and also helps call attention to potential differences between human rights and more mainstream film festivals.

Kathleen Scott was charged with producing a bibliography on film festivals and activism. As with our previous bibliographies, we encouraged the inclusion of popular items: reports and reviews of film festivals, press releases from festivals and even articles from their websites. The field of film and activism, and indeed of film festivals and activism, is, however, still nascent and undefined. With a handful of exceptions, the scholarship addressing topics of witnessing, human rights and activism, tends to focus on reportage and social media rather than film; and when film is the topic, the focus is more on representation and matters of trauma and memory. These issues are significant, to be sure, but we nonetheless wished to collect information on film culture and activism, paying attention to circuits of distribution and exhibition as much as to representation. To this end, the bibliography includes works that explore the ways film and screen media have been used for advocacy alongside the works on activism and film festivals. The interests intersect, and the variety of methodologies on display should be of use to scholars of media-based activism, scholars of film festivals and activists themselves.

Rounding out the Resources section is the latest update on scholarship in the field of Film Festival Studies provided by the conveners of the Film Festival Research Network, Skadi Loist and Marijke de Valck. By valuably adding sources, they too, as usual, investigate the challenges of categorisation, this time within a burgeoning area of scholarship.

Works Cited

Iordanova, Dina and Ruby Cheung (eds) (2010) *FFY2: Film Festivals and Imagined Communities*. St Andrews: St Andrews Film Studies.

Iordanova, Dina (2011) 'The Resources: Necessary Groundwork', in Dina Iordanova and Ruby Cheung (eds) *FFY3: Film Festivals and East Asia*. St Andrews: St Andrews Film Studies, 189-95.

Porybná, Tereza (2009) *Setting Up a Human Rights Film Festival Yearbook.* Prague: People in Need.

From Local to Global: The Growing Pains of the Human Rights Watch International Film Festival: An Interview with Bruni Burres, Festival Director (1991-2008)

Alex Fischer

The Human Rights Watch International Film Festival (HRWFF) (www. hrw.org/en/iff) was established in the late 1980s as an outreach program by the independently organised and operated Human Rights Watch (HRW).[1] Over the past 23 years, the New York-based event has steadily grown into a global force that includes the establishment of a second flagship film festival in London and a 20-city U.S. tour, and has hosted special presentations in Buenos Aires, Brussels, Munich, Rio de Janeiro, Sderot (Israel) and Zurich.

The following interview with Bruni Burres, HRWFF Festival Director (1991-2008), explores the early operational workings of the festival. An activist in her own right, Burres provides candid and illuminating conversation on topics ranging from programming to the importance of community events for niche audiences. Burres is currently an executive producer of Pivot Pictures and in recent years has been involved in the Sunny Side of the Doc/Latin America International Documentary Pitching Forum (www.sunnysideofthedoc.com/uk).

This interview was conducted over Skype on 19 January 2011, with Bruni Burres in New York and Alex Fischer located at the University of St Andrews in Scotland.

Alex Fischer: *Can you discuss the history of the Human Rights Watch International Film Festival?*

Bruni Burres: The first festival was convened by a small group of leading figures within HRW, including Marina Pinto Kaufman and Hamilton Fish

Jr., and a few key players in the New York film community, including Wendy Keys (who is now on the Human Rights Watch board). These individuals knew important documentary and fiction films that existed which highlighted critical human rights. A stunning showcase of a dozen high-quality films that featured both historical and contemporary human rights stories was screened that winter [1988] at the cinématheque in the Joseph Papp Public Theater. Several of the films highlighted issues that Human Rights Watch had either worked on or were currently investigating.

The film festival coincided with the Tenth Anniversary of Human Rights Watch as well as the Fortieth Anniversary of the signing of the Declaration of Human Rights. HRW was eager to have the film series celebrate not just our achievements, but also the ground-breaking work that different organisations had engaged with over the past 40 years, and support those that were making a difference.

To my knowledge this series went very well but the idea of a fully-fledged festival wasn't brought up again until 1990 when Hamilton Fish Jr. decided to bring me on board. When I first started, an annual film festival was still just a vague idea, and I put the majority of my efforts into producing a stellar second film series, highlighting new works about Latin America and Eastern Europe. I also worked with Hamilton and others from HRW to think strategically about how we might leverage the event to raise greater awareness about HRW's work with a more diverse public and raise modest funds for the organisation. [This was important] as HRW is a non-governmental organisation that does not accept support from any governments (including the U.S. government) and relies mainly on support from foundations and individuals.

Throughout the year, it was one up-hill battle after another. Thousands of extraordinary cultural events take place weekly in New York. Many of these wonderful events are free. Trying to promote a human rights film series which charges a regular cinema admission per film may sound worthy on paper, and perhaps even educational, but also perhaps dull and gloomy. The 1991 film festival took place on exactly the same week that Bush Sr. invaded Iraq. As a result, the festival received glowing reviews; the audience was still small, yet politically engaged and growing.

We realised that this really was a great way to address a larger public. Using film and video to communicate HRW's exploration of contemporary human issues and debates could likely reach a broader and more diverse audience than HRW's 200-page report or the legal briefing. We also understood early on that these films, or really these stories, put a human face on HRW's work, and that a great film can emotionally move and affect an individual in a way that no legal report can.

Then, in the mid-1990s, there was a turning point. Audiences were diversifying and growing in numbers and the press was beginning to pay attention to each film and video we showcased. Acclaimed *Village Voice* film critic Georgia Brown published a stunning piece: 'If you are going to go to any film festivals in New York throughout the entire year' – she wrote – 'go to the Human Rights Watch International Film Festival for some of the best films you are going to see'.[2] Brown's piece legitimised the HRWFF as a *bona fide* 'film festival' showcasing cutting edge and lost historic gems. This continued press attention allowed us to concentrate on showing great works of cinematic art that highlighted critical contemporary social issues by top veteran artists or excellent emerging artists.

AF: *Were there developments, particularly in regard to activism, that you had not anticipated?*

BB: Yes, in the mid-1990s, with high quality consumer video cameras hitting the markets, many more human rights stories were being filmed, both by experienced filmmakers and by emerging artist and activists. The increase in production and accessibility of human rights media, combined with the recently garnered and unparalleled credibility of HRWFF, inspired others to launch human rights film showcases around the globe. Today we have the Human Rights Network (www.ihrnetwork. org), The Three Continent Film Festival (www.3continentsfestival. co.za), the One World Festival in Prague (www.oneworld.cz/2011) and many other small and large initiatives in countries on every continent including Argentina, Lebanon, Hungary, Peru, etc. Representatives from many of these initiatives attend or reach out to HRWFF seeking advice, encouragement, partnerships, etc. At first, we were in disbelief – so many individuals and small groups wanted to launch their own human rights film festival – but we were always eager to assist, and then thrilled when official and unofficial human rights networks began to emerge. Undoubtedly these festivals and activities continue to spur additional NGOs, activists, artists and concerned citizens to bring great films to their communities.

If we look at the 1990s, great films were being made and people were watching them, feeling depressed and not knowing what to do. But now, since 2005-6, filmmakers in the U.S., in Latin America, Africa and elsewhere have been collaborating with local activists (or becoming activists themselves). Even in the early stages of production [they] were already strategically thinking about what can be done to address some of the critical human rights issues and problems that their film would raise. These filmmakers are keen to not just add a link at the end of the film suggesting which NGOs are working on the problems explored in the film; instead, they believe that their films can be catalysts for a specific call to action or an integral element of a larger human rights campaign addressing the issues. These films provide information as to how individuals can get involved and take action to stop violence against women in Congo, or demand the U.S. Government to ratify the International Criminal Court. Many of these films are catalysts for educating and connecting concerned citizens, helping them to understand how they can make a difference and become involved.

AF: *Since the festival's inception, have both the event and Human Rights Watch changed? What are the advantages of remaining affiliated with the organisation?*

BB: The film festival is still an official part of HRW and what I think makes it different, but still strong, is the fact that HRW is now 40 years old. It is indisputably one of the most effective human rights organisations in the world. It has the ability to name and shame – and its research and reporting are impeccable. It also means films screened at the festival are vetted for their factual accuracy by experts in the field.

For example, we might have a documentary on the former Yugoslavia and the International Criminal Tribunal. Colleagues that work in that region may watch it and say they don't like a particular film or character but will still remain objective and note if the issues raised in the film are truthful. So it is really about getting their input and making sure everything is factually correct. We can disagree about a film/video's style, but if the film is factually correct and the film festival director and selection committee decide to screen the work, it will be shown.

AF: *Has the film festival helped to set up HRW in other countries?*

BB: Yes, definitely. For more than 20 years, the HRWFF has been one of the best and most effective outreach tools for HRW to reach diverse audiences, especially younger audiences.

AF: *The beauty of film festivals is that most individuals in attendance are like-minded and receptive to certain types of films. Is this taken into consideration by the organisers of the HRWFF?*

BB: Yes, it is definitely a way to talk about some difficult issues, and when you watch a film that is an hour or two hours long it's still a relatively short length of time to be brought up to speed on a particular subject and have an engaging conversation about it.

AF: *How was your directorship of the HRWFF different from other humanitarian film festivals operating at that time?*

BB: We never showed a film that highlighted an important issue but was of low artistic quality or merit. So, it is safe to say that the artistic merit of a film was and still is important to me. I've had lots of screaming matches with filmmakers who were upset we didn't programme their film for this very reason. We look at a film in terms of its strength in storytelling. We had a very high standard for our festival and we wanted it to be the highest possible quality so the audience would engage the filmmakers in discussion.

AF: *As the recognition of the festival grew, were more and better films submitted? Did your programming choice expand?*

BB: We did get more submissions, but many were lower in quality, so we would have to weed through it all. It was rare when we couldn't get a film we wanted, but we were not the Cannes Film Festival [www.festival-cannes.com], so we were competing to get a lot of the good films. There were continually issues with scheduling; someone always wanted their film positioned so that they could make the most of their screening. It is because people are now self-distributing their films. Some people just want their film at the festival; others want a particular slot – it is a case-by-case issue.

There are other factors too, like if a film has been shown on television. In this instance we see what the coverage has been like in the U.S. or UK, the date it aired and if the film had big exposure. Since the festival only shows between 25 and 35 films we are more inclined to programme a film that hasn't recently shown in that community.

AF: *Did any operational changes occur during your festival directorship?*

BB: We added sidebars and started a high school section that brought students to the festival, but we also went to the schools. At the end of my directorship we were starting a new project called Adobe Youth Voices, a project sponsored by the software company Adobe. It was a special section dedicated to screening short films made by young filmmakers from around the globe that highlight human rights issues. We also co-operated the Media that Matters Online Film Festival [www.mediathatmattersfest.org] by showcasing their films in our catalogue and on our website.

We also tried to create innovative programming by curating with different types of media. For example, we did some stage readings of plays in London before the films and we always had a photo exhibition along with the festival in New York.

AF: *Can you discuss where HRWFF is currently held?*

BB: First of all, the festival still takes place in New York – that's the flagship festival. The second flagship is London; HRW's second largest office is located there. A section of the New York festival travels across the U.S., licensed for a small fee to any cultural institution, community centre, human rights organisation that wants to host the festival; the fee goes back to the filmmakers. Human Rights Watch does not make money from this project. It is simply a way to assist local communities to host their own human rights film showcase and to give filmmakers the opportunity to have their films shown throughout the U.S. It is also a way for the Human Rights Watch work to gain exposure to a larger and more diverse public without taxing the staff. At this time, due to limitations in distribution rights for films and videos, the HRWFF showcase travels only throughout North America

Individual locations want different things. Smaller, more remote towns may want to programme and design their own festival in which case we discuss what films are available and the fees associated. For all travelling showcases we offer a lot of supplementary material and guidance on how to host a human rights film series in the community, how to promote this type of series with local journalist and audiences, human rights background/contextualisation for all films, how to engage in post-screening discussions on difficult human rights themes, even how to create an e-flyer, and much more. All human rights festivals that organise events through our office always have full support from us.

AF: *In an article published by the International Centre for Transitional Justice (Burres, 2008) you discuss programming and make special mention of* The Sari Soldiers *(Julie Bridgham, U.S., 2008). This film was important, you say, because it helped to 'keep an eye on Nepal'. Could you explain how this type of film was utilised by the HRWFF to raise attention about particular topics or locations?'*

BB: *The Sari Soldiers* is a great film that highlights the complicated recent political transition in Nepal. [Director Julie] Bridgham worked in Nepal for many years in various capacities – filmmaker, activist, educator – spending time with her three main protagonists, all of whom are women, before she ever began filming them. This allowed a strong bond and enormous trust to build between Julie and her main characters.

The result, *The Sari Soldiers*, is an extraordinary entry point into contemporary, post-civil war Nepal, for both the Nepalese and outsiders. It pointed a lens at what happened in Nepal's recent past and what was currently happening as a result of the transition of power from the monarchy and the military to a civilian, bi-partisan government. It was also clear that ordinary citizens were often the victims of the bloody conflict.

It is also a very human story, following the lives of three protagonists: a Maoist, a human rights worker and a woman who was formerly in the military. It really allows an outsider to have a much more intimate understanding of what was happening in the country at that time.

AF: *Can you tell me more about the philosophy of lowering ticket prices for certain groups?*

BB: We've done it at different times. We've also sponsored them. But we are always very respectful and make sure that it isn't charity. For example, immigrants living in New York and London might attend through an outreach group. In this instance, we will meet with the outreach group and discuss how it should be handled so the attendees are empowered and don't feel like they are receiving special dispensation.

AF: *Was there an ideal audience you hoped would attend the film festival? Did you ever say to yourself, 'I wish this type of person would come and see this film'?*

BB: I would say the 'non-converted', but it is so hard to tell. You cannot just look at a person and assume they don't know about a particular issue. When one sees incredibly young people there, I mean under 20 and not college students, that's inspiring. Sometimes you see people and you are not sure why they attended until they talk to you. This is great because you are able to gain a sense of why they attended. Some audience members are not political but come to a screening because they want to see anything dealing with their home country.

AF: *You mentioned that Human Rights Watch has certain goals for the festival such as fundraising and promoting ideas to a wider audience. Did you also have any personal goals while directing the festival?*

BB: Mine were similar to those of the organisation. But, I am also a firm believer that communal experiences with art, music theatre and film are extremely important for people of all ages, especially in the twenty-first century technological world. Today, it is common place for people of all ages to watch feature length and short fiction, documentary and animated works on their iPhones, iPads or PCs. But when a filmmaker truly knows his/her medium and tells an extraordinary story cinematically, the work deserves to be seen on the big screen with a real audience. Furthermore, I believe that communal screenings help individuals explore new ways of thinking about what is a truly 'open and democratic society'. I also think a community setting forces people to step outside their comfort zone. This is important because it moves people away from knee-jerk left, right or centre beliefs.

Building authentic, engaged communities is a big part of my interest in film festivals. I strongly believe that great art – film – can be a powerful agent for social change and I believe that community settings truly encourage this type of engagement; especially around social issues and art.

AF: *As you explained, Human Rights Watch does not accept government money. Who, then, are the key players in this niche arena? What type relationships do you have with other institutes, organisations, businesses, etc., in order to successfully run the film festival?*

BB: Because building communities was so important to me I was always eager and pushing to collaborate with other local New York and London-based cultural and human rights organisations and initiatives such as the African Film Festival, the New Festival [newfest.org/wordpress], New

Fest: The New York LGBT Film Festival [www.newfest.org organised by the New Festival], Cinematropical [www.cinematropical.com], El Museo del Barrio, the International Center for Transitional Justice, the American Civil Liberties Union, etc.

We would co-host a film with the Goethe-Institut or MoMA [the Museum of Modern Art]. It is true we never took any direct funds from a government, but we were open to collaborating with organisations that had. For example, they might recommend a film they thought was 'wonderful', but we would only programme it if it met our selection criteria, not for a political agenda.

AF: *In terms of raising money, what funding/grant programmes did you apply for?*

BB: Film festivals rarely make a profit, no matter how many you organise or how prime the location. You put money in them to produce a project. At best, even if you have sell-out screenings that help to recoup some of that money, there is never enough generated to cover all the costs. So, it is never is an entrepreneurial endeavour.

We work very closely with the development department because they have such a wide net of individuals and foundations. Sometimes the festival would be presented as part of a larger project, other times it was more discrete and presented to individuals. But it was always done hand-in-hand with HRW, and sometimes in collaboration with another programme at Human Rights Watch.

My personal contributions came from the film and music world. I brought Tony Elliott on board. He is the founder of *Time Out* [*Publishing*] and served as the chair of our New York festival at the same time he was launching *Time Out* there [in New York]. This grew into a wonderful relationship. Tony encouraged many of his friends and colleagues around the globe to engage with HRW. And today he serves on HRW's London board. It just goes to show how strongly interwoven our connections can be.

AF: *Staying on the topic of external participants like Tony Elliott, have you encountered any inventive ways by which individuals or businesses have utilised the festival to their own benefit?*

BB: It depends on the situation. If there is another NGO that is very strong on national security and human rights issues, and Human Rights Watch has a strong programme on counter-terrorism issues, it might benefit both to not only present films, but also organise a reception or an educational programme and highlight both organisations' work to the greater public.

So really, if we see an opportunity we will actually co-present with them. For example, when films started coming out about the Abu Ghraib prison we co-operated with the Center for Constitutional Rights [ictj. org]. This organisation used the festival as a platform to launch a book about the subject. So, in this situation we would usually always say 'yes' because it benefits both parties.

AF: *Has being affiliated with Human Rights Watch been an advantage when appealing to known and respected organisations like the Center for Constitutional Rights?*

BB: Yes, most definitely. But I also believe it is because the HRWFF genuinely fills an important niche – one that promotes great works of art and screens incredibly powerful stories about contemporary social or human rights issues.

I feel that it is a beautiful niche and was, when we first started, a unique one. But now the subject of human rights has been integrated into other film festivals like Cannes, the Berlinale [www.berlinale.de], the San Francisco Film Festival [www.sffs.org/sf-intl-film-festival.aspx] and many others. To me, this is great; it is wonderful that more people and established film festivals are interested in highlighting human rights showcases in their events. I view it as a compliment to us at Human Rights Watch International Film Festival and the field as a whole.

There are so many film festivals, and Human Rights Watch International Film Festival is able to remain strong because it is still faithful to its core mission – bringing awareness about human rights abuses through extraordinary storytelling, in a way that challenges each individual to empathise and demand justice for all people. We believe this builds and engages broad and diverse audiences on global human rights issues.

AF: *Are you more interested in securing a great film for the festival or in fostering community-building that occurs around the film?*

BB: There is a sense of pride with the films that are selected, but it's also the educational programmes that are held in conjunction with the screenings. It is about reaching ten new audience members. It is about developing engaging post-screening discussions with the filmmakers and press. We ask ourselves, 'Did the films and discussions inspire blogs?' or 'Did people attend who never would have seen this type of film before?' All these pieces are interconnected with the programme and represent the ingredients we use to determine our idea of success.

AF: *Speaking of ingredients, have you found that world events influenced the festival? For example, the end of the Cold War meant filmmakers could now access both subjects and physical areas that were previously off-limits.*

BB: What is interesting is that right after the fall of the Berlin Wall and the collapse of the Soviet Union a lot of wonderful films that had been made during the Cold War were now available for those outside the Eastern Bloc to see; it was an extraordinarily rich artistic time.

There was suddenly a great opportunity to show recently made films or watch older films through a totally different lense. I would say that was an incredibly rich period; especially the work that came out of East Germany. Many of the films were shot on 35mm with incredible attention to what was in the frame and the larger story being told. These filmmakers had been schooled at the acclaimed Polish and Russian film schools during the Soviet system. They had this traditional style and rigour that really set them apart from Western filmmakers. So, after 1991 if a filmmaker from the former eastern block, who had lived his/her entire life in the East, decided to tell a story about the complexities of the Stasi and what it meant to report on your neighbour, he/she offered a very different perspective than a Western filmmaker's interpretation of this same situation. So, as I said before, it was a pretty rich period.

AF: *Do you have any predictions as to the future of human rights film festivals? Is there such a thing as human rights film festival circuit?*

BB: In the 1990s when Human Rights Watch International Film Festival first started, people from particular backgrounds, such as programmers, would say, 'It is just a festival with an issue and that doesn't necessarily mean the films are any good'. That theory has been turned on its head and no one says that anymore.

Now there is the Human Rights Film Network [www. humanrightsfilmnetwork.org] and other informal networks. I think these networks are growing much stronger. Interestingly, some established filmmakers are not just happy but also very pleased to have their films highlighted at a themed film festival like HRWFF because they know they are going to get enormous attention. They understand that the reputation of the festival is stellar and they are excited to showcase their work in a particular way. I don't think contemporary filmmakers or the international film community believe that a human rights-themed festival will ghettoise their work. For example, when *Before Night Falls* (Julian Schnabel, U.S., 2000) came out, we showed it at a gala in New York and London. It was a big Hollywood-type movie with two movie stars. It was an incredible portrayal of Cuba, so it had lots of implications for the U.S., and Julian Schnabel showed this film at many film festivals and he loved that it was screened at Human Rights Watch, too.

AF: *Can you talk about how you went about programming for the festival?*

BB: An extraordinary network of filmmakers, independent producers, distributors, human rights activists, curators, avant-garde artists just continued to grow. I've been working in the field for over 20 years so I would often have people contact me via fax, e-mail, a message through a human rights colleague in the field, a phone call, an SMS, you name it, and any form of traditional or modern technology was used to tell me about a new, extraordinary human rights film someone had seen or of an amazing filmmaker someone had met. They might recommend I watch a film from a colleague; I mean it's a small world. I still feel very connected with Human Rights Watch because I'm close to John Biaggi, the current director, and the staff. We talk all the time and when possible work on projects together because my work now involves human rights and film. So, as you can see it is very connected.

AF: *To what extent did distributors influence your programming?*

BB: There was always pressure. Sometimes a distributor is keen to have a good film on a historical subject, say a story about WWII, featured at the festival. If we only have 25-35 programming slots annually, we think twice about using one for a historical subject. However, if that film tackles an historical issue in a new and intriguing way, or can be a stunning metaphor for a contemporary human rights issue, this makes the film more appealing to us. But yes, one always has to say no and turn down some films.

So, in turning down a film, one would say, 'It's a wonderful story and highlights an important historical issue but unfortunately it doesn't bring something new to our audiences and over the years HRWFF has showcased extraordinary documentary and fiction works on this subject'. And sometimes, even if the work highlights a contemporary social issue, it is not chosen for the film festival and one has to respectfully say, 'Thank you for sharing with us this work, but no, it wasn't selected', and leave it at that.

There are other times when you are going after the big distributors because you really want to show their new film and they are juggling and trying to determine the best position for the film. It's a business, so I tried not to take it personally. If we can't get a film we really want we create a wonderful programme around the other great films we have got.

AF: *How much did public opinion dictate programming in any particular year?*

BB: It didn't.

AF: *But what if a sponsor tries to influence the festival by asking you to focus on a particular topic?*

BB: That happens very rarely. The truth is, getting sponsorship for the HRWFF was not as easy as it would seem. As an organisation, it is condemned by many countries and dictators, so it's pretty controversial. Also HRW will not take money from certain corporations that have bad practices, labour union issues and the like. But then again, it's not as if these corporations are knocking on HRW's door to give them money!

So, relatively speaking the money is clean. And it does happen that sometimes a board member will say that they like a particular film and you'll need to be very political and diplomatic and agree to look at it to see if it fits the selection criteria.

I've stood by this philosophy and had many heated debates, but it's important.

Works Cited

Burres, Bruni (2008) 'Filmmaking and Human Rights', *International Centre for Transitional Justice*. On-line. Available HTTP: http://es.ictj.org/en/news/features/1748.html (16 May 2011).

Notes

[1]   Human Rights Watch represents a collective of 'watch' committees that were unified in 1988 to become a single umbrella organisation. The oldest of these watch committees is Helsinki Watch, founded in 1978. HRW is known for 'naming and shaming' those who commit crimes against humanity. Although the organisation operates on a global scale, the majority of HWR funding is raised from North American-based charitable donations.

[2]   The *Village Voice* was one of the prominent alternative arts, counter-culture and political publications in the U.S. at the time.

Combining the Foreign with the Familiar: An Interview with Jasmina Bojic, Founder and Director of the United Nations Association Film Festival

Raluca Iacob

The United Nations Association Film Festival (UNAFF, www.unaff.org) was established in 1998 as a project of the Stanford Film Society and the Midpeninsula Chapter of the United Nations Association (UNA). It has grown to become a national project of the UNA-USA, with growing numbers of collaborations with UNA organisations from other countries as well, while at Stanford University it has resulted in the creation of a programme called Camera as Witness, which hosts UNAFF at the University. Based on the belief that film is a powerful tool for advocacy, the film festival aims to familiarise San Francisco Bay Area audiences with global issues and the aims of the UN. The yearly themes of the festival have ranged from the broad, such as 'Building a Society for All Ages' (1999) or 'The Values of Tolerance' (2004) to the more focused, such as 'Population, Migration, Globalization' (2010). A statement from former UN Secretary General Kofi Annan's Nobel Prize acceptance speech reverberates with the UNAFF programme and mission:

> *We understand, as never before, that each of us is fully worthy of the respect and dignity essential to our common humanity. We recognise that we are the products of many cultures, traditions and memories; that mutual respect allows us to study and learn from other cultures; and that we gain strength by combining the foreign with the familiar.*
>
> *(Annan 2001)*

Although the festival's home base is at Stanford University and in Palo Alto, California, where it has run each October since its launch, there is also a travelling festival (www.unaff.org/2011/traveling.html) sponsored by UNA chapters, universities and community organisations around the world, with screenings from Waukesha, Wisconsin, U.S. to Abu Dhabi, UAE, each tailored to the particular needs of that community.

The festival was conceived by educator and film critic Jasmina Bojic, who was interviewed over email in February and March 2011, while she travelled throughout the U.S. with the festival, stopping briefly to attend the eighty-third Academy Awards®.

Raluca Iacob: *How did the United Nations Association Film Festival (UNAFF) start?*

Jasmina Bojic: UNAFF was originally conceived to celebrate the fiftieth anniversary of the signing of the Universal Declaration of Human Rights. I launched the film festival with the assistance and participation of the Stanford Film Society and the United Nations Association Midpeninsula Chapter, a grassroots, community-based non-profit organisation. Both UNAFF and the UNAFF Traveling Film Festival operate through partnerships between local UNA chapters and university student groups. These unique relationships between the festival and the community confirm our commitment to the artists and college youth and enrich the surrounding communities by providing and encouraging interaction and dialogue with academia and filmmakers.

I was inspired to establish UNAFF through my experience as a film critic attending different film festivals and not seeing enough places for documentary films to be presented and discussed. Also, for the last 14 years, I have been teaching the Camera as Witness: International Human Rights Documentaries course through Interdisciplinary Studies in Humanities and International Relations at Stanford University. It gives students a better understanding of international issues and provides them with an opportunity to be involved in discussions in an interdisciplinary environment. The popularity of this class and the students' interest in human rights documentaries was another inspiration to create UNAFF.

RI: *In what ways is UNAFF connected to the United Nations, and how do the UN policies influence the focus and programming of the festival?*

JB: Although UNAFF supports the goals of the UN, it is not politically or financially connected with the UN and is independent in its programming.

UNAFF is a non-profit organisation, which aims to stimulate local understanding of international issues and to facilitate community participation in related change. The festival celebrates films that deal with human rights, environmental themes, population, migration, women's issues, refugees, homelessness, racism, health, universal education, war and peace and other topics related to Human Rights.

RI: *What distinguishes UNAFF from other film festivals (both activist and non-activist), but also, what do they have in common?*

JB: Unlike other film festivals which focus on one theme, one part of the world or one ethnic group, UNAFF is striving to give a cross-section of the world by illuminating numerous issues from various countries, bound together by the common thread of the Universal Declaration of Human Rights. We believe that we live in an interconnected world and that most problems and solutions today are global. Documentaries often elicit a very personal, emotional response that encourages dialogue and action by humanising global and local problems. To further this goal, UNAFF hosts academics and filmmakers from around the world to foster discussions with the audience; it also provides information on how to get involved. This part is probably similar to other activist film festivals. Where UNAFF differs from other activist film festivals resides in its mission to bring awareness about the world, UN issues and all 30 articles of the Universal Declaration of Human Rights.

RI: *In what ways do you think a human rights film festival can lead to action? Does UNAFF encourage such interaction?*

JB: What we have attempted to do with UNAFF over the years is to bridge the gap between awareness and action, to foster a real appreciation of the art of documentary filmmaking, to provide avenues for audiences to deepen their knowledge in select areas of study through the means of panels and guest appearances, as well as to strengthen Stanford's ties to the Palo Alto community as well as the East Palo Alto community. In addition to this, and to complement the screenings, we also organise panels on topics such as climate change and its effect on migration patterns, the pros and cons of deregulation, global health issues in the twenty-first century, immigration issues and children, fair use, free speech and digital future in documentary filmmaking, all of which featured experts in the field. In addition, we established an event headquarters in downtown Palo Alto where audience members could converse with filmmakers about the process of filmmaking, as well as the themes of the films themselves.

RI: *Could you tell us something about this year's edition? What is the selection process for the festival?*

JB: The fourteenth annual edition of UNAFF is slated for 21-30 October 2011, with the opening night in Palo Alto Aquarius Theatre and screenings on the campus of Stanford University (Cubberley Auditorium and Annenberg Auditorium), in San Francisco at the Balboa Theatre and in East Palo Alto at the Boys and Girls Club and the East Palo Alto Prep School.

In June, UNAFF Jury members selected 70 documentaries from 607 submissions. The theme for UNAFF 2011 is 'Education is a Human Right'. The Jury committee members are usually selected on the criteria of artistic and community knowledge and involvement. They are fully independent and have complete freedom of choice in the selection process; the Festival Director, who is in charge of the programming of the festival, is equally independent.

The key points that we look for in the selection of films are: aesthetic value, fresh approach to the subject matter and relevance to our annual theme and our community, but also general Human Rights topics. We receive documentaries from all over the world dealing with every rights issue. Since each region in the world produces films with their own special pacing, style and rhythm, what matters for the screening committee is to think globally and to have patience with each entry.

RI: *Is UNAFF connected to other festivals and/or organisations? How do these relationships manifest themselves?*

JB: Through the UNAFF Traveling Film Festival [UNAFF TFF] – usually a one- to two-day event featuring several UNAFF films from the previous years – we often work with other film festivals, such as the Environmental Film Festival in Washington, DC [www.dcenvironmentalfilmfest.org], the Davis Film Festival [www.davisfilmfest.org], the Belgrade Documentary and Short Film Festival and the ANASY Abu Dhabi Film Awards.

RI: *The UNAFF Traveling Film Festival has been running for a decade now. What are the differences between UNAFF and the UNAFF Traveling Film Festival?*

JB: We introduced the UNAFF Traveling Film Festival (previously called UNAFF Extension Program) in 2000. We were encouraged by the overwhelmingly positive response both from our audiences and the media. The TFF is usually a small event, organised by the local UNA Chapter in association with a community organisation or a local university, which selects several UNAFF films from any of the previous years that highlight their particular areas of interest. Their purpose is to expose local communities to documentaries and issues that they would otherwise have no access to. So far, the year-round screenings of the Traveling Film Festival have taken place in over 20 larger and smaller cities across the U.S., as well as internationally in Paris, Venice, Belgrade, Phnom Penh and Abu Dhabi. We typically suggest that the universities and local community organisations procure the films for their libraries.

RI: *How were these collaborations initiated? Were you asked to participate by the individual international festival bodies or did you approach them for collaboration?*

JB: We usually receive an invitation from the Festival Director, who finds out about UNAFF through the website, from filmmakers or through encounters at different film events. We always try to make collaborations useful for our filmmakers in giving them new venues for outreach and potential distribution for their films.

RI: *Do such instances of UNAFF include the presence of the festival at non-activist/non-human rights film festivals?*

JB: Sometimes. It depends on the local organiser, what kind of issues they want to bring to their audience and if they find an appropriate film in the UNAFF selection.

RI: *Do you have plans to continue and/or expand the presence of the UNAFF Traveling Festival on the international festival network in the next few years?*

JB: Yes. We would like to continue with this valuable programme if we find interest and support.

RI: *You have been organising the UNAFF for a while and have presumably interacted with other human rights film festivals. Is there a human rights film festival circuit?*

JB: There are the Human Rights Watch Film Festival [www.hrw.org/en/iff], the Artivist Film Festival in Los Angeles [festival.artivist.com], the Movies that Matter Film Festival [www.moviesthatmatterfestival.nl], FilmAid Film Festival [filmaid.org]. Unfortunately, we do not have much contact with all the different activist film festivals. When we meet, it is usually cordial and we exchange some ideas, but not much else besides that.

RI: *What is your opinion of such a circuit?*

JB: Ideally, an activist film festival circuit should be bigger and more extensively covered by the media. The International Documentary Association is one of the best means of connecting different film organisations and film festivals as well as organising events where we can meet and exchange experiences.

RI: *What does the existence of a human rights festival circuit add to individual festivals?*

JB: It benefits the filmmakers to have as many screening venues as possible. Although we all compete in finding the best films, we also complement each other and make sure that few good films get ignored. Different programming strategies may bring to the surface different aspects of documentary art and the more festivals there are, the greater the possibility of supporting a variety of aesthetic and political and philosophical approaches.

Wherever documentaries achieve commercial success, we applaud that, and we are extremely happy to see the increased documentary presence in theatres and on television. Many of the films presented at UNAFF eventually get theatrical and broadcast distribution. Once a film becomes commercially successful, its message has been well propagated; yet, we would rather give a chance to a film or topic that would otherwise not be seen.

RI: *Public figures, in the entertainment industry and elsewhere, have been involved in all sorts of activist issues and have presumably drawn* *a lot of attention from the media to those issues. Do such entertainment industry personalities play a role in the decision-making, programming or practices of the film festival?*

JB: UNAFF has an Honorary Committee that includes high-profile industry figures whose international reputations lend it an additional dimension of prestige. They include businessmen like Ted Turner and William Draper III, Hollywood producer Gale Anne Hurd, documentary filmmakers Barbara Trent and Erika Szántó, as well as actors and music stars known for involvement with human rights issues, like Alec Baldwin, Peter Coyote, Lolita Davidovich, Danny Glover, Susan Sarandon, John Savage and Zucchero.

RI: *In the last few years, social media have been central in creating global awareness leading to social action locally and globally. Does UNAFF use the Internet and social media in order to reach out to a wider audience or to encourage activism?*

JB: While UNAFF has been using the Internet since inception, we believe that the current emphasis on the role of social media in recent political movements, while certainly positive, has been somewhat overstated. People organise with the tools they have, and it is the message, not the medium, that ultimately carries the day. We are, of course, eager to extend our capabilities in any possible way, and social media present a valuable outreach tool.

RI: *How does the festival accommodate various stakeholders (NGOs, activists, filmmakers, audiences, programmers, partners)?*

JB: The two stakeholders in the UNAFF, the UNA-USA and the local UNA Midpeninsula Chapter Palo Alto, as well as Stanford University through its Film Society and Camera as Witness program, have supported the film festival throughout the years, and have provided a wonderful opportunity to educate and engage our audience; to present them with a wealth of information about the world and arts while broadening their view of cultures that they would not otherwise have been exposed to. In the process UNAFF has an impact on nourishing democratic discourse and inspiring their involvement in concrete action, as well as preparing the audience for the challenges of their future professional careers. We have always taken pride in the fact that we are helpful to filmmakers, and we try as hard as we can to help them promote their work. While we seek to satisfy as many categories of participants and partners as we are able, we do not compromise out independent programming and selection policy, and we make that clear at the outset of any collaboration or alliance we enter into.

RI: *What is the importance of awards?*

JB: UNAFF gives five awards: UNAFF Grand Jury Award for Best Documentary, UNAFF Grand Jury Award for Best Short Documentary, UNAFF Youth Vision Award, UNAFF/Stanford Video Award for Cinematography and UNAFF/Stanford Video Award for Editing. We hope that these awards and recognition help the filmmakers to find educational, television and international distributors.

RI: *What is UNAFF's ideal audience?*

JB: While we want to inform as many people as possible about the films and issues that we present, our biggest impact is achieved with younger audiences. Their interest in the future of our world, and their potential to influence it, are the largest and we believe that they can benefit most from the types of documentaries that we show.

Each year UNAFF screens films from all over the world – Asia, the South Pacific, Africa, Europe, the Middle East and the Americas. The festival attracts a broad audience from the San Francisco Bay Area and appeals to a broad range of ethnicities, with many people regarding the screenings as a rare chance to see the state of human rights and culture in their own countries of origin.

We intentionally keep admission prices low (free for students, U.S.$5-10 per screening for the general public and U.S.$120 for a festival pass for all ten days), in order to encourage broader participation and access to these rarely seen films. We also stress the importance of free panel discussions and post-screening exchanges between audience and filmmakers.

RI: *Could you give a concrete example of UNAFF reaching out?*

JB: We have the program called UNAFF in Schools. The years from late adolescence through early adulthood are a particularly important period for integrating political values and habits. We believe that the success of any social engagement depends on capturing the attention and the imagination of students at an early stage.

The UNAFF in Schools Program is an important platform for students and educators to creatively imagine, discuss, compare and evaluate contemporary issues.

During the last four editions of UNAFF, a screening and panel have been held at East Palo Alto Prep School. For example, last year we screened a documentary on the poor quality of food choices in school cafeterias. Following the screening the issues raised by the documentary were discussed by a panel comprised of two parents, the filmmaker and specialists on child obesity from the Stanford Medical Centre. We would like to expand this project to a year-long programme with four to six screenings/debates.

We will work closely with teachers to prepare a programme that aligns with the curriculum. Correlating screenings and panel discussions with the curriculum will create an effective combination that will strengthen the education process.

RI: *What is your idea of success?*

JB: I would consider UNAFF a success if all the films that we have screened over the last 14 years do not remain on the shelves of an archive, but are instead adopted by others and used in classrooms, community organisations and in everyday life.

Works Cited

Annan, Kofi (2001) 'Nobel Lecture', *Nobelprize*. On-line. Available HTTP: http://nobelprize.org/nobel_prizes/peace/laureates/2001/annan-lecture.html (26 May 2011).

Hot Docs: A Prescription for Reality:
An Interview with Sean Farnel,
Former Director of Programming
at Hot Docs Canadian International
Documentary Festival

Alex Fischer

Until the northern spring 2011, Sean Farnel was the Director of Programming at Hot Docs – Canadian International Documentary Festival (Hot Docs) (www.Hot Docs.ca), the largest of its kind in North America. Sean has a long history working in film festivals. Shortly after receiving his BFA in Film Studies from Concordia University in Montreal (now known as the Mel Hoppenheim School of Cinema), he took a job at a film festival in his hometown in Northern Ontario. This festival, an outreach programme initiated by the Toronto International Film Festival (TIFF) (tiff.net) provided Sean with experience and enthusiasm for festival work. So much so that he soon became a full time staff member of TIFF. He began programming documentaries at TIFF around 1998-9 and, while neither the audiences nor the programmes for documentary were large at the time, this was a situation that would dramatically change over the next three years. Soon, audiences blossomed and films exploded, bringing new stories and new forms to the screen. In 2001, Farnel partnered with Hot Docs to launch Doc Soup, a series created to bring documentaries to the screen between TIFF and Hot Docs, and by 2005, had joined Hot Docs as its first Director of Programming. He took the primarily regional festival to national prominence, tripling its audience and cultivating a strong programming culture in his six-year tenure (Farnel 2011). His passion for documentary and his work in festivals has made him a highly regarded and much-appreciated figure in the industry. As for the Hot Docs festival itself, the event is well-respected and seen as a top tier event for serious documentary filmmakers, sales agents and distributors from Europe interested in purchasing quality context.

The following interview was carried out via a Skype video call on 2 August 2011, with Alex Fischer in St Andrews and Sean Farnel at his home in Canada.

Alex Fischer: *Although Hot Docs is well known, could you tell us a bit about it all the same?*

Sean Farnel: I think that among the documentary film festival circuit, Hot Docs is one of the leading festivals of its kind. At Hot Docs we would show upwards to a 130 feature documentaries. At TIFF we were only showing 30-35 docs, so the space was limited although at TIFF I was a bit spoiled because all the big name documentaries came to us, we didn't have to do much haggling. For example, Errol Morris would call offering his new film, or Herzog, or Barbara Kopple. Because the documentaries were playing within the context of this major international film festival, you wanted them to have a little pop. So you tended to show the celebrity-driven work, or work by established directors. For example, this year TIFF will open with the U2 Documentary, *The Sky Down* [Davis Guggenheim, U.S., 2011], they are also showing a documentary about Pearl Jam [*Pearl Jam Twenty* (Cameron Crowe, U.S., 2011)]. So, you are working within a different context. This isn't to say they shy away from political work; it's just that there is a different ratio.

But even at Hot Docs this year, we had this goal to expand our audience so we also dabbled in the celebrity-driven work, so, for instance, we showed the Conan O'Brien film [*Conan O'Brien Can't Stop* (Rodman Flender, U.S., 2011)]. Again, Hot Docs is now a big festival with a broad mandate. The trick was to not let a title that had a 'name brand' marketing advantage overshadow the work. That was just as important to us. It was a tricky balance because the media was most attracted to those easier films.

Still, Hot Docs is on the first tier and many filmmakers use the festival to launch films. In terms of the role of festivals in the life of film, I believe filmmakers really only have six months to launch and screen a film at festivals. An ideal scenario would be a launch at an event that is recognised as one of the worlds leading festivals. To me the big four are Sundance [www.sundance.org/festival], Berlin [www.berlinale.de], Cannes [www.festival-cannes.com] and Toronto. Venice [www.labiennale.org/en/cinema] is important but not so much for documentary. Beyond that, specifically for documentary, and just as effective, would be the IDFA – International Documentary Film Festival Amsterdam [www.

idfa.nl/industry.aspx] – and Hot Docs, in the U.S., South by Southwest [sxsw.com] and Tribeca [www.tribecafilm.com/festival]. Launching regionally or domestically is also a good way to start. For instance, if you are an Asian filmmaker, Pusan [www.biff.kr/intro/default.asp] or, even more specifically, if you are a Japanese filmmaker Yamagata [www.yidff. jp] are important events. A filmmakers 'home' festival can be a lifelong source of support and community, so these should not be neglected.

As important as the festival circuit is to the life of an independent documentary, it can also be a very time consuming and unprofitable venture. Which is why I recommend limiting your active participation, for most films, to a six-month window. We also want you to make another film, so you need to get back to work!

AF: *How is the festival funded?*

SF: Hot Docs, like most film festivals in Canada, is primarily funded from three sources: first, by various forms of government, both provincial and local. Typically it was around 30-35 per cent of the budget that came from the government. Then there is 20-25 per cent from corporate sponsorship and earned revenues were 40-45 per cent. So Hot Docs had a higher than average – at least in a Canadian context – reliance upon earned revenues, which represented ticket and pass sales, as well as industry pass and submission fees. More typically it is split into thirds, or such was the case with Toronto and the festival I started at, Cinefest [www.syracusecinefest.com]. It may be different for both of these organisations now. But there is a shift in Canada, and even more so in the United States, as more funding is being generated through philanthropic means, the so-called 'third-sector' or social econonmy.

AF: *What differentiates Hot Docs, or other documentary film festivals, from human rights festivals; and conversely, what may they have in common?*

SF: First of all human rights is in the title of these festivals so they foreground their intentions a lot more. I certainly think that human rights film festivals have more prominent and formal relationships with other human rights events and non-governmental organisations [NGOs]. At Hot Docs these tended to more informal.

Documentary is a broad form, and activists and human rights festivals narrow in on an aspect of that form. Besides being good for political expression, a documentary can also be very poetic and impressionistic. It's really great for personal filmmaking. A film festival like Hot Docs, which is a survey film festival, programmes as much as possible across the documentary spectrum because the festival's mandate isn't just around human rights filmmaking. I guess that's the difference. The unofficial curatorial motto at Hot Docs was, 'Let's show everything a documentary can do'. The notion being, that it can do as much, if not more, than fiction. So it is a very interesting style of filmmaking, expanding beyond the notion of politically or socially engaged filmmaking.

Yet, human rights festivals are a subset of the broader festival circuit and follow a lot of the same rules and patterns within the festival circuit. Obviously, what we were doing at Hot Docs intersected because I believed, and still do, that the core mission of documentary is around human rights and social activism.

I could compare the people that work at Hot Docs and not see a lot of parallels between them and people that work at designated human rights or humanitarian film festivals, but in my experience they tend to be politically engaged people. I include myself in this category too. Obviously this is the reason why I was drawn to documentary. When I began at TIFF, I was pre-screening all the submissions and watching really bad romantic comedies alongside the documentaries. I then realised that if I was going to be a programmer I would inevitably watch this volume of films every year and, frankly, a lot will be bad films. So, in some ways, my decision to focus on documentary was very practical. Even in watching the weaker films I'd be learning something.

AF: *What is the gatekeeper role of the human rights festival programmer?*

SF: Humanitarian film festivals have different criteria sometimes, but film selection is always important. At Hot Docs we would balance the need for compelling subject matter with an interest in film form and aesthetics that human rights film festivals wouldn't necessarily overly concern themselves with because they tend to prioritise subject and content, though that may be an unfair generalisation.

AF: *Do you think the audiences are different?*

SF: The audiences that attend human rights film festivals and documentary film festivals are not that different. I think we draw from the same cross section, essentially. There is a human rights festival in Toronto [the Toronto Human Rights Watch Film Festival[1] (humanrightsfilmfestival.ca)] that has a smaller cross section of the Hot Docs audience.

AF: *What else distinguishes a human rights film festival?*

SF: There is often more emphasis on wrapping a discussion around the film. This offers an opportunity for formalising and contextualising certain issues through the Q&A period. Q&As are crucial and the whole reason for having this type of film festival because they generate discussion and can result in action following the screening. If you don't have this interaction, then the screening is no different than putting the film on television. It just disappears into living rooms. I think the whole point of having this type of film festival is the transfer that takes place from the screen to the audience. This transfer hopefully inspires some form of action.

Human rights film festivals also seem to focus more on getting the subjects to attend the screenings instead of just the filmmaker. This helps to amplify the story. I know at Hot Docs it was always great to have the filmmakers attend, but it was better to have the subject present especially when it was a politically charged film. The audiences seemed to love this atmosphere and Q&As can last as long as the screenings themselves. Even at TIFF, which is a large, corporate, celebrity-driven event, there are political elements. Some of the celebrities come with political agendas, but they are little more than background and don't seem to get the same attention they would at a documentary or activist film festival.

AF: *In his contribution to this book Igor Blažević from One World International Human Rights Film Festival (www.oneworld.cz/2011) wrote: '[festivals] that lack the market and commissioning dimension have no value to filmmakers as they do not help them generate returns and, respectively, do not help them pull off new projects that they will be planning to work on'. Any comments on that statement?*

SF: I don't agree with that. I mean, what is 'value'? I think there is much meaningful value in making a connection with an audience. In fact, I believe that is the primary value for a filmmaker attending a festival. A statement like this creates the impression that markets are the be-all and end-all for filmmakers at a festival, which in my experience isn't true. Even at Hot Docs or IDFA, which have large market components attached, only a small number of filmmakers truly have access. As well, I find many of the markets are silos, disconnected from the main pubic festival.

I think the notion that they have to network and market themselves constantly can distract and deflate filmmakers and devalue the festival experience. They may become concerned when they know a certain distributor or sales agent is at a festival but fails to attend their screening. It is important to understand that market people generally do not go to screenings at film festivals. They want screeners. They are too busy with business and attending dinners. It may happen that they will hear about a film and possibly catch up with it later. There are a lot of great festival experiences to be had that do not have markets attached. As a filmmaker, you have to see a festival with a market as two distinct worlds. Naturally filmmakers should leverage the market aspect of any events they attend that have that component. But don't get consumed by it.

AF: *Another shared festival aspect seems to be awards. What do you think is the significance of awards at a human rights film festival?*

SF: First of all, the role of festivals is to give attention to subjects or film forms that aren't receiving attention already. Awards further amplify this role by focusing that attention on a select number of films in a festival's programme. I'm not sure as to how sustaining the impact of these awards is, but certainly any accompanying cash prizes are helpful to filmmakers. Also, the awards help to legitimise an issue discussed in a film, not to mention giving a feather to put in the cap of your funders.

AF: *Could you explain how you see human rights film festivals advancing human rights?*

SF: It is understood that an informed citizenry always advances human rights. My only reservation at times is that most film festivals are preaching to the converted. So often I wonder how many minds were changed as a result of a screening.

That's me on a cynical day. Most of the time I think of the bigger picture, like if only one person carries on the message from watching film then the cause was moved forward. I know, for instance, that Hot

Docs showed a film called *Your Father's Murderer: A Letter to Zachary* [also known as *Dear Zachary: A Letter to a Son About His Father*, Kurt Kuenne, U.S., 2008] that dealt with a complicated legal case in [the Canadian province of] Newfoundland, and that film led to a legal change in Canada. It took a while, two or three years after it screened at the festival, but it eventually caused a change in legislation. This was due to the awareness that it generated and the fact the right politicians saw the film at the right time. So I know that can happen, which is an incredible thing. I think the politically engaged documentary can be more captivating than print journalism. It is an emotionally powerful form. It is a very visceral form. It is incredibly effective at communicating and moving people emotionally to act.

AF: *Are there ways in which a programmer might help the activist filmmaker achieve his or her goals?*

SF: This is a big deal because a film only plays two or three times and you want a full house. One wants to make the most of that opportunity. Hot Docs does a lot of legwork around a screening, and scheduling was a big part of it. At Hot Docs we have a good publicity team and we would do our best to try and ensure each film got equal coverage. This coverage ranged from news stories to linking a film with a particular organisation. We also do direct outreach so the film would have the correct audience. That is, seeking out people that would be naturally inclined to see a film about a given subject.

Lots of filmmakers are doing their own social media publicity, but you have to be careful not to create too much noise. The main thing is for people to buy into the notion of the festival as a whole. That is, people buy tickets to an annual event that they have confidence in and it is the identity of the event that lifts the films up.

That's why these events are important. You could have a one-off screening in a town that would require huge amounts of resources and only have a few hundred people attend. But if you have an event with a good profile in a city, ideally the people are just going to come because they trust the programmers based upon their previous experiences.

AF: *Who is the ideal audience to attend an activist film?*

SF: An ideal audience would consist of people who don't agree with the premise of the film. It doesn't happen enough because it's tough to have people attend a film they are not going to agree with. I'd like to see us concentrate on figuring this aspect out because it is what these films are all about. It is very rare that you'll get the ideal audience. Let's face it: these films aren't neutral; they are point-of-view films. Those screenings [where] you do have a mix are electric. The Q&As are amazing.

It is also up to the filmmaker in terms of building that conflict within the film. One of the most politically effective films that I've seen is *Episode 3: 'Enjoy Poverty'* [Renzo Martens, Netherlands, 2009]. It's a darkly satirical film about the economics of aid. The filmmaker is sort of the antagonist within the film, and he makes it very difficult for an audience to orientate themselves within a single point-of-view or emotional attachment. I haven't seen a film get under a person's skin like this, ever. It totally makes you flip your thinking. But it's not your typical human rights film. The more conventional approach usually reaffirms an existing position, or sheds light on an unknown issue, or helps you better articulate your opinion, but they very rarely change opinions.

AF: *Could you talk about a film festival's role in educational outreach?*

SF: This is something I'm personally interested in, having researched and developed what later became the learning stream at TIFF [tiff.net/learning]. In its early phase this consisted of screenings and discussions for adults, filmmaking and competitions for young audiences and study guides for schools. It was about getting film to be used as an educational tool. Documentary lends itself so well to study, and with young people using audiovisual material in everyday life, it seemed a perfect fit.

Hot Docs has a very active education programme in which two things happened. First, films were screened at the festival for free for school groups. Second, we have a year-round programme where we would send films into the schools. We try to get guests to accompany the film and we would provide a study guide. We also try to tie the themes into the curriculum as much as possible. We work with educators, but it is still tough because subjects are limited by teaching times. In this respect, we've found that short films work well. A lot of filmmakers are increasingly seeing the educational market as the primary target for their work. And, of course, these are where the future audiences will come from.

AF: *Have some humanitarian causes been more prominent than others at the festivals you attend?*

SF: Obviously a lot of this has to do with either current events, or the exposure of historical injustices. Good examples would be the many films about the war in Afghanistan and Iraq. There was a five-year period where there was a lot of that work. It seems to have tapered off. When I first started programming documentaries 12 years ago there were a lot of films discussing the Holocaust.

When Hurricane Katrina hit New Orleans, there were 20-30 films dealing with that topic over a two-year period, from various angles. The BP [British Petroleum] oil spill in the Gulf of Mexico will probably be the next topic for American filmmakers. These responses to current events are amazing because documentary seems to have created a space that did not exist in journalism before. The fastest turn around for a feature documentary is around a year. So these films come out well after the event has occurred and they are still able to convey new information that did not penetrate the mainstream media and its 24-hour coverage. I have been at festivals where my jaw has dropped because I learn new information on a subject I'm familiar with. For example, films about Guantanamo Bay, such as Alex Gibney's film *Taxi to the Dark Side* (U.S., 2007), fill this space in which thoughtful investigative journalism, at least in the mainstream, has disappeared.

AF: *Based on your experience to date, do you have any advice for the filmmaker or activist?*

SF: In terms of festivals, if I was giving advice, I'd say the first thing a filmmaker needs to do is look for either a major film festival launch or a reputable platform in their own country, as I mentioned above. Of course, one has to be strategic and knowledgeable about the inclinations of festivals, especially as it applies to première policies. For example, if you are a Japanese filmmaker you can première at Yamagata and still have Berlin as your International première. But if you played at Busan first, Berlin probably wouldn't take you because you've already given away your international première. Ideally, you would then play at two or three second-tier festivals that would be your festival run, a great run, actually. Then depending on your desire to really engage politically, you would need to investigate where your film will do the most work in the world, and this really depends on the subject of your film. I think one of the best examples of doing outreach is Julia Bacha who made *Budrus* [Israel/Occupied Palestinian Territory/U.S., 2009] and *Encounter Point* [Ronit Avni and Julia Bacha, U.S., 2006]. She has really got this figured out in terms of a festival launch: six-month festival screening window followed by a series of targeted events and screenings, whilst leveraging social media and making use of all the tools for maximum impact. These screenings don't need to be connected to festivals but, rather, can be special event screenings with organisations and NGOs. The key is to get the profile for the film from an important film festival.

So, *Encounter Point* went from Tribeca to Hot Docs and then it went to Europe and played at a few festivals. But then it also was involved in a number of other screenings including festivals on the human rights circuit. A nice thing about the human rights festivals is that they are less concerned about premières, so that option is always available to filmmakers if they want to have an extended run. This could mean a film could play for up to a year or two – if you have that kind of time.

So the launch window lasts anywhere from three to five months and then the filmmakers need to decide what the run of the film will be. That is, if they want to continue working with the film, because many filmmakers want to start new projects. It all depends on time because it can be an all consuming, full time job just going to film festivals... and, of course, in most cases that doesn't pay the bills.

Works Cited

Farnel, Sean (2011) 'I Work for Documentary', *Ripping Reality*, 19 June. On-line. Available HTTP: http://rippingreality.com/?p=1253 (12 August 2011).

Notes

[1]   This festival is an initiative of the Human Rights Watch Canada Committee.

Just Vision and the Uses of a Festival Circuit: An Interview with Ronit Avni, Executive Director of Just Vision

Leshu Torchin

Ronit Avni is the founder and Executive Director of Just Vision, a not-for-profit, non-partisan organisation dedicated to bringing visibility to Palestinian and Israeli civic leaders who work to end the bloodshed and the occupation, to preserve human rights, to promote reconciliation and to build a sustainable, free and secure future for all. Just Vision seeks to ensure that these people are taken seriously, that their work is given better visibility, locally and globally, and that their efforts are valued and influential. One of the steps Just Vision has taken is the production of two feature-length documentary films, Encounter Point *(Ronit Avni and Julia Bacha, U.S., 2006) and* Budrus *(Julia Bacha, Israel/Occupied Palestinian Territory/U.S., 2009).*[1]

On 21 December 2010, over Skype, we discussed the films and explored how film festivals assisted the organisation's mission.

Leshu Torchin: *What is Just Vision?*

Ronit Avni: Just Vision is a non-profit organisation dedicated to telling stories that you don't hear on the nightly news of Israeli and Palestinian civilians who are committed to non-violence and conflict resolution work. Our international team is based in Sheikh Jarrah (East Jerusalem), New York and Washington DC. Our members are journalists, filmmakers, human rights advocates and conflict resolution experts. We are Israeli, Palestinian, North American – and one Brazilian, Julia Bacha.

Just Vision was founded in 2003 at the height of the Second Intifada after a two-year in-depth research process whereby we interviewed 475 Israeli and Palestinian non-violence leaders, peace builders and human rights advocates, in order to understand what was needed, what they felt was missing and how they could be better supported.

The vast majority of these activists felt invisible to the media and to their own communities. They did not know how to reach supportive audiences internationally; they also didn't necessarily know who else, within their own societies, was out there doing similar work. This was in 2001-3 when many individuals and groups did not have websites. The penetration of the Internet in Palestinian society was limited. People felt they were working in isolation and Just Vision emerged to fill those gaps.

Our primary audiences (in no particular order) are North Americans, Israelis, Palestinians and the wider Arab world. We are also able to reach broader international audiences because film and multimedia are so efficient, so portable and easy to transmit around the world. But those four audiences are our primary targets, because this is where most of the political influence on the subject resides; this is where the greatest number of stakeholders in the conflict and its peaceful resolution live, although in the case of the U.S., that may be changing.

LT: *Could you speak a bit about your use of film as a tool for advocacy and as a means of achieving the organisation's goals?*

RA: We do several things. Currently, film is a preferred medium because it reaches so many millions of people. It's also a great press hook and a way to have unlikely audience members come in and immerse themselves in another reality for 90 minutes. However, film is inherently reductive and it cannot be comprehensive on this or any complex issue, so we complement it with extensive resources on-line. Our website, www. justvision.org, features hundreds of pages of interviews with Israeli and Palestinian peace-builders ['Visionaries' on the site]. These interviews are conducted in the respective mother tongues of the interviewees and translated into the other two languages – so the site is in Arabic, Hebrew and English. Interviewees speak in-depth about the type of work they are doing, how they arrived at it, what lessons they have learned along the way, what mistakes were made and how others can get involved. There are also supporting materials for the films.

Our first film, *Encounter Point*, was released in 2006. The film follows a former Israeli settler, a Palestinian ex-prisoner, a bereaved Israeli mother and a wounded Palestinian bereaved brother, who risk their lives and public standing to promote a non-violent end to the conflict. Their journeys lead them to the unlikeliest places to confront hatred within their communities and fear within themselves. The film explores what drives them and thousands of other like-minded civilians to overcome anger and grief to work for peace and for freedom. It is a film about the everyday leaders in our midst.

Encounter Point began its circuit at the Tribeca Film Festival [www.tribecafilm.com/festival]. It has since screened in 200 cities around the world, and counting, and has reached tens of millions of viewers. It was broadcast in its entirety on Al Arabiya, one of the largest Arabic satellite networks, followed by a one-hour in-depth conversation with the main protagonist, Ali Abu Awwad, and with an Israeli member of Combatants for Peace. It was also broadcast on Latin American HBO, CBC in Canada and excerpts were shown on CNN. The film has been used by community leaders, clergy, politicians, think tanks and even policy makers over the years. Due to its success we ultimately decided to create another film, which was *Budrus*.

We arrived at the idea of making *Budrus* through interaction with audiences during the tour of *Encounter Point*. Israeli audiences, American audiences and other European audiences would often pose the question, 'Where is the Palestinian non-violence movement?' and often the follow-up statement would be something along the lines of 'If Palestinians adopted non-violence there would be peace'. Whereas in Palestinian society, and Arab audiences, but primarily Palestinian society, people would say, 'We've tried non-violence and it failed' referring to the first Intifada. There was so much energy around this disconnect that we decided to look for a story where we knew the Palestinian community was successfully engaging in a non-violent struggle. That led us to the story of *Budrus*. We began production in 2007, even though the events chronicled in the film had taken place in 2003-4. We were able to track down about a hundred hours of footage from human rights defenders and activists who had been in the field and had been present from early on, recording the struggle to save the lands endangered by the construction of the Israeli separation barrier that threatened to uproot 3,000 olive trees and destroy the fabric of the community.

Budrus residents mobilised, uniting and securing the cooperation of various Palestinian political factions (Hamas and Fatah), the leadership of Palestinian women and the cooperation of Israeli and international activists. We found the story to be moving and powerful and yet no one had heard about it. It was not being referenced by any of the leading journalists covering the region. Even people from nearby Ramallah and Tel Aviv had not heard of the story of Budrus. So we decided to make the film.

LT: *It appears that the exhibition circuit had already contributed to the work of Just Vision by providing the crucible for the second film: with the audience comments, you were able to determine what other stories needed to be told. In this regard, how do film festivals contribute to the goals of Just Vision?*

RA: Film festivals were integral to the strategy of getting the message out. We see film festivals as a key component of driving attention and audiences to our work.

Encounter Point debuted at the Tribeca Film Festival, a world-class film festival that was also incredibly supportive; the film did very well there. Peter Scarlet, who at the time was the head of the festival, singled out four of his favourite films on the front pages of the Tribeca programme; he named *Encounter Point* as one of his favourite films – and there were over 200 films in the festival! That enabled us to garner a lot of media attention. So we had wonderful reviews of the film and great press coverage. Programming director David Kwok also helped by scheduling our opening night in the same 800-seat theatre where a blockbuster like *Mission: Impossible III* (J.J. Abrams, U.S., 2006) had opened just weeks before. Because we had done a lot of prior outreach work to publicise the première, we were able to sell out all four screenings at Tribeca. People were lining the blocks to attend.

Tribeca also organised a press conference, which featured our team and four of *Encounter Point*'s main protagonists. This generated terrific press, not just about the film, but also about the people and the issues that it profiles. All kinds of community events took place in conjunction with that première. Around the festival, we were able to reach out to Jewish, Arab, Muslim and Christian networks that brought out folks to screenings, where we also hosted Q&A sessions after each showing. This helped to enhance the message of the film and increase its outreach potential.

From there, the film travelled to the San Francisco International Film Festival [www.sffs.org/sf-intl-film-festival.aspx], to which we took Ali Abu Awwad, who had not been to the United States before; again we received terrific press, along with the 2006 Audience Award for Best Documentary. We then went to Hot Docs [www.hotdocs.ca] in Canada, where the film was acquired by the CBC and subsequently broadcast. We also took it to the Jerusalem Film Festival [www.jff.org.il] and opened on the day the war between Hezbollah and Israel broke out in 2006. We were able not only to sell out the screening and receive a standing ovation, but we also staged a discussion as a follow up to the film that lasted two hours! This was attended by an extremely diverse group of people – Israelis, Palestinians, Orthodox Jews and settlers, Palestinians from the West Bank, devout Muslims and many others. Outside the theatre, people did not want to leave, so there was an opportunity for them to get together in small groups and have a conversation.

We consciously work to attract diverse audiences at a range of festivals; we reach out to local community leaders and potential stakeholders in the conflict, for example: faith-based groups, relevant ethnic communities and their leadership, academics, think tanks and journalists. We also circulate sign-in sheets at every screening so that we can stay in touch with audience members and grow our base; we have built our email list up to thousands of people. Once people have signed up to the list, they help us to spread the world as we move from city to city to screen the film. In fact, even with great reviews in places like *The New York Times* and *The Washington Post,* nothing beats word of mouth. Communities reaching out to their constituents remains a more reliable way of filling the theatres – stronger than even the greatest reviews in high profile newspapers.

After we completed the high profile festival circuit, we pursued a niche circuit of women's film festivals, human rights film festivals, Jewish, Israeli and Palestinian film festivals, and so on. Then we decided to go for a theatrical run. We only had a staff of five at the time. We had no PR budget whatsoever and no distributor. Yet we found amazing audience loyalty as audiences across the U.S. organised theatrical screenings in their communities. We showed the film in 15 cities, where the screenings were organised entirely by audiences passionate about bringing the film to their local theatre. And then we would create interactive programming in the theatre to have conversations, panels or workshops with people there. This was all a result of people coming to see the film at the festivals. So festival showings were truly a launching pad for us.

LT: *Did you follow the same festival trajectory for* Budrus?

RA: With *Budrus* we decided to start the circuit from the East rather than from the West. This time we launched at the Dubai International Film Festival [www.dubaifilmfest.com] in December 2009. There were two red carpet gala films – one was *Avatar* (James Cameron, U.S., 2009) and the other was *Budrus*, an incredible recognition for us. It was an enormous theatre, incredibly elaborate; many of the filmmakers and local community leaders attended. Even villagers from Budrus were in the audience. Queen Noor of Jordan gave the keynote speech and that marked the beginning of her very committed relationship to the film and Just Vision's work. We brought two protagonists to the festival along with our team. It was an amazing experience and we were able to garner attention in both the Arab and the international press. We also launched relationships with other film festivals.

From there on we went to the Berlin International Film Festival [www.berlinale.de], where *Budrus* did very well. All of the major German press covered the film extremely favourably, which led to a distribution deal agreement whereby the film is being taken to over one hundred cities and towns across Germany in this unique hybrid festival-theatrical model that they have there.

The Berlin Film Festival was a key part of our strategy because we were aware that the Israeli press took the festival very seriously. So we hired a local Israeli PR person to cover the film's reception at the Berlinale, a move that generated a great deal of press in Israel. People would just literally translate the Berlin coverage, not having even seen the film, and in this way we were spoken of very highly in many of the Israeli media outlets. Berlin was essential as the festival was something the Israeli press trusted and liked. So here, as in other places, we were able to reach out by knowing who pays attention to what film festival. And we knew that in this instance, Berlin was of greater weight to Israelis than Tribeca.

The circuit for the film also included the Human Rights Watch International Film Festival in London [www.hrw.org/iff/London], where we were able to reach out to local community leaders. We returned to Tribeca where we benefited once again from the programmers' benevolence; they gave us slots that allowed for excellent exposure and outreach. We held panels. We had a ton of press. We brought the protagonists to the screenings. Michael Moore saw the film and engaged with it. We were also able to hold a special discussion for high-level journalists, thought leaders and policy-makers, in conjunction with the New America Foundation, which included a fancy dinner following a screening. We did that twice, once in Tribeca and once at AFI-Discovery Channel Silverdocs in Silver Spring, MD [silverdocs.com]. These events and the in-depth conversation they engendered led to coverage on NPR [National Public Radio], in Newsweek, in The Nation, at ABC News, etc. A lot of pieces came out of these high level meetings. Members of Congress saw the film and helped us to organise a screening on Capitol Hill for over 200 audience members.

The film travelled to the San Francisco IFF [www.sfiff.org/festival], AFI-Discovery Channel Silverdocs and Travers City [www.traversecityfilmfest.org]. Most exciting, possibly, was the screening in Ramallah. We held this on our own, without a festival. Queen Noor came. Israeli Press came. We timed this to happen in advance of the Jerusalem International Film Festival [www.jff.org.il]. And again, we received terrific coverage.

LT: *Is this emphasis on the media coverage tied to Just Vision's goal to shift the discourse on the coverage of the conflict?*

RA: Absolutely. And film festivals are a crucial and often underutilised platform for this purpose.

LT: *The description of the film's movement and the cultivation of relationships with programmers suggest a distinctly strategic approach to travelling through festivals. Would you say there was a festival circuit you identified for the films that aided in achieving your goals?*

RA: Yes. The strategy is to get as much high profile media attention and as many awards as possible in the beginning to legitimate it as a powerful film in order to reach beyond the choir. People who aren't necessarily issue-driven will come to see it because it has been at these reputable festivals. The strategy for *Encounter Point* and for *Budrus* was the same. We start out in non-denominational settings. For example, while our first visit to San Francisco was to the San Francisco International Film Festival, later on we returned for the San Francisco Jewish Film Festival [www.sfjff.org]. We wanted first to get as broad an audience as we could without getting the film pigeonholed as a Jewish film, a Palestinian film, an Arab film or a women's film, before we brought it to audiences with a special interest in those issues.

So if there is a circuit, one begins with the 'A-List' festivals, which are essential for getting to thought leaders, culture bearers and decision-makers. Then there are the niche or specialised festivals, where the constituencies you are reaching care specifically about the issues raised in the film.

And then there are the festivals where we can charge a fee for the screening. We then use the money to make the film available to Palestinian and Israeli audiences and screen it for free. We will often find creative solutions for those who can't afford to pay for the film so that we can bring the film to the communities where it matters most, regardless of their ability to pay.

LT: *How does one reconcile the demands of a festival economy with the demands of the project? Types of films and the premium on premières, for instance?*

RA: I want to be clear that film festival programmers are duty-bound to bring in the best films that they think are relevant to their audiences, to feature a diverse array of films and to include films that stand alone as works of art. That is their primary responsibility and I don't think that should change. However, for those who have made films of social relevance, it's critical not to overlook festival screenings as an opportunity to have a conversation with audiences and reach out to unlikely allies. Programmers want to work with you, especially if you are able to bring in lots of people who don't normally attend the festival, or people who are passionate and interested.

In terms of *Encounter Point,* we were very clear that we wanted to make a film that could stand on its own as a work of art, so that any filmgoer or film buff could go see it and leave thinking that they just saw a great movie, regardless of the issue it tackles. And then, of course, we also hoped people would be inspired by what they saw and would want to learn more and would want to take it back to their communities and use it as a catalyst for learning and involvement. And we've seen both. But we were very clear that in order to achieve these objectives, the film had to be very professionally done and competitive with any other work of art within the medium that year. It had to be able to garner critical attention and positive reviews and win awards so that it would gain legitimacy and be taken seriously by all kinds of people. So even if viewers didn't agree with the message, they could appreciate the intrinsic value of the film as a film.

LT: *Were there any other ways in which film festivals ended up proving a useful site for developing the project or building a base? Any surprises as to what festivals could or couldn't do?*

RA: I cannot understate the benefit of The Good Pitch, which we participated in at [AFI-Discovery Channel] Silverdocs, although this is a roaming event that moves from festival to festival: it's been at Tribeca, San Francisco and elsewhere. It's a component of the Channel 4

BRITDOC Foundation that trains people with films-in-progress to pitch to a collection of activists, philanthropists and broadcasters – people who can help further the social issue films (see britdoc.org/real_good/pitch).

They brought on Judith Helfand and Robert West of Working Pictures and Sandi DuBowski, so it's a powerhouse of a team. We were selected to pitch in 2009 and it had a huge impact on our film in terms of meeting people. From this, people from the Sundance Institute came on board, and we also met several other funders who became involved.

I was surprised by the degree to which people became champions of the film – some programmers were so passionate about our work. They became friends and allies who were on the lookout for opportunities and who remained in touch with us. They are invested in the success of the films they select; and that is a terrific benefit.

Notes

[1]   JustVision reaches out to a broad donor base, including secular Jewish, Muslim and Christian communities. It receives contributions from a wide range of sources. Film funding for *Encounter Point* and *Budrus* has come from over 300 individuals and family foundations (mostly, but not exclusively based in North America), from private and public foundations, and in-kind donations of services. DVDs for home viewing are available through JustVision at www.justvision.org/purchase. Those wishing to organise a screening are invited to email screenings@justvision.org.

'Connect Me with Activism and Film Practice, Not Activism and Film Festivals!': An Interview with Želimir Žilnik, Filmmaker

Greg DeCuir, Jr.

Želimir Žilnik (b. 1942; www.zilnikzelimir.net) embodies the notion of an activist filmmaker in a very profound way. His enduring rebellious spirit was nurtured in the ciné-clubs of the 1960s in Yugoslavia, where he worked alongside such acknowledged radical filmmakers as Dušan Makavejev and Živojin Pavlović.

From early on Žilnik highlighted the struggle of the disenfranchised. Always present wherever there is social controversy and injustice, his social diagnostic projects can be traced back over several decades: to 1971 for example, when he invited several homeless men to stay in his flat in Crni film (Black Film, Yugoslavia, 1971); or to 1968 and another short documentary film called Pioniri maleni (Little Pioneers, Yugoslavia, 1968) which depicts the plight of youths living on the streets.[1]

As one of the first filmmakers to raise issues such as the discrimination against Gastarbeiters in Germany in the 1970s or the unfair treatment of minorities and migrants across the new Europe today, Žilnik relies on taking as much as possible directly from reality. Many of his films are documentaries, but they often take the form of docu-dramas, which blend a provocative semi-fictional narrative with the use of non-professional actors in their actual places of residence or work. His deceptively simple aesthetic allows him to create urgent street-level communiqués on current problems.

At the height of the Yugoslav wars of secession, for example, Žilnik engaged in a series of subversive staged provocations that exposed the overwhelming nationalism and violence of the Serbian society of the time. For his acclaimed Tito po drugi put među Srbima (Tito Among the Serbs for a Second Time, Yugoslavia, 1993) he hired a Tito impersonator to walk the streets of Belgrade in full costume while he captured the reactions of people on camera. Responses ranged from the incredulous to the bizarre unloading of personal trauma and memories onto the surrogate Tito. Žilnik has called this production a 'happening' rather than a film. His Marble Ass (Yugoslavia, 1995) was one of the first films to showcase gay subculture and the existence of gay prostitutes on the streets of Belgrade. After the film premièred to a packed house at the Sava Center in Belgrade, homophobic crowds gathered to shout their displeasure at the film. In response, Žilnik invited all gays, lesbians and prostitutes to join him on stage and make their voices heard; the call provoked a stampede of people rushing to the stage in a powerful show of solidarity.[2]

Žilnik's work is not in commercial distribution; it is mainly seen in the context of special organised screenings and other guerrilla distribution events. Festivals have also been instrumental in Žilnik's career, from Oberhausen (www.kurzfilmtage.de) and Berlin (www.berlinale.de) to Rotterdam (www.filmfestivalrotterdam.com/en) and the Diagonale Film Festival in Graz (www.diagonale.at). Yet Žilnik still sees festivals as secondary to activism. He speaks of an 'extended activism' that requires a deep and dedicated commitment over time; a lifestyle that comes to be on display within the full oeuvre of a filmmaker and stretches through a lifetime. The various political commitments one makes over time form a unity that is greater than the sum of their parts; the filmmaker returns to highlight the injustice, exploitation and exclusion that have concerned him all his life. At present Žilnik is exploring current social matters such as human trafficking, poverty, social upheaval and intolerance – themes that have repeatedly figured in his films since the first ciné-club productions of the 1960s.[3]

This interview took place in several stages. I first caught up with Žilnik in May 2011 while he was lecturing in one of many video workshops he organises. During a screening break in this workshop we sat down for a talk at the Student City Cultural Center café in Belgrade. Shortly thereafter in June we followed up with a phone conversation and an e-mail exchange.

Greg DeCuir, Jr: Tell us about your first festival experience as a filmmaker.

Želimir Žilnik: My beginnings were in the amateur film clubs in the early 1960s. Festivals were the first places where I got reactions to the films

I was showing. For me and my colleagues that was cause for great excitement. The second important thing was the way we communicated in the former Yugoslavia. All around the country – in Belgrade and Novi Sad (Serbia), in Zagreb and Split (Croatia) and in Ljubljana (Slovenia) – the ciné-clubs organised film festivals. In addition to watching the films, we had debates. Those debates were somehow the first articulation of what we would today call alternative film.

GD: *What were those amateur ciné-clubs like?*

ZZ: Amateur film clubs had been organised in Socialist Yugoslavia as a form of what was called 'people's activism'.[4] This was not an official part of the cultural sector but rather a part of skills training. Ciné-clubs offered a space free from ideology. The people in charge of the ciné-clubs were not socialist realist artists, they were more old-fashioned technicians. Nobody asked you, 'What is your topic?'. They asked, 'How well did you light the material? Did you use the right ingredients to develop the print?'. Therefore, everything that came out on the screen in these amateur film festivals was actually very different from the official cinema. We felt that we were a movement opposing everything that was coming from the state-owned studios. Some filmmakers that I met at film festivals, like Karpo Godina from Ljubljana, Lordan Zafranović from Split and Rajko Grli from Zagreb, later became close friends. On many occasions we worked together. A great plus in this environment was that members of the previous generation who had already passed through the ciné-club practice – Živojin Pavlović, Dušan Makavejev, Marko Babac – were on the juries and took part in those debates. We felt they were better judges than you could find in official, professional film festivals.

GD: *Your first international festival award came in 1968, when the documentary* Nezaposleni ljudi *(The Unemployed, Yugoslavia, 1968) won the Grand Prix at Oberhausen. The film exposed the ills of state socialism in a context where the very existence of such problems was being denied. Can one say that the Oberhausen Film Festival assisted you in bringing up important concerns?*

ZZ: The Oberhausen Film Festival was one of the brightest windows in the world of short and documentary film at the time. Getting an invitation from them was particularly exciting, as Oberhausen was a special place, located in the middle of industrial Germany where the unions had been very strong. It was one of the biggest centres of iron production in Germany and had been the site of the main weapons industry for the First and Second World Wars. The atmosphere there was extremely open. They invited cinema from all the socialist states, as well as the best films from the U.S., Europe and Latin America. I saw the films of radical Cuban filmmaker Santiago Alvarez there and also American independent films. The many uprisings and social movements of the period were reflected in the films shown there. In 1968, there were huge debates among young German filmmakers about burying the cinema of their fathers.

GD: *Just a year later, you were awarded the Golden Bear at the Berlin International Film Festival (www.berlinale.de) for your debut feature Rani radovi (Early Works, Yugoslavia, 1969), which connects its title to the early work of Karl Marx. It is a bold film that exposes the difficulties of reaching out to the masses and the mismanagement of the political system in Yugoslavia. Made on the heels of May '68 in Paris, the Belgrade student demonstrations in June 1968 and in the aftermath of the Prague Spring liberalisation and subsequent military intervention in Czechoslovakia, your stated goal for the film was to reflect the spirit of various student protest movements.[5] This particular award is often seen as an important expression of solidarity. What was the political climate?*

ZZ: The festival programme was great. When I got my award there were also a lot of debates. In Berlin, they had had a lot of student protests. I was only there for a few days but I remember daylong discussions at the festival.

GD: *In the 1970s your work was blacklisted in Yugoslavia and you immigrated to Germany in order to avoid further persecution. Did you make films on inconvenient topics while in Germany?*

ZZ: After emigrating I became involved in a sort of 'activist film cell', if one can describe the German filmmakers cooperative and the New German Cinema that was linked to it in this way. Also, at this stage in my career festivals became of less importance as an exhibition outlet. In Germany, I made a number of shorts, often focusing on the plight of guest workers living in the country. These short films primarily played in commercial cinemas before the presentation of a feature-length film.

GD: *How has the role of film festivals changed from the 1960s when you first began making films to the present day?*

ZZ: In the early 1960s film festivals were the place where new films were invited. The press was very open to new film tendencies. If you compare the critical reaction from that period with European television today, especially German television, things were much more open back then. They had more space in the press in those days, so the criticism was better.

GD: *What does it mean to be an activist filmmaker?*

ZZ: The biggest surprise is the effect of a film. Whenever you address a topic – whether it is exposing an individual or a situation, or focusing on someone who is excluded from the public sphere and whose voice is not heard – you think that it would be good to help people to articulate their position. But you never dare to say that it will change the environment. Only in very few cases have my films had some sort of public impact.

GD: *Your films have appeared at more than 50 festivals, yet you maintain that you have never seen anything like activism associated with these festivals.*

ZZ: They express solidarity, but that's it. Festivals cannot engage deeply with every film in their line-up. There is usually a small press conference for a few hours, but nothing more. It takes risk to be an activist. I am still waiting to receive an invitation from a festival that runs such risk.

To me, activism is everything that one does to launch a low budget project: the pre-production arrangements, the contact with the subjects of the film, the build up toward a public debate, and so on. I call this 'prior activism' in that it takes place before the film is finished and released.

My recent film, *Stara škola kapitalizma* (*The Old School of Capitalism*, Serbia, 2009), for example, speaks of factory dissent and the exploitation of workers by a new class of corrupt post-socialist capitalists. The activist element here is mostly found in aspects that remain invisible and that took place prior to the film coming out. I spent several years making short documentaries on the subject which were not given attention in the media. We shot three documentaries and no one wanted to broadcast them. The workers organised screenings and produced DVDs as part of their protest. These small steps gradually led to a situation where we finally provoked a discussion on television. In recent months, the 'new capitalists' we exposed – international drug dealers and war profiteers among them – were investigated and arrested. The feature grew from the experience of that research and my earlier activist work in the field.

My relationship to festivals, and the state of festivals themselves as cultural institutions, has changed over the years. Indeed, it is hard for me to speak of film festivals and activism because I don't know exactly what film festival activism is. Festivals do not directly produce activism and neither are they the direct product of activism. Directors come as guests and are invited if their film has triggered a certain reaction or debate in the country of origin and the festival wishes to support the director, maybe to facilitate the film's release if such a release is denied in the home country. Sometimes the finished film is launched in the country of the festival to demonstrate respect or solidarity, be it for political or aesthetic reasons. Still, when the Cannes Film Festival [www. festival-cannes.com/en.html] programmes such works, it is not for the films in question, but rather for the sake of the festival's image.

In my experience the idea of festivals as a 'place of activism' had greater significance before the fall of the Berlin Wall and before Internet communication. For many of us from Eastern Europe, the Oberhausen Film Festival was the place to gain support during a period when our films were suppressed at home. There was a possibility of expressing some form of solidarity with directors who were fighting for a change in cultural politics. Today, festivals are the only stage for non-commercial films.

GD: *How do you close the gap between making a film and provoking action afterwards?*

ZZ: I think the film makes it by itself. We didn't control what happened with films that were structured around provocation, such as *Tito Among the Serbs for a Second Time*. For us that was the biggest surprise.

GD: *Do you normally seek out a certain type of film festival for your work?*

ZZ: To be honest, I'm not very good at that. I go to big festivals, like for instance Rotterdam. Usually I wait for invitations.

GD: *Your films address painful issues of today's reality in ex-Yugoslavia. Are you involved with domestic festivals?*

ZZ: In the last 20 years I decided not to be a part of the film scene in Serbia. The cinema infrastructure collapsed. Furthermore, it became necessary to negotiate with politicians and the like. During that time I have never even applied to festivals in Serbia because the system is rotten.[6] I am not a part of the industry machine. I produce and distribute my films using my own network, writing letters to filmmaker friends asking for support, sometimes in exchange for territorial rights. This is activism as well.

GD: *Since 1996 you have organised and led more than 20 video production workshops across the former Yugoslavia, instructing young people in ways to change the world through a responsible use of the camera. Do you see this work as another manifestation of your activism?*

ZZ: In the last decade or two I've been asking myself about the prospects that exist for youngsters. Today they rarely have opportunities like those that were available to us, even back in the so-called dogmatic socialist times. For instance, many of us amateurs had the chance to be noticed at festivals. It was after seeing our work at such festivals that production companies invited us to make more films.

GD: *Are there any prospects for a film festival activism today?*

ZZ: It's difficult to say. For the people coming to the festivals the films are the most important things. Film activism is more relevant to the shooting location, the contact you have with the participants in the film and public debate, rather than festivals. The real film activism occurs in places like Iran where there is a repressive regime that would silence the voices of artists and other dissenters. Festivals, however, do not share the risk of filmmakers who put their lives on the line, but rather profit from it. Connect me with activism and film practice, not activism and film festivals!

Works Cited

Gržinić, Marina (2006) 'Early Works', in Dina Iordanova (ed.) *Cinema of the Balkans*. London: Wallflower Press, 65-72.

Turković, Hrvoje (2009) 'Paralelni, alternativni i subkulturni opstanak – neprofesijski dokumentarizam u Hrvatskoj I Parallel, Alternative and Sub-Cultural Survival – Non-Professional Documentary Filmmaking in Croatia', in Inesa Antic (ed.) *ZagrebDox – International Documentary Film Festival/Međunarodni festival dokumentarnog filma 2009*. Zagreb: Factum, 175-81.

Notes

[1]   There was no officially acknowledged homelessness in Yugoslavia at the time.

[2]   *Marble Ass* won a Teddy Award at the 2005 Berlin Film Festival.

[3]   The Kenedi series, a longitudinal multi-installment project chronicling the trials and tribulations of Kenedi Hasani, a young Serbian Rom (Gypsy) deported from Germany, is one of the most important cinematic documents on the situation of Roma, Europe's most sizable and extensively discriminated-against ethnic minority. So far the series includes *Kenedi se vraca kuci* (*Kenedi Goes Back Home*, Serbia and Montenegro, 2004), *Gde je bio Kenedi 2 godine* (*Kenedi, Lost and Found*, Serbia and Montenegro, 2005) and *Kenedi se zeni* (*Kenedi is Getting Married*, Serbia, 2007).

[4]   This idea of a 'people's activism' went under the name 'narodna tehnika' and was first established as a workshop-type series in 1948 by the Central Committee of the Yugoslav Communist Youth League. It was an initiative designed to administer technical training for amateurs in a variety of fields – a sort of 'enlightenment' process designed to make various technologies accessible to the citizenry and educate (see Turković 2009). A number of leagues were created as a result of this initiative, including the League of Photo Amateurs (Savez foto amatera) which, in 1949, changed its name to the Yugoslav League of Photo/Ciné-amateurs (Savez foto-kino amatera Jugoslavije).

[5]   On this important film see the essay by Marina Gržinić (2006).

[6]   In 2010, Žilnik was a panellist at the Subversive Film Festival in Zagreb, Croatia (www.subversivefilmfestival.com). In July 2011, his newest film *Jedna žena – jedan vek* (*One Woman – One Century*, Serbia, 2011) premièred at the Motovun Film Festival in Croatia (www.motovunfilmfestival.com).

How to Leverage a Film Festival:
An Interview with Judith Helfand,
Filmmaker and Co-founder of Chicken
& Egg Pictures and Working Films

Leshu Torchin

Judith Helfand is an award-winning filmmaker whose commitment to humour, social justice and entertaining media is evident in her films A Healthy Baby Girl *(U.S., 1997), about her exposure to DES,*[1] *her cancer and its impact on her family;* Blue Vinyl: A Toxic Comedy *(with Daniel B. Gold, U.S., 2002), about the hazards of biochemical pollution; and* Everything's Cool *(with Daniel B. Gold, U.S., 2002), about global warming. Although for many, 'sustainability' refers predominantly to environmental issues, for Helfand, these include creating sustainable economies, communities and documentary production. Her collaborative projects include Chicken & Egg Pictures (www.chickeneggpics.org) and Working Films (www.workingfilms.org). The former, co-founded with Julie Parker Benello and Wendy Ettinger, supports women filmmakers with grant funding and creative mentorship. The latter was co-founded with Robert West, a veteran film festival programmer and educator, and aims to enhance the activist potential of films by working with filmmakers and non-government organisations (NGOs) to develop strategic community engagement campaigns and education programmes. Together they have developed Story Leads to Action, a monthly event that unites Chicken & Egg-supported and/or Working Films-trained filmmakers with New York-based activists, educators and organisers and specially invited audiences to brainstorm and develop 'community/audience engagement strategies' for both works-in-progress and completed films. These screenings followed by directed (and interactive) discussions and workshops often led by Helfand, also take place at film festivals, including AFI-Discovery Channel Silverdocs Festival (www.silverdocs. com), DOC-NYC (www.DOCNYC.net) Sheffield Doc/Fest (www. sheffdocfest.com) in 2011.*[2]

In 2009, at the University of Wisconsin-Madison, Helfand partnered with Gregg Mitman to teach a class called Community Engagement through Film. They developed this class in the wake of the first Tales from Planet Earth environmental film festival in Wisconsin (2007; www. nelson.wisc.edu/tales), in order to produce a more 'community driven' festival where 'numerous partners [...] actively shape and use the festival as a platform for community engagement' (Helfand and Mitman, 2009: 1).

We spoke on 17 August 2011 following a screening of shorts – including The Barber of Birmingham *(Gail Dolgin and Robin Fryday, U.S., 2011) (barberofbirmingham.com/), a project which she joined as a producer in order to help complete the film – at the 15th Annual DocuWeeks (www.documentary.org/docuweeks2011), a showcase that provides week-long theatrical engagements for documentaries in New York and Los Angeles so that they may qualify for Academy Award® consideration.*

Leshu Torchin: *Could you explain what you did in the University of Wisconsin-Madison class to 'leverage' the power of Tales from Planet Earth?*

Judith Hefland: The students each chose a film featured in the Tales from Planet Earth festival that they felt spoke to their own interests and passions. The goal was to leverage the press attention of the selected film and the festival, to heighten the public's interest in the film and to link the story on screen to the work of local grassroots organisations in the community, who early on had come on board as community partners to the festival. They knew that these films, while not specifically about their local work, would speak in powerful and personal ways to their supporters and members. So the work of the students was to figure out what would be useful 'asks' of the audiences at the screenings that would support the organisations; what kind of action or activity could help 'move the dial' (i.e. advance the cause and make some change).

The core idea behind leveraging a film festival is to take the moment when a community of hearts and minds – a film festival audience – is caught up in a story and thinking 'Oh gosh, what can I do?'. In collaboration with the organisations our students created intentional, useful 'to dos' that were linked to the film's main narrative or linked to a local equivalent of the story. In a situation like Madison, Wisconsin, the festival films highlight stories that resonate with the people in the cinema even if they are typically about somewhere else. In the post-screening Q&A we say, 'While you're looking at this really hard issue – like poverty or hunger – and finding compassion and empathy for those who live far away, we're going to introduce you to an organisation that's dealing with this very same issue *here* – an issue you might not see because you don't live on that side of town or because you rarely go farther than four blocks away from campus'. In a college town like Madison, like in many places, poverty and deep inequality are often invisible and hard to 'see' unless you consciously look.

Our goal is to take something that is highly visible in the movie, link it to something that might be invisible in the community, and move the latter into the frame. This idea, which we've been experimenting with at Working Films since our founding, is one of the things that I am most proud of. It's a model for leveraging the power, reach and possibilities of a local film festival especially when it is linked to a university or college campus. In order to support our partner organisations, we sought ways to embed opportunities for supporting their on-going work – making these some of the 'to-dos' or 'asks'. Once we solidified these 'asks' we identified and reached out to local institutions, vendors, companies and people who had the capacity, clout and interest to support a film festival. But instead of being asked to support direct 'hard' festival costs, we invited them to specifically support the engagement efforts connected to the films and our partner organisations. This became a model for what Gregg and I saw as a new brand of festival sponsorship – linked to the goals of sustainability – one that celebrated the power of storytelling, stimulated the local economy and helped build a more sustainable community all at once. Instead of the traditional exchange of money and resources for a credit in the festival trailer, a logo on a swag bag and an ad in the catalogue (some of which we still did), the 'buy in' was that their money, contributions and commitment went directly to the engagement projects and community partner organisations.

We were able to do this because Festival Director Gregg Mitman had done a stellar job of fundraising; the festival was fully funded, the filmmakers' plane tickets all paid for and all the movies were free to the public. With that work done, what we wanted to do was to elevate and celebrate our grassroots partner organisations by finding ways for them to gain support and patronage from local businesses, institutions and/or vendors – the kind of access and support they could build on after the festival. One example: the Student Union at UW-Madison and a local micro-brewery committed to buy jam and pickles from Porchlight, a local non-profit organisation that trains and hires formerly homeless people to produce high-end condiments sourced from local farmers.

The sustainability went something like this: we strived to connect the film issues with local concerns; we built on that by linking these to the work of local community partners and supported them by getting press/public interest in their work as well as support from institutions and businesses (what I consider to be mega consumers/vendors) who would contribute to the projects, initially because of the film festival, but hopefully for the long haul.

To get these larger festival 'sponsors' (as opposed to 'partners') from the community, we used the leverage employed by many festivals: publicity and 'getting your name in lights'. We linked this part of the effort to our production class – which was made up of non-filmmakers for the most part, students with rigorous environmental studies rather than filmmaking background. Their core project: each one produced a film festival trailer – two-to-three minute mini-docs that linked to the themes and issues of a programmed film. Before each film, we screened one of the trailers whose sponsorship credits included names of festival funders, local community partner organisations and the community/ festival sponsors. In all of the radio interviews we did, we mentioned, praised and celebrated the community/festival sponsors and the projects and organisations they were supporting. In this context they were much more than patrons of the arts; they were patrons of the community. Best of all was that these relationships and the respectful reciprocity born out of the long-term relationships nurtured by the Nelson Institute for Environmental Studies at UW-Madison (NIES), could thrive way beyond the festival. Such community building contributes to the longevity and effectiveness of a film festival.

LT: *Could you expand on this reciprocity?*

JH: A student made a trailer called *More Jam, More Jobs* about Porchlight, which was also linked to a series of films in the fest about 'green jobs'. The inspiration was another student in our class who wanted to persuade her sorority to use their annual consumption of jam as a way to support the work of a local organisation that offered more than just jam – jobs. This was truly a model 'to do' for building a sustainable community. You need jam? Buy the jam from Porchlight. You need pickles? They sell those too. And every time you buy a jar of jam or pickles, you're helping to turn a programme into a job.

And the benefits go further. Porchlight describes this exchange as '[providing] meaningful, confidence-building employment opportunities to our clients and also [supporting] local, sustainable agriculture and the farms and producers who grow healthy food in Wisconsin' that they source from (www.porchlightinc.org/porchlightproducts). We invited the heads of the student union and held the event where the students made presentations, at the micro-brewery (gratis with food). The event included a tasting, and both of them ended up making an order. Up until then, the University was only buying from SYSCO – a big conglomerate with no local ties. Sustainability, economic justice and local pride were all direct outcomes; the students were thrilled, the University became an even better neighbour and, hopefully, more jobs were created along with more jam and press for all

LT: *You mentioned connecting distant issues to the local community. Do you have any examples of that?*

JH: One of the best things we did was with a film about hunger – *The Hunger Season* [Beadie Finzi, UK, 2008], set in Swaziland. A team of two students came up with this idea called 'Share the Shares'. The goal was to get people to sponsor partial or whole shares of winter vegetables for food pantries so that they would have enough fresh produce to distribute in the winter when all they usually have are starches and canned vegetables.[3] We used this film and engagement project to address the issue of local hunger, an issue that is invisible in a landscape of plenty. The students teamed up with two local food pantries, which were also local community/festival partners. Determining the need for fresh produce in winter, they approached the local Community Supported Agriculture (CSA)[4] to find out if they could pursue 'Share the Shares'. This alternative food network was available but not cheap and not generally accessible to people going to food pantries for assistance. The students were very successful; they raised almost all of the winter shares from community sponsors, with the last bit coming from the festival audience.

We were also able to link this global issue about hunger in Africa directly to Wisconsin – one of the reasons the festival director chose the film – was because the cornmeal that is part of the U.S. Food Aid program in the movie is grown and ground in Wisconsin. Tales from Planet Earth and Working Films invited the company who ground and bagged the corn meal to bring a bag to preview screenings in a church, which also acted as Madison's largest food pantry. After the screening, we served the corn meal, the same meal the audience saw the kids eating in the film and hosted roundtable discussions about the causes and solutions to hunger, both global and local.

Following the meal, the students got up and said, 'Here's the deal. We're not asking you to support the Swazi community featured in the film; the filmmaker is already doing that through direct gifts from film sales. We want to address hunger here in Madison, because as invisible as hunger is over there, it's equally invisible here'. That's when they asked the audience to support Share the Shares – to insure that both pantries, one on the North Side, near campus, and the other on the South Side serving the immigrant Latino community, received a winter's share of fresh CSA non-perishable produce. This model also supported the local farmers. Sponsors and audiences were inspired to give, and the impact was 100%.

These are models that can travel with a movie to festivals and other screening contexts.

LT: *Attention seems key in leveraging a festival.*

JH: Press is a big part of the strategy. Local press is important for any film festival – and for everyone involved. It's the local hook that will help the non-famous filmmakers get in the press – and there are more non-famous filmmakers at most festivals than famous ones. Meanwhile, the festival outreach person, programmers and directors need to prove that they are bringing in a new cross section of the public that has never been to the festival before. They need and want to be able to say that they've brought people in who've never seen an independent film outside of a multiplex; that they've brought together members of the community who've never before sat in the same room at the same time; that they are reaching new audiences and creating safe spaces to talk about uncomfortable issues. Festivals need to find ways to stand behind their mission statement and heighten their profile beyond their core fans. And filmmakers committed to using their films in engaged ways are just what they need to do that.

Meanwhile, local press desperately want to write about their hometown festival and how the films and filmmakers might relate to their community. Filmmakers and festivals want coverage beyond the Arts pages – because there is just so much room/opportunity there. You do that by finding the local angle to a film, finding the local cause and finding local, informed activists or 'eye witnesses' working on the 'issue' who can be interviewed.

LT: *Were there particular challenges or issues that arose in a university-based film festival like Tales from Planet Earth?*

JH: It was a really interesting amalgam. I loved the opportunity to play out all these ideas in a small town, especially where there are established relationships that have been shepherded and nurtured over time. Such relationships are precious to a university especially if there is an authentic desire to bridge a town-gown divide exacerbated by class divisions. And with my colleagues that was the case. We were not just sending students out to 'learn from them' and then leave with the 'goods', which can often happen with traditional 'service learning'. The model Gregg was determined we pursue, in the spirit of University of Wisonsin-Madison, is 'doing with' over 'doing for'. There were challenges: Are we showing the films in the right venues? Is the university sponsorship enough of a reason to screen all the films on campus? Will the audiences we want (and who really might want to/need to) attend feel comfortable and 'safe' enough to come? Or will it just be the people who already feel at home on campus? What are the implications of easy accessible parking, no parking or paid parking? How do we ensure that the students go to events off campus (those not in our class) and do so with deep respect, interest and openness? How do we make sure they feel 'safe' and welcomed?

LT: *At Madison, the students chose from pre-selected/vetted films and community partner organisations; is there any advice you might offer to a filmmaker without this assistance?*

JH: 'Don't wait for the film festival to do the job that you can truly help them do better.' In most cases, festival outreach and audience engagement is a volunteer job; or, there is one paid person responsible for far too many films than they can deal with or do engagement for. They choose panels and engagement events that are press worthy, timely and linked to organisations that can bring in audiences. You can bet that that one over-worked 'outreach' coordinator will probably welcome a developed event that brings in unlikely, new and/or underserved audiences. At Chicken &Egg and Working Films, we recommend that filmmakers apply to a festival with a panel or programme suggestion attached to their film – don't wait for the festival to make these connections. If you have NGO partners, think about bringing them with your lead characters, to serve as part of your Q&A and to help promote the screening. If you do… your film festival tour becomes a film festival strategy built around 'leveraging'. There are 'A-list' festivals, obviously, but by mindfully choosing festivals where you can organically link a film's story with a community, you can help turn any festival into an 'A-list' festival. High profile or not, the festivals will draw press if you make that dynamic link between your film and the story on the screen, to the community that is hosting you to some sort of a campaign or tour.

Let's take for example the film *Semper Fi: Always Faithful* (Tony Hardmon and Rachel Libert, U.S., 2011), about long-term water contamination at the Marine Corps Base in Camp Lejeune, North Carolina and a former Marine's fight for justice. Executively produced by Chicken & Egg, it is about to launch a North Carolina screening tour and national engagement campaign co-developed and co-managed by Working Films The film's non-festival première will be in Jacksonville, North Carolina, where the story is based. The film will then go on a tour to those U.S. cities with the largest populations of retired Marines, who we know were among the one million base members exposed over 20 years. As an extension of the film's festival run, they are targeting cities that have film festivals, are close to military bases. But the concern for this pollution goes beyond those living in the camps, as one in five Americans lives within 10 miles of a military installation. With geography and military bases as navigator this is a potential 'programme in a box'.

Linking the Camp Lejeune story and applying it to a matrix of festivals near bases will bring this urgent story to light as it directly reaches out to its most important audiences where they live. Do that, and it's very easy for a film festival to say 'YES' and for local, regional and even national press to say 'YES', and to see the link as an opportunity.

And now you're bringing festivals a programme, and the programmer thinks, 'Phew! I'm going to do this really engaged thing and I won't have to do all of that work!'. You've given them a handcrafted press story and a new community of people to reach. I know that this sounds like more work than applying to a festival, but this is all about an applied festival strategy. Many times, if you do this homework and groundwork they will take your movie because you showed them the relevance of your film and you did work they would not have had the time or even the connections to do.

And what do you get from it? Well, you will most likely get a beautiful screening room, with good projection and good sound (that you don't have to rent, manage or have set up). These venues won't be as politicised as a 'vets against pollution' meeting or even a 'town hall' screening. The screenings will be linked to arts and culture, which means the organisers and community members get a neutral space and get to feel important because this film which is touring the country – is being shown in their community, independent of their organisation – is in some way about them.

But once you ally yourself with partners, you're on their timeline. Filmmakers can only do festivals for so long. There's a certain period of time in which I do the film festivals, and after a year or so (or less), it's not about the film festival timeline any more, and it's not about the broadcast timeline: it's about the organising timeline. So I use film festivals in that first year in a very strategic way, when the film is fresh and it's new – when I'm figuring out the best strategy. I like to think of film festivals as laboratories where you can experiment. This means – some things are going to stick, find synergy and others won't. So I'll figure it out: 'That didn't work, but this did, so let's do this where it's most strategic'. That's the point at which I leave the festival circuit for the organising circuit. And when I say 'I', I mean 'I' as a working filmmaker, offering my/our best practices to others.

Works Cited

Helfand, Judith and Gregg Mitman (2009) 'Community Education through Film', Syllabus- University of Wisconsin-Madison. On-line. Available HTTP: www.workingfilms.org/downloads/Class%20Syllabus_1.pdf (17 August 2011).

'Posts Tagged "Tales From Planet Earth"' (2011), *Working Films* website postings. On-line. Available HTTP: http://workingfilms.org/blog/?tag=tales-from-planet-earth (17 August 2011).

'Silverdocs! Story Leads to Action' (2011), *Stone Soup Films* website posting, 24 June. On-line. Available HTTP: http://www.stonesoupfilms.org/silverdocs-story-leads-to-action (17 August 2011).

Notes

1   DES refers to Diethylstilbestrol, a synthetic estrogen prescribed between 1940 and 1970 to pregnant women at risk of miscarriage. In utero exposure was later discovered to cause a rare form of vaginal cancer and various other health issues.

2   The people at Stone Soup Films recorded and posted the Story Leads to Action panel at AFI-Discovery Channel Silverdocs on their website (see 'Silverdocs! Story Leads to Action' 2011).

3   Food pantries are organisations that distribute food to feed the hungry – either directly, or through other agencies.

4   Community Supported Agriculture offers a way for consumers to buy food directly from local or nearby farmers.

The Human Touch: Review of *Setting Up a Human Rights Film Festival*

Alex Fischer

Setting Up a Human Rights Film Festival: A Handbook for Festival Organizers Including Case Studies of Prominent Human Rights Events, Tereza Porybná (ed.) (2009) Prague: People in Need. ISBN 978-8086961-64-4. The book is available as a free download from www.oneworld.cz/2011/userfiles/file/OW-cookbook_web.pdf

The production of film festivals is a complex and challenging subject about which to write, but One World's Handbook on *Setting Up a Human Rights Film Festival* is a superb example of getting it right. Comprehensive and well thought out, this volume communicates the ideas of credible and experienced practitioners. Based upon the 'plentiful experiences gathered during 11 years of organizing the One World festival, as well as the know-how of several other important human rights festival organizers' (8), the wealth of knowledge and practical wisdom presented here is simply astounding.

The book is divided into four sections and addresses the experiences of a group of seasoned practitioners based at the Prague headquarters of the One World Human Rights Film Festival (OWHRFF) and directors from the One World global network; from launching the film festival to running the One World affiliate festivals. All write in a candid but instructional tone that is peppered with anecdotes and warnings for those who are contemplating starting, or have just started, their own human rights-focused film festival. The book is signposted by large headings enabling easy navigation of its 232 pages. Equally practical is the unified formatting of each chapter within its respective section; all chapters within the 'Setting Up a Human Rights Film Festival' section come with a useful 'Timeline' indicating when action should be taken regarding the topics discussed. An additional practical advantage is the fact that the book is available as a free download; this makes it easily accessible and is in line with the philosophy of the organisation of contributing to an 'interconnected world' (4).

The expertise of the individual authors is a major strength of the book.

For example, Igor Blažević (founder of the OWHRFF) contributes his expertise in two chapters: 'How to Start' and 'Raising Funds to Support a Human Rights Film Festival'. Similarly, Monika Štěpánová (the Director of the Czech Centre in Bucharest, Romania), Alphonse Apoti Makove (founder of the Kenyan-based Dunia Moja) and Marko Popovic (co-founder of Free Zone Festival in Belgrade, Serbia) provide detailed accounts of their unique experiences in organising human rights film festivals.

The two chapters by festival veteran Igor Blažević are a must read. Not only does he provide valuable advice, but he also explains how human rights film festivals are fundamentally different from mainstream festivals. Central to his argument is the role the former fulfil as sites of 'information and testimony rather than art and entertainment' (15). He emphasises the importance of establishing a specific festival identity and warns first time festival directors of the pitfalls of being overly-ambitious; he talks of seemingly trivial, yet hugely important matters, such as the need to set the festival date well in advance, the importance of choosing an appropriate name and venue, as well as the proper programme size.

Understanding how to frame an event is central to its future success. Blažević notes that due to the challenging nature of the topics they raise, human rights film festivals could potentially face more difficulties when building a support base than more generalised film festivals; it is extremely important that human rights film festival organisers present their event in a proactive context so as to increase the likelihood of gaining support from potential sponsors and funding agencies.

The only failure of the chapter is Blažević's insistence that first-time organisers should not waste 'time, energy and funds from [their] meagre resources on programming' (18) and instead solicit the help of established human rights film festivals for films. While this advice does have benefits, it must be taken with caution as such action could instil a welfare-type attitude of dependency, which could weaken the festival and ultimately limit the creative and curatorial responsibility of the organisers. It is often said that a film festival lives and dies by its programming; it is therefore better to earn a unique reputation than to become a mirror image of some other larger event.

Blažević's second contribution to the book is a thoughtful discussion on finding the money needed to facilitate an event. Full of great advice, this chapter discusses how to approach possible sponsors such as NGOs, embassies and private companies. He recommends avoiding red carpet ceremonies that can be a drain on resources and invites film festival organisers to remain flexible as to where possible sources of funding might be found. For example, he explains how certain government mandates concerning environmental issues can be used to broaden and diversify an event's financial base. Such awareness can help to strengthen the festival's ability to remain financially resilient in difficult or low-income years. Blažević also notes the challenges in building a support base for human rights film festivals, as these are events that need to raise difficult issues and topics (this view has been echoed by other festival directors interviewed here, such as Bruni Burres).

Unlike in the other chapters in this section, however, Blažević does not give any instruction as to when financial planning should commence. This is a major oversight as the planning of grant applications is a long, drawn-out process that can catch novice film festival organisers unaware. Similarly, mention needs to be made of the commitments and key performance indicators that dictate funding and the importance of organisers having a clear understanding as to what needs to be delivered and when. Failure to fulfil such obligations can jeopardise future funding and needs to be taken seriously if the film festival hopes to retain a sense of continuity.

A significant proportion of the book is geared towards preparing festival organisers for unforeseen and potentially disastrous incidents. Tereza Porybná, who discusses production and technical support issues, is obviously well-accustomed to dealing with crises and presents a logical game plan that would help prevent embarrassing situations, ranging from lost films to dead mobile phone batteries. She also highlights the importance of recognising those individuals and companies who helped facilitate the event.

Public relations specialists Karla Štěpánková and Filip Šebek discuss the specifics of media campaigns related to festivals. Their 'golden rule' of dealing with any media organisation is 'understanding them as much as possible' (84). Yet knowing exactly what the media want is difficult and subject to a number of conditions. This chapter presents an impressive range of information detailing the types of print deadlines associated with different kinds of publications, as well as the importance of providing clear and precise answers to questions posed by the press. Štěpánková and Šebek do an excellent job of pointing out the importance of cataloguing press clippings and articles to be used for future events. Such publicity is important in legitimising the event and conveying to sponsors the potential press coverage the event is capable of generating. And such attention to detail is a handy habit for the budding festival organiser to cultivate.

As film festivals are social constructs, they are intrinsically linked to the experiences of their participants; good or bad, these experiences ultimately contribute to the reputation of an event and can have long-lasting influence with regard to future involvement. Contributions that make suggestions for good practice in setting up guest services (Tereza Porybná) and educational outreach activities (Ludmila Součková) highlight further important matters. Other subjects covered here relate to the operational procedures of film festivals as a whole and include detailed advice on catalogue design, as well as useful practical recommendations (e.g. to physically mail out thank you cards at the conclusion of the event).

The second two sections of the book (Case Studies and The One World Tour Affiliated Festivals) feature seven first-person accounts by human rights film festival organisers from around the world. Each author provides unique and personal insight as to the challenges they have overcome in facilitating activist film festivals in environments that can often be qualified as demanding or unsympathetic. The case study on the South Caucasus Documentary Film Festival of Peace and Human Rights stands out as an example of the power of a film festival for breaking down barriers in order to promote human rights. Martina Tichov, the Tbilisi-based festival coordinator, presents an extremely well written and engaging narrative about this travelling festival's role in promoting peace and understanding in the complex conflict-ridden region of the Caucasus.

The case studies – discussing events located or coordinated out of Argentina, Burkina Faso, Georgia, Germany, Kenya, the Netherlands, Romania and Serbia – present a wealth of information and assist in understanding the intricacies of film festival operation in a variety of cultural contexts. These texts, written mainly with practitioners in mind, nonetheless represent a solid contribution to developing the theoretical framework for our understanding of film festivals and their role in society. Each case study is a firsthand account that reveals social ties and struggles that often remain invisible to outsiders.

The Appendix of the volume includes sample budgets and media plans that provide a great resource for neophyte film festival organisers.

Simple and straightforward, these samples can act as a basic frame in which to develop a more comprehensive and individualised festival plan. There is also a list of human rights film festivals, as well as a list of the various awards presented at specific festivals, with hyperlinks provided for those who might want to investigate further.

This handbook on *Setting Up a Human Rights Film Festival* is an excellent resource for organisers entering the field. The advice and wisdom offered by the various authors is sound and should provide operational advantage for those willing to implement its recommendations.

The organisers of the One World Human Rights festivals network should be applauded for their contribution to film festival studies, as this publication not only represents a solid resource, but also marks an important shift in how practitioners view the impact of their work on the world around them. Indeed, film festivals should not be confined to performing as sites of exhibition alone, but should also be capable of producing knowledge and shaping opinions within contemporary film culture and society at large.

Bibliography: Films, Film Festivals and Activism

Kathleen Scott

Abrash, Barbara (2006) 'Making Your Documentary Matter: Public Engagement Strategies That Work', *Center for Social Media*. On-line. Available HTTP: http://centerforsocialmedia.org/sites/default/files/documents/pages/mydm_06_report_0.pdf (20 July 2011).

Andes, Sheryl Rose M. (2010) 'A Peek at the Winners of the *Most Gender-Sensitive Film Award* of the Metro Manila Film Festival', *Dalumat Ejournal*, 1, 2, 23-33.

Archibald, David and Mitchell Miller (2011) 'From Rennes to Toronto: Anatomy of a Boycott', *Screen*, 52, 2, Summer, 274-80.

Arcodia, Charles and Michelle Whitford (2006) 'Festival Attendance and the Development of Social Capital', *Journal of Convention & Event Tourism*, 8, 2, 1-18.

Armatage, Kay (2009) 'Toronto Women & Film International 1973', in Dina Iordanova with Ragan Rhyne (eds) *FFY1: The Festival Circuit*. St Andrews: St Andrews Film Studies, 82-98.

Aufderheide, Pat (2003) 'Frameworks for Action: The Changing Business and Policy Environments', in Karen Hirsch (ed.) *In the Battle for Reality: Social Documentaries in the U.S.* On-line. Available HTTP: http://www.centerforsocialmedia.org/sites/default/files/Battle_for_Reality3.pdf (18 July 2011).

Bao, Hongwei (2010) 'Enlightenment Space, Affective Space: Travelling Queer Film Festivals in China', in Mikako Iwatake (ed.) *Gender, Mobility and Citizenship in Asia*. Helsinki: Department of World Cultures, University of Helsinki, 174-205.

Barlow, Melinda (2003) 'Feminism 101: The New York Women's Video Festival, 1972-1980', *Camera Obscura*, 18, 3, 54, 3-38.

Barrett, Michael, Charlie Boudreau, Suzy Capo, Stephen Gutwillig, Nanna Heidenreich, Liza Johnson, Giampaolo Marzi, Dean Otto, Brian Robinson and Katharine Setzer (2005) 'Queer Film and Video Festival Forum, Take One: Curators Speak Out', *GLQ: A Journal of Lesbian and Gay Studies*, 11, 579-603.

Benson, Michael (1997) 'Tear Gas and Etiquette', *Sight & Sound*, 7, 7, 22-26.

Berry, Chris (2009) 'When Is a Festival Not a Festival?: The 6th China Independent Film Festival', *Senses of Cinema*, 53. On-line. Available HTTP: http://www. sensesofcinema.com/2009/festival-reports/when-is-a-film-festival-not-a-festival-the-6th-china-independent-film-festival (18 July 2011).

Betsalel, Ken and Mark Gibney (2008) 'Human Rights Watch 2007 Traveling Film Festival', *Human Rights Quarterly*, 30, 1, 205-8.

_____ (2009) 'Re-storying Justice Through Human Rights Film: A Selection of Films from the 2008 New York Human Rights Watch Film Festival', *Human Rights Quarterly*, 31, 2, 552-7.

Blažević, Igor (2009) 'How To Start', in Tereza Porybná (ed.) *Setting Up a Human Rights Film Festival*. Prague: People in Need, 14-23.

'Boulder International Film Festival Call-to-Action' (2011), *Boulder International Film Festival*. On-line. Available HTTP: http://www.biff1.com/call-to- action. html (11 June 2011).

Brauerhoch, Annette (1987) 'Jenseits der Metropolen: Frauenfilmfestivals in Créteil und Dortmund' I 'Beyond the Metropolis: Women's Film Festival in Créteil and Dortmund', *Frauen und Film*, 42, 94-100.

Bronkhorst, Daan (2004) 'The Human Rights Film: Reflections on its History, Principles and Practices', *Amnesty International Film Festival*. On-line. Available HTTP: http://www.amnesty.nl/filmfestival/essay.doc (23 June 2011).

Brouillette, Sarah (2011) 'Human Rights Markets and *Born into Brothels*', *Third Text*, 25, 2, 169-76.

Brown, Mark (2008) 'Bafta Bitterness after Film about Disability Axed', *The Guardian*, 8 February. On-line. Available HTTP: http://www.guardian. co.uk/uk/2008/feb/08/film.filmnews (10 November 2011).

Burres, Bruni and Heather Harding (2007) 'Human Rights Filmmaking Today', *Visual Anthropology*, 9, 329-33.

Burton, Julianne (1975) 'The Old and the New: Latin American Cinema and the (Last?) Pesaro Festival', *Jump Cut*, 9, 33-5.

Cacoulidis, Cleo (2009) 'The View from Here: Middle Eastern Cinema at the 49th Thessaloniki International Film Festival', *Bright Lights Film Journal*, 64. On-line. Available HTTP: http://www.brightlightsfilm. com/64/64feststhessaloniki.php (22 June 2011).

Chiu, Belinda and Carlo Arreglo (2011) 'The Intersection of Theory and Practice: Environmental Sustainability and Social Justice at the Finger Lakes Environmental Film Festival (FLEFF)', *Environmental Communication: A Journal of Nature and Culture*, 5, 2, 221-7.

Clarke, Pamela and Lee Knifton (2009) 'The Scottish Mental Health Arts and Film Festival: Promoting Social Change Through the Arts', *A Life in the Day*, 13, 3, 10-13.

Córdova, Amalia (2009) 'Festival Exchanges and Circulation in the Online South', *In Media Res*. On-line. Available HTTP: http://mediacommons. futureofthebook.org.imr/2009/05/05festival-exchanges-and-circulation-online-south (18 July 2011).

de Jong, Wilma, Martin Shaw and Neil Stammers (eds) (2005) *Global Activism, Global Media*. London: Pluto, 2005.

De Vita, Pablo (2009) 'Ecology – a New Film Genre?', *Miranda Global*. On-line. Available HTTP: http://www.miradaglobal.com/index.php?option=com_co ntent&task=view&id=1116&Itemid=9&lang=en (4 August 2011). Originally published as 'Ecología, ¿un nuevo género cinematográfico?', *Criterio*, 2353, October 2009. On-line. Available HTTP: http://www.revistacriterio. com.ar/cultura/ecologia-¿un-nuevo-genero-cinematografico/ (4 August 2011).

Diawara, Manthia (1994) 'On Tracking World Cinema: African Cinema at Film Festivals', *Public Culture*, 6, 2, 385-96.

Ditmars, Hadani (1997) 'Talking Too Much with Men', *Sight & Sound*, 7, 4, 10-12.

Dowell, Kristin (2006) 'Indigenous Media Gone Global: Strengthening Indigenous Identity On- and Offscreen at the First Nations/First Features Film Showcase', *American Anthropologist*, 108, 2, 376-84.

Drinkwater, Mark (2008) 'Disability Issues Hit the Big Screen', *The Guardian*, 13 February 2008. On-line. Available HTTP: http://www.guardian.co.uk/society/2008/feb/13/disability.filmfestival?intcmp=239 (10 November 2011).

FICMA (International Environmental Film Festival- Barcelona) (2011) *FICMA: When Reality Surpasses Fiction*. On-line. Available HTTP: http://www. ficma.com/editorial.php (10 June 2011).

Gamson, Joshua (1996) 'The Organizational Shaping of Collective Identity: The Case of Lesbian and Gay Film Festivals in New York', *Sociological Forum*, 11, 2, 231-61.

Gellhorn, Joyce (1991) 'The First Annual International Environmental Film Festival: A Viewer's Perspective', *Journal of Environmental Education*, 22, 3, 12-15.

Ginsburg, Faye (1994) 'Embedded Aesthetics: Creating a Discursive Space for Indigenous Media', *Cultural Anthropology*, 9, 2, 365-82.

Gregory, Sam (2006) 'Transnational Storytelling: Human Rights, WITNESS, and Video Advocacy', *American Anthropologist*, 108, 1, 195–204.

Gregory, Sam, Gillian Caldwell, Ronit Avni and Thomas Harding (eds) (2005) *Video for Change: A Guide for Advocacy and Activism*. London and Ann Arbor, MI: Pluto Press and WITNESS.

Gündoğdu, Mustafa (2010) 'Film Festivals in the Diaspora: Impetus to the Development of Kurdish Cinema?', in Dina Iordanova and Ruby Cheung (eds) *FFY2: Film Festivals and Imagined Communities*. St Andrews: St Andrews Film Studies, 188-97.

Hammer, Barbara (1998) 'Turning 20: The Festival International de Films de Femmes de Créteil', *The Independent: Film and Video Monthly*, 21, 7, 18-19.

Hartzell, Adam, (2003) 'The Deaf Film Festival (Review)', *The Film Journal*, 5. On-line. Available HTTP: http://www.thefilmjournal.com/issue5/deaf.html (1 September 2011)

Harvey, Penny (1993) 'Ethnographic Film and the Politics of Difference: A Review of Film Festivals', *Visual Anthropology Review*, 9, 1, 164-76.

Haslam, Mark (2004) 'Vision, Authority, Context: Cornerstones of Curation and Programming', *The Moving Image*, 4, 1, 48-59.

Haslem, Wendy (2008) 'A Report on the 2nd Human Rights Arts and Film Festival', *Senses of Cinema*, 50. On-line. Available HTTP:http://www.sensesofcinema.com/2009/festival-reports/human-rights-aff-2008 (7 June 2011).

Hesford, Wendy S. (2005) 'Kairos and the Geopolitical Rhetorics of Global Sex Work and Video Advocacy', in Wendy S. Hesford and Wendy Kozol (eds) *Just Advocacy? Women's Human Rights, Transnational Feminisms, and the Politics of Representation*. New Brunswick, NJ: Rutgers University Press, 146-72.

Hiller, Eva and Renate Holy (1976) 'Festival of Women's Films New York 1976', *Frauen und Film*, 10, 49.

Himpele, Jeff (1996) 'Film Distribution as Media: Mapping Difference in the Bolivian Cinemascape', *Visual Anthropology Review*, 12, 1, 47-66.

Hinegardner, Livia (2009) 'Action, Organization and Documentary Film: Beyond a Communications Model of Human Rights Videos', *Visual Anthropology Review*, 25, 2, 172-85.

Hogan, Mél (2008-2009) '21 Years of Image & Nation: Legitimizing the Gaze', *Nouvelles vues sur le cinéma québécois*, 10, 1-30. On-line. Available HTTP: http://www.melhogan.com/PUB/PUB-NVCQ10.pdf (25 May 2011).

Howard, Cerise (2009) 'Turning X in an XXY World: The 10th Mezipatra Queer Film Festival', *Senses of Cinema*, 53. On-line. Available HTTP: http://www.sensesofcinema.com/2009/festival-reports/turning-x-in-an-xxy-world-the-10th-mezipatra-queer-film-festival (15 May 2011).

_____ (2010) 'Going South in 2010: Thinking Global, Talking Local: The 24th Fribourg International Film Festival', *Senses of Cinema*, 55. On-line. Available HTTP: http://www.sensesofcinema.com/2010/festival-reports/going-south-in-2010-thinking-global-talking-local-the-24th-fribourg-international-film-festival (15 May 2011).

Huang, Yu Shan (2003) '"Creating and Distributing Films Openly": On the Relationship between Women's Film Festivals and the Women's Rights Movement in Taiwan', *Inter-Asia Cultural Studies*, 4, 1, 157-8.

Hüchtker, Ingrid (1992) 'Die verfluchte, die geliebte Öffentlichkeit: Pressearbeit für ein Frauen-Film-Festival (Ein Fallbeispiel mit Conclusio)' I 'The Cursed, the Beloved Public: Press Relations for a Women's Film Festival (A case study with conclusion)', in Gruppe Feministische Öffentlichkeit (ed.) *Femina Publica: Frauen-Öffentlichkeit-Feminismus*. Köln: PapyRossa, 203-18.

Human Rights Human Wrongs Film Festival (2010). *Report: Norway's (and Scandinavia's) First Human Rights Film Festival*. On-line. Available HTTP: http://www.humanfilm.no/report.pdf (24 July 2011).

Hwang, Yun Mi (2010) 'Under the Migrant Lens: Migrant Worker Film Festival in South Korea', in Dina Iordanova and Ruby Cheung (eds) *FFY2: Film Festivals and Imagined Communities*. St Andrews: St Andrews Film Studies, 121-35.

International Center for Transitional Justice (2008). *Filmmaking and Human Rights*. On-line. Available HTTP: http://www.ictj.org/en/news/features/1748. html (23 July 2011).

International Forest Film Festival (2011) *International Forest Film Festival Film Guide*. On-line. Available HTTP: http://www.jhfestival.org/forestfestival/forestfilm-final.pdf (14 June 2011).

Iordanova, Dina (2010) 'From the Source: Cinemas of the South', *Film International*, 8, 5, 95-9.

_____ (2010) 'Mediating Diaspora: Film Festivals and "Imagined Communities"', in Dina Iordanova and Ruby Cheung (eds) *FFY2: Film Festivals and Imagined Communities*. St Andrews: St Andrews Film Studies, 12-44.

Jasny, Barbara, Guy Riddihough, Eric Stokstad and Laura M. Zahn (2008) 'Seeing Green on the Silver Screen', *Science*, 320, 5875, 450-1.

Jayyusi, Lena (1978) 'The Middle East Film Festival', *MERIP Reports*, 69, 21-3.

Juhasz, Alexandra (2006) 'The Future Was Then: Reinvesting in Feminist Media Practice and Politics', *Camera Obscura*, 61, 21, 1, 53-7.

June, Jamie (2004) 'Defining Queer: The Criteria and Selection Process for Programming Queer Film Festivals', *CultureWork*, 8, 2, 1-5.

Kajinic, Sanja (2010) '"Battle for Sarajevo" as "Metropolis": Closure of the First Queer Sarajevo Festival According to Liberal Press', *Anthropology of East Europe Review*, 28, 1, 62-82.

Kim, Jeongmin and Sunghee Hong (2007) 'Queer Cultural Movements and Local Counterpublics of Sexuality: a Case of Seoul Queer Films and Videos Festival', *Inter-Asia Cultural Studies*, 8, 4, 617-33.

Kim, Soyoung (2005) '"Cine-mania" or Cinephilia: Film Festivals and the Identity Question', *UTS Review: Cultural Studies and New Writing*, 4, 2, 174-87. Reprinted in Chi-Yun Shin and Julian Stringer (eds) *New Korean Cinema*. New York: NYU Press, 79-91.

Klawans, Stuart (2006) 'Local Hero', *The Nation*. On-line. Available HTTP: http://www.thenation.com/article/local-hero (20 June 2011).

_____ (2002) 'Global Rights: The Movies', *The Nation*. On-line. Available HTTP: http://www.thenation.com/article/global-rights-movies (15 June 2011).

Kleinhans, Chuck and Julia Lesage (1986) 'Havana Film Festival Report New Latin American Cinema', *Jump Cut,* 31, 70-1.

Knegt, Peter (2011) 'Whole Foods Market Launches Monthlong Film Festival', *indieWIRE*. On-line. Available HTTP: http://www.indiewire.com/article/whole_foods_market_launches_monthlong_film_festival (20 June 2011).

_____ (2009) 'Short Films, Big Issues at Media That Matters', *indieWIRE*. On-line. Available HTTP: http://www.indiewire.com/article/short_films_big_issues_at_media_that_matters (4 June 2011).

Lehrer, Jeremy (1997) 'Bringing Abuses to Light: The Human Rights Watch International Film Festival Focuses the Public Eye on Human Rights Abuses', *Human Rights Magazine,* 14. On-line. Available HTTP: http://www.americanbar.org/publications/human_rights_magazine_home/irr_hr_summer97_lehrer.html (19 May 2011).

Lobato, Heidi (2009) '"Of Course Human Rights Are Not Sexy"', in Tereza Porybná (ed.) *Setting Up a Human Rights Film Festival*. Prague: People in Need, 130-5.

Loist, Skadi (2011) 'Precarious Cultural Work: About the Organization of (Queer) Film Festivals', *Screen*, 52, 2, 268-73.

Lucas, Peter (2008) 'Human Rights Films Seeing Peace Education: Case Study Brazil', in Kelvin Shawn Sealey (ed.) *Film, Politics and Education: Cinematic Pedagogy across the Disciplines*. New York: Peter Lang Publishing, Inc., 107-24.

Marris, Emma (2006) 'Grizzly, Dodos and Gore Put Science on Film', *Nature*, 439, 7079, 902.

McLagan, Meg (2003) 'Principles, Publicity, and Politics: Notes on Human Rights Media', *American Anthropologist*, 105, 3, 605-12.

____ (2006), 'Introduction: Making Human Rights Claims Public', *American Anthropologist*, 108, 1, 191–195.

McLeod, Michael (2007) 'Give Peace a Chance', *Orlando Sentinel*, 16 Sept. 2007, F1, F3. On-line. Available HTTP: http://www.peacefilmfest.org/ uploads/pdfs/orlando_sentinel_09-16-2007.pdf (18 August 2011).

McWilliam, Kelly (2007) 'We're Here All Week: Public Formation and the Brisbane Queer Film Festival', *Queensland Review*, 14, 2, 79-91.

Miller, Nicole (2008) 'Projecting Hope and Making Reel Change in Africa', *Human Rights Quarterly*, 30, 3, 827-38.

Millward, Rachel (2011) 'Birds Eye View Festival: And Woman Created Films for Both Sexes...', *The Guardian Film Blog*. On-line. Available HTTP: http:// www.guardian.co.uk/film/filmblog/2011/mar/08/birds-eye-view-film-festival (20 June 2011).

Morris, Gary (2001) 'San Francisco's 2001 Human Rights Watch International Film Festival', *Bright Lights Film Journal*, 23. On-line. Available HTTP: http://www.brightlightsfilm.com/32/humanrights.php (20 June 2011).

____ (1998) 'Cultural Makeovers: Tranny Fest 1998', *Bright Lights Film Journal*, 32. On-line. Available HTTP: http://www.brightlightsfilm.com/23/trannyfest. php (20 June 2011).

Norman, Marc (2000) 'Public Education Through Community-Based Film Programs: A Report on the Environmental Film Festival in the Nation's Capital', *The Journal of Environmental Education*, 31, 2, 28-30.

Novak, Ivana (2010) 'Branding Representations: What Dokufest Has To Say About Reinventing Tradition: The 9th International Documentary and Short Film Festival (Dokufest)', *Senses of Cinema*, 56. On-line. Available HTTP: http://www.sensesofcinema.com/2010/festival-reports/ branding-representations-what-dokufest-has-to-say-about-reinventing-tradition-the-9th-international-documentary-and-short-film-festival-dokufest (7 June 2011).

One World Film Festival (2011), *Film Festival One World 2011 Final Report*. On-line. Available HTTP: http://www.oneworld.cz/2011/userfiles/file/One_ World_2011_Final_Report.pdf (19 July 2011).

Orlin, Theodore S. (2009) 'The Films of the Third International Human Rights Film Festival Albania, (IHRFFA), 2008', *Human Rights Quarterly*, 31, 1, 290-3.

Pócsik, Andrea (2008) 'Their Life and Our Vicarious Experiences: On Human Rights Films and Festivals', *Politics and Culture*, 2.

Porton, Richard (2009) 'Toronto International Film Festival Update', *Cineaste*, 34, 4. On-line. Available HTTP: http://www.cineaste.com/articles/toronto-international-film-festival-daily-update (22 June 2011).

Porybná, Tereza (ed.) (2009) *Setting Up a Human Rights Film Festival*. Prague: People in Need. On-line. Available HTTP: http://www.oneworld.cz/2011/userfiles/file/OW-cookbook_web.pdf (29 July 2011).

Quinn, N., et al. (2011) 'The Impact of a National Mental Health Arts and Film Festival on Stigma and Recovery', *Acta Psychiatrica Scandinavica*, 123, 1, 71-81.

Rangan, Pooja (2010) 'Some Annotations on the Film Festival as an Emerging Medium in India', *South Asian Popular Culture*, 8, 2, 123-41.

Rastegar, Roya (2008) 'Queer Film and Video Festival Forum, Take Three: Curators Speak Out', *GLQ: A Journal of Lesbian and Gay Studies*, 14, 1, 121-37.

_____ (2009) 'The De-fusion of Good Intentions: Outfest's Fusion Film Festival', *GLQ: A Journal of Lesbian and Gay Studies*, 15, 481-97.

Reynaud, Bérénice (2009) 'Men Won't Cry – Traces of a Repressive Past: The 28th Vancouver International Film Festival', *Senses of Cinema*, 54. On-line. Available HTTP: http://www.sensesofcinema.com/2010/festival-reports/men-won%e2%80%99t-cry%e2%80%93-traces-of-a-repressive-past-the-28th-vancouver-international-film-festival (15 May 2011).

_____ (2010) 'The Image and its Discontent: The 29th Sundance Film Festival and the 18th Pan African Film and Arts Festival', *Senses of Cinema*, 55. On-line. Available HTTP: http://www.sensesofcinema.com/2010/festival-reports/the-image-and-its-discontent-the-29th-sundance-film-festival-and-the-18th-pan-african-film-and-arts-festival (15 May 2011).

_____ (2011) 'Take the A Train and Don't Look Back: The 30th Sundance Film Festival and the 19th Pan African Film and Arts Festival', *Senses of Cinema*, 58. On-line. Available HTTP: http://www.sensesofcinema.com/2011/festival-reports/take-the-train-and-don't-look-back-the-30th-sundance-film-festival-and-the-19th-pan-african-film-and-arts-festival (1 May 2011).

Rhyne, Ragan (2007) 'Pink Dollars: Gay and Lesbian Film Festivals and the Economy of Visibility', unpublished PhD thesis, New York University, U.S.

_____ (2011) 'Comrades and Citizens: Gay and Lesbian Film Festivals in China', in Dina Iordanova and Ruby Cheung (eds) *FFY3: Film Festivals and East Asia*. St Andrews: St Andrews Film Studies, 110-24.

Rich, B. Ruby (1993) 'Reflections on a Queer Screen', *GLQ: A Journal of Lesbian and Gay Studies*, 1, 1, 83-91.

_____ (1999) 'Collision, Catastrophe, Celebration: The Relationship between Gay and Lesbian Film Festivals and their Publics', *GLQ: A Journal of Lesbian and Gay Studies*, 5, 1, 79-84.

____ (2006) 'The New Homosexual Film Festivals', *GLQ: A Journal of Lesbian and Gay Studies*, 12, 4, 620-25.

Robinson, Brian (2011) 'The Pride and the Passion', *Sight & Sound*, 21, 4, 12-13.

Robinson, David (1971-72) 'When is a Dirty Film...?', *Sight & Sound*, 41, 1, 28-30.

Rodríguez, Gloria (2010) 'Project Introduction Text: Ojo al Sancocho', *Sustainable Everyday Explorations*. On-line. Available HTTP: http://www.sustainableeverydayexplorations.net/project-introduction-text-ojo-al-sancocho (10 May 2011).

Sarkar, Bhaskar and Janet Walker (eds) (2009) *Documenting Testimonies: Global Archives of Suffering*. New York: Routledge.

Segal, Jérôme (2010) 'Identities and Politics at the Vienna Jewish Film Festival', in Dina Iordanova and Ruby Cheung (eds) *FFY2: Film Festivals and Imagined Communities*. St Andrews: St Andrews Film Studies, 198-217.

Simanowitz, Stefan (2011) 'Theartsdesk in Western Sahara: The World's Most Remote Film Festival', *The Arts Desk*. On-line. Available HTTP: http://www.theartsdesk.com/index.php?option=com_k2&view=item&id=3744%3Atheartsdesk-in-western-sahara-at-the-worlds-most-remote-film-festival&Itemid=29 (20 July 2011).

Slocum, J. David (2009) 'Film and/as Culture: The Use of Cultural Discourses at Two African Film Festivals', in Dina Iordanova and Ragan Rhyne (eds) *FFY1: The Festival Circuit*. St Andrews: St Andrews Film Studies, 136-52.

Snyder, Sharon L. and David T. Mitchell (2008) 'How Do We Get All these Disabilities in Here? Disability Film Festivals and the Politics of Atypicality', *Canadian Journal of Film Studies | Revue Canadienne d'Études Cinématographiques*, 17, 1, 11-29.

Straayer, Chris and Thomas Waugh (2006) 'Queer Film and Video Festival Forum, Take Two: Curators Speak Out', *GLQ: A Journal of Lesbian and Gay Studies*, 12, 599-625.

Strandgaard Pedersen, Jesper, and Carmelo Mazza (2011) 'International Film Festivals: For the Benefit of Whom?', *Culture Unbound: Journal of Current Cultural Research*, 3, 139-65. On-line. Available HTTP: http://www.cultureunbound.ep.liu.se/v3/a12 (23 July 2011).

Swimelar, Safia (2010) 'Human Rights through Film: An Essay and Review of Selected Films from the Human Rights Watch 2009 Film Festival', *Human Rights Quarterly*, 32, 4, 1069-78.

Tam, Xavier (2010) 'Hear Me?! Deaf people also have cultural citizenship!' *The First HKI Deaf Film Festival*. On-line. Available HTTP: http://www.hkidff.com/hkidff_2010/arts_20100903.html (20 September 2011).

Tang, Denise Tse Shang (2009) 'Demand for Cultural Representation: Emerging Independent Film and Video on Lesbian Desires', in Olivia Khoo and Sean Metzger (eds) *Futures of Chinese Cinema: Technologies and Temporalities in Chinese Screen Cultures*. Bristol and Chicago: Intellect, 169-90.

Tilsner, Jamison (2008) 'A Festival That Matters', *Tubefilter*. On-line. Available HTTP: http://news.tubefilter.tv/2008/05/30/a-festival-that-matters/ (22 June 2011).

Torchin, Leshu (2010) 'Traffic Jam: Film, Activism and Human Trafficking', in William Brown, Dina Iordanova and Leshu Torchin (eds) *Moving People, Moving Images: Cinema and Trafficking in the New Europe*. St Andrews: University of St Andrews, 218-36.

Tracton, Sarah (2008) 'Finding An(other) Audience: Accessible Cinema and The Other Film Festival', *Metro*, 159, 50-3.

Walter, Cornelia (2010) 'Absolut nicht obsolet: Frauenfilmfestivals sind leider noch immer kein Anachronismus' I 'Absolutely Not Obsolete: Women's Film Festivals Are Still Not an Anachronism- Sadly' , *Short Report: KurzfilmMagazin*, 30-5. On-line. Available HTTP: http://www.ag-kurzfilm. de/shared/doc/upload/page/384/page_de_384_a3.pdf (19 July 2011).

Wheatley, Catherine (2008) 'Where Distributors Fear to Tread', *Sight & Sound*, 18, 3, 10-11.

White, Patricia (2006) 'The Last Days of Women's Cinema', *Camera Obscura*, 21, 145-51.

_____ (1999) 'Queer Publicity: A Dossier on Lesbian and Gay Film Festivals, *GLQ: A Journal of Lesbian and Gay Studies,* 5, 1, 73-93.

Whiteman, David (2002) 'Impact of The Uprising of '34: A Coalition Model of Production and Distribution', *Jump Cut*, 45, Fall. On-line. Availabe HTTP: www.ejumpcut.org/archive/jc45.2002/whiteman/index.html (29 August 2011).

_____ (2003) 'Reel Impact: How Nonprofits Harness the Power of Documentary Film', *Stanford Social Innovation Review*, 1, 1, Spring, 60-63.

_____ (2004) 'Out of the Theaters and into the Streets: A Coalition Model of the Political Impact of Documentary Film and Video', *Political Communication*, 21, 1, January, 51-70, January 2004.

_____ (2007) 'The Evolving Impact of Documentary Film: Sacrifice and the Rise of Issue-centered Outreach', *Post Script: Essays in Film and the Humanities*, special issue on 'The Current State of Documentary Filmmaking', 26, 3, Summer, 62-74.

Whiteman, David and Barbara Abrash (2001) 'The Uprising of '34: Filmmaking as Community Engagement', *Wide Angle*, 21, 2, 87-99.

Willemen, Paul (1981) 'Pesaro: The Limitations and Strengths of a Cultural Policy', *Framework*, 15/16/17, 96-8.

Wilson-Goldie, Kaelen (2008) 'Forbidden Images', *Sight & Sound*, 18, 3, 10-11.

Yang, Yang (2010) 'De "Queer" à "Tongzhi": Etude comparative transnationale des festivals de films thématiques ayant trait aux questions de la sexualité et du genre en Belgique et dans les trois Chines' | 'From "Queer" to "Tongzhi": A Comparative Study of Transnational Thematic Film Festivals Related to Issues of Sexuality and Gender in Belgium and in the Three Chinas', unpublished Master's thesis, Universite libre de Bruxelles.

Zielinski, Ger (2008) 'Furtive, Steady Glances: On the Emergence and Cultural Politics of Lesbian & Gay Film Festivals', unpublished PhD thesis, McGill University, Montreal, Canada. On-line. Available HTTP: http://digitool.library. mcgill.ca/webclient/StreamGate?folder_id=0&dvs=1321954881879~999 (10 November 2011).

_____ (2009) 'Queer Film Festivals', in John C. Hawley and Emmanuel S. Nelson (eds) *LGBTQ America Today: An Encyclopedia*. Westport, CT: Greenwood Press, 980-4.

Zimmermann, Patricia R. (2000) *States of Emergency: Documentaries, Wars, Democracies*. Minneapolis and London: University of Minnesota Press.

Table 1: Human Rights Film Festivals

This table is representative but not comprehensive.

Est.	Name	Location and other details	Website
1985	Vermont International Film Festival	Burlington, VT, United States	www.vtiff.org
1988	Human Rights Watch International Film Festival	New York, NY, United States and London, United Kingdom since 1996	www.hrw.org/en/iff
1992	Amnesty International Film Festival	San Francisco, CA, United States (Founded in Seattle, WA, United States)	www.amnestyusa.org/filmfest
1995-2006	Amnesty International Film Festival (Succeeded by Movies that Matter)	Amsterdam, Netherlands	www.amnesty.nl/filmfestival
1996	Seoul Human Rights Film Festival	Seoul, South Korea	sarangbang.or.kr/hrfilm
1997	DerHumALC International Film and Video Festival on Human Rights	Buenos Aires, Argentina	www.imd.org.ar
1998	United Nations Association Film Festival	Travelling festival; various locations worldwide	www.unaff.org
1999	One World - International Human Rights Documentary Film Festival	Prague, Czech Republic	www.oneworld.cz
1999	Perspektive - Filmfestival der Menschenrechte/Perspektive: International Human Rights Film Festival Nuremberg	Nuremberg, Germany (Biennial until 2007; since then annual)	www.filmfestival-der-menschenrechte.de

2000	Media that Matters	Mobile: New York, NY, United States followed by tours, DVDs and on-line streaming.	www.mediathatmattersfest.org
2001	Amnesty International Film Festival Victoria	Victoria, Canada	www.amnestyfilmsvictoria.ca
2001	Human Rights Nights	Bologna, Italy	www.humanrightsnights.org
2001	Watch Docs: Human Rights in Film	Warsaw, Poland (Mobile since 2003)	www.watchdocs.pl
2003	Document – International Human Rights Documentary Film Festival	Glasgow, Scotland	documentfilmfestival.org
2003	Festival de cine y derechos humanos	Barcelona, Spain	www.festivaldecineyderechoshumanos.com/festival-de-cine-y-derechos-humanos-2.html
2003	Festival de cine y derechos humanos	San Sebastian, Spain	www.cineyderechoshumanos.com/2011/es/presentacion
2003	Festival du Film des Droits de l'homme	France, Paris	www.alliance-cine.org/paris
2003	Festival Internacional del Cine Pobre (Poverty)	Gibara, Cuba	www.cubacine.cult.cu/cinepobre
2003	Festival International du Film et Forum sur les Droits Humains	Geneva, Switzerland	www.fifdh.org/?lan=en&rubID=1
2003	Global Peace Film Festival	Orlando, FL, United States	www.peacefilmfest.org

Year	Festival	Location	Website
2003	Human Rights Film Festival	Zagreb, Croatia	humanrightsfestival.org
2003	Tri Continental Human Rights Film Festival	Mobile: Johannesburg, Durban, Pretoria, Cape Town, South Africa	www.3continentsfestival.co.za
2004	Artivist Film Festival	Los Angeles, CA, United States	www.festival.artivist.com
2004	Docudays	Kiev, Ukraine	docudays.org.ua/2010/en
2004	Festival Ciné droit Libre	Ouagadougou, Burkina Faso,	festivalcinedroitlibre.blogspot.com
2004	Festival des Libertés	Brussels, Belgium	www.festivaldeslibertes.be/index2011_launch.php
2004	Verzio International Human Rights Documentary Film Festival	Budapest, Hungary	www.verzio.org
2005	Cinema e Diritti	Naples, Italy	www.cinemaediritti.org/associazione
2005	El Festival Internacional de los Derechos Humanos 'Bolivia, el Séptimo Ojo es Tuyo'	Sucre, Bolivia	www.festivalcinebolivia.org
2005	New Zealand Human Rights Film Festival	Mobile: Auckland, Christchurch, Wellington, New Zealand (2005 and 2006 only)	www.humanrightsfilmfest.net.nz
2005	The International Human Rights Film Festival in Albania	Tirana, Albania	www.ihrffa.net
2006	A Film for Peace Festival/Un film per la pace festival	Medea, Italy	www.unfilmperlapace.it

283

2006	Guth Gafa International Documentary Film Festival	Donegal Gaeltacht, Ireland	www.guthgafa.com
2006	Montreal Human Rights Film Festival (MHRFF)	Montreal, QC, Canada	ffdpm.com/2010/index_presentation.php
2006	Movies that Matter (Successor to Amnesty International Film Festival)	The Hague, Netherlands	www.moviesthatmatterfestival.nl
2006	Pravo Ljudski	Sarajevo, Bosnia and Herzegovina	www.pravoljudski.org
2006	Un Film Per La Pace	Lestizza, Italy	www.unfilmperlapace.it
2007	Ad Hoc: Inconvenient Films	Vilnius, Lithuania	www.nepatoguskinas.lt/lt/2011
2007	Addis International Film Festival	Addis Ababa, Ethiopia	www.addisfilmfestival.org
2007	Human Rights Art and Film Festival	Australia (Mobile)	hraff.org.au/festival-info/about
2007	Nationality: Human	South Caucasus (Mobile and periodic)	www.ya-chelovek.caucasus.net/_about.html
2007	New York Roma/Gypsy Human Rights Film Festival	New York, NY, United States	www.gypsyfilms.org
2007	Steps: International Rights Film Festival	Kharkov, Ukraine	www.cetalife.com.ua/eng/index.htm
2007	Take One Action Film Festival	Edinburgh and Glasgow, UK	www.takeoneaction.org.uk/events/festival

2008	Bahrain Human Rights International Film Festival	Bahrain, Manama	No official page, Facebook group: www.facebook.com/group.php?gid=486412715219
2008	Persistence Resistance	India, New Delhi	www.persistenceresistance.in
2008	This Human World	Vienna, Austria	www.thishumanworld.com
2009	Rencontres méditerranéennes cinéma et droits de l'homme	Rabat, Morocco (Biennial)	www.rmcdh.ma
2010	Activist Film Festival	Brisbane, Australia	www.colmanridgepresents.com.au/activist-film-festival
2011	Autumn Human Rights Film Festival	Kabul, Afghanistan	www.ahrfestival.org
2012	AfricanBamba Human Rights Films and Arts Festival	Thiaroye, Senegal	africanbamba.webs.com

Listing provided by Beatriz Tadeo Fuica

Table 2: Indigenous Film Festivals

This list is representative but not exhaustive.

Est.	Name	Location	Website
1975	American Indian Film Festival	San Francisco, CA, United States	www.aifisf.com
1979	Native American Film + Video Festival	New York, NY, United States (Biennal; triennal from 1997 to 2006)	www.nativenetworks.si.edu
1980	Amiens International Film Festival (Thematic showcases on Native peoples of the Americas since 1995)	Amiens, France	www.filmfestamiens.org
1985	Festival Internacional de Cine y Video de los Pueblos Indigenas	Rotational and Mobile: Latin America, followed by local and European Showcases	www.clacpi.org (not exclusive website)
1990	Présence authoctone First Peoples' Festival Film & Video Showcase	Montreal, QC, Canada	www.nativelynx.qc.ca
1991	Two Rivers Native American Film and Video Festival	Minneapolis, MN, United States	www.walkerart.org/archive/C/A673451D17E5BD7B615F. htm
1995	Native American Film + Video Festival	New York, NY, United States (Triennial)	nativenetworks.si.edu/nafvf/index.aspx
1997	Sami Film Festival	Kautokeino/Guovdageaidnu, Norway	www.samifilmfestival.no

1999	Geografías Suaves/Soft Geographies	Mérida, Yucatan, Mexico (Biennial)	yoochel.org
1999	IMAGeNation Aboriginal Film & Video Festival	Vancouver, BC, Canada	vcn.bc.ca/imag Official site down: imag-nation.com
1999	The Skábmagovat - Indigenous Film Festival	Inari, Finland	www.skabmagovat.fi
2000	Message Sticks Indigenous Film Festival	Mobile: Sydney, Australia with a national tour	www.blackfellafilms.com.au/messagesticks
2000	Premio Anaconda al Video Indígena	Rotational and Mobile: Latin America (Biennial)	www.clacpi.org
2001	Festival of Native Film & Culture	Palm Springs, CA, United States	www.accmuseum.org
2001	imagineNATIVE Film + Media Arts Festival	Toronto, ON, Canada	www.imaginenative.org
2001	Weeneebeg Aboriginal Film and Video Festival	Moose Factory, ON, Canada	www.weeneebeg.ca
2001	Winnipeg Aboriginal Film and Video Festival	Winnipeg, MB, Canada	aboriginalfilmfest.org
2003	Denver Indigenous Film & Arts Festival	Denver, CO, United States	www.iiirm.org
2003	Festival de Cine de los Pueblos Indígenas	Chaco Province, Argentina	festivaldecineindigenaenchaco.blogspot.com/2010/01/indigenous-peoples-film-festival.html

2004	INDIANER INUIT: The North American Native Film Festival	Stuttgart, Germany (Periodic: 2004, 2007, 2009, 2012)	www.nordamerika-filmfestival.com
2004	Red Nation Film Festival	Los Angeles, CA, United States	rednationfilmfestival.com
2004	All Roads Film Festival	Washington, DC, United States	events.nationalgeographic.com/events/all-roads/about
2005	Cowichan International Aboriginal Film Festival	Cowichan, Canada	aff.cowichan.net/?about-us,25
2005	Festival de Cine y Video Indígena	Morelia, Mich, Mexico	fecvi.com
2005	Indigenous World Film Festival	Anchorage, AK, United States	www.alaskanative.net/en/main_nav/plan_visit/calendar_events/indigenous_wff
2005	The Dreaming-Australia's International Indigenous Festival	Various locations in Australia	www.thedreamingfestival.com
2005	Wairoa Maori Film Festival	Wairoa, New Zeland	www.manawairoa.com
2006	Dreamspeakers Film Festival	Edmonton, Canada	www.dreamspeakers.org
2007	Native Spirit Film Festival	London, UK and Madrid, Spain	www.nativespiritfoundation.org
2007	Nepal International Indigenous Film Festival	Kathmandu, Nepal	ifanepal.org.np/
2007	The Festival of Indigenous African - Language Films	Akure, Nigeria	fiafng.com/index.php
2008	Cherokee International Film Festival	Tulsa, OK, United States	www.internationalcherokeefilmfestival.com
2008	Encuentro de Producciones	Carchi, Imbabura, Pichincha (mobile),	www.imagendelospueblos.net/2010

2009	ABYA YALA: Rencontres de cinéma amérindien	France, Tournefeuille, Toulouse, Montpellier, Avignon, Paris Saint Ouen, Forcalquier, Marseille (mobile)	www.apatapela.org
2009	Daupará Muestra de Cine y Video Indígena	Bogotá, Colombia	daupara.org
2009	Festival Internacional de Cine y Video Indígena 'Mirando desde nuestra raíz' (Formerly 'Muestra de Video y Documental Indígena en Puebla')	Mobile: Puebla, Puebla, Mexico and Los Angeles & Fullerton, CA, United States	www.wix.com/ficvi2011/cinearte
2009	Native & Indigenous Film Festival (NAIFF) aka Festival dokumentárních filmů o domorodých lidech v Brně	Brno, Czech Republic	www.naiff.eu
2011	Festival de cine y video Rodolfo Maya	Indigenous reserves of Cauca, Colombia	festivalrodolfomaya.blogspot.com

Listing provided by Beatriz Tadeo Fuica and Amalia Córdova.

Table 3: Lesbian, Gay, Bisexual, Transgender and Queer Film Festivals

This list is representative but not exhaustive.
For a list of more LGBT/queer film festivals go to: www.queerfilmfestivals.org.

Est.	Name	Location	Website
1977	Frameline: San Francisco International LGBT Film Festival	San Francisco, CA, United States	www.frameline.org
1981	Reeling: Chicago Lesbian and Gay International Film Festival	Chicago, IL, United States	www.reelingfilmfestival.org
1982	Outfest: Los Angeles Gay & Lesbian Film Festival	Los Angeles, CA, United States	www.outfest.org
1982	Pittsburgh International Lesbian and Gay Film Festival	Pittsburgh, PA, United States	www.pilgff.org
1984	Ljubljana Gay and Lesbian Film Festival	Ljubljana, Slovenia	www.ljudmila.org/siqrd/fglf
1986	BFI London Lesbian and Gay Film Festival	London, United Kingdom	www.bfi.org.uk/llgff
1986	Festival MIX MILANO di Cinema Gaylesbico e Queer Culture	Milan, Italy	www.cinemagaylesbico.com
1986	MIX Copenhagen LesbianGayBiTrans Film Festival	Copenhagen, Denmark	www.mixcopenhagen.dk

1986	Torino International Gay and Lesbian Film Festival	Turin, Italy	www.tglff.com
1986	Brussels Lesbian and Gay Film Festival	Brussels, Belgium	www.fglb.org
1987	Austin Gay & Lesbian International Film Festival	Austin, TX, United States	www.agliff.org
1987	Connecticut Gay & Lesbian Film Festival	Hartford, CT, United States	www.outfilmct.org
1987	MIX NYC: The New York Queer Experimental Film Festival	New York, NY, United States	www.mixnyc.org
1987	Out on Film: Atlanta's LGBT Film Festival	Atlanta, GA, United States	www.outonfilm.org
1988	image+nation: Montreal International LGBT Film Festival	Montreal, QC, Canada	www.image-nation.org
1989	Newfest: The New York LGBT Film Festival	New York, NY, United States	www.newfest.org
1989	Hong Kong Lesbian and Gay Film Festival	Hong Kong	www.hklgff.hk/en
1989	Paris International Lesbian and Feminist Film Festival	Paris, France	cineffable.fr/en
1989	Vancouver Queer Film Festival	Vancouver, BC, Canada	www.queerfilmfestival.ca
1990	Fresno Reel Pride Film Festival	Fresno, CA, United States	www.reelpride.com

Year	Festival	Location	Website
1990	Lesbisch Schwule Filmtage Hamburg I International Queer Film Festival	Hamburg, Germany	www.lsf-hamburg.de
1990	Honolulu Rainbow Film Festival	Honolulu, HI, United States	www.hglcf.org
1990	Inside Out: Toronto LGBT Film and Video Festival	Toronto, ON, Canada	www.insideout.ca
1990	Tampa International Gay & Lesbian Film Festival	Tampa, FL, United States	www.tiglff.com
1991	Melbourne Queer Film Festival	Melbourne, Australia	www.mqff.com.au
1991	Reel Affirmations: Washington DC's International LGBT Film Festival	Washington, DC, United States	www.reelaffirmations.org
1991	Skeive Filmer/Oslo Gay & Lesbian Film Festival	Oslo, Norway	www.oglff.org
1991	Vinokino Lesbian & Gay Film Festival	Turku, Finland	www.vinokino.fi/en
1992	Tokyo International Lesbian & Gay Film Festival	Tokyo, Japan	www.tokyo-lgff.org
1993	Mardi Gras Film Festival (Queer Screen)	Sydney, Australia	www.queerscreen.com.au
1993	MIX Brasil	São Paulo, Brazil	www.mixbrasil.uol.com.br
1994	identities. Vienna's Queer Film Festival	Vienna, Austria	www.identities.at

Year	Festival	Location	Website
1994	Out in Africa: South African Gay & Lesbian Film Festival	Cape Town and Johannesburg, South Africa	www.oia.co.za
1994	Chéries –Chéri: Paris Gay, Lesbian, Trans Film Festival	Paris, France	www.ffglp.net
1995	Out Takes: A Reel Queer Film Festival	Wellington, New Zealand	www.outtakes.org.nz
1995	North Carolina Gay & Lesbian Film Festival	Durham, NC, United States	www.carolinatheatre.org/ncglff
1995	Philadelphia QFest	Philadelphia, PA, United States	www.qfest.com
1996	LesGaiCineMad: Madrid International Lesbian & Gay Film Festival	Madrid, Spain	www.lesgaicinemad.com
1996	Q Fest: Houston Gay & Lesbian International Film Festival	Houston, TX, United States	www.q-fest.org
1996	Roze Filmdagen: Amsterdam Gay & Lesbian Film Festival	Amsterdam, Netherlands	www.rozefilmdagen.nl
1996	Seattle Lesbian & Gay Film Festival	Seattle, WA, United States	threedollarbillcinema.org/programs/SLGFF
1997	Pink Apple: Lesbian & Gay Film Festival	Zurich and Frauenfeld, Switzerland	www.pinkapple.ch
1997	Queersicht: Lesbian & Gay Film Festival	Bern, Switzerland	www.queersicht.ch
1998	Miami Gay and Lesbian Film Festival	Miami, FL, United States	www.mglff.com

Year	Festival	Location	Website
1998	Q Cinema: Fort Worth Gay & Lesbian International Film Festival	Fort Worth, TX, United States	www.qcinema.org
1999	reelout queer film + video festival	Kingston, ON, Canada	www.reelout.com
2000	Mezipatra Queer Film Festival	Brno and Prague, Czech Republic	www.mezipatra.cz
2000	Seoul LGBT Film Festival	Seoul, South Korea	www.selff.org
2002	Q! Film Festival	Indonesia	www.q-munity.org
2003	Southwest Gay and Lesbian Film Festival	Albuquerque and Santa Fe, NM, United States	www.closetcinema.org
2006	TLVFest: Tel Aviv's International LGBT Film Festival	Tel Aviv, Israel	www.tlvfest.com/en
2007	Iris Prize	Cardiff, United Kingdom	www.irisprize.org
2007	Llamale H: Uruguay International Film Festival of Sexual and Gender Diversity	Montevideo, Uruguay	www.llamaleh.org
2007	QDoc Portland Queer Documentary Film Festival	Portland, OR, United States	queerdocfest.org
2008	Bok-o-Bok/Side-by-Side LGBT International Film Festival	Saint Petersburg and other cities in Russia	www.bok-o-bok.ru
2008	Sarajevo Queer Festival	Sarajevo, Bosnia and Herzegovina	www.sbsff.com/en www.queer.ba
2009	Diversidad Sexual/Sexual Diversity: A Week of Gay Cinema	Havana, Cuba	No website

Listing provided by Beatriz Tadeo Fuica and Skadi Loist.

295

Table 4: Film Festivals Related to (Involuntary) Migration[1]

This table is representative but not comprehensive

Est.	Name	Location and other details	Website
2001	International Exile Film Festival	Gothenburg, Sweden	www.exilefilmfestival.com
2004	FiSahara: Festival de Cine del Sahara	Western Sahara (mobile)	festivalsahara.com
2005	UNHCR Refugee Film Festival	Tokyo, Japan	unhcr.refugeefilm.org
2006	Cultural/Migrant	South Korea (mobile)	www.mwff.org
2007	Australian Refugee Film Festival	Australia (mobile)	www.australianrefugeefilmfestival.org
2007	Refuge in Films	London, United Kingdom	www.refugeinfilms.org/index.php
2008	Unchosen (Trafficking)	Multi-sited: Bristol, Bath and Keele,	unchosen.org.uk
2011	Na Wa Festival (Trafficking)	United Kingdom	en.adesuwa.org/nawa-festival.html

Listing provided by Beatriz Tadeo Fuica

[1] Some of the festivals mentioned here are not on-going. Many are one-offs (such as the excellent Moving Worlds: Cinemas of Migration in Dublin, Ireland in December 2010; www.fomacs.org/mw/fomacs1.html) or have experienced difficulties in continuing on a regular basis. See, for example, our case study of the Migrant Worker Film Festival in South Korea in the bibliography (Hwang 2010) and Leshu Torchin's chapter on various events that tackle human trafficking in this volume, as well as Torchin, 2010.

Table 5: Disability and Health-Related Festivals

This list is representative but not exhaustive

Est.	Name	Location and other details	Website
1982	SUPERFEST International Disability Film Festival	Berkeley, CA, United States	www.culturedisabilitytalent.org/superfest
1993	Annual Rendezvous with Madness Film Festival	Toronto, ON, Canada	www.rendezvouswithmadness.com/about
1994	ImagéSanté	Liège, Belgium (Biennial)	www.imagesante.org/en/about-the-festival/history
1995	Wie Wir Leben / The Way We Live International Short Film Festival	Munich, Germany (Biennial)	www.abm-medien.de
1997	KynnysKINO	Helsinki, Finland (and mobile) (Biennial)	www.kynnyskino.info
2001	London International Disability Film Festival	London, United Kingdom	www.hibiscusredfilm.com
2001	International Disability Film Festival	Calgary, AB, Canada	www.ptff.org/ptff_main/2011-festival.html
2002	Breaking Down Barriers Film Festival	Moscow, Russia (Biennial)	festival-eng.perspektiva-inva.ru
2003	Assim Vivemos - Brazil's International Disability Film Festival	Mobile: Rio de Janeiro, Brasilia, Sao Paulo, BRAZIL (Biennial)	assimvivemos.com.br/wp
2003	Cinema Touching Disability	Austin, TX, United States	www.ctdfilmfest.org

Year	Festival	Location	URL
2003	Festival Clin d'œil	Reims, France (Biennial)	www.clin-doeil.eu
2003	The Sprout Film Festival	New York, NY, United States	www.gosprout.org/film
2004	disAbilities Film Festival & Speaker Series	Buffalo, NY, United States	www.disabilityfilmfest.org
2004	Reel Life Disability Film Festival	Detroit, MI, United States	www.katrinadisability.info/wordpress/?page_id=14
2004	The Other Film Festival	South Melbourne, Australia	www.otherfilmfestival.com
2006	Toronto International Deaf Film and Arts Festival	Toronto, ON, Canada (Periodic)	www.tidfaf.ca
2007	Scottish Mental Health Arts and Film Festival	Glasgow, United Kingdom	www.mhfestival.com/index.php
2008	Cinemobile	Seville, Spain	www.escenamobile.es
2008	Festival Internacional de Cine sobre la Discapacidad. Fundación Anade	Madrid, Spain	www.fundacionanade.org
2008	ReelAbilities: NY Disabilities Film Festival	New York, NY, United States	www.reelabilities.org
2009	International Health Film Festival	Kos, Greece	www.healthfilmfestival.gr
2009	We Care FilmFest	New Dehli, India Mobile	www.wecarefilmfest.net
2010	UK Disability Film Festival Day	London, United Kingdom	www.disabilityfilmfestival.eu/Pages/submit.html
2010	ABÃRA International Disability Film Festival	Dublin, Ireland	www.dochas.ie/abara

Listing by Beatriz Tadeo Fuica

Table 5a: Deaf Film Festivals

Note: Deaf festivals have been listed as a subsection in order to recognise Deafness as disability (facing attendant social prejudices and barriers) and as culture, organised around shared language.

This list is representative but not exhaustive

Est.	Name	Location and other details	Website
1998	Deaffest, Deaf Film and TV Festival	Wolverhampton, United Kingdom (no 2005 edition)	deaffest.co.uk
2000	Dövfilmfestival (Deaf film festival)	Stockholm, Sweden	www.dovfilmfestival.nu
2003	Deaf in the Picture	Amsterdam, Netherlands (Every 4 years)	www.deafinthepicture.nl/en/about
2003	Maine Deaf Film Festival	Portland, ME, United States	mainedeaffilmfest.com
2008	D.C. Deaf Film Festival	Washington, DC, United States	dcdeaf.org/asflfilm/home.html
2010	Hong Kong International Deaf Film Festival	Wan Chai, Hong Kong, PRC	www.hkidff.com

Listing by Beatriz Tadeo Fuica

Thematic Bibliography on Film Festival Research: Update 2011

Skadi Loist & Marijke de Valck

It has been another year of fervent research into film festivals, which has seen the publication of more than 100 new texts. This is the fourth update of the annotated bibliography on film festival research published in the *Film Festival Yearbook* series. In this update, we only list newly published writing (and some older texts that came to our attention since the previous publication). Each entry appears only once, classified under one thematic category. Where more categories were applicable, we selected the category that seemed most suitable. For the complete bibliography, including annotations for categories and subcategories, we kindly refer the reader to the on-line publication at www.filmfestivalresearch.org. As the Web version is not subject to restrictions of length, some entries there appear listed under several categories to reflect the diversity of themes they address. On-line we also offer additional resources, such as a compilation of festival listings, titles of BA/MA theses written on the topic and syllabi of classes taught on film festivals.

The division into 11 general categories has remained unaltered; however, we have made two changes/additions to the level of subcategories. First, we have administered a further distinction in the (7) Programming section. The category has now been divided into three subcategories: (7.1) Issues of Festival Programming; (7.2) Interviews with Programmers; and (7.3) Film Festivals and Questions of Aesthetics. The third subcategory responds directly to the recent trend among film festival scholars of scrutinising the ways in which festivals influence film production aesthetically. We believe that the new heading reflects more adequately the important work currently being carried out on the notion of festival films and on the genre of international art cinema. Secondly, we have changed and added subcategories in the section on Specialised Film Festivals (9). We have added new pieces on specialised genre-based festivals (9.2), such as archive and mental health film festivals, taking into account the academic analysis of issues relevant to these themed events. We have also renamed the former subsection (9.4) Online Film Festivals as Film Festivals and New Media Platforms. This change acknowledges the emergence of a number of film festivals dedicated to new media content and platforms, such as film festivals focusing on iPhone or mobile products. Although not many (academic) studies are available on this topic yet, we anticipate that this will change in the near future.

All entries contribute to the development of the field of film festival studies. Nevertheless, we want to give special mention to four publications. 1) *Film Festivals and East Asia* (edited by Dina Iordanova and Ruby Cheung), the third installment in the *Film Festival Yearbook* series, which delves into the booming business of East Asian film festivals and brings together a diverse range of perspectives on what is arguably the most promising corner of the festival circuit today. Indeed, the largest increase in new writing entered under any category this year has been in the Asian section (6.2); 2) *The Film Festival Dossier*, edited by David Archibald and Mitchell Miller, in which the leading film studies journal *Screen* picks up on the trend towards film festival research and brings together several important contributions dedicated to the politics and economics of the film festival operation; 3) Cindy Wong's *Film Festivals: Culture, People, and Power on the Global Screen*, a new monograph on film festivals published by Rutgers University Press in the 2011 northern summer; and 4) SooJeong Ahn's monograph *The Pusan International Film Festival, South Korean Cinema and Globalization* published by Hong Kong University Press in winter 2011.

We thank everybody who helped us compile this update. Please keep alerting us to new work on film festivals for the next update.

1. Film Festivals: The Long View

Gass, Lars Henrik (2007) 'Wie viel Kunst braucht der Film?' | 'How Much Art Does Film Need?' (bilingual) *Short Report: KurzfilmMagazin*, 37-41.

Kim, Dong-Ho (2010) *Mr. Kim Goes to Festivals*. Busan: Busan International Film Festival/Dong-Ho Kim.

McGill, Hannah (2011) 'Film Festivals: A View from the Inside', *Screen*, 52, 2, 280-5.

1.1 a) Film Festival Theory

Ahn, SooJeong (2011) *The Pusan International Film Festival, South Korean Cinema and Globalization*. Hong Kong: Hong Kong University Press.

Archibald, David, and Mitchell Miller (eds) (2011) 'The Film Festival Dossier', *Screen*, 52, 2, 249-285.

_____ (2011) 'The Film Festival Dossier: Introduction', *Screen* 52, 2, 249-52.

Iordanova, Dina (2011) 'The Resources: Necessary Groundwork', in Dina Iordanova and Ruby Cheung (eds) *FFY3: Film Festivals and East Asia. St Andrews: St Andrews Film Studies, 189-95.*

Rangan, Pooja (2010) 'Some Annotations on the Film Festival as an Emerging Medium in India', *South Asian Popular Culture*, 8, 2, 123-41.

Segal, Jérôme (2010) 'Film Festivals', in Liana Giorgi (ed.) *European Arts Festivals: Cultural Pragmatics and Discursive Identity Frames.* EURO-FESTIVAL Project, 150-221. On-line. Available HTTP: http://www.euro-festival.org/docs/Euro-Festival_D3.pdf (20 January 2011).

Wong, Cindy Hing-Yuk (2011) *Film Festivals: Culture, People, and Power on the Global Screen.* New Brunswick, NJ: Rutgers University Press.

1.1 b) Reports and Responses to Film Festival Studies

de Valck, Marijke, and Skadi Loist (2011) 'What Is New in Film Festivals Studies: Thematic Bibliography on Film Festival Research – Update 2010', in Dina Iordanova and Ruby Cheung (eds) *FFY3: Film Festivals and East Asia.* St Andrews: St Andrews Film Studies, 276-92.

1.1 c) Book Reviews

Bâ, Saër Maty (2010) 'Slicing Mangos in Wilayas during Newroz: Tongues Untied on Very Real Events' [review of *FFY2: Film Festival and Imagined Communities*], *Film International*, 8, 4 (#46), 82-4.

Bosma, Peter (2010) 'Film Festival Yearbook 1: The Festival Circuit & Film Festival Yearbook 2: Film Festivals and Imagined Communities', *Tijdschrift voor Mediageschiedenis*, 13, 183-5.

Fischer, Alex (2010) 'Dina Iordanova and Ruby Cheung (eds), Film Festivals and Imagined Communities. Dundee: St Andrews Film Studies, 2010', *Screening the Past*, 28. On-line. Available HTTP: http://www.latrobe.edu.au/screeningthepast/28/film-festivals-and-imagined-communities.html (24 October 2011).

Hutcheson, Linda (2011) 'Film Festival Yearbook 1: The Festival Circuit/Dekalog 3: On Film Festivals', *Scope*, 20, June. On-line. Available HTTP: http://www.scope.nottingham.ac.uk/bookreview.php?issue=20&id=1290 (24 October 2011).

Page, Anna (2011) 'Film Festival Yearbook 3: Film Festivals and East Asia', *Viewfinder*, 83, June, 27.

1.2 Political Aspects of Film Festivals (History)

Archibald, David, and Mitchell Miller (2011) 'From Rennes to Toronto: Anatomy of a Boycott', *Screen,* 52, 2, 274-9.

Gourmelen, Arnaud and Ralph Eue (2010) 'Die Stunde Null der Cinephilie: Das Festival du Film Maudit (1949) und das Rendez-Vous de Biarritz (1950)', *Recherche Film und Fernsehen,* 7 and 8, 58-71.

Gregor, Ulrich (2008) 'Filmfestival-Chronik des Jahres 1968: Berlin, Cannes, Venedig, Knokke', *Recherche Film und Fernsehen,* 3, 36-8.

Moine, Caroline (2005) 'Le fascisme ordinaire au festival de Leipzig: Documentaire et déstalinisation en RDA', in Kristian Feigelson (ed.) *Caméra politique: Cinéma et stalinisme,* Theorem 8. Paris: Presse Sorbonne nouvelle, 228-39.

_____ (2009) 'Une Allemagne malgré tout? Le festival international du film documentaire de Leipzig, 1955-1990', in Antoine Fleury and Lubor Jílek (eds) *Une Europe malgré tout, 1945-1990: Contacts et réseaux culturels, intellectuels et scientifiques entre Européens dans la guerre froide.* Bruxelles/Berlin: Lang, 297-316.

Pisu, Stefano (2008) 'L'Unione Sovietica alla Mostra internazionale d'arte cinematografica di Venezia (1932-1953)', unpublished PhD thesis. Cagliari: Università degli Studi di Cagliari. On-line. Available HTTP: http://veprints.unica.it/67/ (1 December 2011).

1.3 General Academic Studies on Festivals (Not Only Film Festivals)

Finkel, Rebecca (2009) 'A Picture of the Contemporary Combined Arts Festival Landscape', *Cultural Trends,* 18, 1, 3-21.

Getz, Donald and Tommy Andersson (eds) (2009) *Festival Management.* Special Issue of *Scandinavian Journal of Hospitality and Tourism* 9, 2/3.

Giorgi, Liana (ed.) (2011) *European Arts Festivals: Strengthening Cultural Diversity.* Luxembourg: Publications Office of the European Union. On-line. Available HTTP: http://ec.europa.eu/research/social-sciences/pdf/euro-festival-report_en.pdf (15 June 2011).

_____ (ed.) (2010) *EURO-FESTIVAL Project. European Arts Festivals: Cultural Pragmatics and Discursive Identity Frames.* WP3 Main Report. EURO-FESTIVAL Project, July 2010. On-line. Available HTTP: http://www.euro-festival.org/docs/Euro-Festival_D3.pdf (20 January 2011)

Giorgi, Liana, Monica Sassatelli and Gerard Delanty (eds) (2011) *Festivals and the Cultural Public Sphere.* London/New York: Routledge.

2. Festival Time: Awards, Juries and Critics

Stringer, Julian (2011) 'Japan 1951-1970: National Cinema as Cultural Currency', in Dina Iordanova and Ruby Cheung (eds) *FFY3: Film Festivals and East Asia*. St Andrews: St Andrews Film Studies, 62-80.

3. Festival Space: Cities, Tourism and Publics

Grunwell, Sandra S., and Inhyuck 'Steve' Ha (2008) 'Film Festivals: An Empirical Study of Factors for Success', *Event Management*, 11, 4, 201-10.

Grunwell, Sandra S., Inhyuck 'Steve' Ha and Bonnie S. Martin (2008) 'A Comparative Analysis of Attendee Profiles at Two Urban Festivals', *Journal of Convention & Event Tourism*, 9, 1, 1-14.

Ooi, Can-Seng, and Jesper Strandgaard Pedersen (2010) 'City Branding and Film Festivals: Re-Evaluating Stakeholder's Relations', *Place Branding and Public Diplomacy*, 6, 4, 316-32.

Segal, Jérôme (2011) 'International Film Festivals in European Cities: Win-Win Situations?', in Liana Giorgi (ed.) *European Arts Festivals: Strengthening Cultural Diversity*. Luxembourg: Publications Office of the European Union, 37-45. On-line. Available HTTP: http://ec.europa.eu/research/social-sciences/pdf/euro-festival-report_en.pdf (15 June 2011).

Terry, Neil, Anne Macy and James K. Owens (2009) 'Bikers, Aliens, and Movie Stars: Comparing the Economic Impact of Special Events', *Journal of Business & Economics Research*, 7, 11, 73-80.

5.1 Markets and Funds

Benghozi, Pierre-Jean and Claire Nénert (1995) 'Création de Valeur Artistique ou Économique: Festival International du Film de Cannes au Marché du Film', *Recherche et Applications en Marketing*, 10, 4, 65-76.

Cheung, Ruby (2011) 'East Asian Film Festivals: Film Markets', in Dina Iordanova and Ruby Cheung (eds) *FFY3: Film Festivals and East Asia*. St Andrews: St Andrews Film Studies, 40-61.

de Valck, Marijke (2010) 'Filmfestivals, Coproductiemarketen en de Internationale Kunstcinema: Het CineMart-Model van Matchmaker onder de Loep', *Tijdschrift voor Mediageschiedenis*, 13, 2, 144-56.

Falicov, Tamara (2010) 'Migrating from South to North: The Role of Film Festivals in Funding and Shaping Global South Film and Video', in Greg Elmer, Charles H. Davis, Janine Marchessault, and John McCullough (eds) *Locating Migrating Media*. Lanham, MD: Lexington Books, 3-21.

Ross, Miriam (2011) 'The Film Festival as Producer: Latin American films and Rotterdam's Hubert Bals Fund', *Screen*, 52, 2, 261-7.

5.5 Festivals as Organisations

Loist, Skadi (2011) 'Precarious Cultural Work: About the Organization of (Queer) Film Festivals', *Screen*, 52, 2, 268-73.

Rüling, Charles-Clemens, and Jesper Strandgaard Pedersen (2010) 'Film Festival Research from an Organizational Studies Perspective', *Scandinavian Journal of Management*, 26, 3, 318-23.

Strandgaard Pedersen, Jesper, and Carmelo Mazza (2011) 'International Film Festivals: For the Benefit of Whom?', *Culture Unbound: Journal of Current Cultural Research*, 3, 139-65. On-line. Available HTTP: http://www.cultureunbound.ep.liu.se/v3/a12 (17 June 2011).

6. Trans/National Cinemas

Chan, Felicia (2011) 'The International Film Festival and the Making of a National Cinema', Screen, 52, 2, 253-60.

Iordanova, Dina (2010) 'From the Source: Cinemas of the South', *Film International*, 8, 5, November, 95-9.

6.1 Europe

Čulík, Jan, and Emma Čulík (2010) 'Karlovy Vary International Film Festival 2009: A Remarkable Showcase of Contemporary Cinema', *Studies in Eastern European Cinema*, 1, 1, 119-26.

Holighaus, Alfred (2011) 'Der jüngste deutsche Film auf Festivals', in Thomas Schick and Tobias Ebbrecht (eds) *Kino in Bewegung: Perspektiven des deutschen Gegenwartsfilms*. Wiesbaden: VS Verl. für Sozialwissenschaften, 337-40.

Jacob, Gilles (2011) *Citizen Cannes: The Man Behind the Cannes Film Festival*. Oxford: Phaidon.

Moine, Caroline (2003) 'Le festival du film documentaire de Leipzig, un lieu d'échanges culturels international? Entre mythe et réalité', *Relations internationales*, 116, 559-71.

_____ (2004) 'Gone with the Eastern Wind: Glasnost in 1980s East European Film', *Film International*, 2, 2, 6-13.

Pescatore, Guglielmo (2002) 'Pesaro e i nuovi festival', in Gianni Canova (ed.), *Storia del cinema italiano. Vol. XI. 1965/1969*. Venice/Rome: Marsilio/Edizioni di Bianco e Nero, 520-5.

Willemen, Paul (1981) 'Pesaro', *Framework*, 15/16/17, 96-8.

6.2 Asia

Bell, James (2011) 'North Korea's Pyongyang International Film Festival', in Dina Iordanova and Ruby Cheung (eds) *FFY3: Film Festivals and East Asia.* St Andrews: St Andrews Film Studies, 166-74.

Berry, Chris (2007) '10 Years Young: The Shanghai International Film Festival', *Senses of Cinema,* 45. On-line. Available HTTP: http://www. sensesofcinema.com/2007/festival-reports/shanghai-iff-2007 (15 September 2010).

_____ (2009) 'When is a Film Festival not a Festival? The 6th China Independent Film Festival', *Senses of Cinema,* 53. On-line. Available HTTP: http://www.sensesofcinema.com/2009/festival-reports/ when-is-a-film-festival-not-a-festival-the-6th-china-independent-film-festival (15 September 2010).

Beumers, Birgit (2011) 'Between Europe and Asia? A Chronicle of the "Eurasia" International Film Festival (Kazakhstan)', in Dina Iordanova and Ruby Cheung (eds) *FFY3: Film Festivals and East Asia.* St Andrews: St Andrews Film Studies, 175-85.

_____ (2011) 'Table 10: Film Festivals in Central Asia and the Asian Part of the Former USSR', in Dina Iordanova and Ruby Cheung (eds) *FFY3: Film Festivals and East Asia.* St Andrews: St Andrews Film Studies, 262.

Chen, Yun-hua (2011) 'Taipeh Film Festival: Creation of a Global City', in Dina Iordanova and Ruby Cheung (eds) *FFY3: Film Festivals and East Asia.* St Andrews: St Andrews Film Studies, 142-53.

_____ (2011) 'Table 6: Film Festivals in Taiwan', in Dina Iordanova and Ruby Cheung (eds) *FFY3: Film Festivals and East Asia.* St Andrews: St Andrews Film Studies, 255-7.

Cheung, Ruby (2011) 'East Asian Film Festivals: Film Markets', in Dina Iordanova and Ruby Cheung (eds) *FFY3: Film Festivals and East Asia.* St Andrews: St Andrews Film Studies, 40-61.

_____ and Alex Fischer (2011) 'Table 2: East Asian Festivals by Decade', in Dina Iordanova and Ruby Cheung (eds) *FFY3: Film Festivals and East Asia.* St Andrews: St Andrews Film Studies, 247-9.

Chua, Dave (2011) 'Table 9: Film Festivals in Singapore', in Dina Iordanova and Ruby Cheung (eds) *FFY3: Film Festivals and East Asia.* St Andrews: St Andrews Film Studies, 261.

Davis, Darrell William, and Emilie Yueh-yu Yeh (2008) 'Festivals, Events and Players', in *East Asian Screen Industries.* London: BFI, 140-64.

Dorman, Andrew, and Alex Fischer (2011) 'Table 3: Festivals Featuring Significant East Asian Cinema Content', in Dina Iordanova and Ruby Cheung (eds) *FFY3: Film Festivals and East Asia.* St Andrews: St Andrews Film Studies, 250-2.

Fischer, Alex (2011) 'Do Vodka and Sake Really Mix? An Interview with Natalla Shakhnazarova, Executive Director of Pacific Meridian: Vladivostok International Film Festival of Asian Pacific Countries', in Dina Iordanova and Ruby Cheung (eds) *FFY3: Film Festivals and East Asia*. St Andrews: St Andrews Film Studies, 234-8.

_____ (2011) 'Bibliography: Film Festivals and East Asia', in Dina Iordanova and Ruby Cheung (eds) *FFY3: Film Festivals and East Asia*. St Andrews: St Andrews Film Studies, 267-75.

_____ (2011) 'Table 13: Monetary Value of Awards at Select Festivals in East Asia', in Dina Iordanova and Ruby Cheung (eds) *FFY3: Film Festivals and East Asia*. St Andrews: St Andrews Film Studies, 265-6.

Hwang, Yun Mi (2011) 'Table 8: Film Festivals in South Korea', in Dina Iordanova and Ruby Cheung (eds) *FFY3: Film Festivals and East Asia*. St Andrews: St Andrews Film Studies, 259-60.

Iordanova, Dina (2011) 'East Asia and Film Festivals: Transnational Clusters for Creativity and Commerce', in Dina Iordanova and Ruby Cheung (eds) *FFY3: Film Festivals and East Asia*. St Andrews: St Andrews Film Studies, 1-33.

Iordanova, Dina and Ruby Cheung (eds) (2011) *FFY3: Film Festivals and East Asia*. St Andrews: St Andrews Film Studies.

Knee, Adam, and Kong Rithdee (2011) 'Tourism and the Landscape of Thai Film Festivals', in Dina Iordanova and Ruby Cheung (eds) *FFY3: Film Festivals and East Asia*. St Andrews: St Andrews Film Studies, 154-65.

Lee, Sangjoon (2011) 'Table 1: The Asia-Pacific Film Festival (from 1954)', in Dina Iordanova and Ruby Cheung (eds) *FFY3: Film Festivals and East Asia*. St Andrews: St Andrews Film Studies, 242-6.

Ma, Ran (2011) 'Table 4: Film Festivals in Mainland China', in Dina Iordanova and Ruby Cheung (eds) *FFY3: Film Festivals and East Asia*. St Andrews: St Andrews Film Studies, 253.

_____ (2011) 'Table 5: Film Festivals in Hong Kong', in Dina Iordanova and Ruby Cheung (eds) *FFY3: Film Festivals and East Asia*. St Andrews: St Andrews Film Studies, 254.

Marlow-Mann, Alex (2011) 'Table 7: Film Festivals in Japan', in Dina Iordanova and Ruby Cheung (eds) *FFY3: Film Festivals and East Asia*. St Andrews: St Andrews Film Studies, 258.

Martin, Adrian (2011) 'News for Whom? Critical Coverage of the 10th Jeonju International Film Festival', in Dina Iordanova and Ruby Cheung (eds) *FFY3: Film Festivals and East Asia*. St Andrews: St Andrews Film Studies, 81-9.

Mediarta, Agus (2007) 'Konfiden and the Promotion of Indonesian Short Films', *Inter-Asia Cultural Studies*, 8, 2, 308-9.

Nornes, Abé Mark (2011) 'Asian Film Festivals, Translation and the International Film Festival Short Circuit', in Dina Iordanova and Ruby Cheung (eds) *FFY3: Film Festivals and East Asia*. St Andrews: St Andrews Film Studies, 37-9.

Teh, David (2008) 'The Art of Interruption: Notes on the 5th Bangkok Experimental Film Festival', *Theory, Culture & Society*, 25, 7-8, 309-20.

Zahlten, Alexander (2010) 'Meta-, Hyper-, Inter-, Super-, Anime, World Creation, and the Role of Film Festivals', in Eija Niskanen (ed.) *Imaginary Japan: Japanese Fantasy in Contemporary Popular Culture*. Turku: International Institute for Popular Culture, 20-5. On-line. Available HTTP: http://iipc.utu.fi/imaginaryjapan/Zahlten.pdf (14 July 2011)

6.3 Africa

Bâ, Saër Maty (2010) 'Affective Power/Formal Knowledge: Diaspora, African Cinema, and the Film Festivals outside Africa', *Film International*, 8, 5 (#47), 54-69.

Dovey, Lindiwe (2010) 'Table 1: African Film Festivals', in Dina Iordanova and Ruby Cheung (eds) *FFY2: Film Festivals and Imagined Communities*. St Andrews: St Andrews Film Studies, 266-7.

English, James F. (2011) 'Festivals and the Geography of Culture: African Cinema in the "World Space" of its Public', in Gerard Delanty, Liana Giorgi and Monica Sassatelli. Abingdon (eds) *Festivals and the Cultural Public Sphere*. New York: Routledge, 63-78.

6.6 Australia

Hope, Cathy, and Adam Dickerson (2011) '"Give It a Go You Apes": Relations Between the Sydney and Melbourne Film Festivals, and the Early Australian Film Industry (1954–1970)', *Screening the Past*, 30. On-line. Available HTTP: http://screeningthepast.com/?p=256 (9 June 2011).

7. Programming

7.1 Issues of Festival Programming

Chan, Felicia and Dave Chua (2011) 'Programming Southeast Asia at the Singapore International Film Festival', in Dina Iordanova and Ruby Cheung (eds) *FFY3: Film Festivals and East Asia*. St Andrews: St Andrews Film Studies, 125-41.

van Hemert, Tess (2011) 'Searching for a Feminist Voice: Film Festivals and Negotiating the Tension between Expectation and Intent', *eJournalist*, 11, 1. On-line. Available HTTP: http://ejournalist.com.au/v11n1/VanHemert.pdf (18 May 2011).

Vick, Tom (2011) 'Washington, Pusan, Rotterdam, Udine and Back: Programming East Asian Films for American Audiences', in Dina Iordanova and Ruby Cheung (eds) *FFY3: Film Festivals and East Asia*. St Andrews: St Andrews Film Studies, 90-8.

7.2 Interviews with Programmers

Cheung, Ruby (2011) 'We Believe in "Film as Art": An Interview with Li Cheuk-to, Artistic Director of the Hong Kong International Film Festival (HKIFF)', in Dina Iordanova and Ruby Cheung (eds) *FFY3: Film Festivals and East Asia*. St Andrews: St Andrews Film Studies, 196-207.

Fujiwara, Chris (2011) '"It's Very Simple. We Like to Give the Audience the Chance to See Good Films": An Interview with Hayashi Kanako and Ichiyama Shozo of TOKYO FILMeX', in Dina Iordanova and Ruby Cheung (eds) *FFY3: Film Festivals and East Asia*. St Andrews: St Andrews Film Studies, 214-33.

Lee, Seunghee (2011) 'A Platform to the World: An Interview with Kim Ji-seok, Programme Director of the Pusan International Film Festival (PIFF)', in Dina Iordanova and Ruby Cheung (eds) *FFY3: Film Festivals and East Asia*. St Andrews: St Andrews Film Studies, 208-13.

7.3 Film Festivals and Questions of Aesthetics

Andrews, David (2010) 'Art Cinema as Institution, Redux: Art Houses, Film Festivals, and Film Studies', *Scope: An Online Journal of Film & TV Studies*, 18. On-line. Available HTTP: http://www.scope.nottingham.ac.uk/article.php?issue=18&id=1245 (12 December 2010).

Majumdar, Neepa (2011) 'Importing Neorealism, Exporting Cinema: Indian Cinema and Film Festivals in the 1950s', in Saverio Giovacchini and Robert Sklar (eds) *Global Neorealism: The Transnational History of a Film Style*. Jackson: University Press of Mississippi, 178-93.

8. Reception: Audiences, Communities and Cinephiles

Unwin, Elinor, et al. (2007) 'Getting the Picture: Programme Awareness amongst Film Festival Customers', *International Journal of Nonprofit and Voluntary Sector Marketing*, 12, 3, 231-45.

9.1.1 LGBT/Queer Film Festivals

Bao, Hongwei (2010) 'In Search of Lesbian Continuum: Lesbian Public Space through "Women 50 Minutes"', in Mikako Iwatake (ed.) *New Perspectives from Japan and China*. Helsinki: Department of World Cultures, University of Helsinki, 136-64.

____ (2010) 'Enlightenment Space, Affective Space: Travelling Queer Film Festivals in China', in Mikako Iwatake (ed.) *Gender, Mobility and Citizenship in Asia*. Helsinki: Department of World Cultures, University of Helsinki, 174-205.-

Rhyne, Ragan (2011) 'Comrades and Citizens: Gay and Lesbian Film Festivals in China', in Dina Iordanova and Ruby Cheung (eds) *FFY3: Film Festivals and East Asia*. St Andrews: St Andrews Film Studies, 110-24.

____ (2011) 'Table 12: Gay and Lesbian Film Festivals in East Asia', in Dina Iordanova and Ruby Cheung (eds) *FFY3: Film Festivals and East Asia*. St Andrews: St Andrews Film Studies, 264.

Tang, Denise Tse Shang (2009) 'Demand for Cultural Representation: Emerging Independent Film and Video on Lesbian Desires', in Olivia Khoo and Sean Metzger (eds) *Futures of Chinese Cinema: Technologies and Temporalities in Chinese Screen Cultures*. Bristol/Chicago: intellect, 169-90.

9.1.2 Women's Film Festivals

Walter, Cornelia (2010) 'Absolut nicht obsolet Absolut nicht obsolet: Frauenfilmfestivals sind leider noch immer kein Anachronismus' I 'Absolutely Not Obsolete: Women's Film Festivals Are Still Not an Anachronism – Sadly' (bilingual), *Short Report: KurzfilmMagazin*, 30-5. On-line. Available HTTP: http://www.ag-kurzfilm.de/shared/doc/upload/page/384/page_de_384_a3.pdf (1 March 2011).

9.2 a) Film Genre

Fantasy Film Festivals

Dellert, Frederike (2011) 'Kontroverse Pioniere: Zur Kuration des Fantasy Filmfest', *Schnitt*, 2 (#62), 35-6.

Horror Film Festivals

Hills, Matt (2010) 'Attending Horror Film Festivals and Conventions: Liveness, Subcultural Capital and "Flesh-and-Blood Genre Communities"', in Ian Conrich (ed.) *Horror Zone: The Cultural Experience of Contemporary Horror Cinema*. London/New York: I.B. Tauris, 87-101.

9.2 b) Type

Documentary Film Festivals

Nornes, Abé Mark (2011) 'Bulldozers, Bibles and Very Sharp Knives: The Chinese Independent Documentary Scene', in Dina Iordanova and Ruby Cheung (eds) *FFY3: Film Festivals and East Asia*. St Andrews: St Andrews Film Studies, 101-9.

____ (2011) 'Table 11: Documentary Film Festivals in Asia', in Dina Iordanova and Ruby Cheung (eds) *FFY3: Film Festivals and East Asia*. St Andrews: St Andrews Film Studies, 263.

Archive Film Festivals

Drubek-Meyer, Natascha (2010) 'Do We Need Archive Film Festivals?', *Art Margins: Contemporary Central & East European Visual Culture*, 6. On-line. Available HTTP: http://www.artmargins.com/index.php/6-film-a-video/585-do-we-need-archive-film-festivals-film-review-article (31 March 2011).

9.2 c) Length

Short Film Festivals

Denier, Christian (2010) 'Für die freie Verbreitung von Kurzfilmen' I 'For the Unrestricted Circulation of Short Films' (bilingual), *Short Report: KurzfilmMagazin*, 27-9. On-line. Available HTTP: http://www.ag-kurzfilm. de/shared/doc/upload/page/384/page_de_384_a3.pdf (1 March 2011).

Höhne, Maike Mia (2010) 'Licht auf Film: Das erste Mal' I 'Light on Film: The First Time' (bilingual), *Short Report: KurzfilmMagazin*, 24-6. On-line. Available HTTP: http://www.ag-kurzfilm.de/shared/doc/upload/page/384/page_de_384_a3.pdf (1 March 2011).

9.2 d) Social Concern Festivals

Disability Film Festivals

Tracton, Sarah (2008) 'Finding An(other) Audience: Accessible Cinema and The Other Film Festival', *Metro*, 159, 50-3.

Environmental Film Festivals

Norman, Marc (2000) 'Public Education through Community-Based Film Programs: A Report on the Environmental Film Festival in the Nation's Capital', *The Journal of Environmental Education*, 31, 2, 28-30.

Human Rights Film Festivals

Torchin, Leshu (2010) 'Traffic Jam: Film, Activism and Human Trafficking', in William Brown, Dina Iordanova and Leshu Torchin (eds) *Moving People, Moving Images: Cinema and Trafficking in the New Europe*. St Andrews: University of St Andrews, 218-36.

Mental Health Film Festivals

Clarke, Pamela, and Lee Knifton (2009) 'The Scottish Mental Health Arts and Film Festival: Promoting Social Change through the Arts', *A Life in the Day*, 13, 3, 10-3.

Quinn, N., et al. (2011) 'The Impact of a National Mental Health Arts and Film Festival on Stigma and Recovery', *Acta Psychiatrica Scandinavica*, 123, 1, 71-81.

9.4 Film Festivals and New Media Platforms

Patmore, Chris (2011) 'iPhone Film Festivals', *Film & Festival*, 27, 16-7.

10. Publications Dedicated to Individual Film Festivals

Lloyd, Matthew (2011) *How the Movie Brats Took Over Edinburgh: The Impact of Cinéphilia on Edinburgh International Film Festival, 1968-1980*. St Andrews: St Andrews Film Studies.

Porton, Richard (2010) 'The Toronto International Film Festival at the Crossroads', *Cineaste*, 36, 1, 32-5. On-line. Available HTTP: http://www.cineaste.com/ articles/the-toronto-international-film-festival-at-the-crossroads (5 January 2011).

Segal, Jérôme, and Christine Blumauer (2011) 'Cannes: A French International Festival', in Gerard Delanty, Liana Giorgi, and Monica Sassatelli (eds) *Festivals and the Cultural Public Sphere*. Abingdon, New York: Routledge, 156-72.

11. On-line Resources

Dynamics of World Cinema – Resources, on-line research material website. On-line. Available HTTP: http://www.st-andrews.ac.uk/worldcinema/index. php/resources/research (24 October 2011).

Film Festival Life, website and blog with festival listings and spotlights. On-line. Available HTTP: http://www.blog.filmfestivallife.com (1 December 2011).

St Andrews Film Studies
International Advisory Board

CPSIA information can be obtained
at www.ICGtesting.com
Printed in the USA
LVHW011716180421
684845LV00010B/700

9 780956 373052